RIGHT FROM WRONG

Why Religion Fails and Reason Succeeds

MARK ALAN SMITH

PROMETHEUS BOOKS

Prometheus Books
An imprint of Globe Pequot, the trade division of The Rowman & Littlefield Publishing Group, Inc.
4501 Forbes Blvd., Ste. 200
Lanham, MD 20706
www.rowman.com
Distributed by NATIONAL BOOK NETWORK

British Library Cataloguing in Publication Information Available

Library of Congress Cataloging-in-Publication Data
Names: Smith, Mark A. (Mark Alan), 1970– author.
Title: Right from wrong : why religion fails and reason succeeds / Mark Alan Smith.
    Description: Lanham, MD : Rowman & Littlefield, [2022] | Summary: "Is there a non-religious method for discovering the elements of an objective morality? Yes, Smith argues, the worldview of humanism"—Provided by publisher.
Identifiers: LCCN 2022005675 (print) | LCCN 2022005676 (ebook) | ISBN 9781633887640 (cloth) | ISBN 9781633887657 (epub)
Subjects: LCSH: Apologetics. | Christianity—Controversial literature. | Ethics. | Humanism. | Science. | Reasoning.
    Classification: LCC BT1103 .S635 2022 (print) | LCC BT1103 (ebook) | DDC 239—dc23/eng/20220625
LC record available at https://lccn.loc.gov/2022005675
LC ebook record available at https://lccn.loc.gov/2022005676

∞™ The paper used in this publication meets the minimum requirements of American National Standard for Information Sciences—Permanence of Paper for Printed Library Materials, ANSI/NISO Z39.48-1992

CONTENTS

Contents

FOREWORD

The Case for Science and Reason Determining Right from Wrong

Michael Shermer

WOULD YOU RATHER SURVIVE AND FLOURISH OR SUFFER AND DIE AN early death? An answer for this general question follows from your preferences to these specific choices: Would you rather be satiated or starving? Quenched or thirsty? Healthy or disease ridden? Free from pain or racked in chronic agony? Face fairness and justice or cruel and unusual punishment? Free from chains or yoked in chattel slavery? Prospering in a democracy or struggling in an autocracy? Working in a capitalist or communist economy? Enjoy civil liberties or be refrained from volitional actions? Express yourself freely or be censored on what to think and say? Be knowledgeable or ignorant? Employ reason or irrationality? In short, would you rather live in North Korea or South Korea? East Germany or West Germany during the Cold War?

The questions virtually answer themselves because we know most people in most circumstances nearly everywhere in the world answer them the same way. How do we know? By asking them (through polls and surveys) and observing them through empirical social science and scholarly history. In laboratories and historically, most people everywhere and everywhen almost always engage in behaviors that satiate their hunger, avoid disease and pain, pursue health and longevity, escape bondage to freedom, and seek knowledge instead of ignorance. Why? Because it is in our nature to so desire.

That exceptions come to mind—the masochistic pursuit of pain as a form of pleasure, for example, or hunger strikes in protest of injustice, or totalitarian regimes that program their citizens under threat of torture or death to respond otherwise—only reinforces the point that under normal conditions such preferences are universal and therefore built into human nature. That autocrats and dictators must build walls and concentration camps to maintain their power is empirical evidence for an unmistakable human preference. These examples from history and current events serve as natural experiments that allow us to employ the comparative method of empirical science to draw provisional conclusions about right and wrong. Here is how I outlined it in an essay in my 2020 book *Giving the Devil His Due*:

> *It is my hypothesis that in the same way that Galileo and Newton discovered physical laws and principles about the natural world that really are out there, so too have social scientists discovered moral laws and principles about human nature and society that really do exist. Just as it was inevitable that the astronomer Johannes Kepler would discover that planets have elliptical orbits—given that he was making accurate astronomical measurements, and given that planets really do travel in elliptical orbits, he could hardly have discovered anything else—scientists studying political, economic, social, and moral subjects will discover certain things that are true in these fields of inquiry. For example, that democracies are better than autocracies, that market economies are superior to command economies, that torture and the death penalty do not curb crime, that burning women as witches is a fallacious idea, that women are not too weak and emotional to run companies or countries, and, most poignantly here, that blacks do not like being enslaved and that the Jews do not want to be exterminated.*

Why?

My answer is that it is in human nature to struggle to survive and flourish in the teeth of nature's entropy, and having the freedom, autonomy, and prosperity available in free societies—built as they were on the foundation of Enlightenment philosophers and scientists seeking to discover the best way for humans to live—best enables individual sentient beings to live out their evolved destinies. My moral starting point is *the survival and flourishing of individual sentient beings*, by which I mean the evolved instinct to live and to have adequate sustenance, safety, shelter, bonding, and social relations for physical and mental health. Any organism subject to natural selection will by necessity have this drive to survive and flourish. If it didn't, it would not live long enough to reproduce and would no longer be subject to natural selection.

As I document in *The Moral Arc*, the moral progress we have witnessed over the centuries—the abolition of slavery, torture, and the death penalty; the expansion of rights to Blacks, women, children, workers, gays, and now trans/LGBTQ—has its origin in the scientific and reason-based concept that the world is governed by laws and principles that we can understand and apply, whether it is solar systems, ecosystems, political systems, economic systems, or social and moral systems.

Unfortunately, such arguments as mine are shared by few people. Most scientists and philosophers, for example, do not think there can be objective right and wrong, and so they lean toward cultural relativism and subjective morality, or simply punt on the issue and defer to Stephen Jay Gould's NOMA, or Nonoverlapping Magisteria, which grants religion a free pass from scientists and philosophers who, he argued, should stay in their own domain of empiricism and reason. But the vast majority of people still hold to religious beliefs about right and wrong, and tacitly, if not overtly, invoke Divine Command Theory: God commands it therefore it is moral, or God forbids it therefore it is immoral. And they even seem to agree with secular scientists and philosophers that without God "anything goes," so either way we are left with moral relativism.

Right from Wrong shows not only the folly of religious arguments about morality, but outlines a secular system that enables us to identify an objective morality, "one that rises above any particular individual or society," in the words of the author Mark Alan Smith. In these pages Smith adroitly demonstrates that "God's supposed revelation in the Bible is, in fact, a poor guide to morality," and that "to any person holding modern values, the Bible contains horrifying provisions condemning homosexuality and supporting genocide, patriarchy, slavery, collective punishment, and capital punishment for minor offenses." Of course, most modern religious believers are thoroughgoing Enlightenment moralists who have mostly embraced the moral progress over the centuries (albeit slowly), so as Smith shows, "Christian apologists have eliminated the unsavory verses and passages by essentially rewriting what they call the Word of God." Smith then shows that modern Muslims do the same with the Quran.

The core of this brilliant treatise is to provide a rational answer to a common question believers ask, which Smith allows a YouTuber to voice: "I've always wondered what people who don't believe in the Bible and the descriptions of right and wrong in there . . . on what do you base your personal ways of determining what's good and bad?" *Right from Wrong* provides an answer, namely what Smith calls *inclusive deliberation*. "Deliberation is a form of reason in which people gather information, make arguments, evaluate evidence, and listen to the perspectives of others," he writes, and therefore "this deliberation must include all kinds of people. To the extent that racial, ethnic, gender, or religious minorities are excluded from participating through legal or social means, any seemingly deliberative process will be tilted against their ideas and interests."

Objective knowledge about right and wrong can be approximated through the deliberation process that incorporates diverse voices—the Universal Declaration of Human Rights being a type specimen—but that bucks the millennium-long tendency for religious-based communities to each proclaim knowledge of objective moral truths, despite the fact that they often contradict one another. Historically, such conflicts were resolved on battlefields in conflicts that decimated entire populations, with the sixteenth- and seventeenth-century European wars of religion being just one example among many. There has to be a better way, and there is. You are holding one in your hands, as Smith demonstrably shows that "moral claims are now more likely to be established through inclusive deliberation rather than blind appeals to a holy book. Future moral progress hinges on whether we can improve the quality and scope of our deliberations."

Amen, brother.

PREFACE

Westerners are secular in most respects. We turn to scientists, not religious leaders, to explain the origins of disease, the causes of earthquakes, and the movements of stars. Religion is largely irrelevant to business, which operates according to the principles of accounting, management, marketing, and so forth. You would probably do a double take—and maybe even run for the exit—if you saw your pilot praying for your plane's safe journey while you boarded. We expect pilots and other professionals to uphold the standards of their training and education and to put their religious commitments to the side while performing their jobs.

Yet when Westerners think about general questions of morality, they often turn to religion for answers. Morality is the one domain of life that seems to fall within the special province of religion, even to many nonbelievers. Paleontologist Stephen Jay Gould, himself an atheist, nevertheless granted jurisdiction over "questions of ultimate meaning and moral value" to religion.[1] Gould isn't alone in that sentiment. If the issue of fundamental right and wrong is at stake, you can be sure that someone will invoke religious concepts. In the West, where Christianity is the dominant religion, these moral debates frequently revolve around Christian doctrines. Christians routinely proclaim that morality derives from God, who uses the Bible (according to Protestants) or both the Bible and Church tradition (according to Catholics) to tell us how we ought to live.

I will argue in this book that God's supposed revelation in the Bible is, in fact, a poor guide to morality, at least when we consider the Bible in its totality. Many Christians avoid the problem of what the Bible teaches by remaining blissfully ignorant of it. Others go to great lengths to reconcile what they believe with what the Bible actually says. To anyone holding modern values, the Bible contains horrifying provisions condemning homosexuality and supporting genocide, patriarchy, slavery, collective punishment, and capital punishment for minor offenses. Christian apologists have eliminated the unsavory verses and passages by essentially rewriting what they call *the Word of God*. Modern Muslims, I will show, have done the same with respect to the Quran.

My goals in this book, however, reach beyond explaining the intellectual gymnastics through which the world's two largest religious groups justify their scriptures. I aim to provide a secular alternative allowing us to identify an objective morality, one that rises above any particular individual or society. Every nonbeliever must confront the question a woman in the audience posed to an atheist in one of the popular atheist-Christian debates on YouTube: "I've always wondered what people who don't believe in the Bible and the descriptions of right and wrong in there . . . on what do you base your personal ways of determining what's good and bad?"[2] This book gives my answer.

The first thing to note is that my personal conception of right and wrong is irrelevant. I will instead describe the process through which humanity as a whole, rather than me acting alone, can discover the elements of an objective morality. The crucial component of that process is what I call *inclusive deliberation*. Deliberation is a form of reason in which people gather information, make arguments, evaluate evidence, and listen to the perspectives of others. Although it frequently happens face to face or through online exchanges, deliberation can also occur with printed materials, and it extends across different societies and eras.

To be trustworthy, this deliberation must include all kinds of people. To the extent that racial, ethnic, gender, and religious minorities are excluded from participating through legal or social means, any seemingly deliberative process will be tilted against their ideas and interests. The ideal of objectivity cannot be approximated unless the deliberation incorporates diverse voices. Over the past three centuries, new participants have entered the discussion, and humanity has reached a consensus on many issues, such as the inherent wrongness of slavery, genocide, and torture. The Universal Declaration of Human Rights, adopted in 1948 with the support of people around the world, is a prime example of what inclusive deliberation can deliver.

My approach also explains why the Bible and Quran so often give commands that we now recognize as immoral. The core problem is that those texts did not emerge from a process of inclusive deliberation. They instead reflect the parochial views of their authors, who failed to represent the diversity of all human beings. We have made moral progress since the writing of the Christian and Muslim scriptures because of mass literacy and education, the rise of democratic institutions, and broader participation in moral discussions. In short, moral claims are now more likely to be established through inclusive deliberation rather than blind appeals to a holy book. Future moral progress hinges on whether we can improve the quality and scope of our deliberations.

The Practice of Christian Apologetics

THE *FRONTLINE* DOCUMENTARY "TWO AMERICAN FAMILIES" PROFILES A pair of working-class families through twenty years of their personal and financial struggles. One set of parents, Tony and Terry Neumann, spoke in the mid-1990s about the growth of disorderly and even violent behavior among many teenagers in their neighborhood. The neighborhood's changing character forced the Neumanns to worry about the futures of their own children. They were doing everything they could, Tony explained, to ensure that their two sons and one daughter would "grow up to be good kids."[1]

The Neumanns relied on religion to help their children learn how to behave properly. Tony and Terry were active members of their parish, and all three of their children were baptized and confirmed into the Catholic Church. For generations, many Americans have found similar kinds of community support in congregations large and small. Sociologists have discovered that people often attend church more frequently as they move through early adulthood, establish a stable home, and begin having children.[2] People who previously lost touch with their religious tradition may return to it to provide instruction for their offspring. Believing that morality ultimately comes from God, they value their religious community for its assistance in imparting God's teachings to their children.

This assumption that morality comes from God is widely held among Christians of all stripes. Believers who are unsure about all the scientific, historical, and supernatural claims of their scriptures nevertheless typically retain their faith in a God who tells us how to distinguish right from wrong. They may or may not believe that the earth is less than ten thousand years old, or that Jesus was born of a virgin, but they commonly fear that society would collapse if everyone became atheists. Atheists are one of the least popular groups in America and many other countries, a pattern scholars have attributed to public suspicions that atheists lack a moral code.[3] We need a God, many people assume, to give us morality.[4]

Christian apologists have developed this claim more formally and extensively. Within a religious context, an apologist is someone who offers a reasoned defense, or apology, of the beliefs, doctrines, and scriptures they hold dear. Christian apologists often cite as motivation for their efforts a line from 1 Peter 3:15, "Always be ready to make your defense to anyone who demands from you an accounting for the hope that is in you."[5] The context of the surrounding verses involves accepting Jesus as one's Lord, and so the author of 1 Peter seems to be instructing his readers to explain their religion to non-Christians.

Apologetics is thus a term widely used and embraced within the Christian community. People who want academic training in the field can pursue degree programs, typically at the master's level, at Christian colleges and seminaries such as Trinity Western University in Canada, Maryvale Institute in the United Kingdom, and Biola University and Liberty University in the United States. Students can also take undergraduate courses in apologetics at many Christian colleges, and churches routinely teach the subject through sermons, workshops, study groups, and Sunday school lessons. Lay people who hear about "apologetics" for the first time often mistakenly think it involves apologizing for improper behavior or illegitimate beliefs, a tendency that critics have unfortunately encouraged by using the term pejoratively. To the contrary, Christian apologists aim to explain, justify, and defend their faith, not apologize for it. Throughout this book, I will engage with the arguments and evidence they have offered on a range of topics.

One such topic is the divine origins of morality, which Plato addressed over 2,400 years ago.[6] Updated for a monotheistic context, "Euthyphro's dilemma"—named after a character in one of Plato's dialogues—asks whether an action is moral because God commands it, or

THE PRACTICE OF CHRISTIAN APOLOGETICS

if God commands the action because it is moral. If we choose the first alternative, then God resembles an authoritarian father who tells his children what to do "because I said so." Whatever God commands, including murder and incest, would then become moral and obligatory through his authority alone. We might therefore be tempted to choose the second alternative in which God relies on concrete reasons why something is right or wrong, and those reasons are the basis for his commands. If so, we could skip the need for a divine being altogether and appeal to the same reasons to which God himself is bound.

Christian apologists know they must confront Euthyphro's dilemma, and they have developed what they think is a third option. As explained by philosopher William Lane Craig, "God's own nature is the standard of goodness, and His commandments are expressions of His nature. In short, our moral duties are determined by the commands of a just and loving God."[7] Frank Turek, another well-known apologist, asserts that "the buck has to stop somewhere, and it stops at God's unchanging moral nature. In other words, the standard of rightness we know as the Moral Law flows from the nature of God Himself—infinite justice and infinite love."[8] Other apologists take a similar tack.[9]

This apparent solution to Euthyphro's dilemma fails because it merely pushes the problem back one level. We can ask whether something is moral because God's nature led him to command it, or whether God commanded it because his nature must be moral. If the former, then something becomes moral because of God's arbitrary nature and the commands that reflect it; if the latter, then we can bypass God's nature and affirm the morality to which he too must conform. Calling God "the paradigm and locus of moral value," as Craig does, serves only to distract us from the fundamental challenge Plato identified.[10]

Yet the problem runs deeper because the apologists' attempted solution violates one of the cardinal rules of logic. Craig asserts that "God, as the greatest conceivable being, must be perfectly good."[11] God's nature, then, necessarily includes the property of being morally perfect, allowing his nature to stand as the foundation of morality.[12] Anyone who pauses to consider Craig's claims, however, will see that he is offering an object lesson in circular reasoning. Craig uses the concept in question—morality—to define God's nature, then turns around and cites God's nature as the basis for that very same morality! Beyond convincing himself that this fallacious response solves Euthyphro's dilemma, Craig has somehow slipped it past numerous interlocutors through his books, articles, and debates.

The errors in Craig's approach compound when he starts adding details to the morally perfect nature that God must embody. Craig declares it "impossible" that God would ever command rape or child abuse; to Craig, those possibilities have the same logical status as a "round square."[13] Because he has made specific moral qualities axiomatic to God's nature, Craig engages in circular reasoning when he invokes God's nature as the foundation for morality. Craig and other apologists who take this approach have unknowingly chosen the second option of Euthyphro's dilemma by incorporating an external and independent morality into their definition of God. We could instead work directly with that morality without needing to filter it through God's nature.

HOW CHRISTIANS TRY TO LEARN GOD'S MORAL RULES

Let's suppose a Christian apologist ignores Euthyphro's dilemma and decides to plunge ahead anyway. Even if morality flowed from God's nature, that fact alone would not take us very far. The mere existence of morality cannot guide human behavior if we do not understand its parameters. An objective morality rooted in God's nature would be worthless unless he told us which actions are required, forbidden, and optional under different circumstances. Otherwise, God would be a celestial Joseph McCarthy, supposedly holding a list of dos and don'ts in his metaphorical pocket but refusing to share it with humanity. We need to know what counts as moral before we can act appropriately.

One means through which God could communicate to human beings is personal revelation. Millions of Christians regularly pray, and many of them sincerely believe they can feel God's presence and hear his commands. Perhaps God could use these interactions to tell believers the rules of morality. Suppose a Christian woman, after deep and prolonged prayer, says she learned from God that adultery in her case would not be wrong so long as her husband never found out about it. Would the people hearing her story believe that she received the message from God and understood it correctly? Probably not, but they can't prove otherwise because nobody but her has access to whatever might have transpired during her prayer. This example illustrates the core problem with personal revelation: There is no way to either confirm or disconfirm what a person says God communicated privately. Personal revelation by itself cannot tell us the content of morality.

Christian apologists do not actually invoke personal revelation as a means to know the content of morality, but they do cite a different type of revelation. The apostle Paul stated that Gentiles "show that what the law requires is written on their hearts, to which their own conscience also bears witness" (Romans 2:15; see also Hebrews 10:16). According to Paul and the anonymous author of Hebrews, God implanted his moral code onto every human heart, which means that people enter the world with a basic knowledge of good and evil. C. S. Lewis in *Mere Christianity* stressed this point by asserting that all people, no matter when they were born or what society they grew up in, share a common morality.[14]

So far, so good for the Christian apologist, but how do we resolve the moral disagreements that invariably arise? For example, should we torture people accused of crimes to force them to reveal information about themselves and others who may have broken the law? No less an authority than Augustine of Hippo, arguably the most influential theologian in Christian history, thought so.[15] Pressed to defend his belief, Augustine might well have stated that God designed humans such that they would know instinctively the rightness of torture. Modern Christians, however, would condemn any justice system that used torture as a routine practice. Who's right in this dispute? The assertion that God wrote a moral code onto all human hearts gives us no answers. Such a claim works at a general level for matters on which everyone agrees, but it cannot handle the numerous moral conflicts that exist within and between societies. For this reason, the Christian apologists who mention Romans 2:15 do not use it to address any disputed moral questions.[16]

Christians thus need a source of revelation that everyone can access and that includes the details necessary to resolve moral conflicts. Does such a source exist within the Christian worldview? Yes: the Bible.

Catholics would add Church tradition, constructed and affirmed by popes, councils, and theologians, as an additional way for God to communicate his teachings. Catholics and Protestants agree, however, on the Bible's authority for moral questions, disagreeing only on whether it is the *sole* authority. Through careful study of the Old and New Testaments, Christians assert, we can learn the rules for proper behavior.

At least, that's what they claim in principle. In practice, Christians refuse to accept the Bible's authority on many matters of morality, as I will show in later chapters. The Bible was written over a span of several hundred years during the Iron Age, and its various books reflect the time and place of their writing. Many of the Bible's commands and stories are barbaric, and the God it depicts commonly acts in ways that make him worthy of scorn rather than worship. What can Christians do when they learn about a God who orders genocide, condones slavery, requires the death penalty for trifling offenses, and punishes people because of their membership in a group? What about all the other immoral features of the Bible?

Apologists think they have good answers, and they have produced voluminous writings to explain and defend the Bible. I have studied their works over the last few decades, initially as a believer and later to sustain my intellectual interests. I eventually came across the *Encyclopedia of Bible Difficulties* by theologian Gleason Archer, who taught for over forty years at leading seminaries in America. One of his lines stuck with me. In a section titled "Recommended Procedures in Dealing with Bible Difficulties," Archer offered his readers several pointers. The first one begins, "Be fully persuaded in your own mind that an adequate explanation exists, even though you have not yet found it."[17]

To see the full implications of Archer's seemingly innocuous statement, consider an analogy to the realm of criminal justice. When a criminal charge in America isn't either dismissed or resolved through a plea bargain, the jury sifts through the evidence to determine whether the prosecution has proven its case. According to Archer, the Bible must be deemed innocent from the outset, for he tells his readers to assume that "an adequate explanation exists" for any potential problem. The subsequent investigation thus serves only to ratify the believer's starting position. Once they get their creative juices flowing, apologists find it remarkably easy to read the Bible in such a way that their faith never comes under threat.

Archer's words helped clarify for me the entire field of apologetics. He openly acknowledged starting from his conclusion—the Bible and its God will always be exonerated—and then working backward to construct whatever case can be marshaled with the available materials. Other apologists, I gradually realized, follow the same practice without necessarily admitting it to themselves or anyone else. They present their claims in a deductive fashion and imply that their reasoning led them to their conclusions, as opposed to the opposite process whereby they constructed their arguments and evidence to fit the conclusions they already held. Because apologists are usually smart, imaginative, and skilled at their craft, their writings hide the actual process they consciously or unconsciously followed.

For many years I engaged these writings one at a time. That's a valuable exercise for someone who wants to assess the claims of a particular author, but it obscures the patterns within the author's larger genre. Eventually I learned to place apologetic tracts side by side so I could see the similarities in their style and form of argument. After making many such comparisons, I observed that apologists address biblical problems in one or more of four ways: They ignore, rationalize, reinterpret, and/or mystify the offending passages. Anyone who understands these approaches will never read an apologetic work the same way again, for the strategies often jump off the page or screen once you know how to identify them.

THE FIRST STRATEGY: IGNORE

Back when I was a believer from the 1970s through the early 1990s, Christians rarely learned about the Bible's warts and the standard attempts to handle them. Sermons, Sunday school lessons, and youth group discussions focused on the good parts of the Bible, not the bad ones.[18] Church leaders from that period could presume a base level of religious conviction among their congregants and the general public, which allowed them to ignore difficult biblical verses and other threats to Christianity. Had they wanted to offer resources to bolster a person's faith, there were not many options available. C. S. Lewis's *Mere Christianity* and Josh McDowell's *Evidence That Demands a Verdict* were widely known in church circles, and I devoured both of them, but there were few other apologetic books, articles, and essays targeted at a lay audience.[19]

The religious landscape in America and other Western countries is radically different today. Take the most basic indicator: The percentage of Americans who self-identify as Christian declined from 87 percent in 1990 to 64 percent in 2021.[20] Meanwhile, atheists have become more numerous and visible in public and intellectual life, and many of their challenges to Christianity revolve around the Bible. Whereas an earlier generation of Christian leaders could safely dismiss those voices without comment, following the same path would be foolish today. Whether among their friends, on the Internet, in the media, or on a college campus, ordinary Christians invariably hear about problems in the biblical text. Christian leaders therefore have to teach them how to respond.

The field of apologetics now offers abundant resources for that effort. Many of the most talented and articulate Christian leaders of our era, such as William Lane Craig, Robert Barron, James White, Karl Keating, David Robertson, Frank Turek, Robert Spitzer, Trent Horn, R. C. Sproul, Greg Koukl, Hugh Ross, Amy Orr-Ewing, Ravi Zacharias, Alisa Childers, John Piper, Larry Taunton, Ken Hamm, and Matt Slick, have either founded or worked for apologetics ministries. These ministries explain and defend Christianity and its scriptures through books, websites, lectures, videos, conferences, podcasts, interviews, museums, and radio shows. Reflecting its wide reach, rank-and-file Christians often encounter that material firsthand, and they hear the underlying arguments indirectly through sermons, study groups, and other programming at their churches. Other Christian leaders produce apologetic works for both scholars and the general public from within seminaries, Christian colleges, and other academic institutions. This group includes such luminaries as Sean McDowell, Richard Bauckham, Peter Kreeft, Wayne Grudem, Alvin Plantinga, Nancy Pearcey, Scott Hahn, Gary Habermas, Paul Copan, Alister McGrath, Norman Geisler, and John Lennox. Finally, people such as Lee Strobel, Patrick Madrid, Justin Brierley, Dinesh D'Souza, Hank Hanegraaff, Eric Metaxas, J. Warner Wallace, and Timothy Keller have contributed to apologetics as independent authors, radio hosts, or clergy members.

Thanks to the persistence of these and other writers, the field of apologetics has created a wealth of resources in readily accessible formats. For most moral objections to the Bible, a committed Christian could locate a reply from an apologist without much effort. Not every apologetic work addresses every problem—there isn't enough space, even in a long book, to do so—but the field as a whole usually gives possible responses. So where does this leave the strategy of ignoring problematic biblical verses? Sometimes it proceeds in exactly the same way it did in earlier generations. Many of the Bible's flaws receive no attention whatsoever from leading apologists, whose readers thereby remain unaware that the problems even exist. In the following chapters, I will explain some of these problematic passages that apologists rarely if ever address.

Apologists also use a sophisticated variant of the Ignore strategy that directs the reader's attention to other verses that supposedly resolve the difficulties. Rather than squarely confronting the questionable verses, apologists sometimes discuss others from elsewhere in the Bible, allowing them to change the subject in their favor. When this tactic succeeds, it has the same effect that misdirection does for stage magicians. With people's attention focused in one place, they overlook what is happening elsewhere.

In comparing apologetics to magic in using this strategy, I do not mean to imply that apologists are trying to deceive their readers and listeners. In fact, apologists are almost always committed Christians who believe what they are saying. The processes at work here involve self-deception, not strategic deception. Apologists convince themselves that they have solved the problem, and misdirection can help them persuade others, too.

THE SECOND STRATEGY: RATIONALIZE
Rather than ignoring a problematic passage outright or bypassing it through misdirection, an apologist can instead try to rationalize it, a strategy that builds on something people commonly do in their everyday lives. An adolescent caught in a wrongdoing defends his behavior by

saying, "Everybody else is doing it." Confronted with evidence that she reneged on her promise, a woman replies, "Let me explain." An employee fired for poor job performance complains that his boss is biased against him. A student who performed poorly on a test mutters under her breath that it was unfair.

Apologists similarly try to rationalize difficult biblical passages by arguing that the implications are not what they seem. You can frequently recognize this strategy through its opening words of the sort, "First of all, we need to understand that . . ." After reading an introduction of that kind, you can be sure that a rationalization will follow. Apologists construct these rationalizations not just to persuade their readers and listeners but also to live with themselves. Nobody wants to worship a God who acts immorally and gives immoral commands. When encountering biblical passages that would cause the average person to recoil in horror, apologists often start rationalizing to relieve the psychological discomfort they would otherwise feel.

Considered from the standpoint of the audience, rationalizing resembles the practice of "spinning" in the fields of politics, journalism, marketing, and public relations. Technology writer Margaret Rouse defines spin as "the selective assembly of fact and the shaping of nuance to support a particular view of a story."[21] An apologist can rationalize or spin the Bible by finding a positive slant on a passage and burying anything negative. Rationalizing through spin sometimes involves trying to reframe the whole issue to give listeners and readers a different way to think about it.

In one of their most common moves, apologists try to rationalize the Bible by exploring the verses' context. Context is obviously important when reading any text, and a thoughtful reader of the Bible will consider matters such as who is speaking, who is listening, the type of genre, the historical situation, and the verses before and after the ones in question. This approach turns into rationalization when it becomes an excuse for the God of the Bible issuing immoral commands or behaving in immoral ways. For example, an apologist might claim that God didn't really mean some of the things he said in the Bible. Instead, the argument sometimes goes, God secretly knew that practices such as slavery were wrong but did not reveal his knowledge in the Bible.

Attention to context can also lead apologists astray if it involves asserting that a particular behavior was acceptable in the ancient world but would be unacceptable for modern societies. An apologist thus excuses what the Bible says by limiting its application and relieving today's Christians from needing to obey it. This approach has a major downside for apologists, though. Proclaiming that something was moral only in another time and place is a form of moral relativism, a no-no for apologists who want to defend a universal morality. Apologists thus have to be careful when trying to rationalize biblical passages, lest they inadvertently adopt a stance of moral relativism.

THE THIRD STRATEGY: REINTERPRET

For any given translation of the Bible, the words are fixed but the interpretations are not. Apologists often reinterpret passages by putting new glosses on them, thereby departing from the history of Christian interpretation. The most important break in that history came after the onset of the Age of Reason and the Enlightenment. Some scholars consider these two periods to be one and the same, but others—and I count myself among them—find it helpful to see the periods as separate but linked.[22] The Age of Reason can be usefully dated to the work of René Descartes, especially his *Discourse on the Method* (1637). Prior to Descartes, philosophy was not an independent branch of knowledge and served instead, in the words of the great theologians Anselm of Canterbury and Thomas Aquinas, as a "handmaiden" to theology.[23] Descartes undertook the grand project of founding knowledge on reason alone, thereby casting aside the reliance on faith, authority, and tradition that was dominant within medieval universities. Thomas Hobbes and Baruch Spinoza followed Descartes in seeking to understand through reason alone the origins of political authority and the nature of the self and the universe.

The end of the seventeenth century was a transitional period between the Age of Reason and the Enlightenment. In the small window between 1687 and 1690, John Locke penned foundational political and philosophical tracts and Isaac Newton published his transformative scientific theories. The Enlightenment would fully bloom in the eighteenth century through the works of, among others, Montesquieu, Voltaire, David Hume, Cesare Beccaria, Immanuel Kant, Marquis de Condorcet, Adam Smith, and Mary Wollstonecraft. By rejecting mere tradition and emphasizing science, reason, progress, universalism, and the need to back all claims with evidence, these Enlightenment authors gave people a new way to understand themselves and the world around them. Most importantly for present purposes, the Enlightenment offered a vision of universal human rights. The working out of this vision helped undermine monarchy, despotism, slavery, restrictions on religious liberty, and beliefs in hereditary social classes.

One can see the influence of these periods through the biblical interpretations that came before and after them. Although they typically deny it, the apologists of today are children of the Enlightenment. They have absorbed Enlightenment values of reason, liberty, equality, tolerance, and human rights, which they import into their readings of the Bible. When trying to wiggle out of a biblical passage teaching a flawed morality, apologists rarely examine the full history of Christian interpretation, and for good reason. In many cases, their readings depart from all the interpretations before the Age of Reason and the Enlightenment.

To understand these interpretations, we must examine the writings of premodern Protestants and Catholics. From the very beginning of Christianity, there were always theologians, bishops, monks, and leaders of local churches who carefully read and tried to understand the books later collected in the Old and New Testaments. Those efforts continued during and after the Reformation in both Protestant and Catholic communities. By compiling and analyzing the most influential interpretations over many centuries, we can assess whether apologists are reinterpreting the Bible to make it consistent with modern values. When tackling a biblical passage teaching what the ordinary reader would consider a flawed morality, apologists need to ask themselves the following question: Did premodern Christians ever offer your favored interpretation? If not, you need to seriously consider whether you are deluding yourself into making the text say what you want it to say.

It's possible, of course, that every single interpreter throughout the span of over sixteen centuries made a mistake, and scholars may have found instances of those errors. Rigorous research on the historical and linguistic context has allowed scholars to understand the meaning of certain biblical passages better than their predecessors did.[24] However, I will show in later chapters that the apologists of today routinely offer their own readings without bothering to engage the history of Christian interpretation. Reinterpretation is a standard practice in apologetics, not a one-off event or some kind of exception.

In stressing the need for apologists to study their forebears from before the Age of Reason and the Enlightenment, I hope to encourage them to be more reflective about their interpretations. Does the Bible really mean what you're claiming, or are you searching for something—anything—to salvage the text and the morality of the God who supposedly inspired it? How can you explain why Augustine of Hippo, Anselm of Canterbury, Thomas Aquinas, Martin Luther, John Calvin, and other leading lights in the Church, plus all the lesser-known but equally learned figures writing over many centuries, never offered your interpretation? Isn't it the height of arrogance to think that everyone before modern times missed the real meaning of one passage after another but that you have no obligation to tell us why they're wrong?

Needless to say, I don't expect apologists to take the bait and entertain these questions. If they spent time studying the history of Christian interpretation, they would be forced to grapple with what the Bible meant to people who hadn't unconsciously read Enlightenment values into it. They would confront the fact that the Bible's morality, while praiseworthy in many places, is downright despicable in others. Christians and non-Christians alike have improved on the Bible's morality by embracing Enlightenment values, which apologists have imported into their biblical interpretations to such an extent that they have essentially rewritten the text in key places. An apologist who regularly examines earlier interpretations and thinks about what the Bible really means would soon become either an unorthodox Christian or, more likely, an ex-Christian.

It's important to note that interpretations from the first sixteen centuries of Christianity are not necessarily correct or even plausible. We can say with certainty, however, that they were not unknowingly constructed to support modern values. Consider, for example, the 137th chapter of Psalms. The chapter revolves around Israel condemning her Babylonian captors, and Psalms 137:8–9 reads: "O daughter Babylon, you devastator! Happy shall they be who pay you back what you have done to us! Happy shall they be who take your little ones and dash them against the rock!" Yikes. It's jarring to see the Bible calling for someone to kill Babylonian children who played no part in conquering Israel. The great theologian Jerome, whose life straddled the fourth and fifth centuries, spotted the problem with these verses. He crafted an allegorical interpretation holding that the "little ones" in question were not actual Babylonian children but rather the evil thoughts in our hearts, and to "dash them against the rock" was not a physical process but rather the mental activity of overcoming sin.[25] Whatever else you might say about Jerome's interpretation, it cannot be the product of a modern worldview.

Jerome's allegorical approach to the Bible, which seems like a clever way to handle its moral atrocities, nevertheless finds only limited support among Christian leaders of the twenty-first century. James White, director of Alpha and Omega Ministries, states emphatically that "allegorical interpretation destroys the authority of the text of Scripture." An allegorical interpretation "can never be verified by others working with the same text" and ultimately rests "not on the text itself but the mind of the interpreter who 'sees' things in it."[26] Ian Paul, a theologian, minister, and adjunct professor at Fuller Theological Seminary, criticizes allegorical interpretations for "pulling the text into the world of the reader, instead of taking the reader into the world of the text."[27] He observes further that there is no logical stopping point once a person adopts the method of allegorical interpretation. If one part of the Bible can be interpreted allegorically, then why not another, including foundational aspects of Christianity such as the resurrection?

Although apologists generally agree on these dangers of allegorical readings, they can easily find other ways to reinterpret problematic passages. A person can work within the text and still stretch its meaning beyond what the original author or previous interpreters would have accepted. Through one of their most brazen methods, apologists can simply deny the message of the text or assert that the passage means the opposite of what it says. It's debatable whether we should dignify such readings by calling them "interpretations." In these instances the apologist writes a defense of the Bible that thoroughly misrepresents its actual content.

At other times, apologists reinterpret the Bible by inserting certain details into their descriptions. When you read an apologist's summary of a passage, you'll often discover that it includes something not present in the Bible itself. With these minor additions, apologists can dramatically change the Bible to make the God lying behind it look better. The additions are easy to spot because you can simply compare the apologist's summary with the verses in question. Equally important, you can consult the commentaries that Christians offered before the Age of Reason and the Enlightenment to see that the reinterpretation has no grounding in earlier Church history.

THE FOURTH STRATEGY: MYSTIFY

The mystify strategy has its origin in the Bible itself, for Romans 11:33 states, "O the depth of the riches and wisdom and knowledge of God! How unsearchable are his judgments and how inscrutable his ways!" Similar statements can be found in other biblical passages, most notably in the book of Job. The English poet William Cowper wrote a hymn in 1773 based on this idea and coined a memorable phrase. His first stanza reads:

> God moves in a mysterious way
> His wonders to perform;
> He plants his footsteps in the sea
> And rises upon the storm.[28]

The Catechism of the Catholic Church (CCC) similarly refers to mysteries of the faith in several places. For example, CCC 237 states that God's "inmost Being as Holy Trinity is a mystery that is inaccessible to reason alone or even to Israel's faith before the incarnation of God's Son and the sending of the Holy Spirit."[29] The website GotQuestions.org, which works within evangelical Protestantism to answer common questions about God, the Bible, and Christianity, states that "God's methods often leave people totally bewildered. . . . The processes God uses, the interplay of human freedom and God's sovereignty, and God's ultimate summations are far beyond what the limited human mind can understand."[30] Both Catholics and Protestants, then, accept that God's ways are sometimes puzzling to human beings.

That agreement among diverse groups of Christians notwithstanding, apologists normally do not defend the Bible by pointing to mystery. Because it's an admission that they cannot mitigate or justify the moral flaws in a biblical passage, even the apologists who use the mystify strategy typically combine it with the others. Apologists sometimes attempt one or more of the other strategies first and then invoke God's mysterious ways only when there are no more straws left to grasp. The force of their argument becomes, "In case all my defenses of this passage have failed, let me close off further discussion by appealing to mystery."

The mystify strategy thus undermines one of the core principles of intellectual life: the idea that all claims can be evaluated and potentially falsified or refuted. Most of the time, apologists adhere to the ordinary norms of inquiry and explain their positions on God, the Bible, and Christian doctrine in great detail. They insist we can understand God's nature, what he communicated through the Bible, and how we can achieve eternal salvation. In fact, they argue, we can even know God's rules about what consenting adults can and cannot do in the privacy of their bedrooms. Apologists do not invoke mystery—a confession of ignorance—until they exhaust their other options and get trapped in an intellectual prison of their own making. The mystify strategy then serves as their Get Out of Jail Free card. Apologists who play that card think they can appeal to mystery to eliminate any problem posed by the Bible or their religion more generally. If no one objects, apologists insulate their beliefs from further scrutiny by relying on an enigma that neither they nor anyone else can comprehend.

The apologists using this strategy normally do not name it because the phrase "God moves in mysterious ways" has become somewhat tainted in recent years. When William Lane Craig faces a tough question during a debate with an atheist, for example, he will sometimes justify God's questionable commands, actions, or inactions by asserting that God had a "morally sufficient reason" that Craig does not claim to know or understand.[31] That's just another way of saying that God moves in mysterious ways. Similarly, pastor and best-selling author Tim Keller responded to a question about universal salvation by pointing to two contradictory biblical teachings, saying that the Bible doesn't indicate how "both of those things can be true together." He continued by stating, "Just because I can't see a way doesn't prove there cannot be any such way."[32] Keller thus invoked the concept of a mystery without mentioning the phrase "God moves in mysterious ways."

Now that we understand the Mystify strategy and the other three, we can move past a stale debate over whether the Bible should be interpreted "literally" or "metaphorically." The difference between literal and metaphorical interpretations most often arises with respect to miracles. For example, is the Bible claiming that creation took place over six literal days, or is it giving a metaphorical account of a longer and more complex process? Are the biblical authors asserting that Moses really parted the Red Sea, or are they taking poetic license with a traditional story? Some Christians dispute the literal accounts of these and other miracles and instead offer metaphorical readings. Discussions about the Bible's moral teachings, however, follow a different track. When apologists feel uncomfortable with some aspect of the Bible's morality, they rarely dismiss it by making a metaphorical interpretation. Instead, they Ignore, Rationalize, Reinterpret, and/or Mystify what the Bible says.

THE STRATEGIES IN PRACTICE

A concrete example will help illustrate how apologists use the four strategies, and the story of Elisha, the boys, and the she-bears works well for this purpose. As described in the book of 2 Kings, the prophet Elijah ascended to heaven on a whirlwind, and his wonder-working mission then fell to his protégé, Elisha. What the prophet Elisha did next in 2 Kings 2:23–25 will raise the eyebrows of even the most devout believer:

He went up from there to Bethel; and while he was going up on the way, some small boys came out of the city and jeered at him, saying, "Go away, baldhead! Go away, baldhead!" When he turned around and saw them, he cursed them in the name of the LORD. Then two she-bears came out of the woods and mauled forty-two of the boys. From there he went on to Mount Carmel, and then returned to Samaria.

This is not the kind of story that clergy members include in homilies or inspirational sermons, for the God it depicts exacted a vicious punishment on forty-two boys for acting like, well, boys. As I grow older and lose some of my hair, I can understand Elisha taking umbrage at some young whippersnappers taunting him as "baldy." However, did God really need to send she-bears from the woods to maul the boys? It's hard to determine who was more petty in this situation—the prophet who cursed the boys or the God who delivered the punishment, but it doesn't matter. Either way, the Bible is portraying a profoundly immoral response to the offense.

I don't recall ever encountering this story when I was a Christian. It has become better known in recent years, and it now regularly attracts the attention of apologists. One of them is David Lamb, a professor at the Missio Seminary in Philadelphia, Pennsylvania. Lamb wrote a popular book titled *God Behaving Badly: Is the God of the Old Testament Angry, Racist and Sexist?*[33] You can probably guess that Lamb's answer to his question is no. His book found a receptive home within the evangelical community, where reviewers praised his "common-sense, clear-thinking interpretation" and thanked him for "equipping the reader to answer tough questions about God's character."[34]

Lamb addresses many problematic passages of the Old Testament, including the story of Elisha, the boys, and the she-bears. By confronting the story directly, Lamb forgoes the "Ignore" strategy, but his response draws from each of the other three. Lamb correctly observes that the Hebrew word translated as boys can also refer to youths or adolescents.[35] From there, his account goes off the rails. He reinterprets the text by adding the detail that the boys (or youths) were actually a "teenage gang" who threatened the prophet's life.[36] Lamb then rationalizes the violence against them on grounds that insults were a serious matter in ancient societies. Strong norms of honor and authority in Elisha's homeland meant that "within his cultural context his behavior was justified."[37] Lamb doesn't seem to realize that he has waded knee-deep into the morass of moral relativism, where there is no universal standard to condemn a behavior occurring in a particular society. He also seems unsure of his own attempts to "Reinterpret" and "Rationalize" the text, because he admits that he doesn't "fully understand the severity of God's violent reaction."[38] You'll recognize his confession as a version of the "Mystify" strategy.

Other Christian apologists who interpret this story take the same broad approach as Lamb, especially his emphasis on the threat the boys or youths posed to Elisha.[39] All of these interpretations share one important characteristic: They were constructed in modern times. Tucked away in just three verses within a relatively obscure part of the Bible, the story was not a regular feature of biblical study before the Enlightenment. The commentators who did address it felt no need to insert a line about the boys or youths being a street gang who threatened the prophet's life.

Those commentators included some of the most learned clergymen in England. The Westminster Assembly, which commissioned a commentary on the entire Bible largely from within the Reformed tradition, gives us an important index of pre-Enlightenment sentiment. The prophet Elisha was "not doing anything to provoke" the boys into insulting him, the commentators observed, and "to be bald-headed is no just cause of any scorn." Coming from their home in Bethel, the boys were "children of idolaters" who sinfully uttered a "blasphemous scoff" of God's prophet: "The sin was great in itself, greater in regard of the person against whom it was committed"—making the punishment a "just judgment."[40]

English theologian Matthew Poole subsequently offered his own commentary on the Bible. Noting that Bethel "was the mother-city of idolatry," Poole stressed that the insult reflected these idolaters' "impiety and hatred of God and his prophets." The boys were fully accountable for their actions, for they "were grown up to some maturity." They mocked not only a man and prophet "but even God himself," making them "guilty of idolatry, which by God's law deserved death."[41]

Why did David Lamb, our modern apologist, interpret the story so differently than the Westminster commentators, Matthew Poole, and others in Christian history? To answer this question, we must link back to theologian Gleason Archer's first rule for handling difficult Bible passages. Recall that Archer insisted that God and the Bible will always be acquitted of all charges, with individual Christians sharing responsibility to build the best possible case for that predetermined outcome. The Christians of earlier centuries did not struggle with the story in 2 Kings because it and the rest of the Bible offered sufficient justification for the punishment. The boys from Bethel, a city full of idolaters (1 Kings 12:25–33; 2 Kings 23:15–20), bowed to idols and worshipped false gods, meaning that they repeatedly violated the first and second of the Ten Commandments. As noted by the Westminster commentators and Matthew Poole, the boys also mocked God's prophet and thereby committed blasphemy, a grievous sin punishable by death (Leviticus 24:16). God therefore gave them the punishment they deserved.

David Lamb, however, chose not to invoke this answer provided in the Bible. As a child of the Enlightenment, he almost surely embraces the principle of religious freedom, even for pagans and atheists. To the ears of most people in the West, and possibly Lamb himself, the concepts of idolatry and blasphemy sound faintly ridiculous. Religious freedom includes the right to make idolatrous or blasphemous statements in the public square or—ahem—in books such as this one. Other scholars have explored the complicated history of Christianity and religious freedom in great detail, and I'll return to it in chapter 5, but a short summary here will suffice. After suffering occasional persecution as a religious minority under Roman rule, Christians turned the tables once they achieved numerical and political dominance in the Roman Empire and later throughout Europe. Christians proceeded to sporadically persecute pagans, heretics, and Jews for over a millennium. Amid the carnage from religious wars during the sixteenth and seventeenth centuries, some Christians then made important contributions to the political and philosophical case for religious freedom.[42]

For present purposes, what matters is that Western societies now cherish religious freedom as a foundational principle, and Lamb formed his values within that environment. In his five-page response to the story in 2 Kings, he does not even mention the facts that pre-Enlightenment commentators cited to justify the boys' punishment: their idolatry and blasphemy. To someone like Lamb who upholds the principle of religious freedom, those offenses are insufficient for a just God to unleash she-bears onto the boys. Lamb therefore must take a different path to his predetermined destination of salvaging the Bible, so he reinterprets the story to turn the boys or youths into a thuggish gang who threatened the prophet's life. Even here the punishment is excessive—God did not have to send wild animals to maul them—but this is the best explanation Lamb can offer. He also rationalizes the passage based on the context of the times and then deploys every apologist's fallback strategy of mystification.

I don't question Lamb's sincerity in trying to explain this story. In his book he comes across as earnest, thoughtful, and good-natured, and he undoubtedly believes his proposed solutions to the Elisha story and other problems in the Bible. Nevertheless, he's blinded by faith and doesn't recognize all the contortions he has made to defend the Bible's moral system and uphold its God as fair, kind, generous, just, and merciful. Perhaps a close study of pre-Enlightenment commentaries on the Bible would convince him that he's reading into the text rather than drawing from it.

We'll see in the next chapter that contortions like Lamb's are standard fare among apologists. No matter what kind of immorality the Bible teaches, apologists always find a way to justify it. Now that we understand how their strategies work, we can proceed to a deeper dive into some of the most morally flawed biblical passages.

CHAPTER 2

How Christian Apologists Whitewash the Bible

LET'S SUPPOSE YOU DECIDE TO INVENT A NEW RELIGION. BEFORE determining its precise content, you search for models from throughout human history. You soon learn that, a few exceptions notwithstanding, any respectable religion must have some kind of God or gods. You are tempted to design your religion around gods because they afford endless opportunities for you to tell stories to regale your followers. In those stories the gods will plot against each other, demonstrate extraordinary powers, express the full range of human emotions, and even mate with special human beings. What drama! Each god will have jurisdiction over a specific area—the weather, childbirth, health, love, commerce, death, etc.—and people will commune with the gods through prayers, offerings, rituals, shrines, sacrifices, and pilgrimages.

Yet upon reflection, you start to see the weaknesses of a polytheistic system. The trend around the world over the last two millennia has been toward monotheism, and you wonder whether people will embrace a new religion based on many gods. In an age when most people have at least a rudimentary understanding of science, will anyone accept that different domains of life are each governed by a separate god? A divine realm with a single God, you conclude, is simpler and easier to understand. Your God will possess impressive qualities, including being omniscient, omnipotent, and omnibenevolent. You'll lose some of the storytelling potential inherent to polytheism, but you can always invent secondary divine beings such as angels and demons to spice up the interactions between the material and spiritual worlds.

Thinking further about what a new religion should entail, you realize you must address what is called the "problem of evil." If God is omniscient, he knows about all the evil in the world; if he is omnipotent, he could eliminate it; and if he is omnibenevolent, he would want to do so. The prevalence and persistence of evil might therefore make people question whether your God is real. People who experience or witness suffering will be especially likely to raise challenging questions about God's character. Without a good answer to why God allows so much suffering, your religion might never get off the ground.

While contemplating your response, you find it helpful to distinguish between two kinds of evil. Through natural evil, debilitating diseases kill infants, children, adults, and animals one at a time, while hurricanes, tsunamis, earthquakes, and other natural disasters decimate thousands or even millions in one fell swoop. You can't honestly say that you have a good explanation for natural evil, so you decide to reconsider it at a later date. You then give your full attention to the second category, moral evil. You observe that some people lie, slander, defraud, and steal, while others commit vicious acts including assault, rape, torture, and murder. The scale of atrocities increases when people gather into groups and engage in warfare, conquest, and genocide. The amount of suffering that some humans have inflicted on others since the beginning of recorded history boggles the mind. Why doesn't your God do something about all of this evil in the world?

Fortunately, you think you have a solution: Your God created human beings and intentionally gave them free will. He could have designed automatons who acted according to inborn templates through which they never harmed anyone else, but he wanted humans to treat each other kindly and fairly through their own volition. Without free will, they would deserve neither credit for good actions nor blame for bad ones. Given the wide range of choices available to them, some humans will invariably cause others to suffer, but that's the price of freedom. If God instead forced certain behaviors or prevented people from acting upon their desires, they would be merely puppets on a string. In order for an action to have meaning, you conclude, it must be freely chosen.

CHRISTIAN APOLOGISTS AND THE FREE WILL FRAUD

My account above is not hypothetical, for Christian groups and leaders use the same logic to explain why moral evil exists. As stated in the Catechism of the Catholic Church, "Angels and men, as intelligent and free creatures, have to journey toward their ultimate destinies by their free choice and preferential love. They can therefore go astray. Indeed, they have sinned. Thus has *moral evil*, incommensurably more harmful than physical evil, entered the world. God is in no way, directly or indirectly, the cause of moral evil. He permits it, however, because he respects the freedom of his creatures and, mysteriously, knows how to derive good from it."[1] Apologetic works by individual Catholics and Protestants make similar points.[2] Apologists offer many explanations for natural evil, but free will is typically either their first or only answer for moral evil.

Curiously, most apologists do not cite a single biblical passage to sustain these claims about God, free will, and moral evil.[3] Other apologists do quote verses where a person demonstrated the freedom of choice, but they fail to offer any biblical grounding for their crucial point that God does not interfere with free will.[4] Their omission should give us pause. It's almost as if apologists have pulled a solution out of thin air to extricate themselves from a sticky situation. If you were inventing a God from scratch, you could make a move of that sort and easily cover your tracks. You could design God to have whatever characteristics necessary to resolve the problem of evil, then write the solution into the holy book that your followers would accept as his inspired Word. Christian apologists, however, don't have that option. They're stuck with the Bible passed down through the ages and the God it portrays. Therein lies the problem.

Ordinarily, apologists insist that we derive our understanding of God from the Bible. As explained by the late Tim LaHaye, an evangelical minister and coauthor of the bestselling *Left Behind* books, "One of the major purposes of Bible study is to know God, for as we have seen, He reveals Himself to us through His Word."[5] *Nelson's Illustrated Bible Dictionary* similarly tells its readers they can grasp God's character "by examining His attributes as revealed in the Bible."[6] According to the online evangelical ministry GotQuestions.org, "The Bible, God's word, tells us what God is like and what He is not like. Without the authority of the Bible, any attempt to explain God's attributes would be no better than an opinion."[7]

Given that they instruct other Christians to learn about God from the Bible, why do apologists violate their own rule and engage in special pleading when writing about God's relationship to free will? The answer is obvious: The Bible never states or even implies that God refrains from intervening in free will. In fact, the Bible shows God doing the exact opposite on many occasions. Most famously, God pledges that he will harden Pharaoh's heart, inflict calamities on the Egyptians, and free the Israelites from slavery (Exodus 7:3–4). God then proceeds to fulfill each part of his promise. The story unfolds in a back-and-forth manner whereby God hardens Pharaoh's heart at key moments (Exodus 9:12, 10:20, 10:27, 11:10, 14:8), while Pharaoh hardens his own heart at other times (Exodus 8:15, 8:32, 9:34).

This is but one example, for God continues to interfere with free will in many other biblical passages. In Deuteronomy 2:30, God hardens King Simon's heart so that the king will block the Israelites from crossing his land. During Joshua's conquest of the Promised Land (Joshua 11:20), God hardens the hearts of Joshua's adversaries to ensure they will fight Israel and get slaughtered. In 1 Samuel 18:10–11, God sends an evil spirit that causes Saul to throw his spear and attempt to pin David to the wall. The apostle Paul in Romans 9:17–18 links back to the Exodus story to make the more general point that God "has mercy on whom he chooses, and he hardens the heart of whomever he chooses." Intervening in free will, Paul assures us, is not a one-time event but rather a routine feature of God's providence over the world.

What can we conclude from the fact that apologists writing about the problem of evil overlook all of these verses? This is a textbook case of the "Ignore" strategy that I explained in chapter 1. If you can't find any biblical basis for believing that God has a principled objection to interfering with free will, just avoid the Bible entirely and hope nobody notices. We have a word for that: cheating.

Probing Deeper into the Problem of Evil

Christian apologists use many other deceptive tactics. They commonly write sections, chapters, or entire books asking the same question I have posed: Why does God allow evil?[8] It seems like a reasonable question until you realize it contains a hidden assumption. Asking a loaded question ("Are you still beating your wife?") is a rhetorical ploy in which the questioner dictates the possible answers by presuming something unjustified or unproven. An apologist who asks the loaded question "Why does God allow evil?" has assumed that God never *causes* evil. With that possibility ruled out by sleight of hand, the apologist then tries to explain why God allows evil. As I have shown, apologists cannot answer their own question while maintaining fidelity to the Bible, but the problem runs deeper because they have bypassed the tougher challenge.

One of the clearest examples of God causing evil occurs in Romans 13:1: "Let every person be subject to the governing authorities; for there is no authority except from God, and those authorities that exist have been instituted by God." Paul's account in this verse is entirely consistent with the Old Testament, where God chooses the leaders in Israel and other nations (see also Proverbs 8:15–16). Note that Romans 13:1 says that all governing authorities, not just the good ones, assumed power through God's intervention. The implications are profound. According to the Bible, God gave political authority not only to Mandela, Lincoln, and Cyrus the Great, but also to Hitler, Stalin, Pol Pot, and every other tyrant across human history. God was therefore a direct contributor to human misery of all kinds, up to and including genocide. Moreover, because he is omniscient, God knew in every instance that his actions would lead to thousands or millions of deaths.

Interestingly, apologists rarely comment on Romans 13:1, perhaps because atheists and humanists have not consistently challenged them on it.[9] In any case, we can imagine a number of responses. An apologist might assert that God does not actually kill anyone through genocide but merely opens the door for political leaders to carry it out. Strictly speaking, that's true according to Romans 13:1, but God doesn't get off the hook that easily. If a person brought to a children's summer camp a pedophile with a long history of acting on his desires, would you hold the facilitator blameless for any sexual assaults the pedophile commits? If not, then why should we absolve God of responsibility for giving governmental authority to mass murderers? In a court of law, we would convict him of millions of counts of aiding and abetting murder. Although it's not as bad as pulling the trigger, aiding and abetting is still a serious offense.

With one option foreclosed, an apologist could turn to the "Mystify" defense. Maybe God has a plan we don't understand and he paves the way for governmental atrocities so that he can accomplish a larger purpose. God's ways are beyond our comprehension, the reasoning goes, and he uses genocide to bring his divine plan to fruition. If you're willing to accept that story, you have to believe the ends justify the means. That's a questionable morality for humanity, but it's even worse for God. A human being might be tempted to commit a heinous act—say, killing one person—for the greater good of saving ten others. For an omnipotent God, such a choice would never arise. Remember, this is a God who can supposedly create the universe out of nothing, cause seas to part, arrange miraculous healings, and bend the will of whomever he chooses. If God wanted to, he could turn a raccoon into a carrot; that's what it means to be omnipotent. Unless you abandon the concept of divine omnipotence, you have to admit that God could find some means other than genocide to accomplish whatever ends he was seeking.

Possibly anticipating this objection, R. C. Sproul, one of the most famous American theologians of the last half-century, tries another tack. After accepting that Romans 13:1 means what it says, Sproul deploys the "Rationalize" strategy: "We have to distinguish, however, between a government ordained by God and a government approved by God. God did not approve of Nero and Stalin, but it was His design that they come to power. God gives us wicked rulers as part of His judgment on our sins."[10] Let's pause to break down Sproul's response. According to Sproul, God installs genocidal dictators in office but does not approve of their actions, as if that's supposed to relieve God of any responsibility for the outcomes. Would we exonerate a man morally or legally for aiding and abetting mass murder if he said he disapproved of the result? If not, why should we hold God to a lower standard? The problem becomes even worse when we realize that God, being omniscient, can fully anticipate the consequences of his actions.

The second part of Sproul's rationalization says that "our sins" justify God giving us tyrannical rulers. The problem here is a wild mismatch between the offenses and the punishment. Not everyone gets eliminated through genocide, just those who belong to the wrong race, ethnicity, religion, or political affiliation, and who live under a regime that demonizes them as a threatening and detestable outgroup. If "our sins" merit someone being exterminated through starvation, gunshots, machetes, or gas chambers—itself a dubious proposition—then why do most people get off scot-free while only minority groups face punishment? Despite Sproul's best attempt to rationalize Romans 13:1, God still comes across as arbitrary and despotic, a divine being who aids and abets genocide.

GOD COMMANDING GENOCIDE

In other places in the Bible, God goes one step further and actually *commands* genocide. Questions surrounding genocide in the Bible continue to attract scrutiny from believers and nonbelievers alike. In contrast to Romans 13:1, which they usually ignore, apologists regularly write about God ordering the Israelites to kill all the Canaanites and the other nations living in Canaan, a region including parts of modern-day Jordan, Israel, Syria, and Lebanon.[11] The details of the biblical accounts do not make for cozy bedtime reading. In Deuteronomy 7:1–2, Moses relays the communication he received from God: "When the Lord your God brings you into the land that he clears away many nations before you—the Hittites, the Girgashites, the Amorites, the Canaanites, the Perizzites, the Hivites, and the Jebusites, seven nations mightier and more numerous than you—and when the Lord your God gives them over to you and you defeat them, then you must utterly destroy them. Make no covenant with them and show them no mercy." Deuteronomy 20:16–17 continues: "But as for the towns of these peoples that the Lord your God is giving you as an inheritance, you must not let anything that breathes remain alive. You shall annihilate them—the Hittites and the Amorites, the Canaanites and the Perizzites, the Hivites and the Jebusites—just as the Lord your God has commanded."

Lest readers think this was just idle talk, the Bible records the Israelites fulfilling part of God's command during Moses's lifetime, including
the slaying of King Sihon and the Amorites: "So they killed him, his
sons, and all his people, until there was no survivor left; and they took
possession of his land" (Numbers 21:35). Most of the genocide occurred
under the leadership of Moses's successor: "Joshua turned back at that
time, and took Hazor, and struck its king down with the sword. Before
that time Hazor was the head of all those kingdoms. And they put to the
sword all who were in it, utterly destroying them; there was no one left
who breathed, and he burned Hazor with fire. And all the towns of those
kings, and all their kings, Joshua took, and struck them with the edge of
the sword, utterly destroying them, as Moses the servant of the Lord had
commanded" (Joshua 11:10–12).

Readers who encounter this material for the first time are often
shocked that it appears in the Bible, let alone through God's direct
order. Seasoned apologists, however, have seen it all before. How can
they justify God's behavior? Before we examine their writings, we know
from chapter 1 that they will use one or more of four strategies: "Ignore,"
"Rationalize," "Reinterpret," and "Mystify." It turns out the "Rationalize" and "Reinterpret" strategies serve their purposes well here, for they
typically insist that the event in question involved capital punishment,
not genocide—thereby making it defensible.[12] To most apologists, the
Israelites were merely the instrument God used to punish the assorted
Canaanite peoples for their wickedness and debauchery. As stated by
Clay Jones, who has held academic appointments in apologetics, "The
Bible is unambiguous concerning what sins they committed, including
idolatry, incest, adultery, child sacrifice, homosexuality, and bestiality."[13]
With that litany of offenses, apologists assert, God was fully justified in
bringing the death penalty, especially after he gave them four hundred
years to repent.

Many apologists also argue that the biblical writers exaggerated in
reporting that "there was no one left who breathed" in the Canaanite
towns. This may well be an area where modern scholarship has gained
insights into the text that interpreters missed through most of Christian history. While poring over proclamations, historical records, and

archeological evidence, scholars have discovered that it was common in the ancient Near East for victorious armies to inflate the number of casualties they inflicted. The true level of destruction was usually much lower than what their leaders claimed.[14] Placed in its historical context, apologists note, any conquest of the sort the Bible describes probably fell short of total destruction.[15]

Biblical support for this view comes from descriptions of Canaanites in later stories, implying that some of them survived the onslaught. Had they all been eliminated, as a literal reading of the conquest narrative would suggest, the Canaanites could not have continued to interact with the Israelites. Of course, actions can be genocidal even if there are some survivors. As defined by the Convention on the Prevention and Punishment of the Crime of Genocide, which has been ratified by 152 countries, a genocide occurs through actions intended to destroy a religious, ethnic, national, or racial group "in whole or in part."[16] The conquest of Canaan would qualify as a genocide even if the biblical writers exaggerated the level of destruction.

Perhaps recognizing this problem, Christian philosopher and theologian Paul Copan takes his reasoning in a different direction. Copan's book *Is God a Moral Monster? Making Sense of the Old Testament God* is one of the most widely cited works of Christian apologetics from the last decade. Christian reviewers praised his book for "answering many of the hard questions that arise from the Old Testament"[17] and for defending a biblical morality "that is liberating and awe-inspiring."[18] Demonstrating the book's prominence within the apologetic community, William Lane Craig sometimes points his debate audiences to it when he receives a difficult Old Testament question.[19] One Christian ministry even gave copies to its donors.[20]

It will thus be worthwhile to consider how Copan handles the genocide of the Canaanite nations. Like other apologists, Copan stresses their wickedness as justification for God levying the death penalty on them. Copan also asserts that the people "targeted for destruction were political leaders and their armies rather than noncombatants."[21] According to Copan, the towns the Israelites attacked were military outposts, not population centers. As he builds his case, Copan implicitly invokes two principles widely accepted today: people must be punished for serious offenses, and armies should not kill civilians. If he can convince the reader that the biblical stories adhere to these rules, he will have succeeded in rationalizing the unspeakable violence depicted therein.

Copan apparently doesn't realize that the details of the conquest place his two principles in direct conflict with each other. If the Canaanite nations brought the death penalty upon themselves through their grievous sins, why should noncombatants be exempted from judgment? Justice would dictate that everyone who committed the sins, not just soldiers, deserved to die. Indeed, it would be a miscarriage of justice to let guilty parties—people who had sacrificed their own children and committed many other sins—walk away with no punishment. Copan's work shows us how difficult it is to keep your story straight once you start rationalizing the Bible. When apologists keep adding new rationalizations, they can easily find themselves caught in a contradiction.

Having failed to spot the contradiction in Copan's approach, some later apologists have adopted it wholesale.[22] Other apologists, however, are willing to grant that women, children, the elderly, and other people who were not the primary combatants died during the Israelites' conquest. In his own famous defense of the massacres, William Lane Craig asserts that the slaughtered children went straight to heaven, a clever way of rationalizing their deaths.[23] Two other well-known apologists, Seth McDowell and Jonathan Morrow, freely acknowledge that they have no explicit biblical basis for saying so, but they agree with Craig that the children are now spending eternity with God.[24]

We see here another danger of the "Rationalize" strategy, in that it often solves a problem only to create a different one. If Craig, McDowell, and Morrow are right, then the Israelites did the children a huge favor by killing them. The attacks occurred before what McDowell and Morrow call the children's "age of accountability" when they would become responsible for their decisions.[25] Had the children escaped with other Canaanites into the countryside, they almost surely would have grown up to be pagans and idolaters—all non-Israelites fell into those categories—and they would therefore be ticketed for an afterlife in hell.

By slaughtering the children, the Israelites gave them a gift that literally keeps on giving forever.

Think for a moment about the implications of this position. It means that one of the most humane things an individual can do, whether in Canaan or elsewhere, is to kill a child. Doing so ensures the victim a place in heaven, whereas letting the child live risks the possibility of them suffering eternal punishment in hell. Why take a chance on the child's everlasting torment when you know a simple shooting, stabbing, or poisoning can guarantee the child an afterlife of infinite bliss with God? For that matter, why not use the authority of the state to mandate abortion? If a fertilized egg counts as a person from the moment of conception, as conservative Christians believe, then both the woman and the doctor perform a humanitarian service by undertaking an abortion. An aborted fetus instantly joins God in heaven, but all bets are off if it passes through infancy and childhood to become an adult who may or may not die with a faith in Christ.[26] Attempts to rationalize the Bible often cause apologists to fall into traps of this sort.

KILL ALL AMALEKITES

You probably didn't notice the misdirection I created in the last section. I introduced the subject of God commanding genocide and then immediately began discussing the Canaanite peoples. In proceeding this way, I tried to model the misdirection common in the works of Christian apologists. Their books often cover the Canaanites within a section, chapter, or multiple chapters, after which the apologist moves on to other topics. However, the God of the Bible actually commands the Israelites to exterminate two different groups: the assorted Canaanite nations and also the Amalekites. When apologists talk about the former but not the latter, they are using the "Ignore" strategy. Why do apologists so rarely discuss the genocide of the Amalekites?

This oversight leads one to suspect the apologists have something to hide. Recall that nearly every apologist rationalizes the Canaanite massacres by saying that they were examples not of genocide but rather capital punishment for people who committed abominable sins such as incest, bestiality, and child sacrifice. Can apologists recycle the same explanation for the nation of Amalek? Let's examine Deuteronomy 25:17–19 to see why not. Speaking through his prophet Moses, God says to the Israelites: "Remember what Amalek did to you on your journey out of Egypt, how he attacked you on the way, when you were faint and weary, and struck down all who lagged behind you; he did not fear God. Therefore when the Lord your God has given you rest from all your enemies on every hand, in the land that the Lord your God is giving you as an inheritance to possess, you shall blot out the remembrance of Amalek from under heaven; do not forget." Notice that God here is commanding a later generation to kill the descendants of the Amalekites who attacked the Israelites during their journey out of Egypt.

After more than four centuries have passed, God works through his prophet Samuel to instruct the Israelites to carry out his long-standing order. When reading this passage (1 Samuel 15:1–3), pay careful attention to the justification God gives for why the Israelites had to eliminate the Amalekites: "Samuel said to Saul, 'The Lord sent me to anoint you king over his people Israel; now therefore listen to the words of the Lord. Thus says the Lord of hosts, "I will punish the Amalekites for what they did in opposing the Israelites when they came up out of Egypt. Now go and attack Amalek, and utterly destroy all that they have; do not spare them, but kill both man and woman, child and infant, ox and sheep, camel and donkey.'" In that passage's key sentence, God says, "I will punish the Amalekites for what they did in opposing the Israelites when they came out of Egypt."

Saul then fulfills most of the order in 1 Samuel 15:7–9: "Saul defeated the Amalekites, from Havilah as far as Shur, which is east of Egypt. He took King Agag of the Amalekites alive, but utterly destroyed all the people with the edge of the sword. Saul and the people spared Agag, and the best of the sheep and of the cattle and of the fatlings, and the lambs, and all that was valuable, and would not utterly destroy them; all that was despised and worthless they utterly destroyed."

You can see why apologists don't want to talk about these verses. They cannot point to child sacrifice or sexual sins to rationalize the Amalekites' slaughter. The texts of Deuteronomy 25:17–19 and 1 Samuel 15:1–3 clearly state the reason why the Amalekites had to die: intergenerational punishment. Over four hundred years after the nation of Amalek attacked Israel, the Israelites levied the punishment God commanded at that earlier time. This would be like the British of today invading and decimating the French to retaliate for offenses France committed under King Louis XIII. Fortunately, we have long since abandoned the barbaric beliefs that would justify such behavior. We now think a person is accountable only for their own actions, not those of distant ancestors. Instead of defending the biblical concept of intergenerational punishment, most apologists plead the fifth. They talk about the genocide of the Canaanite nations, which they believe (incorrectly) they can explain, while ignoring the more difficult case of the Amalekites.

It will be instructive to engage one of the relatively few apologists who does address the Amalekites. Paul Copan, whom we met earlier as the author of *Is God a Moral Monster?*, devotes nearly three chapters to the Canaanites. He covers the Amalekites in only one and a half pages, but he differs from most apologists by at least saying *something*.[27] Although Copan ordinarily quotes verbatim the verses under consideration, he deviates from his usual practice here, and we learn why when we read his discussion. Copan uses the "Reinterpret" strategy, which is easier to implement if readers do not have the full text of the biblical passages at their fingertips. I doubt he is trying to deceive his readers, but the effect is the same regardless of his intentions. Perhaps unconsciously, Copan seems to realize that quoting directly from the verses will undermine his case.

How does Copan reinterpret the slaughter of the Amalekites? After briefly mentioning that the Amalekites attacked Israel during an earlier era, Copan refers to a few verses unrelated to the later genocide suggesting that "they continued to be a thorn in Israel's side for generations."[28] Rather than relying on the Bible's stated reason of intergenerational punishment, which is explicitly given in Deuteronomy 25:17–19 and 1 Samuel 15:1–3, Copan claims that God punished the Amalekites for both previous *and* continuing offenses. Like magazines that airbrush photographs to highlight a person's best features and hide any blemishes, Copan edits the story in a subtle yet powerful way to make it more palatable.

We can examine how Christians understood the Bible before modern times to see that Copan's interpretation was invented after the onset of the Enlightenment. It will be useful to start with the Puritans because they were familiar with the biblical story in question, and yet they felt no need to change the reason why the Amalekites had to be killed. John Winthrop, one of the Puritan founders of the Massachusetts Bay Colony, drew from the story the lesson that God's commands must be "strictly observed."[29] The influential Puritan minister Cotton Mather thought that the slaughter of the Amalekites provided a model for the colonists' own wars against Indian tribes.[30] Interpreters from earlier in Christian history also saw nothing objectionable about the massacre. Thomas Aquinas, for example, did not try to reinterpret it to eliminate the intergenerational nature of the punishment. He focused instead on condemning Saul for deciding "to offer in sacrifice the fat animals of the Amalekites against the commandment of God."[31]

Which brings us back to Paul Copan. Unlike his predecessors, Copan apparently cannot bear to think his God would punish people to atone for their ancestors' sins. He therefore inserts a crucial detail into the story to change its meaning. Copan's revisionist history flows out of the intellectual and moral worlds he inhabits. During and after the Enlightenment, people developed new ideas about crime and punishment. Virtually everyone now deems it immoral to punish someone because of their membership in a group, or because their distant ancestors committed certain offenses, and yet the God of the Bible often punishes in precisely those ways. I address this issue in greater depth in chapter 4. Many of the Bible's moral flaws stem from its tendency to reduce individuals to the groups to which they belong, and this matter deserves the longer treatment I give it there. For now, it's sufficient to note that Copan reinterprets the Bible to avoid having to acknowledge how its God behaves.

THE BIBLE'S SUPPORT FOR SLAVERY
In ways similar to how they handle genocide, apologists can choose from the four strategies of "Ignore," "Rationalize," "Reinterpret," and "Mystify" to address what the Bible says about slavery. By "slavery," I mean what is technically called "chattel slavery," a practice through which one person

owns another as property that can be used, sold, given as a gift, or passed down to descendants. As historians David Eltis and Stanley Engerman explain, this is what most people mean by the term "slavery."[32] Apologists typically examine slavery in the Old Testament before turning to the New Testament, and I'll do the same.

One source of confusion is that the Old Testament uses the same word—עֶבֶד in Hebrew or *eved* when written in the Roman alphabet—to refer to either an indentured servant or a slave. Classical Hebrew contained less than nine thousand unique words, compared to about one hundred seventy-one thousand for modern English.[33] Stemming from the different sizes of their vocabularies, a single Hebrew word can map onto multiple English words with different shades of meaning. Translators respond to this dilemma for the case at hand by making one of three choices: always translate *eved* as slave, always translate *eved* as servant, or translate *eved* according to the context. The New Revised Standard Version follows the first of those options, as we can see in the key verses: "When you buy a male Hebrew slave, he shall serve six years, but in the seventh he shall go out a free person, without debt" (Exodus 21:2). Subsequent verses in Exodus add some conditions and details, and similar rules reappear in Deuteronomy 15:12: "If a member of your community, whether a Hebrew man or a Hebrew woman, is sold to you and works for you six years, in the seventh year you shall set that person free." Although many English translations of Exodus and Deuteronomy follow the NRSV in using the term *slave*, we know from the surrounding text that the situation described is indentured servitude. These and other verses stipulated that the buyer had to free the servant after six years, or during the Jubilee occurring once every forty-nine or fifty years (Leviticus 25:8–10, 40). Israelites could also become indentured servants if they were sentenced as punishment for theft (Exodus 22:1). Finally, sometimes people voluntarily became servants so that they could live under the care and protection of someone from their extended family (Leviticus 25:35, 39–41).

We find entirely different rules in Leviticus 25:44–46: "As for the male and female slaves whom you may have, it is from the nations around you that you may acquire male and female slaves. You may also acquire them from among the aliens residing with you, and from their families that are with you, who have been born in your land; and they may be your property. You may keep them as a possession for your children after you, for them to inherit as property. These you may treat as slaves, but as for your fellow Israelites, no one shall rule over the other with harshness." Unlike the verses in Exodus and Deuteronomy, the ones here in Leviticus refer to actual slavery. The text explicitly states that enslaved people can be treated as property and willed to one's offspring, and there is no provision requiring them to be released after six years.

Why do Exodus 21:2 and Deuteronomy 15:12 describe indentured servitude, whereas Leviticus 25:44–46 authorizes slavery? Is this a contradiction? No, because the verses refer to two different classes of people. Indentured servitude was reserved for fellow Hebrews, whereas slavery applied to people from "the nations around you." Leviticus 25:46 stressed this distinction in saying that you may turn foreigners into slaves, but you cannot rule harshly over other Israelites. The Old Testament described one other way through which foreigners can become slaves, namely warfare: "When you draw near to a town to fight against it, offer it terms of peace. If it accepts your terms of peace and surrenders to you, then all the people in it shall serve you at forced labor. If it does not submit to you peacefully, but makes war against you, then you shall besiege it; and when the Lord your God gives it into your hand, you shall put all its males to the sword" (Deuteronomy 20:10–13). The verses state that people who surrender during a military conflict become your slaves (see also Numbers 31:1–47). As non-Israelites, these prisoners of war did not have to be set free after six years.

Having studied the most important Old Testament verses, we are now ready to examine how apologists try to wiggle out of the problems the Bible has created for them. This is not merely an academic matter, for momentous consequences hang in the balance. If the Bible endorses slavery, one of the most brutal institutions human beings have ever created, why should we trust it as a moral guide on anything? Similarly, if God authorized slavery through his scriptures, how can he be considered morally good? Wouldn't his behavior mean that he deserves contempt rather than adulation? Apologists attempt to address these questions through several types of answers.

Through their opening salvo, apologists often apply the "Ignore" strategy and talk about indentured servitude while skipping past slavery. That's the approach taken by Hank Hanegraaff, a Christian author and radio host who earned the nickname "Bible Answer Man." In *The Complete Bible Answer Book*, he writes: "A myth propped up by secular skeptics is that Scripture sanctions slavery. Nothing could be further from the truth." While discussing the Old Testament, Hanegraaff makes one main point: "Because bankruptcy laws did not exist, people would *voluntarily* sell themselves into slavery."[34] He is certainly right that heavily indebted Israelites did sometimes sell themselves to other Israelites and become indentured servants. However, Hanegraaff fails to mention the foreigners purchased as permanent slaves (Leviticus 25:44–46) or the prisoners of war who were enslaved "voluntarily" only because the other option available to them, according to Deuteronomy 20:10–13, was mass slaughter. Those two biblical references to slavery are linked because most of the foreigners offered for sale in the ancient world entered the international slave trade through military conquests.[35]

Other apologists do mention slavery, but only after spending many more pages on indentured servitude. Writing in *The Politically Incorrect Guide to the Bible*, Robert Hutchinson declares that "the Old Testament is unquestionably anti-slavery."[36] To defend his bold assertion, Hutchinson talks extensively about the system of indentured servitude. Almost as an afterthought, he then briefly mentions the verses involving slavery in Leviticus. Similarly, Paul Copan devotes considerably more attention in his book to indentured servitude in the Old Testament than to slavery.[37] In Steve Halbrook's book *God Is Just: A Defense of the Old Testament Civil Laws*, you can't help but notice his extensive coverage of indentured servitude, but you have to search carefully to find him discussing slavery.[38]

Is focusing on indentured servitude a convincing way to acquit the Bible from the charge of authorizing slavery? As a parallel, imagine a man on trial for both jaywalking and murder. He spends most of the court's time on the former allegation, and he carefully explains why jaywalking is not a serious crime. In fact, he argues, there are situations in which jaywalking is the morally correct behavior. After droning on endlessly about jaywalking, he then briefly attempts to defend himself against the murder accusation. Would anyone serving on the jury be persuaded by the man's attempt to dodge the serious charge by concentrating instead on the lesser one? How can apologists get away with similar reasoning when they devote far more space and attention to indentured servitude than to slavery? Wouldn't anyone who examines the Bible see through this ruse?

To grasp why apologists deploy the "Ignore" strategy here despite its obvious flaws, it helps to understand the larger forces at work. The primary purpose of apologetics is not to convert non-Christians but rather to bolster the faith of people who already believe. Many apologetic works reveal this purpose through their titles that presume a Christian audience, such as William Lane Craig's *On Guard: Defending Your Faith with Reason and Precision*; Gregory Koukl's *Tactics: A Game Plan for Discussing Your Christian Convictions*; and Norman L. Geisler and Thomas Howe's *When Critics Ask: A Popular Handbook on Bible Difficulties*.[39] No doubt apologists relish the prospect of reaching the broader population with their works, and they often ask Christians to steer their non-Christian friends and family members to relevant videos, books, and websites. As a practical matter, however, the vast majority of people who consume apologetic resources are already Christians.

Much of this consumption happens through the ordinary channels of communication in churches and Christian communities. Christian leaders continually worry that believers will question or lose their faith, and they rely on apologetics as a tool to keep people in the fold. Nancy Pearcey, a noted author on the Christian worldview, pinpointed the problem over a decade ago: "To be effective in equipping young people and professionals to face the challenges of a highly educated secular society, the church needs to redefine the mission of pastors and youth leaders to include training in apologetics and worldview."[40] Many churches now make apologetics a central part of their sermons, Bible studies, and youth groups. J. Warner Wallace, a homicide detective who has lent his talents to apologetics, explains that his work involves "vaccinating" the next generation of Christians. By exposing young people to common objections to Christianity, he hopes to equip them to retain their faith throughout their entire lives.[41]

THE AUDIENCE FOR SLAVERY APOLOGETICS

Once we see that fellow Christians are their primary audience, we understand why apologists often get away with the "Ignore" strategy when addressing the Bible and slavery: They are preaching to the choir, quite literally in many instances. Christians may have heard it stated that the Bible justifies slavery, but most of them probably have not studied the matter closely. Apologists can therefore offer a comforting message: "Don't worry about it, the Bible establishes indentured servitude, not slavery." Most Americans learned in grade school that early immigrants to the American colonies often arrived as indentured servants, and apologists benefit from drawing an implicit parallel with the Bible. For someone with the will to believe, such a message might be good enough to keep them from doubting their faith or investigating the matter any further.

Most of the time, there's no one present to challenge apologists who use the "Ignore" strategy in this way. A notable exception happens on the stage of a formal debate. Over the last two decades, churches, seminaries, universities, and other organizations have hosted many debates pitting a prominent atheist against a Christian apologist. One such debate took place on October 1, 2016, between David Smalley and Matt Slick.[42] David Smalley is an atheist, stand-up comedian, and the host of the *Dogma Debate* podcast whose topics include religion, politics, and science. His debating opponent Matt Slick is one of the best-known apologists in America. As a young minister in 1995, Slick founded the Christian Apologetics and Research Ministry (CARM), which pioneered using the Internet to disseminate apologetic materials. Even today, Google searches for "apologetics" from within the United States commonly reach Slick's website as the top non-Wikipedia option. Complementing the work of his Internet ministry, Slick is the longtime host of a Christian radio show broadcast on stations throughout America.

During the debate Smalley made a passing reference to slavery, and Slick responded by talking about indentured servitude. Slick offered the analogy of professional athletes who sign a contract to play for one team for a specified number of years. The Bible, he stated, recorded the workings of a similar system, and the servants were released after six years or during the Jubilee. Slick continued: "You never find in scripture that it says that a master owns a slave. It's always said he's the master. Ownership is always referred to of animals and property, and it's never used in the Bible of people, in the context of what we call slavery."[43] Smalley did not address Slick's claim because the debate turned to other matters, but the issue arose again during the question-and-answer period. It just so happened that the audience included Matt Dillahunty, who was slated to debate Slick the following night. A leading voice in the atheist community, Dillahunty for many years has hosted a webcast and cable-access television show called *The Atheist Experience*. He is a frequent public speaker who travels around the United States for talks and debates.

Dillahunty began posing his question, but he got no further than his introduction: "So Matt, earlier you said the Bible never refers to slaves as property."[44] Sounding like a man caught with his pants down, Slick immediately interrupted Dillahunty: "To the best of my knowledge, that's correct. If you've got a verse, I'll check it out." During his long tenure as a Christian apologist, Slick had probably found himself in many discussions where nobody had the background necessary to question his claims. A different situation existed here, for he knew he had a worthy adversary in Dillahunty. Slick therefore channeled his inner lawyer and sought to defend his earlier statement ("To the best of my knowledge, that's correct") without perjuring himself. The rest of the dialogue proceeded as follows:

> Matt Dillahunty: "Leviticus 25:45 and 46, you'll buy your slaves from the heathens that surround you, they shall become your property. The Hebrew word there, by the way, is achuzzah, which is Strong's 272, which is used earlier in that same, same chapter, or actually Leviticus 10 I believe, to refer to houses and property."
> Matt Slick: "OK."
> Matt Dillahunty: "Would that mean that you are incorrect?"

Matt Slick: "If that's the case, then yes. Hold on, what's the verse? I'll go research it."

Matt Dillahunty: "Leviticus 25:45 and 46."

Matt Slick: "OK."[45]

During this exchange, Slick pretended not to know that the verses in Leviticus refer to slaves as property, saying that he would go research the matter. His denial doesn't pass the sniff test. Anyone who reads his posts, articles, reports, and books will discover that he has an encyclopedic knowledge of the Bible. During much of the last three decades, he has worked in apologetics *for a living*. Are we really supposed to believe he doesn't understand what is written in Leviticus 25:45 and 46?

As it turns out, we have more than circumstantial evidence to prove that Slick was lying. His website at CARM discusses the verses in Leviticus—the same ones Dillahunty mentioned during the debate—in a post titled, "You May Buy Slaves?" Slick asserted that, "in the fallen world that mankind had created, slavery was a reality. God permitted its existence and worked within its system."[46] Lest you wonder whether he developed his thinking *after* the debate, the post is dated from 2008, several years before his exchange with Dillahunty.

I'm willing to give Slick the benefit of the doubt and assume he's not a pathological liar. Why would a man who is presumably honest most of the time feel the need to lie during a debate? Slick's behavior demonstrates what's at stake in the controversy over the Bible and slavery. If the Bible fails to give us the right answer on such a simple moral issue as slavery, it will lose much if not all of its moral authority. Given the importance of this matter, you can see why an apologist like Slick would be tempted to deny—despite knowing otherwise—that the Bible ever treats human beings as property. Other apologists don't actually lie in this way, but they nevertheless mislead their readers by deploying the "Ignore" strategy. By focusing so much on indentured servitude in the Old Testament and so little on slavery, they make it seem like there's no problem worth discussing.

The New Testament offers them no help, for it too treats slavery as an ordinary human institution. Not a single New Testament author condemns slavery. To the contrary, the epistles take slavery for granted and prescribe the respective duties of slave and master. Titus 2:9–10 reads, "Tell slaves to be submissive to their masters and to give satisfaction in every respect; they are not to talk back, not to pilfer, but to show complete and perfect fidelity, so that in everything they may be an ornament to the doctrine of God our Savior." Ephesians 6:5–9 and Colossians 3:22–24:1 give similar commands, adding that masters should treat their slaves justly and fairly.

Meanwhile, 1 Timothy 6:1 tells enslaved people to "regard their masters as worthy of all honor." By way of comparison, can you imagine the Bible saying that someone should regard a man running a stolen-goods operation to be "worthy of all honor"? Surely such a man would not be honorable, and yet the Bible instructs those held in bondage to believe the exact opposite about masters who steal their labor. Furthermore, the gospels contain stories referring to the enslaved being sold, beaten, or killed (Matthew 18:24–34; Matthew 24:45–51; Luke 12:47–48). The fact that the biblical writers could refer to slavery in such a nonchalant manner speaks volumes about their blithe acceptance of it.

RATIONALIZING WHAT THE BIBLE SAYS ABOUT SLAVERY

In trying to finesse the Bible's support for slavery, apologists can also use the "Rationalize" strategy. Writing for the Stand to Reason ministry, for example, Melinda Penner makes the common apologetic observation that slavery in the Bible "was not race-based," and nobody was enslaved because of the color of their skin.[47] To demonstrate that this is a rationalization, we could ask her whether slavery would be acceptable so long as it happened within rather than across races. She would almost surely declare the practice immoral regardless of whether it involved members of one race enslaving those of another. Apologists such as Penner who talk about race in this context are engaging in a diversionary tactic, for they would not accept any kind of chattel slavery.

In any event, Penner's statement is misleading because biblical slavery was usually tied to ethnicity, a concept closely related to race. Recall that God told the Israelites to never treat one of their own as property, but he permitted them to hold foreigners as chattel slaves (Leviticus 25:44–46). In other verses (Deuteronomy 20:10–13 and Numbers 31:1–47) God gave the Israelites permission to enslave prisoners of war who were, almost by definition, members of other ethnic groups. Slavery in other ancient societies, including the Greco-Roman world of the New Testament, was also practiced along ethnic lines. Historians such as Brooke Newman, Lukas de Blois, and R. J. van der Spek have shown that most chattel slaves originated as prisoners of war from conflicts between different ethnic groups, with smaller numbers acquiring their status by being born into it or sentenced for a crime.[48] Thus, apologists are splitting hairs when they try to rationalize biblical slavery on grounds that it wasn't based on race, when we know full well that it was usually based on ethnicity.

Christian writer Wayne Jackson offers another rationalization, saying that biblical slavery was more humane than other ancient systems or the later ones of the New World.[49] Many people dispute this point.[50] For one thing, every slave system includes both generous and harsh slaveholders, along with huge variation in the kinds of work enslaved people perform. A house slave on a Southern plantation might well have led a better life than an agricultural slave toiling for twelve hours a day in ancient Israel or Rome. For the sake of argument, however, let's suppose that Jackson is correct. What difference does it make? Would rape be acceptable in a particular case if the perpetrator used less force than the rapists from another time and place? The essence of slavery is one person owning another. You can't hide that reality by appealing to verses commanding the master to treat his slave kindly, especially when other verses allow him to beat his slave so long as the person does not die within a day or two (Exodus 21:20–21).

A still further attempt at rationalization holds that God secretly knew slavery was wrong but chose not to reveal his knowledge in the Bible. Appealing to God's hidden knowledge is a convenient way to ensure that no matter what the Bible says, all goodness must spring from God. If God did something moral in the Bible, such as telling people to love each other, the apologist points to that command as an indicator of

God's true character. If God did something immoral, such as authorizing slavery, the apologist claims that God secretly knew better but accommodated himself to human sinfulness in allowing the practice. So long as nobody notices the game being played here, the apologist creates a situation of heads I win, tails you lose.

Robert Hutchinson took this approach and called slavery God's "concession to the hardness of human hearts in the brutal world of the ancient Near East."[51] In inspiring the words of the Bible, God "did not signify approval but merely the recognition of slavery as a worldly reality."[52] Matt Slick echoed Hutchinson in the post I mentioned earlier by insisting that God's statements in the Bible did not reflect his true beliefs, for God "works within the fallen system to bring about His will."[53] The apologists Sean McDowell and Jonathan Morrow reckon that "influence takes time and moral progress is often painfully slow," so God did not use the Bible to express his true beliefs about slavery. Instead he set forth principles that would eventually lead people to abolish the practice.[54]

Despite their surface appeal, these rationalizations fall flat because they require a God radically different than the one described in the Christian scriptures. In other words, they are rationalizations imposed on the Bible rather than derived from it. When we read the actual text, we see that the God of the Bible is no shrinking violet who refrains from expressing his will or intervening to bring justice to the world. To punish humanity for its wickedness, for example, he unleashed a flood to kill everyone except Noah and his family (Genesis 6–8). When the northern kingdom of Israel was wracked with disobedience and immorality, God sent the Assyrians to conquer it (2 Kings 17:1–23).

Beyond these and other punishments indicating that he took justice seriously, we encounter in both the Old and New Testaments a God prescribing his commandments in great detail. He routinely prohibited certain practices while mandating others. Had he wanted to declare slavery immoral, all God had to do was include a command saying, "Thou shalt not own slaves." True, putting such a statement on the books would not have immediately ended the practice, just as forbidding adultery did not eliminate all instances where somebody cheated on their spouse. Nevertheless, God could have stated that slaveholding was a grievous sin. It strains credulity to think that a God who declared his will on dozens of other issues with clarity and precision suddenly became mealymouthed on slavery.

When All Else Fails, Reinterpret the Bible

If Christian apologists cannot whitewash the Bible's support for slavery through the "Ignore" or "Rationalize" strategies, perhaps they can "Reinterpret" it. Many apologists have done so by trying to turn Exodus 21:16—which says you cannot kidnap and sell someone, an offense punishable by death—into a more general proclamation against slavery. Christian author and pastor Jack Wellman reinterprets the verse in precisely this way: "People might be surprised to learn that the Bible does not condone slavery at all, even in the Old Testament as many falsely claim. Even in the first laws that God gave, God abhorred the capturing of people to make them slaves. Exodus 21:16 states, 'Anyone who kidnaps someone is to be put to death, whether the victim has been sold or is still in the kidnapper's possession.' God not only forbids slavery, He gives them the death penalty for it. That's how serious God sees slavery as."[55]

Wellman and others who use the same approach fail to distinguish between the different ways someone can become enslaved. It's true that Exodus 21:16 bans kidnapping a free person and selling them into slavery. Wellman seems to think this was some kind of moral innovation of the Bible; it was not. Every ancient society in the Near East had similar laws and norms. In Babylonia, Assyria, Egypt, Greece, Persia, and Rome, you could not legally walk through a town or village, kidnap a free person, and sell them into slavery. All of these societies instead followed the Israelite practice (Deuteronomy 20:10–13; Numbers 31:1–47) and allowed the permanent enslavement of prisoners of war, with no kidnapping required.[56] Chattel slavery was for foreigners, especially those who surrendered during warfare, not for members of your own society.

Compounding their misunderstanding of Exodus 21:16, apologists also try to reinterpret 1 Timothy 1:10. You'll recall that Hank Hanegraaff disputed that the Bible supports slavery by asserting, "Nothing could be further from the truth." His key evidence from the New Testament is 1 Timothy 1:10. According to Hanegraaff, "The Bible denounces slavery as sin. The New Testament goes so far as to put slave traders in the same category as murderers, adulterers, perverts, and liars (1 Timothy 1:10)."[57] The author of 1 Timothy (traditionally believed to be Paul) does indeed list several kinds of sinners in the relevant verse. One possible translation, preferred by Hanegraaff, includes "slave traders" on the list.

Is Hanegraaff correct that 1 Timothy 1:10 demonstrates that the Bible is antislavery? The Greek word in question is ἀνδραποδισταῖς, or *andrapodistais* when written in the Roman alphabet. *Andrapodistais* is the plural form of *andrapodistes*. As documented in *The KJV New Testament Greek Lexicon*, an *andrapodistes* is "a slave-dealer, kidnapper, man-stealer." The entry explains further that the term refers to "one who unjustly reduces free men to slavery" or "one who steals the slaves of others and sells them."[58] From that definition we know that Paul was not condemning everyone who enslaved or sold another person. He referred instead only to kidnapping and enslaving a free person (the same crime as Exodus 21:16), and the stealing of another person's slaves. Those behaviors were already illegal, but again it was considered ethical in ancient societies, including Israel and Rome, to enslave prisoners of war. Warfare was sufficiently common in the ancient world, not to mention today, to provide endless opportunities for anyone wanting to enslave defeated soldiers. Far from offering a moral improvement, then, Paul simply reaffirmed the accepted reasons in the ancient world whereby a person could and could not be made a slave. Just as they did for Exodus 21:16, Hanegraaff and other apologists have reinterpreted 1 Timothy 1:10 to make its application far more expansive.

How can we know for sure that apologists have reinterpreted Exodus 21:16 and 1 Timothy 1:10? Because Christian writers before the Enlightenment did not think those verses prohibited all forms of slavery. The Puritans are an illuminating test case, for they sought to build a society in the American colonies based on the Bible alone. In 1641 the largest of the early New England colonies, Massachusetts, elaborated its rules about slavery in its law code. Their law code specified that slavery must be restricted to "lawfull Captives taken in just warres, and such strangers as willingly selle themselves or are sold to us."[59] Another provision stipulated that "if any man stealeth a man or mankind, he shall surely be put to death."[60] In other words, the Puritans followed the Bible to a T. They allowed slavery for prisoners of war (Deuteronomy 20:10–13; Numbers 31:1–47) and for foreigners who sold themselves or were offered for sale (Leviticus 25:44–46), while requiring the death penalty for kidnapping and enslaving a free person (Exodus 21:16).

The Puritans had the opportunity to implement their rules about slavery. Historian Edmund Morgan shows from surviving records that they "enslaved the Indians whom they captured in the Pequot War and in King Philip's War. Many of these Indians they sold in the West Indies and in return brought back Negroes (captured, presumably, in equally just wars), for Negroes were more docile than Pequots or Mohawks or Narragansetts."[61] John Winthrop, one of the colony's founders and himself a slaveholder, recorded in his diary that the Puritans traded their captured Indians for "salt, cotton, tobacco, and Negroes."[62] Clearly, the Puritans read Exodus 21:16 and 1 Timothy 1:10 not as a prohibition on all slavery but rather a ban on kidnapping and enslaving a free person, and they read Deuteronomy 20:10–13, Numbers 31:1–47, and Leviticus 25:44–46 to specify the conditions under which a person could be enslaved.

The apologists who interpret the Bible differently do not try to explain why they think the Puritans got it wrong. That oversight speaks to a more general phenomenon in apologetic works. Apologists often imply that they hold the definitive biblical interpretation on slavery without bothering to engage their predecessors who addressed the same issues during the first sixteen centuries of Christianity.[63] More commonly, at least in books, an apologist will include some number of endnotes.[64] When you read the endnotes, however, you discover something remarkable. You invariably find citations to other modern apologists, but rarely to any pre-Enlightenment Christians. The field of apologetics is thus a closed circle: One apologist cites another, and yet few of them check to see whether any writers from before 1700 endorsed their preferred interpretation. That's just as well, because apologists surely don't want to know the answer. In researching this book, I have searched extensively but have not found any Christians before 1700 who pointed to Exodus 21:16 or 1 Timothy 1:10 as evidence that the Bible opposes chattel slavery in all its forms.[65]

To the contrary, from the dawn of Christianity up to the Enlighten-ment, leading voices in the Church typically followed the Bible in accept-ing slavery within certain limitations. During the first few centuries, some Christians called on slaveholders to free their slaves, but those same Christians rarely questioned the institution of slavery itself.[66] The medi-eval Church worked to forbid the practice of holding fellow Christians as slaves while continuing to bless the enslavement of non-Christians.[67] The most influential theologian of that era, Thomas Aquinas, justified slavery through the concepts of natural law.[68] Slavery eventually gave way to serfdom in Europe, but not because of any biblically based movement demanding its end. Instead, persistent warfare among feudal lords led them to favor serfs, who provided military service, over slaves.[69] With its individual plots of land offering serfs an incentive to work hard, serfdom also proved to be a sustainable agricultural system.[70]

When slavery returned in the colonies that Portugal, Spain, France, and England established in the New World, leaders in the Church veered between upholding and rejecting the practice, depending on which groups were being enslaved. Consistent with long-standing doctrines, Pope Eugene IV (1435 and 1436) attacked the enslavement of Christians in the Canary Islands but did not object to enslaving non-Christians.[71] Following in the same tradition, Pope Nicholas V (1452) authorized the enslavement of pagans, Muslims, and Africans, three groups who comprised the laborers for Portuguese colonies.[72] Pope Paul III (1537), however, departed from a long line of rulings from popes and councils in denouncing the enslavement of a non-Christian people, the native inhabitants of the Americas.[73]

The minority of pre-Enlightenment Christians such as Pope Paul III who opposed enslaving a non-Christian group rarely cited biblical passages for support. Instead, they made theological arguments that sometimes alluded to the Bible without ever grappling with the specific parts dealing with slavery. Stated another way, they believed that God took their side of this issue, but they did not claim the same for the Bible. Writing in approximately the year 380, Gregory of Nyssa established this basic means of arguing the issue. He offered a vigorous theological justifi-cation for his position that included only a passing reference to the book of Genesis.[74] The relatively few Christians in the medieval period who deemed it immoral to keep non-Christian war captives as slaves also did not cite the Bible for support, and neither did Pope Paul III in 1537.[75]

The justifications for antislavery positions changed once the Enlightenment was underway. Unlike their predecessors, Christian abolitionists of the eighteenth and nineteenth centuries *did* assert that the Bible mandated their positions, and they wrote extensively about the biblical passages dealing with slavery. In fact, the abolitionists developed many of the fanciful interpretations that the apologists of today have recycled. I'll address the Christian abolitionists in greater detail in chapter 5, where I'll praise their convictions and commitment to social progress, which unfortunately came at the expense of their own intellectual honesty. For present purposes, I'll simply note that they read the Bible in ways wholly unprecedented in Christian history. As I've shown in the preceding pages, one has to engage in mental acrobatics through the "Ignore," "Rationalize," and "Reinterpret" strategies to whitewash what the Bible says about slavery. If they run out of material, apologists can always throw up their hands and invoke the "Mystify" strategy, saying that no one can fully understand the Bible's support for slavery.

THE BIBLE AND CAPITAL PUNISHMENT

Apologists also have to get creative when discussing capital punishment, a subject the Bible covers in great detail. The Old Testament requires the death penalty for offenses including not only murder but also adultery, blasphemy, bestiality, cursing a parent, breaking the Sabbath, male-to-male sexual activity, bearing false witness during the trial for a capital crime, and for a woman discovered on her wedding night not to be a virgin.[76] Although they commonly regard the behaviors on that list as serious sins, today's Christians invariably recoil from the prospect of executing people who commit them. That's true for liberal Christians, as one might expect, but also for conservatives. None of the major organizations representing conservative Christians, including the Family Research Council, Christian Coalition, and Alliance Defending Freedom, advocate the death penalty for the full range of biblical offenses, and neither do conservative denominations such as the Southern Baptist Convention,

Assemblies of God, and the Seventh-day Adventist Church.[77] That fact should lead us to wonder about the consistency of their positions. Conservative Christians routinely call homosexuality a sin and oppose same-sex marriage and nondiscrimination laws, yet they rarely if ever demand that gays be arrested, tried, and executed. How can they claim to follow the Bible's teachings while rejecting what it says about capital punishment for homosexual acts?

In a departure from how they handle genocide and slavery, their answer reaches deep into Christian history. From the earliest days of the apostles, Christians had to figure out which parts of the Old Testament still applied and which did not. In Romans 13:9, Paul affirmed certain principles from the Hebrew scriptures: "The commandments, 'You shall not commit adultery; You shall not murder; You shall not steal; You shall not covet'; and any other commandment, are summed up in this word, 'Love your neighbor as yourself.'" In his letter to the Galatians, however, Paul rejected any requirement of circumcision for Gentile Christians. The Council of Jerusalem, as described in Acts 15, reached the same conclusion while upholding prohibitions on fornication, idolatry, eating meat containing blood, and eating meat from animals that had not been sacrificed properly. 1 Colossians 2:16 differs in saying that Christians cannot be condemned for violating the Jewish law "in matters of food and drink or of observing festivals, new moons, or sabbaths." Meanwhile, Jesus in Matthew 5:17–18 declared that he came to fulfill rather than abolish the law, implying that it remained in place.

Building on the work of previous theologians, Thomas Aquinas elaborated the most popular way to reconcile these biblical provisions. Aquinas divided the Old Testament provisions into three categories: ceremonial, judicial, and moral. Ceremonial laws structured how Jews worshipped God and included circumcision, sacrifices, festivals, and food preparation. Judicial laws referred to matters within the purview of political authorities, especially crime and punishment. Moral laws covered everything else and included most of the Ten Commandments, restrictions on sexual behavior, and other rules about how people relate to each other. Aquinas held that Christians must adhere to the Old Testament's moral laws, which existed prior to God's covenant with the Jews, but Christians need not obey the ceremonial and judicial laws because Jesus already fulfilled them through his death and resurrection.[78] Modern apologists such as Bill Jones, Amy Orr-Ewing, and Thomas Schreiner take the same general approach as Aquinas, though they borrow from the Westminster Confession of Faith in calling the second category "civil" rather than "judicial."[79]

Note that this solution requires three nonoverlapping categories: A particular topic is exclusively ceremonial, civil, or moral. Crucial implications follow for the death penalty. By classifying it as a civil rather than a moral issue, apologists think they can bypass the Old Testament rules. In no other context, however, would anyone deny that capital punishment is a moral issue. Indeed, most observers would call it one of the leading moral controversies of the last several decades. For example, college textbooks bearing titles such as *Contemporary Moral Problems*, *Contemporary Moral Arguments*, *Analyzing Moral Issues*, and *Disputed Moral Issues* cover the philosophical, legal, and sociological aspects of issues dividing Western societies.[80] These textbooks usually include a chapter on capital punishment. Similarly, in 2010 the Gallup organization asked Americans whether various behaviors and policies were "morally acceptable" or "morally wrong."[81] Demonstrating its status as a subject of moral concern, capital punishment was among the issues covered.

The Gallup survey demonstrates the futility of trying to separate moral and civil matters. True, some governmental policies have no moral content, such as the choice about whether we drive on the left or right side of the road. Most policies, however, both reflect and affirm a particular moral stance. Budgets, for example, are expressions of values, for they indicate the level of government concern for different problems, programs, and goals. Relatedly, debates over taxes, climate change, gun control, and the minimum wage revolve not just around facts but also values and therefore morals. When we make something illegal—whether it's fraud, embezzlement, discrimination, assault, slavery, kidnapping, torture, or murder—we need the government to administer and enforce the laws. Capital punishment also requires state administration, but that doesn't remove it from the realm of morality. It's precisely because capital punishment raises profound moral questions that people debate whether to use it and, if so, for which crimes.

Once we recognize that capital punishment is both a civil *and* a moral issue, we gain insights into what apologists are doing. In defending the Old Testament's approach to capital punishment while insisting those rules no longer apply, apologists are using the "Rationalize" strategy. As always, the "Rationalize" strategy allows apologists to excuse what otherwise appear to be immoral biblical commands. Yes, they say, it would be wrong to execute a person today for adultery, blasphemy, male homosexuality, or the other items on the Old Testament's expansive list, but those rules were appropriate for ancient Israel. That's an odd position to take for someone who claims to believe in a moral code that applies throughout history and across different societies.

Apologists rarely invoke the term "moral relativism" when discussing capital punishment, but they should. The *Stanford Encyclopedia of Philosophy* defines moral relativism, in the sense relevant here, to mean that "the truth or falsity of moral judgments, or their justification, is not absolute or universal, but is relative to the traditions, convictions, or practices of a group of persons."[82] Under moral relativism, each culture or subculture has its own moral code on subjects such as incest, homosexuality, usury, and female genital mutilation, and we cannot state that any of them are objectively right or wrong. Claiming that Old Testament provisions for capital punishment were right for ancient Israel but wrong for modern times is a prime example of moral relativism.

With this background in place, we can now dissect a standard apologetic line. In their writings and debates, apologists often accuse atheists of adhering to moral relativism. Phil Fernandes, an apologist, pastor, and president of the Institute of Biblical Defense, asserts that "consistent atheists are moral relativists—since they deny the existence of God (the absolute moral Lawgiver), they deny the existence of absolute moral laws."[83] Some atheists welcome the charge and do not consider it an insult.[84] Other atheists, including me, are moral universalists who believe we can discover moral rules that hold for all individuals and societies.[85] Christian apologists almost always claim that they are also moral universalists, but their approach to capital punishment indicates otherwise.

Before hurling accusations at atheists, they need to ponder the message of Matthew 7:3: "Why do you see the speck in your neighbor's eye, but do not notice the log in your own eye?"

GROUNDING MORALITY IN A GOD

It will be useful to conclude the chapter with some reflections on the big picture. Many people believe, without thinking about it carefully, that morality has no foundation unless God exists. Theism is superior to atheism, the assumption goes, because it allows us to establish an objective morality. I disputed this point in the last chapter by explaining why theists cannot solve "Euthyphro's dilemma" without resorting to circular reasoning. In this chapter I have explained a second and more complicated problem for theists, one that leads them to deny the God depicted in their scriptures.

These scriptures matter greatly because any moral code rooted in a divine being would be worthless unless he communicated it to humanity through sources anyone could access. When they read the holy books he supposedly inspired, however, theists discover a God who often acts immorally and gives immoral commands.[86] The only way Christians and other theists can square the circle is to deny the contents of their scriptures, a maneuver that apologetic works inadvertently encourage. Apologists start from the premise that their God will always be exonerated from wrongdoing, no matter what their scriptures actually say. If they abandoned their belief that God is morally perfect, they might be forced to discard their religion altogether.

To protect their assumption of a morally perfect God, Christian apologists read the Bible through the "Ignore," "Rationalize," "Reinterpret," and "Mystify" strategies. When deployed by an apologist with a vivid imagination, these strategies can solve any problem the Bible poses. Apologists have proven that if you torture the Bible long enough, it will confess to whatever you want it to say. They have thereby sidestepped the biblical God who interferes with free will, gives political power to dictators, engages in intergenerational punishment, orders genocide, authorizes slavery, and requires the death penalty left and right. In this chapter I have covered only a sampling of the Bible's moral flaws, but they are sufficient to illustrate how apologists use their four strategies. After cycling through the apologists' washing machine, God comes out looking clean and pure.

Apologists find it necessary to make their intellectual moves because the Bible embodies an Iron Age morality with both good and bad parts. Ancient Christians and Jews created a God in their own image, imposed their morality onto him, and wrote that description into their scriptures. Thankfully, as I'll explain in later chapters, humanity has made many moral advances since biblical times. If today's Christians wanted to write a new Bible, they could depict a God who proclaims a defensible morality. Needless to say, Christian leaders won't be firing up their computers to undertake such an effort anytime soon. Having ruled out the most straightforward solution, apologists instead create a new God in their own image by twisting the words of the existing Bible. If they manipulated the Bible just once, their actions would not merit much attention. Unfortunately, there is no end to the intellectual gymnastics they will perform to salvage the God of the Bible.

A person cannot avoid this problem by following a different Abrahamic religion. To borrow a line from Gordon Gekko's comparison of troubled companies in *Wall Street*, each of the other Abrahamic religions is just a dog with different fleas. Because it shares scriptures with Christianity, Judaism faces many of the same difficulties and requires the Ignore, Rationalize, Reinterpret, and Mystify strategies to obtain a God worthy of worship. Judaism thus takes us no closer than Christianity to a God who can serve as the source of morality. Meanwhile, within Islam, the Quran and the hadith justify such immoral practices as jihad, slavery, child marriage, wife beating, and the death penalty for apostates.[87] If you want a blueprint for universal morality, you won't find it in the writings of Islam. Like Christians and Jews, Muslims have to engage in elaborate contortions to downplay or eliminate the offending material in their texts.

In chapter 8 I'll address the question of whether nontraditional forms of Christianity, Judaism, and Islam can contribute to the search for a universal morality. For now, I need to make a different kind of transition. In the first two chapters, I have shown why theism cannot provide an adequate foundation for morality. My ultimate goal, however, is not to tear down but to build up. In the next chapter, I will therefore make my positive case for why atheism leads us to humanism, which then gives us morality.

CHAPTER 3

Discovering Morality through Inclusive Deliberation

ATHEISTS ARE STRIKINGLY UNPOPULAR, ESPECIALLY IN AMERICA. WHEN asked several years ago whether they "would disapprove if my child wanted to marry" an atheist, 44 percent of Americans said yes, much greater than the number for African Americans (23%), Jews (18%), and Hispanics (13%).[1] Only 58 percent of Americans would vote for a well-qualified candidate from their party who happened to be an atheist, whereas many more would vote for someone who was Catholic (93%), female (92%), Black (92%), Mormon (81%), or gay or lesbian (74%).[2] Many atheists report being ostracized from their families after publicly declaring their nonbelief in God,[3] and résumés that mention a person's affiliation as an atheist are less likely to get a response from prospective employers.[4]

These negative attitudes toward atheists reflect a common belief that they readily lie, cheat, and steal when it serves their interests. Research documenting those perceptions has been conducted by psychologist Will Gervais, who developed a clever test to capture beliefs about who commits the greatest number of moral transgressions. He found that Americans think atheists are much more likely than members of groups defined by race, religion, and sexual orientation to commit murder, engage in incest, kick a dog, cheat at cards, disrespect an employer, eat human flesh, ridicule an obese woman, and renounce national and family ties.[5] In a country where nearly half the population deems it "necessary to believe in God to be moral," as one survey indicates, atheists seem to threaten order and decency.[6]

As it turns out, Christian apologists are usually more generous than the general public when talking about atheists. William Lane Craig speaks for many of his colleagues in holding that "a belief in God is not essential to living a moral life."[7] Directing his comments to other Christians, Craig acknowledges that atheists can and do "live good moral lives—indeed, embarrassingly, lives that sometimes put our own to shame."[8] Matt Slick, president and founder of the Christian Apologetics and Research Ministry, goes even further in stating that "atheists, generally, are honest, hardworking people.... Atheists are capable of governing their own moral behavior and getting along in society the same as anyone else."[9] On a personal level, apologists such as Larry Taunton have often established enduring friendships with people who deny the existence of God. Taunton, a vocal defender of Christianity through his organization Fixed Point Foundation, movingly describes his relationship with the noted atheist Christopher Hitchens.[10]

Despite these charitable attitudes toward atheists as individuals, apologists routinely attack *atheism* as an idea. Virtually all apologists claim that atheism offers no foundation for an objective moral code, and therefore no reason to believe that objective morality even exists. As a result, apologists argue, atheists can neither justify their own moral actions nor urge similar behaviors by others. Rice Broocks, a pastor, writer, and cofounder of the Every Nation family of churches, picks up this line of argument: "If there is no God, there couldn't possibly be a transcendent morality that everyone should obey."[11] The absence of a transcendent morality, in turn, would lead individuals and societies to create a free-for-all. In the eyes of Dennis Prager, a columnist, radio host, and creator of the PragerU videos on YouTube, such an outcome is inevitable because "without God there is no good and evil."[12]

Other apologists challenge atheists to explain where their moral beliefs come from. Christian philosopher Chad Meister wonders, "What grounds the atheists' moral positions? What makes their moral views more than hunches, inklings, or subjective opinions?"[13] Craig Hazen, founder of the MA program in Christian Apologetics at Biola University, asks of atheists, "What makes your moral standard more than a subjective opinion or personal preference? What makes it truly binding or obligatory?"[14] Writing for Ravi Zacharias International Ministries, J. M. Njoroge summarizes the apologists' thinking: "Can we really make sense of objective morality without God?"[15]

A related issue involves what happens to society if people become atheists. If atheists lack a foundation for objective morality, the spread of nonbelief could easily lead to increases in debauchery, disease, and death. In one of their favorite debating lines, apologists often pin the blame for various atrocities of the twentieth century on atheism. Stalin, Mao, and Pol Pot were all atheists, and their regimes caused millions of deaths through famines, warfare, genocide, and politically motivated executions. Christian authors such as Dinesh D'Souza and Larry Taunton attribute the deaths to those leaders' allegiance to atheism.[16]

Are they right? Should we fear that the growth of atheism in our own societies will instigate a new wave of killing? The answer is no, because atheism has no positive content of its own and therefore cannot cause anything, at least not by itself. Atheism merely describes one belief a person denies, not the full set of beliefs they affirmatively hold. To understand why people act as they do, we need to investigate what replaces the belief in God and other supernatural agents. Depending on the commitments a particular atheist holds, we will observe a huge range of behaviors.

In the cases of Stalin, Mao, and Pol Pot, the guiding principles for their lives were provided by Marxism-Leninism. This ideology justified limiting civil liberties, restricting private property, concentrating power in the state, and using violence to achieve political ends. However, there is no necessary reason why an atheist would want to embrace the ideas that motivated these rulers. A simple fact proves the point: Of the millions of atheists living in the West today, very few are Marxist-Leninists. Scholars of sociology and religious studies such as Christel Manning, Elizabeth Drescher, and Phil Zuckerman have analyzed survey data, conducted in-depth interviews, and examined both historical and contemporary documents to learn about the lives and beliefs of Western atheists. In all of this research, Marxism-Leninism is not even a blip on the radar screen.[17]

Besides their mistake in attributing the crimes of Stalin, Mao, and Pol Pot to atheism, Christian apologists also err in calling atheism a "worldview." Philosopher Peter Kreeft, one of the leading Catholic apologists in America, wrote an entire book distinguishing between the "theist worldview" and the "atheist worldview."[18] Jason Lisle, a writer for Answers in Genesis, deems atheism an "irrational worldview,"[19] while philosopher Alister McGrath asserts that atheism is not a "credible worldview."[20] Pastor and author Lance Waldie argues that "the atheistic worldview cannot account for logic, morality, or science,"[21] and the influential apologists Norman Geisler and Frank Turek assert that "the atheist's worldview . . . actually requires more faith than the creationist's."[22]

All of these statements suffer from the same false assumption that there is such a thing as an "atheist worldview." We need to recognize instead that atheism is simply the belief that neither God nor any other divine beings exist. That's it. The definition of atheism assumes nothing else, and atheists themselves disagree on fundamental matters. Some are libertarians; some are not. Some are environmentalists; some are not. Some are feminists; some are not. Comedian and actor Ricky Gervais puts the matter well: "Saying 'Atheism is a belief system,' is like saying 'not going skiing is a hobby.'"[23]

Because atheism is not a worldview or belief system, it gives people little guidance on understanding and interacting with the world. Most importantly, atheism offers no insights on how a person should think and act. To learn what motivates a particular atheist, once again we must examine what replaces a belief in divine beings. The usual answer today is humanism. As historian Callum Brown and other scholars have shown, most atheists in the West endorse the core ideas of humanism, even if they don't regularly use that term.[24] Speaking for myself, I openly identify as a humanist and prefer the label as the best summary of my beliefs, though I call myself an atheist, too. Atheism describes what I don't believe; humanism describes what I do believe. Unlike atheism, humanism is a worldview and can structure a person's life.

So What Is Humanism?

Humanism has carried many different meanings since the term first entered common usage during the Renaissance. The best way to learn what humanism means today is to ask self-described humanists and the organizations representing them. As explained by Humanists UK,

"Roughly speaking, the word humanist has come to mean someone who:

- trusts to the scientific method when it comes to understanding how the universe works and rejects the idea of the supernatural (and is therefore an atheist or agnostic)

- makes their ethical decisions based on reason, empathy, and a concern for human beings and other sentient animals

- believes that, in the absence of an afterlife and any discernible purpose to the universe, human beings can act to give their own lives meaning by seeking happiness in this life and helping others to do the same."[25]

One can find similar definitions in allied associations throughout the Western world, including Humanist Canada, Humanist Association of Germany, Council of Australian Humanist Societies, American Humanist Association, Union of Freethinkers of Finland, and the Secular Humanist League of Brazil. In the United States, Brazil, and some other countries in North and South America, the modifier "secular" is frequently attached to yield "secular humanism." Indeed, the Council for Secular Humanism, publisher of the magazine *Free Inquiry*, is one of the leading US organizations working in this area. In most Western countries, however, the adjective "secular" is considered redundant when describing "humanism."[26] For that reason, hereafter I will use the term "humanism" to include what others call both "humanism" and "secular humanism."

With these terminological matters resolved, we can see that humanism touches upon many important subjects and helps its adherents navigate all aspects of life, of which moral beliefs and actions are the most important for this book. A humanist claims we can establish a moral code through reason, argument, and evidence. An action does not become moral because of what somebody feels, what's written in a holy book, what authority figures say, or what people have traditionally believed. Morality instead has to be rationally defended using the best tools available to humanity, which include using empathy to put yourself in the shoes of other people. Philosophy, history, literature, the natural sciences, and the social sciences are all essential in allowing us to discover and defend a comprehensive morality. To learn the principles of right and wrong, along with how to handle concrete situations, people must think, reflect, and deliberate with others. In short, they must deploy reason in all its forms.

This humanistic project quickly butts up against what theists claim as their exclusive province. In the last two chapters, I explained why the truth of right and wrong cannot be established through a God or gods, and here I will explain why morality exists in the absence of supernatural agents. Christian apologists assert that any morality without God must be arbitrary and subjective, reflecting the mere opinions or preferences of a person, group, or society. To see why the apologists are wrong, we first have to distinguish the senses in which something can be objective. The *Oxford English Dictionary* provides two definitions of "objective" relevant to the topic of morality. As we read the definitions, we quickly see their differences:

1. of a person and his or her judgement: not influenced by personal feelings or opinions in considering and representing facts; impartial; detached[27]

2. external to or independent of the mind[28]

Philosophers disagree about whether morality could ever be "external to or independent of the mind," as required for the second definition, if there is no God. Philosophers such as Erik Wielenberg and Michael Martin have argued for yes, while Julian Baggini and Paul Kurtz have argued for no.[29] Regardless of who is right in that debate, human beings in their moral judgments can be objective in the first sense. We can attain moral rules stripped of what the *Oxford English Dictionary* calls the "personal feelings or opinions" that people often use "in considering and representing facts." Many conflicts and controversies revolve around limitations of precisely this kind. When you make a statement or argument and someone replies that you are "not being objective," they are accusing you of bias. If they are right, you have a prejudice or preconception that is clouding your judgment and preventing you from assessing the issue correctly. You aren't seeing the whole picture but only what is visible from your narrow and parochial perspective. With more care in collecting and analyzing the relevant facts, combined with reflection on the principles at stake, you could be objective and thereby arrive at the truth.

Notice the subtle distinction between the two definitions. The first one applies to the way a person reaches a judgment or decision, whereas the second is normally used to describe abstract concepts. Parents mediating disputes between their children try to be objective in the first sense. We use the second sense, by contrast, to refer to "objective reality," something whose ontological status does not depend on any human processes. When applied to morality, the second definition refers to a morality independent of the human mind. Again, philosophers do not agree on whether such a morality could exist in the absence of God. I focus here instead on the first meaning of objectivity, and I will explain how human beings can reach it by following the right processes.

Apologists care greatly about that first definition, for they commonly invoke it when they contemplate a world without God. If there is no God, they fear, then morality becomes "simply one group's opinion"[30] (Rice Broocks), "mere hunches, inklings, or subjective opinions"[31] (Chad Meister), or "a subjective opinion or personal preference"[32] (Craig Hazen). In the rest of this chapter, I will show that apologists are mistaken in their fears. We can construct a morality that rises above the perspectives of particular individuals and societies, making our judgments objective in the first sense.

To make my case, I will begin by examining what individuals can do to limit their subjectivity. Although no one can overcome all of their biases, they can uphold objectivity as an ideal and take steps to move closer to it. I then argue that a morality purged of bias can only emerge from deliberation that welcomes and incorporates the views of people from diverse backgrounds. Morality, then, derives not from any single person but rather from human beings as a collective. I conclude by debunking common Christian objections to a morality without God.

OBJECTIVITY AS AN ASPIRATION

Let's get something out of the way right now: I'm biased, and so are you. This is inevitable given the distinctive biological and environmental forces that shape how each of us thinks and acts. Each person has a unique set of genes (shared for some people with an identical twin) that influences their personality, tastes, and behaviors. Other influences emerge at the societal level. Which society a person grows up in, whether it's ancient India, medieval England, or modern-day Haiti, affects them and their morality in profound ways. Even within a given society, the experiences a person undergoes during childhood, along with the values taught by parents, neighbors, schools, friends, and the media, can leave a lasting imprint on their conception of right and wrong. We also need to account for structural factors related to a person's identity and how others perceive and act toward them. A person's race, class, gender, and sexual orientation affect their life course and their moral beliefs.

The upshot is that we're all biased when we evaluate moral questions. The question is how to respond to this incontrovertible fact. We could choose to wallow in our biases and turn morality into something entirely personal and subjective. Perhaps we should throw up our hands, take a relativistic stance, and assert that everyone lives in their own reality. If someone gives a passionate defense of something we find offensive, such as racism, genocide, or child abuse, we could say "that's true for you but not for me." If we think certain moral views are actually *wrong*, however, we have to figure out how to move beyond the beliefs of one person or society to an overarching morality.

A humanist tackles this challenge by using reason. Fortunately, humanists can draw from thousands of years of thinking from around the world. The Golden Rule offers a useful place to begin. Virtually every religion, society, and ethical system has articulated some version of the Golden Rule. The Golden Rule can be stated either negatively (what you should not do) or positively (what you should do). Buddhism and Confucianism capture the negative version, Judaism and Christianity the positive, and Islam combines both. The founders and prophets of these philosophical and religious movements all express similar ideas: "Hurt not others in ways that you yourself would find hurtful" (the Buddha); "Do not do to others what you do not want them to do to you" (Confucius); "Thou shalt love thy neighbor as thyself" (Moses); "Therefore all things whatsoever ye would that men should do to you, do ye even so to them" (Jesus); and "As you would have people do to you, do to them; and what you dislike to be done to you, don't do to them" (Muhammad).[33]

The fact that so many different people and traditions have discovered the Golden Rule suggests that it is tapping something universal to humanity. Human beings are social animals; except for the occasional hermit, we live in communities. Society after society has learned that the Golden Rule is a useful principle allowing us to not only coexist but also cooperate for common ends. The Golden Rule helps depersonalize morality by forcing each of us to recognize the needs and desires of others. When you consider the perspective of another person, you take a step toward objectivity. Everyone wants to be treated kindly and fairly, and no one wants to be enslaved, raped, assaulted, slandered, or disrespected. The Golden Rule leads us away from our parochial values and interests and toward a principle for behavior that all human beings can embrace.

These considerable strengths notwithstanding, the Golden Rule cannot eliminate subjectivity precisely because it starts with the self. Morality under the Golden Rule extends outward from how a person would and would not want to be treated. So far, so good. But what if other people have their own preferences on these matters? You might think they want what you want, which might be true sometimes but probably not always. Is it really moral to always act toward them in the ways you would prefer, as opposed to the ways they actually desire? A more general problem with the Golden Rule is its simplicity. The Golden Rule is just an aphorism, not a set of detailed guidelines on how to handle specific decisions. A moral principle that could fit onto a refrigerator magnet can only take us so far in our complex, messy world.

A humanist therefore must dig deeper into the history of ethical thought to develop a comprehensive system of morality. We need to flesh out the crucial details telling us how to act, which are left unspecified by the Golden Rule, while preserving its aim of removing the biases of each individual and society. The contractarian (or social contract) school of ethics, as elaborated by John Rawls, offers powerful resources for this effort because it puts the question of bias front and center. Rawls and other contractarians such as Thomas Hobbes, John Locke, and Jean-Jacques Rousseau are best known for their insights into how politics and society should be structured, but they have also thought deeply about what qualifies as moral—the subject of this chapter.

Earlier writers including Plato, Epicurus, and the authors of the Buddhist texts *Mahāvastu* and *Sutta Pitaka* dropped hints of contractarian thinking, and Manegold of Lautenbach (1030–1103) subsequently offered a longer treatment.[34] Thomas Hobbes (1588–1679) is widely credited with expanding the approach. A humanist forerunner, Hobbes provided an account of morality that does not depend on any divine beings. Theorizing instead that humans create morality through common agreement, he asked us to imagine living in a "state of nature" without any rules or government. Within the state of nature, everyone has the freedom to act however they choose, regardless of the effects on other people. Nobody has any protection from others in their property or physical security beyond their ability to retaliate. Any observer can see that such a situation creates "continual fear, and danger of violent death; and the life of man, solitary, poor, nasty, brutish, and short."[35] To avoid these negative consequences, Hobbes argues, rational individuals would voluntarily agree to a moral code to regulate their interactions with each other, and they would empower a sovereign to enforce it.

Reacting to and often challenging Hobbes, John Locke and Jean-Jacques Rousseau offered their own versions of contractarian ethics, and John Rawls reinvigorated the approach at the end of the twentieth century. Instead of the "state of nature" envisioned by his predecessors, Rawls offered the "original position" through which individuals determine the fundamental social and political arrangements of their society. Rawls does not think the "original position" ever did or could exist; it instead serves as a theoretical device for him to determine the rules for a political community that can be rationally defended. Decisions within the original position take place behind a "veil of ignorance," Rawls writes, such that "no one knows his place in society, his class position or social status; nor does he know his fortune in the distribution of natural assets and abilities, his intelligence and strength, and the like."[36] By requiring that people know nothing specific about their lot in life, Rawls ensures that they construct the rules in an objective manner, without influence from personal factors that would otherwise distort their judgment.

This restriction does not mean that individuals enter the original position with no knowledge whatsoever. To give them the means for having an intelligent conversation, Rawls ensures that they understand all relevant facts about "human society," "political affairs," "principles of economic theory," "the basis of social organization," and the "laws of human psychology. Indeed, the parties are presumed to know whatever general facts affect the choice of the principles of justice."[37] Knowing these general facts allows the parties to make thoughtful and reasoned decisions, but not ones that systematically advantage or disadvantage a certain kind of person.

Rawls designed his framework primarily for its political applications, and he called his influential book *A Theory of Justice*. Its core concepts, however, can be easily extended to the overlapping and somewhat broader realm of morality. The original position puts us on a path toward discovering an impartial morality. Behind the veil of ignorance, nobody is special, everyone counts equally, and no one can foresee the place they will hold in society. You can't be biased if you have to choose the moral rules without knowing your talents, your tastes and dispositions, and characteristics such as your gender, class, race, nationality, and sexual orientation. Everyone else is making choices under the same constraints. Thus, even people who wanted to build a system favoring themselves would lack the knowledge necessary to do so. Self-interest does not exist behind the veil of ignorance; or rather, one person's self-interest is identical to everyone else's.

Rawls uses the original position to derive principles of justice regarding the basic liberties available to all and the permissible social and economic inequalities. I will expand his concepts for use in thinking about morality more generally. My goal here is to describe the process to follow, not to specify the content of the moral code that will emerge. To carry my analysis forward, I borrow from Rawls's "veil of ignorance" and pair it with what I call the "fountain of knowledge." The "fountain of knowledge" is similar to but broader than the "general facts" that Rawls allows people to access within the original position. By the "fountain of knowledge," I mean to invoke all forms of practical wisdom and experience, along with the ideas that human beings have developed through the arts, humanities, social sciences, natural sciences, and other branches of knowledge.

Like Rawls, I am proposing a thought experiment, one I hope readers will actively engage. Each person, though biased, can aspire to objectivity. To move closer to that ideal, a person seeks to determine right and wrong from behind the veil of ignorance and in front of the fountain of knowledge. The veil of ignorance allows us to eliminate the influences stemming from our backgrounds, abilities, and positions in society. The fountain of knowledge, meanwhile, gives us the information necessary to address the wide range of situations a system of morality must handle. These twin concepts reinforce each other. From behind the veil of ignorance, you form your moral beliefs based solely on the facts and wisdom flowing from the fountain of knowledge. On the flip side, the more you drink from the fountain of knowledge, the easier it becomes to overcome your biases as the veil of ignorance requires.

STRIVING FOR OBJECTIVITY

A concrete example will help bring these concepts to life. Let's suppose you're a heterosexual who has never felt any sexual attraction to a person of the same sex. You're trying to figure out whether homosexuality, as embraced by consenting adults, should be considered moral or immoral. You step behind the veil of ignorance to remove yourself from the equation. All of the biological and environmental forces that have shaped your views are irrelevant to the question of whether homosexuality is right or wrong. It makes no difference what you've been taught by your family, community, and society, for any particular tradition or culture has no inherent connection to a defensible morality. Your own position as a heterosexual is also irrelevant, for you have to imagine forming your beliefs without knowing whether you will or will not be one of the people attracted to members of the same sex.

While standing behind the veil of ignorance, you imbibe from the fountain of knowledge. You talk to gays and lesbians and ask about their upbringing, interests, hopes, fears, motivations, and daily lives. You read literature by and for gays and lesbians, including articles, essays, memoirs, and novels, and you examine how different societies, both historically and today, have handled issues relating to sexual orientation and behavior. You search for insights in the texts of the world's philosophical and religious traditions. What have writers through the ages said about homosexuality? Do those writers offer persuasive arguments and evidence for their positions? You then examine scientific research on the origins of a person's sexual orientation, and you examine research on homosexual relationships. By comparison to heterosexual relationships, do those between same-sex partners lead to outcomes that are better, worse, or about the same for them and their children? What are the consequences—good, bad, or neutral—for both the individual and society when someone engages in homosexual behaviors? Only after synthesizing all these disparate pieces of knowledge will you be ready to assess whether homosexuality is moral or immoral.

Admittedly, no one has the time to follow the process I have described, at least for the complete set of matters on which we form moral beliefs. Nevertheless, my thought experiment helps clarify what we can do to move closer to the ideal of objectivity on not just homosexuality but the whole panoply of moral questions. First, we can recognize and confront our biases, subsequently changing our moral beliefs when they fail the test of rationality. Thoughtful people should regularly ask themselves, "Do I hold my beliefs because they are actually true, or am I simply parroting what I have learned through socialization? Do my beliefs suspiciously match what you would predict for someone with my heritage, upbringing, talents, and socioeconomic status? Can my beliefs be rationally defended, and if not, what beliefs should I hold?" Morality should be a matter of considered judgment, not the expression of raw feelings or prejudices.

A person can develop a more refined morality, one less tied to their predispositions, by reading, thinking, studying, and talking with others. By exposing yourself to at least a sampling of the diverse ideas that humanity has produced, you will be better positioned to form your moral beliefs through the method of humanism: reason. It's especially valuable when someone stretches beyond their comfort zone to interact—whether in person or vicariously through books, documentaries, or other means—with people and ideas from another time or place. Writers such as Herodotus, Alexis de Tocqueville, and Kwame Anthony Appiah have gained moral insights after moving either temporarily or permanently from one society to another, allowing them to address questions of cultural similarities and differences.[38] Study abroad programs serve the same purpose on a smaller scale. One systematic survey found that 95 percent of participants affirmed that their program "has had a lasting impact on my worldview," and 98 percent said it "helped me better understand my own cultural values and biases."[39]

Yet we need not spend time physically in another society to reap these kinds of benefits. Art, literature, and films produced around the world or closer to home can help a person become more reflective in deciding questions of right and wrong. Practical consequences of this sort are just one of many reasons why the arts and humanities are essential to any enlightened society. Through a jarring image, an appeal to beauty, or a call to recognize complexity, works of art such as paintings, sculptures, and photographs open windows into the human condition and encourage people to grapple with familiar matters in a new way. Similarly, the best novels and movies allow a person to understand the experiences, emotions, and choices of someone else. Seeing the world through the eyes of another, especially someone whose race, values, opportunities, cultural background, or social status differs from our own, often gives us a new perspective on moral questions. We know that the characters are fictional, and yet they can prod our thinking.

Complementing the insights gained from art, literature, and films, the fields of journalism, history, and anthropology also contribute to the fountain of knowledge. Each person can only see and experience a limited part of what is happening in their local community, the nation, and the world at large, which is why we need journalists. After combing through available records and talking to experts, government officials, and ordinary citizens, journalists bring information and events to our attention. Historians do the same for the past by illuminating the lives and times of our predecessors. The experiences of those who are now dead can be accessed only through the tools of history and allied disciplines: gathering sources, critically evaluating them, and constructing the best possible account. Anthropologists bring us a similar depth of understanding for contemporary societies. Through long-term immersion in the language, customs, families, economies, and religions of diverse societies, anthropologists expand our knowledge of how people can and do live. Anthropological findings and perspectives can inform our moral beliefs and choices.

Having stressed how the veil of ignorance and the fountain of knowledge can allow us to overcome our subjectivity, it's only appropriate that I also acknowledge their limitations. First, no one will ever eliminate their biases even if they make a strong effort to do so. These biases shape what information a person seeks, how they interpret it, and what they recall, thereby restricting their ability to draw from the fountain of knowledge. A person who recognizes their biases will surely learn more than a person who does not, but objectivity will necessarily remain an aspiration rather than something any individual can achieve on their own. Second, there are some people who deny their limitations, and they can't be helped by the veil of ignorance or the fountain of knowledge. These kinds of people often gleefully point out the biases they perceive in others while insisting their own views are objective. At the extreme, they might change their minds rarely if ever, refuse to examine evidence or arguments that challenge their beliefs, and treat the notion that they have something to learn as an insult rather than a statement of fact that applies to everyone.

Third and most importantly, I have relied so far on theoretical concepts. We can try to overcome our subjectivity, I have argued, by standing behind the veil of ignorance so that we can construct our morality solely from the fountain of knowledge. If all subjectivity arising from a person's genes, upbringing, position in society, and other influences were removed, and if we had access to the same knowledge, we would converge on the same moral code. The hypothetical nature of my method—the preceding sentence contained two important "ifs"—limits its potential to serve as the foundation for morality. In effect, I have inherited not only the strengths but also the main weakness of the contractarian approach to morality. Way back in 1758, David Hume criticized the social contract of Hobbes, Locke, and Rousseau by arguing that people have no obligation to a hypothetical contract they never promised to obey. According to Hume, we should hold people accountable for their actual promises, not those ascribed to them without their consent.[40] Some contractarians have responded that the contract is implicit; just by living in society, you have tacitly agreed to follow its rules. Philosopher Robert Nozick rejects that claim, quipping that an implicit contract "isn't worth the paper it's not written on."[41]

A Reboot of Social Contract Morality

To my mind, these are powerful critiques that any contractarian must address. I will therefore attempt to preserve what is valuable in contractarian morality while making the approach more practical and concrete. To survive close scrutiny, contractarian morality must apply to not just hypothetical worlds but also real societies past and present, which leads me to modify the approach contractarians normally take. Instead of trying to determine the morality someone would endorse under idealized conditions—whether in the state of nature, the original position, or the alternative I proposed in the preceding pages—let's examine the beliefs people actually hold. Such a move does not force us to abandon the contractarian view that human beings affirm the content of a moral code through shared agreement. Similarly, we can still highlight the problem of subjectivity that Rawls explains, so long as we find an alternative means to handle it.

Consider the subjectivity that results because a person has formed their beliefs within a specific society. Societies vary along many dimensions, including their economic organization: Some are based on hunting and gathering, others are agricultural, and others are primarily a mix of industry and services. Some societies are polytheistic while others are monotheistic, and within those two broad categories, the ways people interact with their God or gods vary enormously. Some societies are individualistic, others collectivist. Amid all these differences in how people live their lives, we should not be surprised to find that societies also vary in their moral systems. Behaviors that are condemned in one society might be deemed acceptable in another. In India, for example, Hindus believe that eating cows is immoral, whereas Americans of many religious stripes treat hamburgers as a staple of their diet.

Underlying all the moral differences between societies, however, are many similarities. Anthropologist Donald Brown explored this question in his book *Human Universals*, and other scholars have carried forward his line of research.[42] I mentioned earlier that virtually every society embraces some version of the Golden Rule, at least for relationships within the group.[43] Owing to its simplicity, the Golden Rule is difficult to apply to complex situations, but it nevertheless provides a useful starting point for morality. Similarly, every society limits who, when, and under what conditions you can kill someone; the belief that you can kill whomever you want, for whatever reason you want, has never existed in any known society.[44] Norms against incest are also universal, even as societies vary on matters of definition, exceptions, and enforcement.[45] Every society values keeping your promises, reciprocating helpful acts, and punishing wrongdoers.[46] Wherever you go, the dead are treated with respect and there are mourning rituals.[47] Around the world, people give special care to infants and children and devote considerable resources to raising the next generation.[48]

What can we conclude from these areas of agreement? The shared beliefs can't be subjective, a matter of mere opinion, precisely because different societies, each with its own way of viewing the world, arrive at the same positions. As a result, what I will call the "basic morality" is universal to humanity. It includes, at a minimum, the Golden Rule, restrictions on killing, theft, and incest, and requirements of reciprocity, punishment, promise keeping, respect for the dead, and care for infants and children.

We don't know when the basic morality first appeared in our human ancestors. Given that other animals show what primatologist Frans de

Waal calls the "ingredients of morality" such as fairness and compassion for other members of their species, the basic morality probably has an evolutionary origin.[49] What we can say is that diverse societies have all had the chance to overturn it, and none have done so. Certain individuals have surely offered a contrary view at moments along the way—asserting, for example, that people should be able to kill indiscriminately, or that our default mode should be lying rather than telling the truth—but those individuals have never won much support from other members of their communities.

Are there aspects of morality beyond the basic morality that extend to all of humanity? Quick thinking suggests not. Moral questions on which societies diverge are, by definition, not included in the basic morality, and people learn the subjective perspectives of their own culture or subculture. Take slavery as an example. From the beginning of agricultural societies until a few hundred years ago, slavery was widely accepted around the world. Among the Incas, Egyptians, Babylonians, Israelites, Aztecs, Arabs, Chinese, Songhai, Turks, Persians, Kongolese, Romans, and Mongols, and later in the Portuguese, Spanish, French, and English colonies, societies practiced slavery with virtually no internal opposition.[50] Beginning in the eighteenth century, however, abolitionist movements mounted forceful opposition and eventually succeeded in outlawing the institution worldwide, though it continues illegally through means such as the sex trade, child labor, debt slavery, forced marriage, and forced migrant labor.[51]

So who is right—the societies that embraced slavery or the ones that have condemned it? Or is slavery a matter of personal or cultural opinion without a definitive right or wrong answer? To stimulate our thinking about these questions, we can turn to the theory and practice of deliberative democracy. Modern democracies suffer from many problems, two of which relate to the quality of the public voice on which governmental authority supposedly rests. People have many ways to register their preferences: They can vote, join interest groups, contact government officials, attend protests and demonstrations, give time or money to campaigns, and talk with others about politics in person or online. Most of these modes of participation are skewed, to varying degrees, toward people who are older, whiter, wealthier, and hold more extreme views than the general population.[52] Meanwhile, most of the expressed opinions are raw and unrefined because people typically avoid discussing politics with those who disagree with them. This problem intensified as it became easier for people to surround themselves with like-minded others through their personal networks and media sources.[53] Thus, the public voice we hear today neither represents the larger population nor reflects careful thinking.

Deliberative democracy, an important area of study in political science and related disciplines, aims to solve these problems. One of the earliest applications came through deliberative opinion polls. In a traditional poll, researchers attempt to draw a random sample of the relevant population, then ask those selected for their opinions about a political issue. Polls of this kind treat people as isolated individuals, and the respondents lack the chance to learn about the issue or discuss it with others. A deliberative poll retains the goal of obtaining a demographically representative sample of the population, but it departs from a traditional poll in important respects. The selected people meet face-to-face to discuss the issue, listen to expert testimony, and study the matter over one or more days. Trained moderators are typically on hand to ensure that everyone participates in the discussions, not just the most passionate or articulate. At the end of a deliberative poll, we obtain opinions that are both representative (because the participants have been selected as a cross-section of the population) and reflective (because the participants have expressed their views after careful deliberation).[54]

Similar procedures have been undertaken in many countries to allow representative and reflective bodies of citizens to make recommendations on government budgets, infrastructure projects, social policies, and initiatives and referenda that voters will decide in an upcoming election.[55] Academic research on these forums demonstrates that the participants take their responsibilities seriously, learn from the experts and each other, and strive to make informed choices.[56] Communication scholar Laura Black reports that participants offer personal stories and experiences, draw from events and news stories, make arguments to defend their positions, and ask factual questions to gather important information.[57]

Political scientists James Fishkin and Cynthia Farrar show that contributors to deliberative polls become more familiar with relevant facts, gain confidence in their political knowledge and abilities, and often change their opinions through the process of talking and learning.[58]

One of the most valuable aspects of these experiments in deliberative democracy is that they bring together people from all walks of life and help the participants break out of their bubbles. Because they use the methods of random and stratified sampling, the forums necessarily include young adults, the middle aged, and the old. In ordinary life, a Caucasian might never have a meaningful conversation with a Black person, but the selection procedures for deliberative democracy ensure that all races are represented in rough proportion to their population averages. The assembled group might include veterans, accountants, factory workers, college students, small business owners, and former or current welfare recipients. Given the many forms of diversity built into the group, someone within it probably has personal knowledge or experience with any issue up for discussion. Before making any decisions or recommendations, the group will hear a wide range of perspectives from each other and the relevant experts. In the eyes of Helene Landemore and other political theorists, diversity in background and experiences increases the ability for a group to synthesize pertinent information and make good decisions.[59]

You might be wondering how the workings of deliberative democracy can inform a reboot of contractarian morality. The linkage becomes clear once we recognize that some of the problems plaguing democracies—unequal participation and relatively little deliberation—also affect how a society articulates its moral code. Some people lack the economic, social, or political power to make their voices heard, so their interests and concerns can get ignored within declarations of what qualifies as right and wrong. Meanwhile, the morality of each individual is often the product of instinct, tradition, or deference to authority rather than reasoned judgment. Deliberative democracy starts from the premise that the public voice on political issues should be formed through representative and reflective means. The same principle, I claim, applies to the moral realm.

Defining Contractarian Morality

With this background in place, I now offer my definition of morality from a contractarian standpoint: *the consensus among individuals and societies regarding right and wrong conduct that would emerge or has emerged after a process of inclusive deliberation.* This definition contains a lot of information, so it's worth pausing to explain its various parts. Any definition of morality would presumably cover the rules and principles for "right and wrong conduct," so mine includes this obvious feature. My definition's contractarian underpinnings are evident in its reliance on a consensus. The consensus has to reach across "individuals and societies" such that it is general to humanity. A consensus does not require unanimity, just a strong majority. In other words, no person, group, or society gets an automatic veto.

The last part of my definition, which stipulates that the consensus only counts if it resulted from "a process of inclusive deliberation," shows my debt to the concepts of deliberative democracy. A morality worth the name rests on deliberation within and between societies—possibly lasting years, decades, or centuries—through which people make arguments, examine evidence, gather additional information, listen to other perspectives, and change their minds when appropriate. The deliberation could be face-to-face but also occurs through the written word as people engage the positions and arguments of both their predecessors and contemporaries. What matters for deliberation is not that people share the same physical space but that they carefully consider the reasons supporting each stance on the question at hand. The written word has the advantage of giving people as much time and space as they need to explain their views and respond to objections. Thus, the deliberative process includes writing and reading relevant books, articles, essays, letters, blog entries, social media posts, and other materials.

Regardless of where it occurs, the deliberation must be inclusive. The crucial point is not that all people participate in the extended conversation—that would be impossible—but that all *kinds* of people participate. It's especially important that the people most directly affected by any moral stance have the opportunity to express their views. Without this wide-ranging participation, any apparent consensus might reflect the subjective preferences of a dominant group rather than the considered judgment of human beings in all their diversity. When the deliberation is inclusive, the result transcends the biased and limited perspectives of any single person or society. The moral positions meeting all the criteria within my definition join with the basic morality and apply to all of humanity. My conception of contractarian morality, then, includes the basic morality plus every moral position that fulfills each part of my definition.

Expressed in this way, contractarian morality is consistent with a core principle of humanism. A humanist, you'll recall, determines what is moral by using reason, and humanists have proposed several ways to derive a reason-based morality.[60] I have offered my own distinctive approach from within the social contract tradition. The veil of ignorance and the fountain of knowledge are powerful tools of reason because they encourage people to strive for impartiality, empathize with others, and draw from available knowledge before venturing any conclusions. As the term is ordinarily used, "reason" is thus something an individual can do on their own. Contractarian morality, by contrast, is communal by its very nature and incorporates the differing ideas, experiences, and sources of knowledge that people carry with them.

Some readers will notice the similarity between my account and the "discourse ethics" of philosopher and social theorist Jürgen Habermas, who sought to establish moral truth through idealized deliberation that meets criteria including open dialogue, the absence of coercion, the freedom to express or challenge any view, and agreement to universalize any claim.[61] The deliberation required for my conception of contractarian morality rests on not only each individual's wisdom and experience but also history, philosophy, literature, and other branches of knowledge. To reach a consensus, people have to study, talk, and learn such that they achieve together what none of them could achieve individually. Deliberation can thus be considered a form of *public* reason, or humanism applied at the community level.

But what if people around the world have grappled with a certain question and yet have not reached a consensus? My definition of contractarian morality addresses that very possibility by referring to the consensus that either "has already emerged" or "would emerge" through inclusive deliberation. In constructing the definition that way, I am trying to maintain a healthy tension between the actual and the ideal. The lack of consensus on an issue could indicate that biases are tainting the judgments people have offered. If some people are unable or unwilling to engage in a deliberative process based on reason, it will be difficult to achieve a consensus. The solution in that case is to keep the conversation going as long as it takes. A future generation might come to see the issue differently, allowing people to reach a consensus that eluded their predecessors.

While waiting for a potential consensus to emerge, people need not refrain from making moral claims. To the contrary, this is the moment when we need a range of people to consider the various stances and the justifications for them. It's possible that one position is right and another is wrong, which we can learn through further investigation. The "right" position in this context is the one that would find a consensus if diverse people took the deliberation seriously and applied reason to the relevant considerations. My definition thus allows morality to exist in a type of Platonic realm that we can access to varying degrees, depending on the quality of our deliberation. Although human beings can never actually achieve the ideal of inclusive deliberation, we can come sufficiently close to give us confidence in certain moral judgments.

As an illustration, consider the societies marked by a consensus that chattel slavery was normal and acceptable. Did the overwhelmingly pro-slavery beliefs in those societies emerge through inclusive deliberation? Hardly. To state the obvious, no one bothered to ask the slaves whether their bondage was justified. Furthermore, the people who defined what qualified as acceptable behaviors did not consider, discuss, and debate the reasons for and against creating a system where some human beings owned others. Slavery instead reflected the raw exercise of power, most commonly (in the ancient world) when victorious soldiers enslaved those they defeated. Other people became slaves because they were born into it or were sentenced to slavery as punishment for a crime.[62] Slavery persisted in some parts of the world but was replaced with serfdom in Europe during the Middle Ages.

When chattel slavery returned in European colonies in the sixteenth and seventeenth centuries and became controversial in the eighteenth and nineteenth, many people participated in the deliberations. Clergy members delivered sermons and homilies on both sides of the question. Philosophers, politicians, and activists wrote essays, pamphlets, and books extolling slavery's vices or its virtues. Abolitionist societies held public meetings and rallied supporters. Most important of all, former slaves joined the discussions. Sometimes their participation happened directly, as when Olaudah Equiano, Mary Prince, Ignatius Sancho, David Walker, Sojourner Truth, Frederick Douglass, and others contributed speeches, letters, pamphlets, and memoirs.[63] Enslaved people also entered the debate as fictional characters in novels, novellas, and plays by authors such as Harriet Beecher Stowe, Dion Boucicault, Herman Melville, and Gertrudis Gómez de Avellaneda.[64] As the push for abolition gained strength in the nineteenth and twentieth centuries, most countries managed to end slavery peacefully. The United States required bloodshed and civil war, and slavery was still legal in a handful of other countries until the second half of the twentieth century.[65]

We now have a global consensus against owning human beings as property, and it is illegal in every country. That consensus was forged through inclusive deliberation over several centuries. Because it exists across myriad lines of difference, the agreement reaches beyond particular individuals and societies. By neutralizing the potential biases through which people might view the question, humanity has moved the debate to a higher plane. Regardless of a person's race, religion, nationality, political ideology, social status, or family background, they almost surely deem slavery a reprehensible institution. Although support for slavery still exists among a tiny percentage of people, most notably the supporters of the Islamic State (ISIS), the consensus is nevertheless robust.

The example of slavery points to a more general phenomenon: Our understandings of right and wrong can change over time, which we should welcome so long as the change occurs after inclusive deliberation. My approach here resembles that of philosopher William Talbott, who views morality as a fallible work in progress emerging over time through diverse sources including experience, intellectual activity, social movements, and the perspectives of ordinary people.[66] The earlier consensus in favor of slavery did not qualify as contractarian because it resulted from certain people exercising power over others rather than a good-faith search for morality among diverse participants. In fact, the principles of contractarian morality undercut many practices that have been widespread throughout human history. Any system whereby one group dominates another through sexism, racism, colonialism, or genocide would be unlikely to emerge from a process that brings all affected people into the conversation on equal footing. Changes in morality that develop when previously excluded voices join the conversation are almost always for the better. Conversely, morality can get worse if it follows from a process becoming less inclusive.

How Morality Resembles Science

This tentative and changeable nature of morality—where a consensus does not guarantee truth, especially if it was reached through flawed means—has clear parallels in the area of science. The connection between these two domains might seem suspect on first glance. Morality is often considered a subject for philosophy, religion, and the humanities, whereas scientific disciplines handle matters amenable to empirical investigation. In recent decades, however, authors such as Edward O. Wilson, Steven Pinker, and Edward Slingerland have called for unifying the different branches of knowledge, and I endorse their project.[67] In fact, my definition of contractarian morality helps crystallize the ways in which scientific and moral knowledge are connected.

One area of overlap lies in the prospects for objectivity. Depending on where scientists received their graduate training and from what advisors, they may be predisposed to certain positions on topics of scientific debate. Other biases reflect the incentives embedded in the system of scientific publication and communication. Given that reviewers and editors resist devoting scarce journal space to papers lacking statistically significant findings, studies confirming the null hypothesis tend to be underreported.[68] Meanwhile, once scientists are on the record advancing a certain claim, the desire to protect their reputation can keep them from accepting new research challenging their conclusions. Scientists can also show biases related to their race, gender, or nationality.[69]

Accordingly, objectivity should be considered a property not of any single scientist but rather of science as a collective enterprise. The norms and protocols of scientific communities are designed to overcome the biases that might affect particular scientists. For example, the scientific method requires scientists to be open and forthright about their procedures, analyses, and data. To publish their research in a respectable journal, scientists must submit to peer review, and scrutiny continues after a paper gets published. Different scientists, each with their own biases and desires for professional advancement, thus serve to check each other. A claim doesn't get accepted as scientific knowledge until it has been hypothesized, tested, evaluated, and then replicated by other scientists. Recent attention has appropriately focused on the last stage of that process. Many findings in psychology, medicine, and other disciplines have failed to replicate and, accordingly, do not count as knowledge.[70] When the right procedures are followed, including a commitment to replication, science as an enterprise can attain an objectivity unavailable to individual scientists.[71]

The same principles hold for morality, where all humans form the relevant community. All people start with preconceptions related to their biology, the society they happened to grow up in, and myriad factors that have influenced them over their lifetimes. We thus need inclusive deliberation so that all moral ideas can be put to the test. Objectivity emerges when different people, each with their own starting points, use logic, evidence, and argument in an open and deliberative process to discover right and wrong. For a moral stance to attain a status beyond subjective beliefs, it must make sense, after rigorous investigation, to human beings in all their diversity. A community of diverse human beings can thus be objective in ways no individuals could accomplish on their own.

Another parallel between science and morality lies in the role of dissenters. Scientists with the relevant expertise define what qualifies as scientific knowledge, but the presence of a consensus does not mean no one disagrees. For example, we can find a handful of card-carrying scientists—people with PhDs in scientific disciplines from reputable universities—who deny evolution, climate change, or the origins of AIDS through HIV, or who believe in ESP, bigfoot, homeopathy, alien abduction, or the claim that vaccines cause autism.[72] A given scientific dissenter might be mistaken but could also serve as the catalyst for driving knowledge forward. In the former category, we could point to Martin Fleischmann and Stanley Pons, whose experiments allegedly demonstrating cold fusion could not be replicated in other labs.[73] In the latter category of dissenters who successfully challenged the status quo, Alfred Wegener—originator of the theory of continental drift who was ridiculed in his own day—is a prime example.[74]

Dissenters are equally important in the realm of morality. In societies where nearly everyone within the dominant group deemed slavery acceptable, there eventually emerged some lonely voices standing on the other side. Beyond the issue of slavery, somebody had to be the first to say it is wrong to engage in torture, burn people accused of witchcraft, or punish the family members of wrongdoers. By forming movements, publicizing their ideas, and pressing their case, dissenters can eventually overturn a prevailing consensus. To determine whether an existing consensus needs to shift, we must subject the ideas of moral dissenters to inclusive deliberation. The community might justifiably reject those ideas—after all, some moral dissenters are cranks—but we won't know for sure until their ideas receive a fair hearing.

Morality is also similar to science in that each involves a process of discovery rather than invention or creation. Scientific advances are driven by evidence that evaded previous scientists who were limited by their methods, instruments, and concepts. For example, the theory of plate tectonics (the successor to continental drift) rests in large part on data that had not been collected or even imagined before the twentieth century. The discovery of mid-ocean ridges and the magnetic alignment of the rocks at various distances could not be explained through the assumption of a static earth. Satellite technology in the twenty-first century has allowed scientists to chart with great precision the small year-to-year movements in the plates.[75] Scientists discovered rather than created these and other pieces of evidence for plate tectonics.

In a like manner, human beings discover the rules of morality through a deliberative process. Deliberation requires establishing and highlighting basic facts relevant to the subject at hand. If the quality of the underlying information improves, so do the judgments that result from the deliberation. The discovery of a better morality can also happen because additional voices joined the discussion. The reasons why it's wrong to hold another person as property were waiting to be discovered, and former slaves and their allies eventually brought those reasons into the open. Similarly, as religious minorities in the last few centuries increasingly pressed the case for why their rights should be respected, members of the dominant religions learned about a perspective that had been hiding in plain sight. Inclusive deliberation thus facilitates a process of moral discovery by improving the flow of information and injecting new ideas into the dialogue.

Science and morality are also connected in that the claims within each of them are provisional and subject to being revised or even overturned. Scientific knowledge rests upon the interplay of theory and data. Through the development of conceptual tools and theoretical frameworks, plus new forms of measurement, analysis, and research design, scientists update their models of the world and demonstrate that all scientific knowledge—including the knowledge accepted today—is fallible. A moral consensus is also fallible, especially when we recognize that deliberation is always imperfect and inclusivity can only be approximated. By engaging a long-standing issue, people sometimes discover that a previous consensus needs to be modified or rejected.

The possibility that some moral understandings will change does not mean that we should embrace a position of moral relativism, which would imply that there are no universal standards and no possibility of moral progress. A relativist would say that the guidelines for proper behavior are subjective in being specific to each individual, community, or era. My position differs in that I have defended a process allowing us to obtain an objective and universal morality. When we discover through inclusive deliberation that moral beliefs must change, we can apply that knowledge retroactively. Through my approach, we can see that people from earlier times and places were wrong in approving of practices such as torture, witch burning, and collective punishment.

Of course, any evaluations of historical individuals and societies must be tempered by acknowledging the fallibility of current beliefs about morality (and science). The germ theory of disease, for example, is supported by a mountain of research. If this theory is right, then people in the past erred when they attributed outbreaks of disease to the humors, stale air, or the evil eye. Similarly, we have reached a moral consensus that no one should be denied social or political rights based on their gender, race, ethnicity, religion, or other aspects of their identity, which means that people from earlier eras who thought otherwise were mistaken. Although it seems unlikely, both the germ theory of disease and the moral principle of equal rights could be fundamentally flawed. Even if we are right about both claims in a general sense, there remain large gaps in our knowledge. We do not fully understand infectious organisms, nor do we know how to apply the principle of equal rights to all aspects of modern polities. Just as scientific research must continue, so too must deliberation over moral questions.

Sometimes sustained deliberation of this kind can unsettle an established consensus. For example, living generations might have reached a consensus whose implementation places harm on future generations. Once the needs of people not yet born are explicitly considered, moral positions might appropriately change. A consensus could also exist that relies on the unjust treatment of nonhuman animals. Focusing on the harm to other sentient beings could cause some people to withdraw their agreement from a previous consensus. Because contractarian morality is provisional rather than final, it ensures that moral innovations can emerge and eventually win additional adherents through persuasion.

RESPONDING TO CHRISTIAN OBJECTIONS

I doubt that Christian apologists reading this chapter will accept the conclusions I have reached, so I will try to anticipate some of their concerns. An apologist might accuse me of saying that morality ultimately reduces to public opinion, making it synonymous with the will of the majority. Anyone who has read this chapter knows I have argued no such thing. I have stressed instead that morality has to be discovered through reason, with inclusive deliberation serving as a means of reason ideally suited to overcoming the initial biases of each person and society. An apologist alternatively could try to undermine my approach by offering a hypothetical scenario. To borrow from an example that William Lane Craig regularly uses, what if the Nazis had brainwashed everyone into approving the Holocaust?[76] Wouldn't my approach force me to acknowledge that consensus as the appropriate grounding for a moral judgment?

To the contrary, my version of contractarian morality accepts a consensus only if it resulted from inclusive deliberation. Neither a hypothetical brainwashing nor the Nazis' actual promotion of their agenda meets the necessary criteria. If the Nazis had tried to defend their policies through open debate rather than totalitarian control of state institutions, massive numbers of people—Jewish and non-Jewish alike—would have vehemently objected both during and after the Holocaust. Hypotheticals about the Nazis brainwashing the whole world give us no more insight into moral questions than hypotheticals about money trees give us into retirement planning.

Even if apologists accepted my point about the need for a consensus to rest on inclusive deliberation, they would still feel uncomfortable with my approach. In particular, they would object that I'm cutting God out of the picture. Ravi Zacharias, one of the most prominent apologists of the last half century, writes: "When you assume a moral law, you must posit a moral lawgiver—the source of the moral law."[77] Similar statements appear in the works of many other apologists, including Phil Fernandes, David Limbaugh, and Doug Powell.[78] The apologists think their line of reasoning takes us straight to God, for who else could give us morality? In fact, apologists often work backward from the presence of moral laws to infer that God must exist.

As a defender of contractarian morality, I reject their claims wholesale. I have argued that morality originates not with God but with human beings, and an analogy might bolster my case. No one doubts that we enact laws through our governments in order to define impermissible behaviors, specify the means of enforcement and judgment, and describe the punishments for those found guilty. If human beings can establish laws of the political variety, why can't we also discover the basis for moral laws? In fact, morality and politics are tightly connected, for moral questions frequently become political questions. Any list of behaviors that a society deems immoral will overlap heavily with the list of behaviors the society declares illegal.

An apologist might respond by questioning the objectivity of the humans who serve as moral lawgivers. In the words of Catholic apologist Christopher Akers, "For a moral system to be truly objective, moral law must stem from a source external to humanity. Otherwise, all we have is subjective human moral opinion, no matter how it is dressed up."[79] Akers assumes that if morality originates with human beings, it must be a matter of opinion. Protestant apologist William Frye makes the point even more strongly in asking, "Is morality real or just opinion or preference?"[80] William Lane Craig similarly worries that "in a world without God, there can be no objective right and wrong, only our culturally and personally relative subjective judgments."[81] My burden in the current chapter has been to show why Akers, Frye, Craig, and other apologists are mistaken.

Some aspects of morality, which I have called the "basic morality," are more than mere opinion because they are shared across all societies. When so many human beings from different cultural backgrounds all agree on something, it cannot be dismissed as just the subjective preference of one person or society. We can augment the basic morality by forging a consensus through inclusive deliberation. In one notable example, representatives from dozens of countries as diverse as Lebanon, Canada, France, India, and the United States participated in drafting and adopting the Universal Declaration of Human Rights (UDHR) in 1948. The UDHR condemns slavery, torture, and arbitrary arrest and demands that all persons be granted equal protection of the law, freedom of speech and religion, and the rights to an education, remunerative work, and an adequate standard of living.[82] Several countries abstained from the United Nations vote on the UDHR, which does not change the fact that it had consensual support around the world. It was approved through an open and deliberative process based on information, discussion, and debate.[83]

The UDHR, which includes many aspects of public and political morality, fits cleanly within my definition of contractarian morality.

To fully address the issue of objectivity for the UDHR or anything else, though, we need to distinguish between the different definitions of objectivity. Something could be objective in the sense of being external to the mind, meaning its existence does not depend on any human processes. Apologists claim that morality without God lacks that kind of objectivity. Such a limitation, they argue, means that morality therefore cannot be objective in the sense of reaching beyond parochial opinions. Apologists thereby link the two definitions, saying that the latter kind of objectivity cannot exist without the former kind. I have argued the contrary in separating the two definitions. Regardless of whether an externally existing morality is a meaningful concept in a purely materialist universe, a point on which philosophers disagree, morality can certainly be objective in the way people ordinarily use the term. If individuals with different beliefs and backgrounds reach a consensus after a process of inclusive deliberation, they have transcended the subjective perspectives with which they began, thereby achieving objectivity in the sense that matters to our everyday lives.

Christian apologists such as Frank Turek fail to make these necessary distinctions. "In order to judge between competing societies," Turek writes, "there must be this objective standard beyond those societies and beyond humanity." Note that Turek here is using "objective" to indicate something external to the human mind, and he then jumps immediately to the other definition: "Without that unchanging objective standard, all moral questions are reduced to human opinion—nearly seven billion human opinions."[84] Turek is now worried about whether morality can be objective in the sense of transcending individual opinions such that it is shared and impartial. As I have shown in this chapter, he is wrong in asserting that morality in the absence of God cannot be objective in this wider meaning.

Recognizing that it offers the main alternative to a morality based on God's commands, other apologists have questioned what reason can accomplish. As stated by Catholic apologist Michael Novak, "If morality were left to reason alone, common agreement would never be reached, since philosophers vehemently—and endlessly—disagree."[85] Novak here makes the common mistake of taking an all-or-nothing position. He's certainly right that philosophers writing about morality use several competing approaches, including consequentialism, deontology, natural law, virtue ethics, and care ethics.[86] Despite those differences in their guiding frameworks, philosophers (and nonphilosophers) have forged a consensus on many moral questions, including the rightness of being kind, showing love, demonstrating bravery, seeking justice, acting generously, and caring for one's family. We also have a consensus on the wrongness of murder, rape, incest, assault, theft, fraud, pedophilia, kidnapping, robbery, arson, slavery, torture, genocide, ethnic cleansing, human sacrifice, arbitrary arrest, collective punishment, and killing civilians during wartime. Of course, those behaviors still happen today; if they didn't, we wouldn't need treaties, laws, police officers, courts, and other enforcement mechanisms. Perpetrators of the forbidden behaviors either belong to the small minority who reject the consensus, find themselves unable to act in ways that match their beliefs, or else think their situations deserve a special exception.

On other issues, we have not reached a global consensus on what the norms should be. The divisive issues include such matters as abortion, contraception, homosexuality, polygamy, blasphemy, gambling, pornography, prostitution, capital punishment, child labor, eating meat, premarital sex, honor killings, assisted suicide, animal welfare, forced marriages, male circumcision, female genital mutilation, corporal punishment of children, and alcohol and drug use. Differing views persist across individuals within each society on some of these questions. Other subjects on that list are controversial within certain societies but not others. These various kinds of contentious issues notwithstanding, the global community has formed a consensus on many moral questions through the use of reason. It's a mistake to assume, as Novak does, that humans cannot resolve any moral issues and must remain forever deadlocked on the ones that divide us.

MORALITY AND THE AFTERLIFE

In the unlikely event that they accepted all of my points above, apologists would still have one card left to play. They could appeal to an important religious concept—the afterlife—to declare the superiority of a God-given morality. After all, what obligation does a person have to obey a moral code discovered and elaborated by human beings? Why should people refrain from behaving immorally if doing so would serve their interests? What constrains someone from acting in ways that harm other people?

One answer is a person's self-regulation. Most people *want* to get along with others and lead a respectable life. Research in psychology and other disciplines finds that the predictors of happiness include building strong relationships, engaging in meaningful work, and participating in one's community.[87] Will a decent person who loses faith in God subsequently become a moral deviant and a social outcast? According to the best research, no. Systematic data indicates that atheists are worse than the rest of the population on some indicators (giving to charity) but better on others (likelihood of going to prison).[88] There is no evidence indicating that the lack of belief in God leads to massive increases in socially destructive behaviors.

A second answer to what keeps people from harming others is that the state stands ready to intervene. Since the days of Thomas Hobbes, the contractarian approach to ethics has sought to discourage malicious behavior by enacting laws and empowering the state to enforce them. Should someone step out of line, they will hear from the state's law enforcement apparatus, which can be strengthened or weakened as necessary to achieve desired ends. If convicted of murder, rape, assault, theft, fraud, or another offense, a person might go to prison, which provides a strong incentive for staying on the right side of the law.

Yet these two answers are incomplete. An apologist could note, correctly, that self-regulation and the criminal justice system work sometimes but not always. Some people have no desire to obey society's rules, and we cannot put a cop on every street corner. Many crimes go unsolved or even unreported, and other moral offenses—such as lying to your friends or family to benefit yourself—are not illegal. Given the limitations of any human means to enforce morality, an apologist could offer the alternative of cosmic justice. God can serve as the watchful eye in the sky, and by controlling a person's destination in the afterlife, he can punish someone who evaded the political authorities on earth. Any moral system without God affords no such solution.

Many apologists, including Sean McDowell and Jonathan Morrow, press this argument to the hilt. They write: "According to the New Atheists, in the end there will be no ultimate justice, no making things right, and no punishment for the wicked. Clever criminals will 'get away with it.'"[89] McDowell and Morrow offer the alternative of justice in the afterlife. Frank Turek echoes their claims: "If there is no God and no afterlife, then *no justice will ever be done.* Thousands of pedophiles who have committed murder over the years will never get justice. They will go to their graves unpunished."[90] William Lane Craig similarly argues, "If life ends at the grave, it ultimately makes no difference whether you live as a Stalin or as a Mother Teresa."[91] Through the afterlife, by contrast, "the scales of God's justice will be balanced. Thus the moral choices that we make in this life are infused with an eternal significance."[92]

McDowell, Morrow, Turek, and Craig are tapping into the common assumption in the West that people who behave morally go to heaven while evildoers go to hell. There is only one problem: That's not what their own religion actually teaches. According to Christian theology, all people are sinners who deserve eternal punishment, and they can be brought into a right relationship with God only through the death and resurrection of Christ. As Paul states in Romans 6:23, "For the wages of sin is death, but the free gift of God is eternal life in Christ Jesus our Lord." For Protestants, those who accept Christ's sacrifice for their sins make it to heaven, while those lacking faith go to hell. For Catholics, the faithful must also maintain their saving grace by participating in the sacraments. In both the Protestant and Catholic traditions, a pedophile, rapist, or murderer who receives God's grace spends eternity with him. Upstanding individuals who refuse God's gift of salvation, a group that presumably includes many readers of this book, get a one-way ticket to hell.[93]

As the holders of advanced degrees in theology who have spent many years or decades studying the subject, McDowell, Morrow, Turek, and Craig know full well what their religion teaches about the afterlife, and yet they can't help themselves. Their rhetorical moves show that apologetics is not a dispassionate search for truth but rather the public relations of people who think they already have it. Since the goals are reinforcement and ideally persuasion, not truth seeking, apologists can rely on the false beliefs the masses hold about how the afterlife works in Christianity. On this and other topics, apologists routinely offer whatever argument seems to work, regardless of whether it makes any sense or accurately reflects the doctrines of their own religion. With the ends justifying the means—they believe they are saving souls—many apologists yield to the temptation to use deceptive tactics. They don't necessarily do so consciously, but their writings nevertheless show that they haven't reconciled what they believe with what they say.

If Christian apologists want to uphold an afterlife with "punishment for the wicked," as McDowell and Morrow put it, they need to find a new religion. Let me recommend Islam, which teaches something close to the works-based righteousness often falsely ascribed to Christianity. The Quran refers in many places to the Islamic equivalent of heaven—جنّة in Arabic, usually written in the Roman alphabet as *Jannah* and translated into English as *paradise*. To enter paradise, a person must proclaim there is no god but God, believe in the angels, and accept God's prophets and revelations.[94] Beyond matters of belief, a person must perform good works such as praying with humility, caring for orphans, and engaging in acts of charity.[95] The Quran even describes a kind of scale, where those whose good deeds outweigh the bad enter paradise. Everyone falling short goes to the Islamic version of hell, either temporarily or permanently.[96]

By envisioning an afterlife that sorts people according to how they lived their lives, Islam gives a more rational solution than Christianity for someone who commits serious offenses yet avoids punishment by the state. Of course, the Islamic solution only works if Islam is, you know, true. If it's not, and if no other religion is either, then it's an unfortunate fact of life—along with death and taxes—that some people will get away with acting immorally. An additional problem for Islam is that Muslims in the West often find the moral rules of their religion hard to swallow. If reaching paradise requires accepting such practices as jihad, slavery, wife beating, denying religious freedom, and banning friendships with non-Muslims, one wonders whether the price is worth it. In chapter 7 I'll return to the subject of how modern Muslims handle the Quran's teachings.

For now, I'll focus solely on Christianity. In the next chapter, I examine changes in morality over the grand scale of two millennia. I aim to explain how both Christians and non-Christians managed to improve on the morality presented in the Bible. Although the Bible's morality is flawed in many ways, we have discovered a new and better morality through the method of humanism: reason.

CHAPTER 4

The Group-Centered Bible and Its God

IN THE BEGINNING THE ISRAELITES CREATED THEIR HEAVENS AND earth. And their surroundings were without form and void, and darkness fell upon the face of their land. And the Israelites said, "Let there be order," and there was order. And the Israelites saw that order, that it was good, and they divided the order from the chaos.

And the Israelites said, "Let us make God in our image, after our likeness, and let him have dominion over the stars in the sky, and over human beings on earth." So the Israelites created God in their own image. And the Israelites saw everything they had made and, behold, it was very good. And on the seventh day they rested.

The Israelites were not done creating, however. The mere existence of a God could only take them so far in binding their community together. They needed to define their God's qualities, tell stories about his relationship with them, and turn him into a father figure who could teach their offspring right from wrong. So the Israelites took the moral beliefs already held by some members of their society and put them on God's lips. Instead of recognizing that it emerged organically among their predecessors and contemporaries, they attributed this morality to God.

Over the succeeding centuries, the Israelites wrote books in which God worked through prophets to relay their moral teachings back to them. The God they created told them which behaviors were required, prohibited, and optional, and he introduced a system of rewards and punishments to encourage compliance. They began treating the books containing God's rules as his direct inspiration. Through its supposed origin in a divine being, their morality thus acquired greater credibility and persuasive power. A moral code created by human beings could always be challenged, but God's rules were final. The Israelites copied, distributed, and passed down to their descendants the books containing that morality.

The Israelites eventually became known as Jews, for they lived primarily in an area called Yehud by the Persians and Judea by the Romans. Amid the political and religious turmoil of the Roman Empire, Judaism spawned a splinter sect, Christianity. Christians inherited from Jews an image of God, and they followed in Jews' footsteps by projecting their own morality onto him. Christians decided to combine the Jewish scriptures with additional books giving God some features distinctive to Christianity. We call the resulting compilation the Bible. Its God reflects the moral vision of many authors, Jewish and Christian, writing over several centuries. Despite some variation from book to book, the God of the Bible prescribes a coherent morality.

Modern Christians have continued this ancient practice of creating a God in their own image and attributing their morality to him, but they face a daunting problem: They cannot write a new Bible from scratch. Sects such as Mormonism treat certain books from the modern era as scripture, but most Christians, whether they identify as Catholic, Protestant, Orthodox, or something else, think the biblical canon has been closed since the fourth century.[1] Whereas ancient Jews and Christians could write books and proclaim they derived their morality from the God portrayed therein, today's Christians don't have that option. They instead have to work within the Bible handed down by their predecessors. Modern Christians wouldn't want to rewrite some parts of the Bible, especially those describing the "basic morality" (see chapter 3) shared across societies. Christians find it easy to ratify the Bible's admirable commands to take care of the poor, follow the Golden Rule, honor your mother and father, and condemn murder, theft, and kidnapping.

The problem arises in how to handle the biblical passages teaching a flawed morality. As I explained in previous chapters, Christian apologists use some combination of four strategies—Ignore, Rationalize, Reinterpret, and Mystify—to address situations where the God of the Bible either acts immorally or gives immoral commands. These strategies allow Christians to uphold a modern morality while claiming allegiance to the Bible. Christians live in the shadow of the Enlightenment, and they have unknowingly absorbed from the secular culture such values as freedom, equality, and tolerance. On issues including slavery, divorce, women's rights, moneylending at interest, and crime and punishment, Christians reject what the Bible says.[2] Christians cannot openly acknowledge that fact, though, so they deploy one or more of their four standard strategies to recreate the God of the Bible in their own image.

In the current chapter I explain why Christians do not accept the Bible as written. I will show that many aspects of modern morality, widely shared among people of diverse religious backgrounds, conflict with the moral code that ancient Jews and Christians wrote into their scriptures. Many of the Bible's problems, I will demonstrate, stem from its authors' excessive tribalism, a single flaw with many manifestations. By exploring that flaw, we can understand why the Bible botches many moral issues and investigate how modern Christians respond to the resulting dilemma.

HUMAN BEINGS ARE TRIBAL

As members of my family can attest, watching sports often brings out my worst qualities. I yell at the screen as if it can hear me. I delude myself into thinking I know more about the game than the managers, coaches, and players. Conveniently ignoring favorable rulings for my teams, I denounce the umpires and referees whenever any close call goes the other way. Most interesting of all, I announce to whoever happens to be listening when "we" score a run or a touchdown. Somehow I feel part of my favorite teams—the Philadelphia Phillies in baseball and Pittsburgh Steelers in football—even though I'm just a fan. Meanwhile, I hold a hostility toward the New York Yankees and New England Patriots that would be excessive even if all their players were child molesters.

I take some solace in knowing I'm not the only irrational sports fan who lets my group loyalty obliterate any semblance of balance, fairness, and decorum. In fact, sports are just one of many arenas that activate the tribal instincts of human beings. People tend to divide others into ingroups and outgroups, then treat the former with kindness and generosity while viewing the latter with suspicion.[3] Such groupishness is precisely what one would expect from a species that evolved in hunter-gatherer bands typically including only a few dozen individuals. Throughout most of human history, people relied on their small bands for assistance with all of life's needs.[4] On the rare occasions when ancient humans encountered them, people from other bands—who talked funny, followed different rituals, and behaved in strange ways—posed a threat to their own group's cohesion or even existence. Over thousands of generations in such environments, the processes of natural selection left us with brains that readily classify people into the categories of us and them.[5]

To see that humans have a strong tendency toward groupishness, one need only examine its recurrence throughout history in all parts of the world. Anthropologists have discovered many societies who have a word for themselves that translates as "people," implying that outgroup members are somehow less than human. Such societies often use demeaning terms to describe others in their vicinity.[6] The Arctic offers a classic example of this phenomenon. Westerners originally called the natives of the region "Eskimos," a term borrowed from a neighboring group that could mean "eaters of raw flesh." The natives refer to themselves as the Inuit, meaning "people."[7]

Further evidence of our tribal tendencies comes from studying babies, who have not yet learned about the specific divisions within their communities. Through the Infant Cognition Center at Yale University, colloquially known as the "Yale Baby Lab," psychologist Karen Wynn and her colleagues have demonstrated that babies just a few months old pick up cues about who is similar and dissimilar to them.[8] For example, babies will sort each other into groups based on seemingly arbitrary preferences for either graham crackers or green beans, then prefer third parties who act kindly toward their ingroup and poorly toward the outgroup.[9]

Adults also show strong tendencies toward being groupish. Psychologist Henri Tajfel, one of the pioneers in this area of study, conducted research in which people formed groups based on a trivial characteristic—preferences for one piece of abstract art over another—and then favored ingroup members when allocating resources.[10] Subsequent scholars documented the same effect even for people who know they entered a group through a coin toss.[11] This body of research is called the "minimal group paradigm," and it identifies the minimum conditions (random chance, as it turns out) necessary for people to create a world of us and them.

At the same time, other research demonstrates that groupishness is a variable rather than a constant. Many factors can either amplify or dampen the extent to which a person thinks and acts in a tribal manner, leading to significant differences in group-related attitudes and behaviors across individuals, situations, and societies.[12] The effects of groupishness are also highly variable. Group loyalties often have the positive consequence of allowing people to cooperate, build trust, and create functioning communities.[13] Only under certain conditions does a generalized distrust of outgroups degenerate into a desire to enslave, kill, or colonize them. As we'll see in the rest of the chapter, the Bible's authors embraced the worst forms of groupishness, and this led them to create a group-centered God.

GROUPISHNESS IN THE BIBLE

When I was in fourth grade, I got into a scuffle with another kid over who had dibs on the swing. Amid some pushing and shoving from both of us, he shouted at me, "Your mama wears combat boots!" I knew this was an insult, but I also found it confusing. My mom indeed would have looked silly in combat boots—I could imagine her wearing them only for a Halloween costume—but the insult still seemed rather weak, as if he couldn't think of anything more cutting. It wasn't until I reached adulthood that I understood what he was saying. During the first world war, I learned, sex workers sometimes followed the troops from camp to camp. Sometime thereafter saying that someone's mother wore combat boots became a way to disparage her character through innuendo.[14] That kid from fourth grade, whether he knew it or not, followed the time-honored practice of insulting a person by accusing them or a family member of deviant sexual behaviors.

I thought of that experience while I was reading the Bible a few years ago. The ancient Israelites lived in a region containing many other ethnic groups, and the Bible told stories about their origins. One such story alleges that Lot, Abraham's nephew, had sex with and impregnated his own daughters after they got him drunk (Genesis 19:30–38). The two daughters subsequently gave birth to the founders of the Moabite and the Ammonite peoples. The story thus served to demean all living members of the Moabites and Ammonites as the descendants of incestuous ancestors. It's one thing for someone to denigrate an individual or their family, as I learned in fourth grade, but another matter entirely to stigmatize a person's entire community. The fact that the Bible traffics in ethnic slurs of that kind speaks to the groupishness of its authors.

The Bible contains a similar story about another ethnic group, the Edomites. The scriptures describe how Esau, father of the Edomites, was so dumb that he sold his birthright to his brother for a bowl of stew (Genesis 25:29–34). It's not hard to imagine ancient Israelites feeling superior to the Edomites upon hearing this joke. It fits the historical prototype of ethnic jokes from around the world that sociologist Christie Davies has explored in great depth.[15] To assert their power through stereotypes, individuals from dominant groups have long told jokes in which the punch line involves a person from a minority group doing something stupid.[16] Enlightened people now consider ethnic jokes based on crude stereotypes to be a form of racism, and yet there they are in the Bible. Another means by which people historically have disparaged members of other ethnic groups is by calling them cockroaches, rats, pigs, or some other kind of animal. Two of the New Testament authors, Matthew and Mark, followed this practice in comparing Canaanites and Syrophoenicians to dogs (Matthew 15:26 and Mark 7:27).

Having read hundreds of books, articles, and blog posts by Christian apologists, I cannot remember them ever addressing these stories about the Moabites, Ammonites, Edomites, Canaanites, and Syrophoenicians. In other words, apologists have generally opted for the "Ignore" strategy to handle the matter. None of the atheist and humanist literature I've read has raised the issue either, so the apologists' nonresponse has allowed them to bury it. Why have the Bible's ethnic insults and jokes failed to provoke a debate? The reason, I suspect, is that the groups the Bible denigrates no longer exist as distinct peoples and therefore lack defenders in the modern world. Had the Bible instead directed its racism toward Kurds, Hungarians, Persians, and the Han Chinese, apologists could not get away with ignoring the issue.

Extending well beyond ethnic insults and jokes, the groupishness of the Bible's authors led them to conceive a God who permitted his followers to enslave people from other groups. Whereas they could hold fellow Israelites only as indentured servants, outsiders could become actual slaves: "As for the male and female slaves whom you may have, it is from the nations around you that you may acquire male and female slaves. You may also acquire them from among the aliens residing with you, and from their families that are with you, who have been born in your land; and they may be your property. You may keep them as a possession for your children after you, for them to inherit as property. These you may treat as slaves, but as for your fellow Israelites, no one shall rule over the other with harshness" (Leviticus 25:44–46). God thus forbade his chosen people from enslaving each other but allowed them to enslave people from the nations around them. Those slaves became property that could be used throughout the owner's lifetime and then passed to descendants. Several New Testament authors took slavery of this kind for granted and proscribed the respective duties of slave and master (Ephesians 6:5–9; Colossians 3:22–24; Titus 2:9–10; 1 Timothy 6:1–2). During the times of both the Old and New Testaments, winning armies commonly enslaved their surviving opponents, who were almost always from different ethnic groups, and then sold them through the international slave market in Israel and other nations.[17]

Although it was not racially based, chattel slavery in the Bible was thus motivated by ethnic divisions. The fact that ancient peoples tended to identify with their own group to the exclusion of everyone else made slavery seem normal and natural. This mentality often led them to regard a different ethnic group in their vicinity as a mass, a phenomenon that social psychologists call "outgroup homogeneity."[18] The outgroup members thereby lost their individuality and were presumed to think and act alike. The New Testament book of Titus followed this practice in embracing a statement calling the inhabitants of Crete "always liars, vicious brutes, lazy gluttons" (Titus 1:12–13). Besides encouraging slavery and racist characterizations of other nationalities and ethnic groups, perceptions of outgroup homogeneity could and did lead to genocide. This happened in the Bible when God ordered the Israelites to exterminate all the Canaanite peoples—adults, children, and infants—to punish them for engaging in bestiality, incest, and other sins.

The Bible's allegations about behaviors occurring throughout Canaanite society cannot be taken at face value, for historians and anthropologists know that every society on record contains internal divisions. People differ from each other on many dimensions, including their propensity to commit crimes and their tastes for deviant sexual behaviors. It's implausible to believe that every single person within the Canaanite nations participated in the practices the Bible alleged. The difficulties become especially pronounced with respect to infants. Are we really supposed to believe they committed abominable sins, let alone through their own volition? Infants nevertheless fell under God's command that "you must not let anything that breathes remain alive" (Deuteronomy 20:16). The Bible treats the Canaanite nations not as collections of individuals with differing interests, values, and behaviors but rather as unified entities that must be eliminated.

OTHER OUTGROUPS IN THE BIBLE

Taking an even more extreme view of the Amalekites, the Bible depicts them as a continuing body extending over several centuries. The Amalekites first appear in the Bible when they attack the Israelites during the escape from Egypt (Exodus 17:8–16). To exact retribution, God orders a future generation of Israelites to kill all the Amalekites living at that time (Deuteronomy 25:17–19), and his promissory note eventually comes due. Working through his prophet Samuel, God instructs the Israelites to exterminate every last Amalekite to fulfill his earlier command (1 Samuel 15:1–3). This is a type of intergenerational punishment, one of the most despicable concepts human beings have ever devised. The Bible's authors envisioned a God who thought it appropriate to kill an entire group of people as punishment for what their ancestors did four hundred years earlier. Retribution of that kind only makes sense if the Amalekites were a single homogenous group not only at a given moment but also over time.

The Israelites' time in Egypt demonstrates a similar tendency for the Bible to view outgroups as a mass. God proves in that story that he can bend anyone's will, and he causes Pharaoh to alternatively decide to keep the Israelites in bondage or release them (Exodus 9:12, 10:20, 10:27). God nevertheless hardens Pharaoh's heart one last time (Exodus 11:10) and then sends a plague killing all the firstborns in Egypt (Exodus 12:29–30). How could infants and children, most of them the offspring of peasants working the fields, possibly be blamed for Pharaoh's actions? Given that he had already demonstrated his control over Pharaoh's will, God did not need to kill the firstborns in order to free the Israelites from slavery. The story indicates that the biblical authors conceived a God who viewed the Egyptians as interchangeable cogs in a machine. It didn't matter which Egyptians God killed, for they lacked any individual identity.

Lest one think only the Old Testament strips individuals of any identity separate from their groups, consider how the New Testament refers to Jews. The book of John, for example, consistently refers to Jesus's opponents simply as "the Jews." In describing the events leading to Jesus's crucifixion, Matthew asserts that the assembled crowd, comprised entirely of Jews, demanded that Pontius Pilate release Barabbas rather than Jesus (Matthew 27:15–23; Luke 23:13–25). Matthew then blames all Jews living at the time, plus their offspring, for Jesus's crucifixion. As Matthew tells the story, the Jews agree and proclaim, "His blood be on us and on our children!" (Matthew 27:25). Paul similarly refers to "the Jews, who killed both the Lord Jesus and the prophets" (1 Thessalonians 2:14–15). These verses in Matthew and 1 Thessalonians enshrined in scripture the Christian belief that all Jews are "Christ killers," a slur that prompted myriad forms of antisemitism in Christian communities over the next two millennia.

Besides its characterizations of Jews, the New Testament encourages an "us versus them" mentality in many other ways. Matthew 12:30 and Luke 11:23 quote Jesus as saying, "Whoever is not with me is against me." You could not construct a clearer statement of us-and-them thinking if you wrote it yourself. Other New Testament books contain similar sentiments, as when 1 John calls the people who have left the community "antichrists" (2:18, 4:1–6), "liars" (2:22), and "children of the devil" (3:10). Even the biblical verses that gesture toward uniting all of humanity presume a group-centered view of the world. Paul proclaims in Galatians 3:28, "There is no longer Jew or Greek, there is no longer slave or free, there is no longer male of female; for all of you are one in Christ Jesus." Paul certainly deserves credit for welcoming people into his community regardless of their ethnicity, gender, or status as slave or free. Nevertheless, Paul—along with his fellow New Testament authors—uses harsh language to describe the people who do not accept his religious claims. In effect, the New Testament replaces existing forms of group identity with a new division based on a person's allegiance to certain religious doctrines.

COLLECTIVE PUNISHMENT IN THE BIBLE

The Bible's group-centered thinking is also apparent in its approach to punishment. To see this, let's suppose a male apologist is enjoying a leisurely Saturday afternoon at home when he answers a knock on his front door. On the other side is a police officer who immediately handcuffs him and announces, "You're under arrest." With a puzzled look on his face, the apologist asks, "On what charge?" The cop was waiting for that question. "Your great-grandfather robbed a store back in 1907, and you must pay for his crime. You're gonna do hard time in the slammer." The apologist is incredulous. "I never even met my great-grandfather! He died long before I was born! How can I be held responsible for what he did? This arrest is outrageous!" The police officer calmly replies, "Look, buddy, I'm just following the same principles for punishment as your own God."

The cop knows of what he speaks. God declares himself in Exodus 20:15 to be "a jealous God, punishing children for the iniquity of parents, to the third and fourth generation of those who reject me." With the offender representing the first generation, that verse pledges divine punishment for the children, grandchildren, and great-grandchildren. Deuteronomy 5:9 records God making the same promise. Numbers 14:18 gives additional information and explains, "The Lord is slow to anger, and abounding in steadfast love, forgiving iniquity and transgression, but by no means clearing the guilty, visiting the iniquity of the parents upon the children to the third and fourth generation."

These verses in Exodus, Deuteronomy, and Numbers are examples of a much larger phenomenon. Scholars use the term *collective punishment* to refer to any divine or human process that punishes people other than, or in addition to, the individual who committed the offense. We can further distinguish between two forms of collective punishment. Through *kin punishment*, God or the governing authorities, or extralegal entities such as vigilantes, gangs, or the mafia, punish family members along with or instead of the offender. Through *group punishment*, retribution flows beyond the offender's family and reaches into their friends, community, nation, or ethnic group, or even to all of humanity. I'll begin by examining kin punishment, which—as we've seen—the God of the Bible explicitly promises.

Kin punishment is not limited to the Bible, for many societies have used it. Before the Roman Empire extended into Europe, for example, Germanic tribes allowed family members of someone suffering an injury to exact revenge on the perpetrator's family.[19] From the Qin dynasty (221–207 BCE) until 1905 CE, Chinese emperors punished the entire families of people who committed serious crimes.[20] The Soviet Union often sent both political prisoners and their relatives to the Gulag.[21] Today, people on every continent condemn kin punishment, and it persists in the legal code of only one country: North Korea. Seemingly modeling its laws directly on the Bible, North Korea in 1948 began punishing the families of political prisoners up to the third generation, and this policy remains in place.[22]

Something resembling kin punishment can happen even in countries whose judicial systems officially reject it. For example, the American policy of attacking suspected terrorists by sending drones, initiated during the administration of George W. Bush and expanded by his successors, has been widely criticized for inadvertently killing the targets' family, friends, and associates as collateral damage.[23] Since the extra killing does not occur intentionally, drone strikes are not examples of kin punishment, but they nevertheless raise troubling moral questions. While campaigning for the presidency in 2015, Donald Trump proposed going much further and intentionally killing the family members of terrorists.[24] He reversed his position later in the campaign and did not implement any such policy during his presidency.[25] Thus, while historically many societies have echoed the Bible in embracing kin punishment, it is relatively rare today and occurs only in isolated instances.

Owing to public awareness of the relevant verses, Christian apologists cannot sweep the Bible's much broader depiction of kin punishment under the rug through the "Ignore" strategy. If apologists failed to confront the problem directly, onlookers could easily conclude that the God of the Bible behaves in ways widely considered immoral today. Through their most common response, apologists try to get God off the hook through the "Reinterpret" strategy. John Piper, a prolific writer and one of the best-known apologists of the last half century, asserts that "the sins of the fathers are punished in the children *through becoming the sins of the children*.... When the father's sins are visited on the children it is because the children are really sinful" and therefore deserve their punishment.[26] Similarly, GotQuestions.org, an online evangelical ministry, claims that "a new generation will tend to repeat the sins of their forebears. Therefore, God 'punishing the children' is simply another way of saying that the children are repeating the fathers' sins."[27]

You'd be forgiven for wondering whether Piper and the writers at GotQuestions.org have acquired a long-lost Bible different from the one you're used to seeing. These apologists have changed the biblical texts, at least in their own minds, to say that the children are committing the same sins as the fathers. The verses in question contain no such statement, but that doesn't stop apologists from reading that meaning into them. Contrary to their assertions, the God of the Bible not only declares himself a believer in kin punishment but also practices it. When Ham sees his father naked, for example, God punishes Ham's son, Canaan, and makes him a slave of his brothers (Genesis 9:20–27). Even if Ham committed some kind of grievous sin by glimpsing his father's naked body, only the concept of kin punishment could justify imposing such a severe penalty on Canaan.

Other examples of kin punishment occur after God establishes his covenant with the Israelites. On one memorable occasion, God splits apart the ground so that it swallows and kills not just Korah, a leader of the rebellion against Moses, but also Korah's entire household (Numbers 16:1–33). God thereby held Korah's wife and children accountable for an action they did not commit. The prophet Isaiah makes a similar statement about the king of Babylon: "Prepare slaughter for his sons because of the guilt of their father" (Isaiah 14:21). Even an infant could get caught in God's system of kin punishment, as the story of David and Bathsheba demonstrates. After David sleeps with Bathsheba and sends his soldiers to murder her husband, God kills the newborn child conceived through the adulterous act (1 Samuel 11:1–12:19). The prophet Nathan relays God's message to David, saying, "Now the Lord has put away your sin; you shall not die. Nevertheless, because by this deed you have utterly scorned the Lord, the child that is born to you shall die" (1 Samuel 12:13–14).

The biblical version of kin punishment also includes the Israelites implementing God's will themselves, as when they stone to death not only Achan, who stole some booty designated for the larger community, but also his sons and daughters (Joshua 7:1–26). According to the biblical text, that combination of punishments satisfied God and allowed him to "turn from his burning anger" (Joshua 7:26). Later in Israelite history, God continues to follow his long-standing rules by using his prophet Hosea to curse the children of Samarians who had sinned against him. Hosea's chilling words leave precious little to the imagination: "Samaria shall bear her guilt, because she has rebelled against her God; they shall fall by the sword, their little ones shall be dashed in pieces, and their pregnant women ripped open" (Hosea 13:16).

FROM KIN PUNISHMENT TO GROUP PUNISHMENT

The God of the Bible doesn't stop at kin punishment, for he also engages in the related practice of group punishment. We have already seen him levying it on outgroups, as when he sends a plague to kill all Egyptian firstborns after Pharaoh refused to release the Israelites. God later demands a genocide of the Amalekites to atone for what their ancestors did four centuries earlier. Interestingly, God also applies group punishment to his chosen people when he kills seventy thousand Israelites because David violated his requirements about how to conduct a census (2 Samuel 24:1–15).

The Bible's authors were not the only people who have justified group punishment by God or human beings. The Statute of Winchester, enacted in England in 1285, legalized the punishing of someone who did not commit a crime. The king and his agents gained the authority to punish an entire *tything*, an administrative unit covering many families, for the crimes of one of its members.[28] Group punishment has also occurred on an ad hoc basis. After the 1984 assassination in India of Prime Minister Indira Gandhi by her Sikh bodyguards, mobs led by Congress Party members attacked Sikh neighborhoods in Delhi, killing thousands of people.[29] In 2016 and 2017, Burmese soldiers burned Rohingya villages, committed rape and other atrocities, and drove men, women, and children across the border into Bangladesh. To justify this brutal form of group punishment, the Burmese government claimed that Rohingya villages were harboring militants who had attacked police stations and killed twelve officers.[30]

Group punishment has been especially common during times of sustained warfare. Near the end of the American Civil War, General William Tecumseh Sherman took the fighting to the Confederate countryside. Through their March to the Sea, Sherman and his troops burned and destroyed houses, fields, factories, mills, warehouses, bridges, and railroads from Atlanta to Savannah.[31] During World War II, Germany punished the communities of individuals who aided Jews or participated in resistance movements, the Soviet Union forcibly relocated to Siberia several ethnic groups containing members who allegedly undermined the war effort, and the United States dropped atomic bombs on Hiroshima and Nagasaki, wiping out both military facilities and civilian populations.[32] Responding to terrorist attacks originating in and from the West Bank, Israel in recent decades has imposed curfews, restricted movement, and destroyed houses and orchards, all of which affect many more people than just terrorists.[33]

Governments have often justified these types of policies with arguments carrying at least a surface plausibility. Given the limited tools at their disposal, governing authorities might decide they need to attack a group that includes—but extends beyond—their specific targets. Take the case of quelling an insurrection that could lead to civil war. Insurgents who melt into civilian populations become nearly impossible to isolate, and group punishment might be the only way to reach them. Similarly, political and military officials may decide that only an attack that kills civilians as collateral damage will lead their opponent to surrender. Although historians continue to debate whether the atomic bombs were militarily necessary, President Truman and his aides insisted they were trying to eliminate any need to invade Japan, an action which would prolong the war and potentially lead to even more deaths.[34]

These justifications notwithstanding, public opinion worldwide over the last several decades has turned against the practice of either targeting civilians directly or engaging in indiscriminate attacks that inevitably kill noncombatants. General Giulio Douhet of Italy, an influential proponent in the 1920s of bombing civilians during wartime, has few followers today.[35] The Fourth Geneva Convention (1949) captured the emerging global consensus for protecting civilian populations. The Burmese government, for its part, faced intense criticism from the global community for its actions in 2016 and 2017. Countries from every region of the world called attention to what the members of the UK Parliament described as a "human rights and humanitarian crisis."[36]

Now deemed immoral when undertaken by a government, group punishment by a God is even worse. God is supposed to be omniscient and omnipotent. Unlike human governments, he always knows with certainty who committed certain offenses and where they are located. If he wished, God could mete out punishments with pinpoint accuracy to ensure that no one else gets caught in the dragnet—and yet the God of the Bible regularly punishes people besides the offenders. This should not surprise us, because he embodies the morality of the authors who created him in their own image. Convinced that group punishment was an acceptable practice, they envisioned a God who shares those beliefs.

Note that the biblical authors did not reject the concept of individual punishment. Societies with kin and group punishment have always instituted them to complement rather than replace punishments targeted at the specific offender. Even in North Korea, the authorities normally punish only the actual person they believe committed a crime.[37] This coexistence of kin and group punishment with individual punishment forecloses one of the responses apologists might offer to salvage the Bible and its God. You'll recall from previous chapters that apologists often try to use the "Ignore" strategy not only to bypass a certain problem but also to shift the focus to something else. For the case at hand, apologists might identify the many instances where God practices or commands individual punishment and then proclaim they have restored his character. Such a move would be a transparent attempt to avoid discussing why the God of the Bible also engages in collective punishment.

In another possible response, apologists might "Reinterpret" one of the examples of God using collective punishment. For example, apologists could assert that the Amalekites had to be slaughtered not because their ancestors attacked Israel but because they committed continuing sins. Although the verses in question explicitly describe the punishment as intergenerational, apologists could nevertheless insert the necessary details into the story to change its meaning. Even if they got away with it for that particular example, they would still have to address all the other instances of the Bible's collective punishment, including Ham and Canaan, Korah's family, Achan's family, the children of the Samarians, the Egyptian firstborns, the Canaanite nations, David's newborn child, and the punishment of the Israelites for David's census.

Backed into a corner, apologists could simply admit that the God of the Bible sometimes levies punishment on one person for the sins of somebody else. Through the "Rationalize" strategy, they could then make excuses for God's behavior. Human beings act immorally in using collective punishment, apologists could argue, but God does not. This response calls to mind the time when Richard Nixon tried to defend his actions by saying, "When the President does it, that means it is not illegal."[38] Only in Bizarro World would someone claim that the bar for morality is lower for God—supposedly a morally perfect being—than for humans. If anything, God should be following a higher rather than a lower standard than we would expect of mere mortals.

The "Mystify" strategy won't work here either. An apologist could assert that God has reasons we will never understand for punishing someone other than the person who commits an offense. The mystify defense contradicts the Christian belief that God is omnipotent, able to snap his metaphorical fingers and cause anything he wants to happen. With powers of that kind, God would never need to use immoral means such as collective punishment to achieve the ends he sought. Instead, he could accomplish his ends directly. An apologist might be ready to cry uncle at this point, but the picture actually gets worse. Moving beyond punishing members of someone's family or group, God sometimes punishes people with no connection whatsoever to the offender, as we'll see in the next section.

PUNISHING ALL OF HUMANITY

Roald Dahl, author of children's classics such as *Matilda*, *The BFG*, and *Charlie and the Chocolate Factory*, was a Christian up to age forty-six. He lost his faith after his daughter Olivia, all of seven years old, died from the brain disorder Subacute Sclerosing Panencephalitis (SSPE).[39] Children with SSPE frequently become forgetful, endure seizures, have hallucinations, struggle with speaking or swallowing, and make uncontrolled jerks with their arms and legs. Before dying, they often become mute, lose control of bodily functions, and fall into a vegetative state.[40] SSPE is one of many diseases, accidents, and ailments that kill children after a long and painful ordeal. How could a just God design a world in which Olivia and others experience such immense suffering? Dahl concluded that no such God actually exists, and he lived the rest of his life as an atheist.

Other people reach the same conclusion after witnessing the massive loss of life and livelihood from natural disasters. No matter where you live, you're vulnerable. Anyone residing near streams or rivers can be overtaken by floods. Coastal areas face dangers from hurricanes and tsunamis, and interior regions are affected by droughts, tornados, and wildfires. People living at the intersection of continental and oceanic plates can be wiped out through earthquakes or volcanic eruptions. All of these types of natural disasters are recurring features of our world. Among the worst tragedies of the twenty-first century, an earthquake in Kashmir snuffed out 100,000 lives, a cyclone left 150,000 dead in Sri Lanka and Burma, a tsunami in the Indian Ocean killed 230,000 and displaced millions in

Indonesia and other countries, and an earthquake in Haiti killed 230,000 and injured 300,000.[41] Every time a natural disaster hits, some people question whether there is a God.

Christian apologists know they have to explain why a good God would create a world with diseases and natural disasters that indiscriminately kill both children and adults. This is often called the problem of "natural evil," which is distinct from the problem of "moral evil" that I addressed at the beginning of chapter 2. One apologetic answer holds that life could not exist at all without natural evil. Rich Deem, who runs a website attempting to reconcile science and religion, takes this approach in claiming that natural evil results from physical laws "necessary for the proper operation of the universe."[42] Most of Deem's fellow apologists reject this solution because it seems to deny God's omnipotence. If God can create the entire universe out of nothing—the greatest possible miracle—then he could surely create an earth without diseases and natural disasters.

A different apologetic argument therefore stresses the value of suffering in allowing people to build character. As summarized by J. Warner Wallace, a homicide detective who has contributed to the field of apologetics, "It's in the face of trials, disasters, and other forms of evil that true courage, compassion, forgiveness, self-sacrifice, and charity are developed."[43] The website for Ongoing Ambassadors for Christ likewise notes that suffering can lead to "our strengthening, encouragement, or discipline."[44] The problem with this approach is the mismatch between who suffers and who benefits. Even if parents can develop virtues by caring for their dying children—a questionable proposition in itself—those parental gains could not possibly benefit the children or somehow justify their deaths.

Recognizing these difficulties, many apologists pin the blame for natural evil on human beings—or rather the first human being, Adam. To set the context for their accounts, I first have to relay a personal story. My graduate program in political science required students to write two major research papers before advancing to a dissertation. One of my fellow students, whose name I have long since forgotten, tried to defend her failure to complete her first paper by blurting out, "The paper didn't get done." I'm reminded of her oddly phrased statement, which implied that she had no control over the matter, every time I hear apologists attribute the origins of natural evil to events in the Garden of Eden.

To see why, consider the writings of Frank Turek, a popular author, speaker, and debater. According to Turek, diseases and natural disasters "are not the result of someone's free will today. But Christianity traces all of our trouble back to a freewill choice of Adam. As a result, we live in a fallen, broken world where bad things happen."[45] Kenneth Boa, founder of Reflections Ministries, echoes Turek in blaming natural evil on "man's rebellion against God. . . . Because Adam fell, the universe likewise was cursed."[46] We hear similar sentiments from Robert Velarde of Focus on the Family, who claims that natural evil "ties into the broad Christian explanation of the human predicament. Paradise has been lost due to human moral shortcomings. As a result, we live in a fallen world, east of Eden."[47]

Did you notice what these apologists are doing? All of them remove God from the equation, saying simply that "bad things happen" (Turek), "the universe was likewise cursed" (Boa), and "paradise has been lost" (Velarde). All three authors are capable of constructing vigorous prose, and they do so elsewhere in their writings. Here they deploy the passive voice or similar constructions to hide the action, which should immediately make us suspicious. Isn't God supposed to be omnipotent and providential, creating the universe and controlling its unfolding through his interventions? When writing about natural evil, why do these apologists strip God of agency, thereby turning diseases and natural disasters into autonomous forces that Adam unleashed?

The obvious answer is that they are trying to explain natural evil while shielding their God from criticism. Like my fellow student who refused to take responsibility for her actions, the apologists write as if natural evil emerged independently from anything God did. If they instead openly stated that God uses natural evil to punish people for Adam's sin, they would alienate actual and potential Christians. Who would want to worship a God who forces people today to pay the consequences of Adam's misdeed? Living in an age that values individual rights, we now think people can be justly punished only for their own behavior, not somebody else's. Just imagine Roald Dahl's reaction if an apologist informed him of God's decree that his daughter had to die because Adam ate the forbidden fruit. Recognizing the weakness of their position, apologists try to turn God into a bit player in the emergence of natural evil.

Unfortunately for them, the Bible portrays a God who often exacts retribution on one person for the sins of another. I have already described how God applies kin and group punishment to both outgroup members and his chosen people, and he engages in similar practices elsewhere in the Bible. Genesis 3:16 says that God causes all women to suffer pain in childbirth because of Eve's sin. This is no small matter given the intensity of the labor pain that women experience. Modern women with access to good health care can get at least some relief, but strong painkillers were unavailable for most of human existence. God also responds in Genesis 3:16 to Eve's sin by levying punishment on subsequent women such that "your desire shall be for your husband, and he shall rule over you." In 1 Timothy 2:11–15, the New Testament reinforces this point about the consequences for all women of Eve's action.

The doctrine of original sin is another example of how God connects the nearly eight billion human beings living today to the events of the Garden of Eden. Rooted in Romans 5:12–14 and the writings of Church fathers Irenaeus and Augustine, original sin remains central to the theology of most Christians, though with differing interpretations of what human beings inherit from Adam and Eve. As stated in the Catechism of the Catholic Church, "Adam and Eve transmitted to their descendants human nature wounded by their own first sin."[48] Protestants have typically believed that people inherit both the sinful nature and the actual guilt of the first couple. The Augsburg Confession, an early statement of Lutheranism, says that "all men are full of evil lust and inclinations from their mothers' wombs" and thus carry "inborn sickness and hereditary sin."[49]

We thus see through pain in childbirth and original sin that group-based thinking is rampant in Christian texts and traditions. The notion of God punishing all of humanity through natural evil fits cleanly as yet another example that apologists must address. If they value intellectual integrity, apologists such as Turek, Boa, and Velarde have two choices. First, they could state forthrightly that God responded to Adam's sin by creating diseases and natural disasters. Should they choose this option, they have to abandon the passive voice in their writings and instead describe a God who accepts responsibility for establishing a system of group punishment. Apologists will probably resist that choice because it makes God look immoral and thus unworthy of worship. Their second option is therefore to find some other way to explain natural evil. We have already seen why some of the standard alternatives fail, but they could always invoke the "Mystify" defense.

Some apologists, in fact, do try to turn natural evil into a mystery. According to Greg Koukl, founder of the Stand to Reason ministry, God had "morally sufficient reasons" to design a world with natural evil, but "we don't have to know what those reasons are."[50] Following the template for the "Mystify" strategy, Koukl here appeals to an enigma lying beyond human comprehension. Matthew Tingblad of the Josh McDowell Ministry takes the same approach in saying, "We rightfully say that our comprehension is nothing compared with God's knowledge and foresight of all the workings of the universe. At the end of the day, we really don't know" why diseases and natural disasters happen.[51]

Because it's a confession of ignorance, the "Mystify" strategy works best when used sparingly. Apologists would rather give concrete answers to the questions posed by current and prospective believers, and both Koukl and Tingblad normally follow that approach. They don't play their Get Out of Jail Free Card until they confront a problem such as natural evil that affords no good solutions. As always with the "Mystify" strategy, they are implicitly telling people, "Don't worry about it, God has it all figured out." Although it's unlikely to win any converts, such a response might be sufficient to preserve the faith of someone who already has a strong will to believe.

GROUPISHNESS TODAY

Even if they succeeded in mystifying the problem of natural evil, apologists would still need to address the ways the Bible traffics in racism, endorses slavery, defends genocide, treats ethnic groups as unified entities, and establishes collective punishment. These are not separate issues but rather different facets of the same problem: the excessive groupish-ness of the Bible's authors. We know from the experiences of every society ever studied that tendencies toward tribalism extend well beyond the Bible. Nevertheless, it's possible for people to mitigate the most harmful features of groupishness, and that's exactly what has happened in modern times. Since the biblical authors penned their final books, and especially since the Enlightenment, human beings have made substantial progress on questions related to group identity and conflict.

Take racist jokes (or insults) as an example. Clearly, they still exist. Some readers of this book may travel in social circles that insulate them from direct exposure to that phenomenon, but the jokes are prevalent in many quarters of society. Data scientist Seth Stephens-Davidowitz has documented several million Google searches in the United States per year where someone looks for jokes involving a racial or ethnic group.[52] Not all such jokes belittle and demean the group, but most do. The difference between modern times and the Bible is that offensive jokes of this kind are no longer considered acceptable among cosmopolitan leaders in business, law, medicine, academia, the media, and—most importantly for present purposes—religion. You can read all the speeches, statements, and encyclicals of twenty-first century popes and archbishops without finding any racist insults or jokes, and yet those forms of racism appear in the holy book that Catholic leaders regard as the Word of God.

Or consider slavery. Reflecting the morality of its times, the Bible authorizes holding foreigners as slaves. Historians estimate that in the Roman Empire of the first century, which provided the backdrop to the New Testament, enslaved people comprised 10–40 percent of the population in Rome and each of the provinces.[53] According to the United Nations, various forms of slavery currently entrap enough people to constitute a far lower 0.5 percent of the global population.[54] The extent of slavery in today's world is reprehensible, but human beings (led, in many countries, by Christians) have nevertheless improved on the Bible by forging a consensus that slavery is not only wrong but one of the worst things a person can do to someone else. Slavery is now illegal in every country, and it persists mainly because—as with other crimes—the authorities have not succeeded in catching every perpetrator.

Genocide represents another important change in norms. The twentieth century was bracketed by the Turkish genocide of the Armenians at the beginning and the slaughter in Bosnia-Herzegovina at the end, with the Holocaust and genocides in Ukraine, China, North Korea, Cambodia, Ethiopia, and Rwanda in between. A genocide in the Darfur region of Sudan marred the beginning of the twenty-first century. The ancient world had its own genocides, including those in the cities of Carthage, Epirus, Babylon, Melia, Mytilene, Hirimme, and Thyrea, plus the Israelites' slaughter of the Canaanite peoples and the Amalekites.[55] A critical difference between ancient times and today rests in the extent to which genocide receives popular approval as a legitimate practice. If they sat down to write a new Bible, modern Christians would surely not portray a God who ordered genocide and demanded its completion.

They would also want to create a God who punishes only individuals, not their families or groups. The Bible's repeated endorsement and depiction of collective punishment is a source of embarrassment for today's apologists. There is no way to reconcile what the Bible says about the morality of kin and group punishment with what people now believe. Fortunately, human beings since the Enlightenment have greatly reduced the incidence of these formerly common practices. Statements of constitutional and statutory rights and their enforcement through courts have given people important protections against being punished for somebody else's offense. International commitments through the Geneva Conventions, the Universal Declaration of Human Rights, and the International Covenant on Civil and Political Rights have put additional pressure on states to refrain from collective punishment.

This moral progress across a range of topics relating to groupishness is halting and uneven but nevertheless real, which raises important questions. How have human beings managed to improve on the Bible's morality? Why are modern people less likely than the biblical authors to demonstrate the worst forms of groupishness? I will return to these questions periodically in the rest of the book. For now, I focus on how reason—the method of humanism—allows a person to recognize the dignity and worth of all people, including those who look, talk, and act differently than oneself.

Philosopher Peter Singer made an important contribution on this score by stressing how reason facilitates what he calls the "expanding circle." Among ancient peoples, including those who wrote the Bible, the circle of who counted as a human being was drawn narrowly. Over the next two millennia, the circle expanded in fits and starts from the family, clan, and tribe to the nation, race, and eventually (for many people) to all humans and even nonhuman animals.[56] I have documented the myriad ways in which the biblical authors demonstrated their groupishness, and other ancient peoples showed the same tendencies. For example, an inscription on a grave from the fifth century BC commended an Athenian soldier who "slew seven men and broke off spear-points in their bodies" and "saved three Athenian regiments." Without a hint of self-consciousness, the epitaph then praised the soldier for "having brought sorrow to no one among all men who dwell the earth."[57] Clearly, the groups the soldier helped defeat did not count as part of "all men who dwell the earth."

Plato was only slightly less groupish than his contemporaries, for he extended the circle from Athens to the other Greek city-states. Using Socrates as his mouthpiece in the *Republic*, Plato declared it immoral in warfare to "destroy the lands and burn the houses" of fellow Greeks, but he deemed it acceptable when fighting non-Greeks to target "the whole population of a city—men, women, and children."[58] Plato was no more enlightened on the issue of slavery. While rejecting the notion that Greeks could legitimately enslave each other, he approved of them owning non-Greeks.[59] The Bible expressed that same sentiment about owning foreigners, but norms have changed immensely since then. Through reason, people increasingly came to recognize that all of humanity has the same claim to respect and basic rights as the members of one's own group. Once your circle expands to include all human beings, practices such as slavery become unthinkable.

THE RISE OF REASON
The widespread use of reason does not appear out of nowhere, however. Certain factors make it easier for modern than ancient peoples to exercise reason and see the humanity of those outside their immediate

communities. One such factor is the amount of mutually beneficial contact between members of different groups. In the ancient world, transportation was difficult and expensive. The common people rarely if ever traveled outside the village where they were born, and stark lines divided one society and ethnic group from another.[60] Multiethnic empires existed in ancient times, but mainly to exact tribute from various provinces that did not interact much with each other. It was unusual in ancient empires, whether the Carthaginian, Egyptian, Incan, Hittite, Macedonian, Persian, or Roman, for someone to move from one ethnically defined province to another.[61] Today, by contrast, most societies contain a mixture of different racial, ethnic, religious, and other identities, and people regularly interact with someone from groups besides their own.

All of this matters because of a well-supported body of research in the social sciences known as the *contact hypothesis*, formalized by psychologist Gordon Allport in 1954. Building on the research of previous scholars, Allport proposed that contact between members of different groups lessens hostility, prejudice, and discrimination, but only under certain conditions. The contact has to involve personal interaction among people holding equal status, which could occur within schools, marriages, families, workplaces, and civic organizations. Contact within hierarchical settings, as when a majority group member hires someone from a minority group as a domestic servant, would not produce the same result. Allport also thought it essential that the intergroup relations arise in situations where people work toward common goals under the protection of the law or authority figures.[62]

Since Allport's time, research in the United States and around the world has confirmed that positive contact improves intergroup relations. For example, a classic study of housing projects that integrated white and Black families, as opposed to keeping the races segregated in separate buildings, found that the white residents developed more favorable attitudes toward Blacks in general, not just their own neighbors.[63] A more recent study showed that white student-athletes who play team sports, and hence often interact with Black teammates, are less likely to hold prejudicial attitudes than their white counterparts who play individual sports.[64] Other studies demonstrate that these effects of positive contact extend beyond racial and ethnic groups and into those defined by sexual orientation and religion. Compared to those with more narrow social circles, heterosexuals who personally know someone who is gay or lesbian are far more supportive of same-sex marriage and are less likely to hold antigay attitudes.[65] Similarly, a person begins to view a religious minority more favorably when someone from their own network of friends and family members belongs to that group.[66]

Based on the results of thousands of studies, we can confidently say that positive contact is one of the best means to alleviate intergroup prejudice.[67] When a person has not previously experienced any such contact with someone from a group, it's easy to hold negative stereotypes that paint all of its members with the same broad brush. Once you get to know people from the group on a peer-to-peer basis, you start to see the complexity and variation within it, which makes you more likely to treat the group as a collection of individuals rather than a single mass. You also learn from members of the group, who probably have different backgrounds and ways of thinking than you do. An extensive body of research shows that interactions between diverse individuals can stimulate creativity and expand the pool of ideas under discussion.[68] Reason involves examining and assessing information, evidence, and arguments, a process that intergroup contact enhances by bringing new perspectives to the table. You can't use reason to evaluate an idea that you never encountered in the first place.

The emergence of mass literacy is another factor that allowed people in modern times to apply reason to a range of matters, including morality and intergroup relations. In the ancient world, reading and writing were confined to the narrow group who comprised the ruling elite, kept records, or had specific professional needs.[69] Most people worked in agriculture, toiling in the fields as either free or enslaved, and they were overwhelmingly illiterate. Various historians estimate the adult literacy rate in the ancient Mediterranean region as no higher than 10 percent.[70] Literacy remained low during the Middle Ages but rose during the Protestant Reformation, the Enlightenment, and the following centuries. Adult literacy stood at 86 percent worldwide as of 2015 and now approaches 100 percent in Western countries.[71]

Literacy matters because it greatly enhances the application of reason. Illiterate people can certainly think, make judgments, draw from experience, and deliberate with others. Nevertheless, their ability to gather and assess information is necessarily limited. The range of ideas that can be accessed through printed or online materials is far greater than anyone could ever absorb in a verbal form. Once you can read, you get transported to other worlds where you see through the eyes of someone else. Facts and perspectives from someone else in one's own society, or from other times and places, build a person's knowledge, stimulate their creativity, and make it easier to discover right and wrong through reason.

In her landmark book *Inventing Human Rights*, historian Lynn Hunt points to a process of just that kind. The scattered gestures toward human rights that appeared in many ancient philosophical and religious texts lacked mass support in those same societies. Why did more robust versions of human rights suddenly come to seem self-evident during the Enlightenment? Hunt identifies literacy as one of the key factors. It became popular in eighteenth-century England and France to read novels by authors such as Samuel Richardson and Jean-Jacques Rousseau, and the practice later spread elsewhere.[72] When you read novels, you learn to put yourself in someone else's shoes, which encourages you to appreciate the lives, struggles, and motivations of people you will never meet. This kind of empathy is a prerequisite to coming to believe that anonymous others should have basic rights.

Hunt acknowledges that the two main statements of universal rights in the eighteenth century—the Declaration of Independence (United States) and Declaration of the Rights of Man and the Citizen (France)—were often honored in the breach. Despite the universalizing rhetoric of those documents, their authors never intended to extend equal rights to women, the enslaved, men without property, and all racial, ethnic, and religious minorities. Still, the sentiments those documents conveyed established ideals to which future reformers could appeal. In countries with widespread literacy, activists could print and distribute literature explaining the case for abolition, civil rights, women's rights, and religious freedom. As Hunt notes, the democracies of today fall short of guaranteeing equal rights across lines of race, gender, and religion, but we have nevertheless greatly improved on what existed from ancient times through the Middle Ages and the early modern period.[73]

THE TRAJECTORY OF GROUPISHNESS

Let me end the chapter by returning to a point I introduced at its beginning: Human beings have a strong tendency to act in a tribal manner. Our brains are wired to divide the people we meet into the categories of Us and Them. That's the bad news. The good news is that our categories are fluid and malleable. We all carry multiple identities—based on religion, gender, occupation, race, ethnicity, nationality, age, interests, region, hobbies, political affiliation, sexual orientation, position within the family, and other variables—such that the composition of the ingroup and outgroup can shift according to what each situation or context makes salient. We can also increase the number of people who count as part of our ingroup. Under the right conditions, we can consider all human beings equally deserving of basic rights and dignity.

I have identified two factors—positive intergroup contact and mass literacy—that have facilitated our ability to break down the barriers to including all of humanity within the circle of concern. No doubt other factors could also be highlighted that have made this transformation possible. The change in worldview that accompanied the expanding circle has engulfed people of all persuasions, including Christians—thereby creating a problem. The Christian scriptures depict a group-centered God who endorses slavery and genocide, treats ethnic groups as undifferentiated masses, and practices kin and group punishment. That's not what people today have in mind when they think of a God who is incapable of behaving immorally.

Christian apologists have responded by recreating God in their own image. Through judicious applications of the Ignore, Rationalize, Reinterpret, and Mystify strategies, they have tried to reformulate the God of the Bible into a morally perfect being who deserves adulation, respect, and worship. In this chapter and the previous ones, I have given many examples of their handiwork. Considered one at a time, each example certainly raises eyebrows, but a charitable reader might withhold comment if the rest of the apologetic case were sound. The problem arises when apologists pile one such example upon another, offering increasingly strained arguments to salvage the Bible and its God. At that point, the field of apologetics degenerates into an elaborate attempt to defend the indefensible.

Science writer and noted skeptic Michael Shermer warns us to beware of smart people, who are good at constructing justifications for beliefs they acquired for nonsmart reasons.[74] Apologists could easily stand as Exhibit A for Shermer's cautionary note. Their intelligence allows them to make an indefensible position sound plausible, at least to committed believers. Backed by strong faith and years of learning, apologists convince themselves that they have solved the problems the Bible poses, and then they try to persuade others. Apologists start from their conclusion that the God of the Bible must always be morally pure, and then they use their talents to figure out how best to defend that conclusion with the four strategies available to them.

What happens if a person begins instead without preconceptions about what the Bible says? Any such study will reveal the Bible to be not the Word of God but rather the words of human beings, specifically ancient Jews and Christians. Drawing from the cultural beliefs and assumptions of their era, they created God in their own image and gave him their morality, an excessively groupish morality that no one in the modern world accepts in its totality. If apologists want to avoid acknowledging these moral flaws in the Bible and its God, they could make one last move in challenging my standing to make any judgments one way or the other. In the eyes of virtually all apologists, atheists such as myself have no grounding for our moral beliefs. If no God exists, isn't it just my opinion that the biblical statements and commands I have discussed are immoral?

I answered that objection in the last chapter, where I appealed to reason and inclusive deliberation as the means by which we can attain a morality stripped of the biases and subjectivity of any person or society. Over the last few hundred years, human beings around the world have deliberated about moral questions within their families, workplaces, neighborhoods, community groups, and national assemblies, not to mention in books and other written materials. Much of that deliberation has focused on the consequences of groupishness, the subject of this chapter. Regardless of their nationality, race, religion, gender, and other identities, people have overwhelmingly concluded that slavery, genocide, and collective punishment are wrong. It's not just my opinion that those practices are immoral; it's the settled consensus that human beings, in all their diversity, have reached after engaging the issues thoughtfully and systematically. Behaviors violating the consensus happen today despite rather than because of the moral beliefs ordinary people hold.

I don't expect devout Christians to accept my claim that morality can be grounded in reason and inclusive deliberation rather than the commands of a God. People do not easily abandon the kind of faith a person needs to believe that God communicated his moral rules and principles through the Bible and, for Catholics, the teaching authority of the Church. When confronted with evidence that the Bible's morality is flawed in many respects, most Christians decide to shoot the messenger and find someone who can bring them better news. Apologists are willing and able to serve in that role.

The difficulty for apologists is that they have to defend the Bible regardless of what it says. Humanists such as myself, by contrast, can evaluate each of its claims and commands on a case-by-case basis. I have read and studied the Bible for most of my life, and I treasure its insights into how human beings can and do live. I applaud its instructions to build strong families, strive for justice, care for the poor, and love your neighbor as yourself. At the same time, I stand with most people today in rejecting its rank tribalism. Humanists can take a balanced view of the Bible, recognizing that it offers moral guidance that should not be discarded lightly. We also see how it contains other content that should be dumped straight into the trash.

If I wasn't there already, that last sentence probably crossed the line into blasphemy. Throughout most of Christian history, denigrating even part of God's revelation would have qualified as such. The Bible requires the death penalty for blasphemers (Leviticus 24:16), and Western countries through the ages have executed many offenders.[75] Legislators and courts gradually reduced the maximum penalty to fines or jail, and they eventually either overturned the laws altogether or left them unenforced.[76]

In any Western country today, there is zero chance the authorities will execute me for committing blasphemy, which raises an important question: How did religious freedom become sufficiently established that even blasphemers and atheists enjoy its protections? How did Christians overcome their own history to become strong advocates for religious freedom? I tackle these and other questions in the next chapter.

CHAPTER 5

Intellectual Dishonesty in Christianity

THE BIBLE IS A COMPLEX ANTHOLOGY. CHRISTIAN LEADERS TYPICALLY insist that readers interpreting it work to avoid common pitfalls. Assuming they do not know the original Hebrew and Greek languages, readers can use a concordance, Bible commentaries, and multiple translations.[1] Christian leaders also advise believers to talk with their pastor or priest to guard against making erroneous interpretations. Although certain fundamentalists take the approach of personalized readings based on "just me and my Bible," most theologians and clergy members strongly recommend working within a community or the entirety of Christian teaching and tradition to gain an accurate understanding.[2]

The standard approach to biblical interpretation also draws a clear distinction between *exegesis*, from a Greek word meaning "to draw out," and *eisegesis*, meaning "to lead into." As explained by theologian Terance Espinoza, "Exegesis tries to listen to the text, and let meaning come from the text itself in its original, historical context."[3] Other theologians stress that readers need to consider matters of grammar, word usage, literary forms, and the culture from which the author was writing.[4] Christian writers such as Wyman Lewis Richardson and S. Michael Houdmann condemn the contrasting practice of eisegesis because it allows "our presuppositions and assumptions to shape our reading of the Bible"[5] such that "the interpreter injects his own ideas into the text, making it mean whatever he wants."[6] Richardson calls it "a sad but true fact" that believers more frequently engage in eisegesis than exegesis, especially "when it comes to culturally unpopular or difficult teachings."[7] According to these and other Christian authorities, readers must avoid twisting the words of the text to suit their own purposes.

I have documented many instances of Christian apologists succumbing to this temptation in my previous chapters. They start from the premise that the God of the Bible must be loving, just, and merciful, which then colors how they handle difficult passages. To downplay God's excessive punishment of sending she-bears to maul forty-two boys who taunted the prophet Elisha for being bald (2 Kings 2:23–25), they revise the story to turn the boys into a street gang threatening violence. To relieve God from any responsibility for giving governmental authority to tyrants (Romans 13:1), they claim he disapproves of the results. To solve the problem of moral evil, they assert that God does not interfere with free will even though the Bible consistently portrays him doing the opposite. They have also manipulated the Bible to hide its many depictions of a God who reaches beyond individuals to punish members of an offender's family or group.

Through eisegesis of that kind, apologists are engaging in intellectual dishonesty, a term that requires some clarification so that readers see what I am and am not claiming. Ordinary dishonesty involves intentionally deceiving others. As my earlier chapters have explained, apologists almost always believe what they are saying, and so we cannot characterize their practices as dishonest in the ordinary sense. I focus here instead on *intellectual* dishonesty, which happens when apologists deceive themselves (and then possibly others) by violating standards of logic, rationality, and open inquiry. Those standards are essential to the practice of critical thinking. Energy and environmental scientist Jonathan Koomey expresses the matter succinctly: "Someone who is intellectually honest follows the facts wherever they may lead, and does so in spite of discomfort, inconvenience, or self-interest."[8]

Intellectual honesty requires drawing conclusions from the totality of the evidence, rather than sifting through the evidence to build a case for the position one held at the outset. Theologian Gleason Archer gives us an object lesson in how not to proceed. He tells his readers who confront challenging material, "Be fully persuaded in your own mind that an adequate explanation exists, even though you have not yet found it."[9] Such advice is an open invitation to intellectual dishonesty. Apologists who want to maintain their integrity must recognize that the biblical authors might have taught a morality or depicted a God different from what modern readers expect. When apologists use the Ignore, Rationalize, Reinterpret, and Mystify strategies to eliminate one biblical problem after another, they are guilty of intellectual dishonesty.

That's a strong claim, I realize. How can anyone know if an apologist has committed the error of eisegesis and crossed the line into intellectual dishonesty? We have to master the details of the biblical materials and their contexts to determine whether the apologist has tried to capture the intent of the original authors or, alternatively, has forced the text into saying something palatable to a person living in the twenty-first century. Investigations of grammar, vocabulary, and literary genre are also essential for allowing us to make informed judgments. Is the apologist stretching the meaning of the text beyond what a typical reader would accept? We should be especially suspicious if the apologist's strained interpretation conveniently gets God or the Bible off the hook for what readers would normally consider to be rank immorality.

To learn whether apologists are imposing their own values onto the text, we must also investigate the history of Christian interpretation. Because apologists are typically intelligent, knowledgeable about the Bible, and proficient at creative writing, they can often make a flawed reading sound plausible. What we really want to know is whether a person who hasn't internalized modern values would interpret the text the same way. How did Christians before the Enlightenment read the relevant passages? If theologians from over sixteen centuries of Christian history never offered the apologist's favored interpretation, we have evidence for a charge of eisegesis. At a minimum, the apologist needs to explain why all of these learned predecessors got it wrong.

Of course, earlier interpreters might have engaged in eisegesis of their own. No matter when and where individuals formed their values, the temptation always exists to make the Bible compatible with what they already believe. Interpreters from the first sixteen centuries of Christianity are useful to us not because they were immune from eisegesis but because they could not have been influenced by the Age of Reason and the Enlightenment, which hadn't happened yet. If a modern apologist offers an interpretation that had little or no support for most of Christian history, we have strong grounds to accuse them of eisegesis.

As we'll see in this chapter, I'm somewhat conflicted about how to evaluate these instances of intellectual dishonesty. Certainly, no one can fully endorse the ways in which apologists manipulate the Bible to fit their preconceptions. Their intellectual dishonesty is a form of shoddy scholarship that undermines the shared mission of everyone who cares about accurate interpretations. Apologists who distort the Bible ought to know better, because they typically have the knowledge and resources to capture both the intent of the original authors and the understandings of Christian interpreters through the ages. Apologetic practices are nevertheless different from lying, which would require intent such that the apologists know their statements are untrue. In matters of textual interpretation, especially of the Bible, outright lying is rare but apologists routinely twist the scriptures to protect a cherished belief or even their entire worldview.

Ironically, the resulting eisegesis can help to reform Christianity from within. Steven Pinker makes a similar point in holding that a religion can get better over time through "woolly allegory, emotional commitments to texts that no one reads, and other forms of benign hypocrisy."[10] Many social movements of the last few centuries have included Christians among their leaders and participants, including movements opposing colonialism and war and supporting abolition, women's rights, labor reform, civil rights, and the expansion of religious liberty.[11] That fact should give pause to anyone who thinks the West would have been better off if its dominant religion had withered on the vine long ago. The Christians involved in the various movements often engaged in intellectual dishonesty, but their skewed interpretations of the Bible nevertheless contributed to social progress.

In the rest of this chapter, I will extend these points by exploring three issues: religious freedom, slavery, and homosexuality. My goal throughout is to show how apologists and other Christians have developed interpretations that deviate from both a careful reading of the Bible and the understandings of their predecessors. These forms of intellectual dishonesty have nevertheless helped to advance freedom, protect vulnerable populations, and promote human flourishing.

THE BIBLE AND RELIGIOUS FREEDOM

Christian apologists regularly proclaim that the Bible requires governments to establish and protect the right to religious freedom. Andrew Walker, who has held leadership positions within the Southern Baptist Convention, argues that "religious liberty exists as a biblical idea."[12] Pastor and author Bart Barber similarly testifies that he is "doggedly committed to the idea of universal religious liberty not because it is American or self-serving but because it is biblical."[13] Hugh Whelchel, who runs an organization applying Christian principles to the workplace and the economy, observes that the Bible does not "comment specifically" on religious liberty, but he nevertheless infers such support from it.[14]

To determine whether these apologists are engaging in eisegesis, we need to examine how Christians through the ages have understood the Bible's teachings on religious liberty. You might be surprised to learn that the early Christians did not search their scriptures to learn how the Roman authorities should handle that subject. As a small and occasionally persecuted group, Christians were not in a position to determine state policies on religious liberty or any other topic. For that reason, it didn't matter what their scriptures said. Christians did, however, advocate on their own behalf. One of the most influential theologians from the first two centuries, Tertullian, pressed the Romans to give Christians the freedom to practice their religion. He did not draw from the Bible to build his case and instead made practical arguments that could apply irrespective of a person's religious commitments. For example, he stressed that "we injure nobody, we trouble nobody" through various prayers, feasts, gatherings, and rituals.[15] He also invoked the principle of fairness: The Romans allowed pagans throughout the provinces to worship the gods of their choosing, but "we alone are prevented having a religion of our own."[16]

In presenting arguments of that sort, Tertullian and other Christians sounded like the members of every other fledgling religion from ancient times to the present. Historian Andrew Pettegree calls religious tolerance a "loser's creed" because minority groups lacking political power invariably support it.[17] Nobody in their right mind would demand of the state, "Come and arrest us, confiscate our property, assault our members, and prevent us from worshipping in the ways we deem appropriate." Religious minorities such as the early Christians just want to be left alone. The Christians' pleas sometimes failed, leading to harassment and violence from local mobs plus empire-wide persecution under emperors Decius (250–251), Valerian (253–260), and Diocletian (303–313).[18] Christians nevertheless steadily gained converts and eventually won over Constantine, the emperor who embraced Christianity as an adult and protected the interests of Christians until his death in 337.[19]

Christian fortunes improved even more in 380 when Emperor Theodosius I worked with his governing partners to make Christianity the official religion of the empire.[20] Christians in the following years had to decide whether the freedom they had long sought for themselves should be extended to other groups. Augustine developed the most extensive answer to this question, and his perspective would shape Christian teachings for over a millennium. His tenure as the bishop of Hippo beginning in 395 coincided with Roman attempts to stamp out paganism and heresy. In opposing these policies, the young Augustine declared in 396 that no one "should against his will be coerced into the Catholic communion."[21] He was concerned about state persecution of a group of heretics known as Donatists who were prominent in his area.

Augustine changed his mind over the next decade by studying the Bible and observing that imperial repression had brought some Donatists back into the fold. He placed great weight on the Parable of the Great Banquet, which appears in the Gospels of Luke and Matthew. In the parable Jesus tells a story about a master or king hosting a lavish dinner, and Jesus later explains that the dinner symbolizes the kingdom of God. The invited guests all make excuses for why they cannot attend. In Luke's version of the parable, the master then instructs his slave to go into the streets and "compel people to come in" (Luke 14:23). In Matthew's version, by contrast, the king instead tells his slaves to "invite everyone you can find" (Matthew 22:9). Augustine prioritized the account in Luke on grounds that it was written later, "when the Church had been strength-ened," and thus offered a parallel to his own times.[22] Augustine defended imperial coercion to promote Christianity and concluded that "men should be compelled to come in to the feast of everlasting salvation."[23]

Augustine pointed to other biblical passages that also justified using coercion to force a person into the right religious practices. For example, God himself punished the Israelites until they obeyed his commands, and he gave fathers the authority to beat their disobedient sons into submis-sion (Proverbs 23:13).[24] To win Paul's allegiance, Jesus blinded him on the road to Damascus and threw him to the ground. Paul then became Jesus's greatest ambassador, demonstrating to Augustine the value of selective violence in bringing a person to faith.[25] Paul subsequently explained how God gave rulers the authority to promote good behavior and punish evil (Romans 13:1–7). As the purveyors of evil doctrines that harmed people and jeopardized their salvation, pagans and heretics therefore deserved persecution in Augustine's eyes.[26]

For Augustine, force could be appropriate depending on its purposes. Moses acted rightly in punishing the Israelites because he was leading them to the proper worship of God. Pharaoh had erred in coercing those same Israelites because his motivations reflected a "lust for power."[27] Augustine offered other examples from the Bible: "The wicked put prophets to death; prophets put the wicked to death. The Jews scourged Christ; Christ also scourged the Jews." The rightness or wrongness of each act hinged on whether the perpetrator was "on the side of truth" or "on the side of iniquity."[28] Dismissing the notion that anyone had the right to propound error, Augustine inferred from the Bible that the advocates of truth could use violence to combat falsehoods. He thereby helped legitimize Roman policies that included destroying and looting pagan temples, criminalizing pagan worship and sacrifice, forcibly closing the churches of heretics, and confiscating their houses and other property.

At the same time, Augustine drew the line at executing heretics. He relied on the Parable of the Tares (weeds) in the Gospel of Matthew, where a sower refrains from pulling up the weeds for fear of inadver-tently killing some of the wheat. Jesus explains that the weeds represent believers in false doctrines, whom God will handle on judgment day.

John Chrysostom, archbishop of Constantinople and one of the Church Fathers, had already interpreted the parable to mean that God "does not therefore forbid our checking heretics, and stopping their mouths, and taking away their freedom of speech, and breaking up their assemblies and confederacies, but our killing and slaying them."[29] Augustine agreed with Chrysostom that the parable allowed lesser actions and prohibited only the killing of heretics.[30] Showing that he took that limitation seriously, Augustine pleaded with Roman administrators to spare the lives of heretics slated for execution.[31]

Augustine is often considered the most influential theologian in Western history. Claimed as an authority by both Catholics and Protestants, he shaped Christian doctrines on subjects including salvation, predestination, original sin, free will and God's foreknowledge, and the operation of the sacraments.[32] He was also the most important contributor to the early development of the Church's position on religious liberty. Inferring from the Bible that nobody had the right to disseminate falsehoods, Augustine pushed to severely limit, by force when necessary, the teaching, preaching, proselytizing, assembly, observance, and worship of pagans and heretics. Augustine's legacy, then, was to develop and defend what historian Perez Zagorin calls "a theory of persecution founded entirely on Christian grounds and supported with numerous examples from the Old and New Testaments."[33]

CHRISTIANITY AND RELIGIOUS SUPPRESSION

Over the next several centuries, Christian rulers worked closely with the Church to eliminate paganism and heresy. A commission of Emperor Theodosius II, who ruled from 429–438, compiled and reissued previous edicts, including one limiting the rights of citizenship "to those who observe the Catholic law." The commission forbade what it called "heathens and schismatics" from worshipping, and it demanded that "the temples be henceforth closed."[34] Leading theologians of this era backed these policies but generally opposed executing anyone on religious grounds. Emperor Justinian, who ruled the eastern half of the empire from 527 to 565, banned pagans and heretics from teaching their beliefs in public or in private.[35]

These policies changed during the medieval era. Most theologians believed in some kind of right to conscience and thought it impossible to compel a person to accept Christian doctrines. The authorities nevertheless sometimes forced Jews and pagans to undergo baptism and convert to Christianity. To explain why he opposed those actions, the English priest, scholar, and poet Alcuin (735–804) declared, "You can persuade a man to believe but you cannot force him. You may even be able to force him to be baptized, but this will not help to instill the faith within him."[36] Theologians thus wanted to persecute heretics not to change their hearts but to prevent them from corrupting other people's faith. Thomas Aquinas spelled out this doctrine, saying that heretics who persist after being twice admonished must be "exterminated thereby from the world by death" in order to preserve "the salvation of others."[37]

This same logic dictated forbidding Jews to proselytize or hold public office. As the Fourth Lateran Council (1215) declared, "It is absurd that a blasphemer of Christ exercise power over Christians."[38] The Council also demanded that secular authorities "exterminate in the territories subject to their jurisdiction all heretics pointed out by the Church."[39] This collaboration between church and state led to the Inquisition, which was conceived as a way to protect the community from the lies peddled by heretics. One of the operating manuals of the Inquisition explained that "punishment does not take place primarily and per se for the correction and good of the person punished, but for the public good in order that others may become terrified and weaned from the evils they would commit."[40]

These understandings continued into the Protestant era. Although Martin Luther broke from Catholicism in many respects, he largely affirmed traditional teachings on religious liberty. Like his predecessors, Luther upheld a right of conscience: "For faith is a free act, to which no one can be forced. Indeed, it is a work of God in the spirit, not something which outward authority should compel or create."[41] He distinguished between the responsibilities of the church and those of the secular government, with the latter charged "to bring about external peace and prevent evil deeds."[42] Preventing evil did not entail trying to coerce someone into violating their conscience: "let the Turk believe and live as he will, just as one lets the papacy and other false Christians live. The emperor's sword has nothing to do with the faith."[43]

For Luther, a person sinned not by believing false doctrines but by proselytizing and teaching them, or by engaging in outright blasphemy. Luther was especially concerned about Jews, whom he ranked among the biggest blasphemers of all. Early in his career, he wrote: "I have come to the conclusion that the Jews will always curse and blaspheme God and his King Christ, as all the prophets have predicted."[44] The mature Luther wrote a scathing attack called *On the Jews and Their Lies*, which included his call for denying them the freedom to spread their blasphemy. Luther advised Christian rulers and leaders to burn synagogues and Jewish schools, raze and destroy Jewish houses, confiscate prayer books and Talmudic writings, deny Jews safe passage on roads, and ban rabbis from teaching "on pain of loss of life and limb."[45]

Luther expressed similar sentiments about blasphemy and heresy in his more temperate writings. In his commentary on the 82nd Psalm, Luther restated the traditional understanding of the Bible that nobody had the right to propound false doctrines: "If anyone were to teach that Christ is not God, but a mere man and like other prophets, as the Turks and the Anabaptists hold—such teachers should not be tolerated, but punished as blasphemers. For they are not mere heretics but open blasphemers; and rulers are in duty bound to punish blasphemers."[46] Luther also called upon rulers to punish those who teach doctrines such as "Christ did not die for our sins" or "there is no hell."[47]

Luther emphasized that his restrictions applied only to what a person expressed in the public sphere: "By this procedure no one is compelled to believe, for he can still believe what he will; but he is forbidden to teach and to blaspheme."[48] In his other writings, Luther followed the Bible (Leviticus 24:16) in requiring the death penalty for blasphemers: "If anyone wishes to preach or to teach, let him make known the call or the command which impels him to do so, or else let him keep silence. If he will not keep quiet, then let the civil authorities command the scoundrel to his rightful master, namely, Master Hans (i.e., the hangman)."[49]

The other great Protestant reformer of the sixteenth century, John Calvin, also took an approach to religious liberty similar to theologians from previous centuries. Calvin defended the freedom of conscience not only for Christians but also for "Turks and Saracens and other enemies of religion," and he did not want "to force them to our faith."[50] He nevertheless called on civil governments to fulfill their biblical responsibility to ensure that there is "no idolatry, no blasphemy against the name of God, no calumnies against his truth, nor other offenses to religion."[51] Calvin thus affirmed the long-standing distinction holding that God gave civil government the authority to regulate behaviors but not beliefs. He noted that "in scripture holy kings are especially praised for restoring the worship of God when corrupted or overthrown."[52]

Like Luther, Calvin followed the Bible in demanding the death penalty for people engaging in blasphemy.[53] He was a rarity among theologians in that he moved beyond advising rulers and into a direct role in governing. At the request of Geneva's city council, he assumed an omnibus position as preacher and magistrate in 1541. Geneva's onerous rules and regulations succeeded in preventing blasphemy until Michael Servetus, a Spanish physician and theologian who denied the Trinity and rejected infant baptism, traveled to the city in 1553. Demonstrating his concern for the crime of blasphemy, Calvin supported Servetus's arrest and subsequent execution. Calvin wrote to a friend that Servetus deserved the death penalty for his offenses against God.[54]

It can be difficult for people raised on Enlightenment values of tolerance, equality, and freedom to understand the mentality of Christian theologians up to and including Calvin. Lacking the insights into the human condition that the modern world has yielded, those theologians were forced to rely solely on the Bible and Christian tradition to determine the permissible kinds of religious speech and action. Nobody, whether Christian or not, would allow an evil person to poison the bodies of their family, friends, and others in their community. Theologians traditionally believed someone who poisoned people's minds had committed just as serious an offense. For over a thousand years, blasphemy and heresy were considered to be means through which an evil person could turn others away from true faith and eternal salvation. Anyone who cared about their fellow human beings had to work to eliminate such practices. Reflecting their stubborn consciences, blasphemers and heretics might be immune to persuasion, but persecuting and even executing them could at least prevent them from leading other people astray.

New ways of thinking about these questions started to emerge in the seventeenth century, with Roger Williams standing as a transitional figure. Williams accepted most of Calvin's theology but departed on questions of church and state. Expanding upon the efforts of Thomas Helwys, John Murton, and others in his era, Williams constructed the first fully developed biblical case for religious liberty in *The Bloudy Tenent of Persecution* (1644).[55] He noted that Paul recognized Caesar's authority on matters related to "civil violence and murder" but not on any "spiritual or church controversy."[56] Williams discounted the experience of Israel's theocracy as purely "figurative and ceremonial," a one-time event with "no pattern nor precedent for any kingdom or civil state in the world to follow."[57] Williams instead stressed biblical examples of pagan rulers who gave their subjects, including Jews, the freedom to worship in their own ways: "Thus Cyrus proclaims liberty to all the people of God in his dominions, freely to go up and build the temple of God at Jerusalem, and Artaxerxes after him confirmed it."[58]

Williams did not address one passage that some theologians had stressed, the Parable of the Great Banquet, but he did discuss the Parable of the Tares. He interpreted it to mean that people practicing the wrong religion must be "let alone" even though they need not be "approved or countenanced."[59] Williams here sounds strikingly modern in conceiving an expansive right for people to worship freely. Going further than his predecessors, he sought to extend the right to "Jews," "Indians," "papists" (Catholics), and "Turks" (Muslims).[60] Elsewhere he adds those with "Paganish" and "anti-Christian" inclinations to his list.[61]

APOLOGETICS AND THE QUESTION OF RELIGIOUS FREEDOM

Almost all of today's apologists take positions on religious freedom closer to Roger Williams than his predecessors dating back to Augustine. In the eyes of David Plott, former president of the International Mission Board of the Southern Baptist Convention, "The same right to religious liberty that should protect followers of Christ should also protect followers of Moses, Muhammad, Krishna and Buddha, as well as those who believe there is no god to follow in the first place."[62] One can see a similar message in the work of Sean McDowell, who teaches apologetics at Biola University and has written extensively on the subject. McDowell affirms "exploring religious questions and living by the answers" as a fundamental right applying to "even those who end up as atheists or agnostic."[63] Perhaps the strongest indicator of apologists' support for religious liberty is their willingness to share the debate stage with atheists, who become blasphemers as soon as they open their mouths.

Apologists struggle, however, to build a persuasive case from the Bible for the religious freedom they hold dear. In his book *Politics According to the Bible*, for example, theologian and apologist Wayne Grudem relies heavily on Jesus's answer to whether someone should pay taxes to the emperor (Matthew 22:15–22).[64] The King James Version translates the crucial part of Jesus's response as: "Render therefore unto Caesar the things which are Caesar's; and unto God the things that are God's" (Matthew 22:21). The passage suggests that a person has different obligations to the state and its rulers than to God, but no Christians before the Age of Reason thought it meant the state had no role whatsoever in restricting religious practices. They did not have to look far to find a biblical warrant for state involvement of that kind. For example, the Bible praised Israelite kings who combated paganism and promoted the worship only of Yahweh. In the New Testament, Paul acknowledged the government's authority to use force to prevent or punish evil (Romans 13:3–4), and Augustine, Aquinas, Luther, and Calvin all believed the evil offenses included blasphemy and proselytizing on behalf of a false religion. Apologists such as Grudem who try to ground a comprehensive right to religious freedom in the "Render unto Caesar" passage are stretching it well beyond what readers accepted over the first sixteen centuries of Christianity's existence.

Other apologists see the freedom of religion as an extension of the freedom of conscience they think the Bible teaches. To defend such a claim, the online ministry GotQuestions.org cites verses in Genesis, Joshua, and elsewhere indicating that "God allows us to choose" which beliefs to hold. The group notes that Jesus did not try to coerce a rich young ruler who was unwilling to give up his wealth to gain eternal life

(Matthew 19:16–23), and other verses teach that "it is the Holy Spirit who changes hearts, not the government."[65] The Christian organization WallBuilders, whose name predates the political career of Donald Trump and does not relate to the US-Mexico border, stresses the examples of Jesus, Paul, and the other apostles. According to WallBuilders, these biblical teachers simply made statements and "hearers then chose whether or not to follow Christianity; there was never any penalty, pressure, or force levied against them."[66]

Before the Age of Reason, however, Christians did not think the freedom of conscience could sustain a more encompassing freedom of religion. Theologians such as Aquinas, Luther, and Calvin viewed laws and norms regulating how a person could act to be compatible with respecting the freedom of conscience. They distinguished behaviors, which the state could restrict, from beliefs, which it could not. Until Roger Williams offered his case for allowing diverse Christian and non-Christian groups to worship freely, theologians thought they had biblical authority to prevent pagans and heretics from worshipping freely. Only in modern times have Christians held that the freedom of conscience allows people not only to believe whatever they want but also say whatever they want in the public square and attempt to recruit others into their religion (or irreligion). That notion was rejected by learned theologians such as Augustine, Aquinas, Luther, and Calvin, all of whom devoted their lives to studying the Bible and theology, understanding God's will, and promoting Christian teachings.

Modern apologists who claim the Bible consistently supports religious freedom overlook evidence to the contrary, such as the Parable of the Great Banquet. It figured prominently in how Augustine thought rulers should deal with heretics. He accepted Luke's version of the parable, which holds that one must "compel" people to enter the kingdom of God, over Matthew's version in which one can only "invite" people.[67] Instead of finding some alternative way to resolve the contradiction between the accounts in Luke and Matthew, apologists writing about religious freedom usually ignore the parable altogether. They also ignore the biblical verses that deem blasphemy and idolatry to be grievous offenses deserving the death penalty (Exodus 22:20; Leviticus 24:16; Deuteronomy 13:1–18).

If God really wanted people to have religious liberty, he could have said so in his scriptures. He could easily have inspired his authors to include a passage saying: "Thou shalt respect the freedom of religion. Ruling authorities must grant each person the right to choose their religion and to change it as conscience dictates. All people can engage in religious proselytizing, observance, worship, and practice, whether privately or publicly, consistent with obeying generally applicable laws. The state shalt not discriminate against any person on grounds of religious affiliation or nonaffiliation. The state shalt also protect religious groups from violence, intimidation, and property destruction initiated by other people in their communities."

The Bible contains no such statements and instead looks exactly as one would expect if it is not the Word of God but rather the words of a particular set of human beings. The first Christians, those who wrote the New Testament and accepted the Old Testament, were a fledgling sect without political power. An omniscient God would have known that their descendants would become politically dominant within a few centuries and would need guidance on whether to grant religious freedom and to whom, and he could have included it within his inspired Word. In conveying their own ideas rather than God's, however, the biblical authors gave only the most general instructions on how to design a political system based on Christian principles. They were apocalypticists who thought God would soon intervene and establish his kingdom on earth, making questions about long-term political arrangements beside the point. Jesus himself had proclaimed that "this generation will not pass away" before God brought his judgment on humanity (Matthew 24:34), and Paul continued that apocalyptic teaching in the churches he founded.[68]

RELIGIOUS FREEDOM IN MODERN TIMES

Support for religious freedom as such simply does not exist in the Bible. If it did, somebody surely would have discovered it during the first sixteen centuries of Christianity, and the apologists of today could point to biblical passages that teach the doctrine clearly. Instead, the commitment to religious freedom within Christianity was a *development* that emerged in a specific cultural milieu. The Wars of Religion—which began in 1522 and continued, in some form, until 1700—killed millions but created no resolution to the conflicts between Catholics, Lutherans, Calvinists, Anabaptists, and other sects. The result was a sense of exhaustion in Europe and a desire to find new ways to manage religious differences. To keep the peace, rulers eventually began to see the appeal of allowing the competing groups to practice their religions freely.[69] Philosophers and theologians, for their part, increasingly came to view religious liberty as a human right, something intrinsic to the dignity and worth of each person.[70]

To be sure, the establishment of religious liberty did not take hold all at once throughout the Western world. Transylvania granted local communities the authority to choose their own preachers as early as 1568 through the Edict of Torda.[71] Poland-Lithuania codified a policy of limited tolerance in 1573, and the Netherlands became a haven for religious minorities after the Union of Utrecht in 1579.[72] Other territories in the succeeding decades retained restrictive policies and sought to squelch dissent. The myths taught to American schoolchildren notwithstanding, the early New England colonies were bastions of religious intolerance rather than freedom. The Puritans of Massachusetts hanged four Quakers for repeatedly violating bans on their preaching.[73] It fell to Roger Williams to make the case for greater religious freedom in the American colonies, and his views prevailed in the Rhode Island Colony he helped found in 1636.[74] The English Civil War (1642–1651) subsequently created the conditions for Levellers, Presbyterians, Independents, and other groups to push for expanding the scope of religious liberty in England.[75]

Over the next two centuries, policies affirming religious freedom became institutionalized throughout the Western world and won strong public approval. The First Amendment to the US Constitution protected people from encroachments on their religious liberty from the national government and eventually from state and local governments.[76] Most countries in Western Europe granted citizenship and legal equality to Jews during the nineteenth century.[77] Restraints on the religious liberty of Unitarians, Catholics, Quakers, atheists, and others were also gradually repealed.[78] Of course, debates continue to this day concerning matters such as when, if ever, religious groups should be exempted from particular laws.[79] Controversy also remains over how to resolve the conflict between religious freedom and other principles such as nondiscrimination on the basis of sexual orientation and gender identity.[80] Nevertheless, virtually everyone in the West now supports a conception of religious freedom much broader than anything theologians and biblical interpreters accepted for most of Christian history.

Today's apologists thus work within a cultural milieu that cherishes religious freedom as a central principle, and they smuggle that principle into their biblical interpretations. They work backward from what they have absorbed from the larger culture to what they are sure the Bible teaches. In other words, they decide what the Bible says before they actually read it. The process begins with their conviction that religious freedom is a fundamental right. They assume that God is good, and so he too must want people to have that freedom. Because the Bible is God's revelation for all mankind, it therefore must teach that everyone has the right to hold, practice, and promote whatever religion (or none) they want. From there, it's a short step to cherrypicking some tangentially relevant verses and proclaiming that they require the government to establish and protect each person's right to religious liberty. You could not find a clearer example of eisegesis if you tried.

We should not veer to the other extreme and conclude that the Bible consistently opposes an expansive vision of religious liberty; rather, anyone who takes the Bible seriously will see that it takes no consistent position on this subject. The first Christians, who expected the world to end within their lifetimes, did not explicitly address religious liberty in their New Testament writings. Intellectually honest Christians readily acknowledge the Bible's important omissions on this score. For example, Luke Timothy Johnson, an accomplished scholar of the New Testament who is himself a Christian, notes that "the Christian scriptures, in short, do not in any direct or obvious way provide support for the contemporary proposition that 'it is a human right to be religious.'"[81] Apologists, however, lack the intellectual honesty that Johnson displays, and so they twist the Bible into saying what they want it to say.

There is a significant upside to this dishonesty. Given their prominence and the extent to which churches disseminate their writings, apologists help shape the beliefs of the entire Christian community. Widespread support for religious liberty from Christian citizens and voters, in turn, helps build a political coalition for establishing and maintaining the relevant policies. It is thus in everyone's interest for Christians to think their scriptures command the ruling authorities to respect a comprehensive right to religious belief and practice.

To demonstrate these shared interests, let me start with myself. I've got a good life in every respect that matters. My parents and brother love me. I have a strong marriage of over twenty-five years, two wonderful children, and a group of trusted friends. As a professor, I have what I believe to be the best job in the world, which allows me to interact with smart colleagues, promising students, and ideas and research across a range of disciplines. I have financial security and, with the exception of three chronic but manageable ailments, good health.

In short, I don't want to die. It would be great if I could at least meet the actuarial averages in life expectancy for someone my age. I especially don't want to meet my demise at the stake or the gallows. For most of Christian history, getting burned or hanged was a realistic possibility for someone pushing views like mine. Until the seventeenth century and beyond, theologians thought the Bible required blasphemers like me to receive the death penalty. Thankfully for me and everyone who cares about my well-being, both Christian leaders and the rank and file no longer believe that.

Stated another way, I much prefer my intellectual adversaries to be apologists from today rather than the first sixteen centuries of Christianity. That's not to say that I expect apologists to soft-pedal their critiques of my arguments and analyses. They might even be tempted to borrow a line from the Bible in calling me a fool for saying there is no God (Psalm 14:1, 53:1). I can live with that, for the unsolicited emails I receive often contain far worse epithets. The one thing apologists won't do, however, is call upon the government to execute me for writing this book. They have come to accept that the freedom of religion includes not only the right to practice any religion or none, but also the right to publicly challenge other people's beliefs, doctrines, and scriptures. Rather than working to get me executed for blasphemy, apologists will focus their efforts on trying to find some holes in my book, and for that I'm grateful.

Members of religious minorities such as Buddhists, Sikhs, Jews, Muslims, and Hindus can also sleep easier in knowing that Christians no longer think the Bible empowers the government to restrict the speech (blasphemy, proselytizing) and actions (worship, observance) of people adhering to what those in power deem a false religion. In fact, Christians themselves have a stake in a shared commitment to religious liberty. Prior to the enactment of protective policies, the "false" religions included new or unorthodox sects of Christianity. By historical standards, many of today's Christians would be branded heretics. Groups such as Mormons, Seventh-day Adventists, and Pentecostals didn't even exist until the nineteenth or twentieth centuries, making them heretics almost by definition. Other self-identified Christians hold heretical beliefs such as reincarnation, and they too benefit from broad protections for religious liberty.[82] In countries with diverse populations, just about everyone can applaud the apologists who read into the Bible their belief that rulers cannot punish nontraditional forms of religious speech and action.

THE BIBLE AND SLAVERY

The upside of Christians' intellectual dishonesty is also evident in how they think about slavery, which the Bible explicitly authorizes. In the ancient world people often enslaved foreigners, especially those who surrendered during battles or were offered for sale through international markets, but generally did not hold members of their own ethnic group as chattel slaves. God gave specific instructions to that effect in the Bible. In the Old Testament, Moses conveyed to the Israelites God's rules allowing them to hold each other only as indentured servants (Exodus 22:1; Leviticus 25:8–10, 40; Deuteronomy 15:12), whereas they could purchase foreigners as chattel slaves to be used, resold at a later date, or passed to descendants (Leviticus 25:39–46). God's prophet also told the Israelites they could not kidnap and enslave a free person (Exodus 21:16), but they could turn prisoners of war into slaves (Deuteronomy 20:10–15).

The New Testament took this basic framework for granted. During the course of his ministry, Jesus commonly encountered slaves and their masters (Matthew 8:5–13, 26:49–56; Mark 14:43–50; Luke 7:1–10, 22:47–53; John 4:46–54, 18:10–11, 18:18–27). He did not ever rebuke the slaveholders or suggest they were doing anything wrong in treating another human being as property. Jesus also regularly referred to slaves and their masters in his parables (Matthew 13:24–30, 18:23–35, 21:33–41, 22:1–14, 25:14–30; Mark 12:1–12; Luke 12:41–48, 14:15–24, 15:11–32, 19:11–27, 20:9–19). In those parables the slaves ran errands, toiled in the fields, and endured beatings from their masters and overseers. Through all the opportunities his storytelling provided, Jesus said nothing negative about the institution of slavery.

This omission cannot be explained by a reticence on Jesus's part to engage in moral instruction. To the contrary, much of his ministry focused on teaching his listeners right from wrong. In just a sample of his teachings, Jesus commanded people to honor their parents (Matthew 15:4; Mark 10:19), turn the other cheek (Matthew 5:38–42; Luke 6:27–31), love one another (John 13:34), love one's enemies (Matthew 5:44), and feed the hungry, clothe the naked, provide hospitality to strangers, and care for those who are sick or in prison (Matthew 25:35–40). Jesus also condemned many behaviors, including getting divorced (Matthew 19:3–12; Mark 10:2–12), charging interest (Luke 6:35), judging others (Matthew 7:1), swearing oaths (Matthew 5:34), getting angry (Matthew 5:21), feeling lust in one's heart (Matthew 5:28), and committing murder, adultery, fornication, theft, or slander (Matthew 15:19; Mark 7:20). Clearly, Jesus was no shrinking violet who declined to speak his mind on moral questions. Had he intended to denounce slavery as sinful, he easily could have done so. By treating slaveholding so nonchalantly in his daily encounters and his parables, Jesus instead left his listeners with the impression that he saw nothing wrong with the practice.

By way of comparison, suppose an ancient sage lived in a society that accepted rape as an ordinary human behavior. During his travels the sage frequently met both rape survivors and their rapists. He proceeded to interact with the rapists as if nothing were amiss. The sage answered their questions, guided their spiritual development, and taught them right from wrong, all without ever mentioning rape. He also told parables in which both rape survivors and rapists appeared as characters, and yet the stories never said anything about rape itself. What would an ordinary person infer from his teaching? Clearly, that the sage was a typical member of his society in that he did not consider rape a moral offense. Anyone hearing Jesus's teaching would similarly think he resembled the rest of his society in accepting slavery.

The apostles also indicated their acceptance. In the book of Philemon, the apostle Paul returned a runaway slave, Onesimus, to his lawful owner. If Paul believed it sinful to hold human beings as property, he could have taken that occasion to express his views. In the book of Colossians, Paul instructed slaves to obey their masters and then told the masters to treat their slaves justly and fairly (Colossians 3:22–4:1; see also Ephesians 6:5–9).[83] Does that sound like the teaching of someone who deemed the whole institution immoral? In what appears on the surface to be contradictory evidence, Paul mentioned slave traders among a list of sinners in one of his other letters (1 Timothy 1:10). Slave traders in the ancient world often behaved illegally by either stealing someone else's slaves or by kidnapping and enslaving a free person. Paul was not alone in disparaging those actions. The city-states of Knossos and Miletos, for example, signed a treaty stating that their citizens would not purchase a free person from the other city-state who had been illegally forced into slavery.[84]

One therefore cannot use 1 Timothy 1:10 to claim that Paul opposed slavery as such. His statements in Philemon, Colossians, and Ephesians indicate instead that he accepted the morality of someone getting reduced to chattel after being defeated in battle or sentenced for a crime, the two most common legal means by which a person became enslaved in the areas of the Roman Empire where Paul lived and traveled. The Romans were continually fighting battles in the far reaches of their empire, and slaveholders stood ready to buy the war captives.[85] Most enslaved people that Paul and anyone else in his society encountered had originally been prisoners of war. Showing that he accepted the laws and customs of his day, Paul referred without further comment to slaveholders who were "members of the church" (1 Timothy 6:2). Paul actually commanded slaves to consider their masters "worthy of all honor" (1 Timothy 6:1; see also Titus 2:9–10 and 1 Peter 2:18–21). If owning another person was inherently sinful, surely the masters would deserve shame rather than honor.

The Bible's support for slavery in both the Old and New Testaments puts apologists in a pickle. God is supposed to be a morally perfect being who used his written revelation to tell us how to behave. After seeing the Bible give the wrong answer to such a simple moral issue as slavery, many people would conclude that God didn't inspire the Bible in its entirety, God isn't good, or God doesn't exist at all. None of those are viable options for a traditional Christian. Apologists therefore propose a fourth alternative: The Bible doesn't actually permit slavery! They use a combination of their standard strategies to make their case. I explained the errors in their reasoning in chapter 2, and I won't rehash the details here. My goal in this chapter is to show that most of their arguments were invented during or after the Age of Reason. Up through the seventeenth century, most Christians viewed slaveholding as a moral practice, and the relatively few who disagreed did not ground their arguments in the Bible.

That last sentence will surely raise the hackles of some Christians, who will be tempted to turn to Google to prove I'm wrong. One can find many erroneous statements on the Internet about what Christian individuals and groups said about slavery at various points in history. If you look carefully, you'll discover that most of the posts, comments, and articles omit links to the primary sources that would allow the reader to verify the information being presented. As explained by biblical scholar Hector Avalos, these problems are not limited to internet materials.[86] Authors of well-known books addressing the topic of Christianity and slavery have sometimes conducted lazy research through which they relied mainly or entirely on secondary sources.

One of the biggest offenders, Avalos shows, is sociologist Rodney Stark, whose books *For the Glory of God* and *The Triumph of Reason* stand as works of apologetics rather than scholarship.[87] Drawing from the secondary literature, Stark characterizes certain Christians from history as uniformly antislavery even as their own writings reveal that they actually opposed only certain forms of slavery as applied to certain people.[88] To make matters worse, other apologists often rely uncritically on Stark's books, at which point the assertions become thirdhand.[89] There is, of course, a better way for an author to proceed: read the primary sources and include citations to them. In my research, I have followed these guidelines for all cases where the sources were originally written in English or exist in English translations.

Failing to read the primary sources is not the only mistake apologists make. They also have a tendency to present a minority view from history as if it was actually mainstream, which is especially problematic for the sixteen hundred years before the rise of an abolitionist movement. Stark and others focus on the scattered antislavery voices from late antiquity and the Middle Ages while ignoring or downplaying the theologians, popes, and councils on the other side. You can make the hitters on any baseball team look impressive if you exclude from consideration the times they strike out, and the same principle applies here. By overlooking the large majority of Christians who believed there was nothing inherently wrong with one person owning another as property, apologists give a selective and biased account of their religion's history. To reach an accurate conclusion, one has to examine a representative sampling of the prominent views from the dawn of Christianity through abolitionism. Accordingly, I will offer a summary that highlights the most influential figures of each era.

CHRISTIAN HISTORY AND SLAVERY

The earliest Christian writings not contained in the New Testament simply extended the messages on slavery contained in Paul's letters. These post-biblical sources were widely known and respected in the ancient world, and the Church Fathers often quoted from them.[90] In the *Epistle of Barnabas*, which most scholars date to shortly after the turn of the second century, the author sounded much like Paul in instructing slaves to "be subject unto thy masters as to a type of God in shame and fear."[91] We hear similar sentiments in the *Didache*, a book of teachings attributed to the apostles, which told slaves to "be subject to your master, as to God's representative, in reverence and fear."[92]

Christian leaders demonstrated their acceptance of slavery in many other ways. Cyprian, a bishop of Carthage during the third century, observed that Christian masters sometimes need to "flog and scourge" a slave to compel obedience.[93] Gregory of Nazianzus, archbishop of Constantinople during the fourth century and a contributor to Trinitarian theology, was himself a slaveholder. He freed most of his slaves in his will and left others to the Church.[94] However, he did not pair his manumission with any statement indicating general opposition to slaveholding, and the Church as a whole sought to protect the rights of masters. In 324 the Council of Granges condemned anyone who "leads a slave to despise his master, to remove himself from slavery, to not serve with good will and respect."[95] In 340 the Synod of Gangra blasted those who use the "pretext of piety" to encourage slaves to run away, scorn their masters, or fail to serve with honor.[96] With representation from throughout Christendom, the Council of Chalcedon later ratified the decisions of previous synods, including the one at Gangra.[97]

The end of the fourth century yielded the first Christian to denounce the entire institution of slavery, Gregory of Nyssa. Nyssa was a small town located in what today is part of Turkey, and Gregory served as its bishop. Lacking the capacity for self-delusion that modern apologists demonstrate, he did not try to assert that the Bible opposed slavery, and he declined to engage with the biblical texts that authorize and regulate the practice. To sustain his case that slavery was immoral, Gregory instead offered a theological argument that included only a passing reference to the book of Genesis.[98] Gregory of Nyssa thereby proved that individual Christians can improve upon the Bible's morality. Christians do not have to believe or accept something just because the Bible teaches it.

Unfortunately, Gregory's antislavery stance remained the minority view within Christianity for well over a millennium. One of his influential contemporaries, Augustine, spent more time addressing the biblical texts, and Augustine did not deny that the Bible supported slavery. He nevertheless tried to contextualize the issue by saying that God's original design in the Garden of Eden involved "not man over man, but man over the beasts."[99] Slavery did not appear in the Bible "until righteous Noah branded the sin of his son with his name."[100] Augustine inferred that "the prime cause, then, of slavery is sin, which brings man under the dominion of his fellow—that which does not happen save by the judgment of God."[101] For Augustine, slavery was God's punishment for human sinfulness.

During the Middle Ages, the most common position within the Church held that Christians could enslave pagans and Muslims but not each other. Balthild of Ascania, who ruled as regent for her eldest son in the kingdom of the Franks, issued a decree banning her Christian subjects from taking fellow Christians as slaves.[102] The Council of Koblenz later sought to spread the policy to a wider area.[103] An important dissenter from this group-based stance of Christians during the Middle Ages was Smaragdus of Saint-Mihiel, a Benedictine monk who wrote the only text from the Carolingian dynasty opposing all forms of slavery. Unlike most of his contemporaries, Smaragdus held that Christians could not enslave non-Christians who surrendered during battles.[104]

Thomas Aquinas subsequently addressed slavery in several places in his *Summa Theologica*, which he wrote between 1265 and 1274. Like Augustine, he attributed slavery in the Bible to the Fall, writing that "in the state of innocence such a mastership could not have existed between man and man."[105] Aquinas deduced that slavery, like a piece of clothing, is not inherent to natural law but stands as an acceptable addition, for both slavery and clothes were "devised by human reason for the benefit of human life."[106] He cited Aristotle to argue that slavery could be justified on grounds of utility "in that it is useful to this man to be ruled by a wiser man, and to the latter to be helped by the former."[107] Aquinas pointed to 1 Timothy 6:1 to affirm that slaves are "bound to earthly masters."[108]

Through the Middle Ages, then, leading voices in the Church held that slavery was biblically and morally permissible, with many writers stressing that enslaved people had to be non-Christians. As feudalism and serfdom spread and the supply of slaves diminished, the practice of slavery nearly disappeared from Europe. It would later return, of course, in the European colonies of the New World. The Portuguese were the first to colonize, and they began their efforts relatively close to home in the Canary Islands. In 1435 Pope Eugene IV issued a ruling forbidding anyone to attack and enslave the recently baptized Christians living there.[109] He followed up the next year with an edict granting the Portuguese the right to conquer and enslave non-Christians in the Canary Islands.[110] In 1455 Pope Nicholas V explicitly allowed the enslavement of pagans, Muslims, and Africans, and he reaffirmed his proclamation three years later.[111] In 1488 one of his successors, Innocent VIII, accepted a gift of Moorish slaves from King Ferdinand of Aragon and then redistributed some of them to cardinals and nobles.[112]

SLAVERY IN THE EARLY MODERN PERIOD

The first major shift in Church doctrine occurred in 1537 when Pope Paul III condemned the enslavement of Native Americans. In his bull *Sublimus Dei*, Paul III did not mention the Bible but nevertheless asserted that Native Americans cannot "be deprived of their liberty or the possession of their property . . . nor should they be in any way enslaved."[113] Paul III was not a consistent opponent of slavery, however, and in 1548 he praised the fruits of slave labor: "from a multitude of slaves, inheritances are augmented, agriculture better cultivated, and cities increased." He denounced the practice of slaves running away to seek freedom, and he upheld the right of citizens in Rome to buy and sell slaves.[114]

As European countries began moving toward large-scale colonization and settlement, the Protestant reformers made scattered references to slavery. While discussing a verse commonly invoked by twenty-first-century apologists, 1 Timothy 1:10, Martin Luther disparaged the form of slavery that begins by kidnapping a free person.[115] Luther said nothing, however, about the kinds of slavery the Bible endorses. John Calvin also commented on 1 Timothy 1:10, and he thought Paul intended to attack only certain behaviors related to slavery rather than the institution per se. Calvin noted: "The Latin word *plagium* was employed by ancient writers to denote the carrying off or enticing the slave of another man, or the false sale of a freeman."[116] In writing about Ephesians 6:5–9, Calvin stressed that the verses referred not to servants but to actual slaves "whom their masters bought with money" for the purposes of "perpetual" bondage.[117] The Bible, Calvin stated, taught that slaves who obey their masters are "doing the will of God."[118]

Protestants of the seventeenth century agreed with Calvin that the Bible approved some forms of slavery. In its commentary on the Bible from within the Reformed tradition, the Westminster Assembly inferred from Leviticus 25:46 that the sons of slaveholders "shall inherit the masterly power" upon their father's death, and slaves "shall abide in bondage as long as they live."[119] The Puritans of Massachusetts wrote the Bible's provisions into their law code. They outlawed kidnapping and enslaving a free person but permitted the permanent enslavement of war captives.[120] Through their wars with various Indian tribes, the Puritans acquired slaves, and they kept some and sold others to middlemen for Caribbean plantations.[121] Some slave traders, however, had long been violating the Bible's ban on kidnapping and enslaving a free person. In 1686 the Catholic Church's Congregation of the Holy Office issued a ruling restating the reasons for which a person could and could not legitimately be made a slave. While condemning the practice of capturing and selling free persons from Africa, the ruling affirmed the morality of slavery in general.[122]

As of 1700, then, not a single Christian on record had cited the Bible as justification for opposing all forms of slavery. That's a remarkable fact. If the Bible's rules, principles, themes, and narrative arc all worked against slavery, why didn't anyone discover that over the previous sixteen centuries? Augustine, Aquinas, Luther, Calvin, and other theologians with towering intellects had read and studied the Bible throughout their adult lives. How did they all miss the teachings that today's apologists are certain the Bible contains? Apologists such as Victoria Johnson often note, as if they are conceding something, that many Christians historically "used the Bible to justify slavery."[123] That analysis has the story backward. Before the Age of Reason, everybody knew that the Bible said one person could own another as property. The interesting development came when some Christians began to use the Bible to justify abolition.

It wasn't until 1701 that Massachusetts judge Samuel Sewall took the first significant step in that direction. After reviewing texts from the Old and New Testaments, he concluded that the Bible, taken as a whole, rejected the institution of slavery.[124] Compared to the slick apologetics on this topic in twenty-first-century books by Paul Copan, Robert Hutchinson, and others, Sewall's presentation lacks polish.[125] Because no one before him had addressed the wide range of biblical texts and concluded that they forbade the ownership of human beings, Sewall had to rely mainly on his own creativity to build his case. Other writers would innovate further in the subsequent decades, and the nineteenth century saw writers such as George Bourne and Albert Barnes arguing that the Bible denounced chattel slavery of any kind.[126]

Abolitionists and the Strategy of Reinterpretation

These reinterpretations helped fuel the abolitionist movement. Christians opposed to slavery threw their energy into organizing, speaking, writing, and protesting, and they often defended their positions with biblical appeals. They tested and honed arguments about why the Bible condemns slavery, and apologists often repeat their claims today. Controversial within their own era but lionized in ours, Christian abolitionists provoked a debate about the Bible. Prominent theologians responded by identifying the errors in their interpretations and conclusions.

One such theologian was John Henry Hopkins, who became an Episcopalian bishop in Vermont in 1832 and later the Presiding Bishop of his entire denomination. Hopkins explained that he had no personal stake in slavery: "If it were a matter to be determined by my personal sympathies, tastes, or feelings, I should be as ready as any man to condemn the institution of slavery; for all my prejudices of education, habit, and social position stand entirely opposed to it."[127] Hopkins refused, however, to allow those prejudices to corrupt his biblical interpretations. He pledged to "submit my weak and erring intellect to the authority of the Almighty" as expressed through the sacred scriptures.[128]

Hopkins had grown weary of the ways abolitionists approached the Bible. They commonly asserted that the Bible allowed only indentured servitude, not slavery. Hopkins refuted them by quoting Leviticus 25:39–46. As the Vermont bishop explained, the text's distinction between the temporary servitude of Israelites and the permanent slavery of heathens and foreigners is "too plain for controversy."[129] Abolitionists also insisted that God showed his contempt for slavery by raising a prophet, Moses, to deliver the Israelites from bondage in Egypt. To demonstrate that the exodus from Egypt said nothing about the morality of slavery, Hopkins observed that Moses described God's provisions for the Israelites to later acquire their own slaves.[130] Finally, abolitionists tried to turn the Bible's general statement of the Golden Rule (Leviticus 19:18; Matthew 7:12) into a specific ban on slavery. Any such move, Hopkins stated, was unjustified because the Golden Rule and support for slavery coexisted in the same text, which would be impossible if the former ruled out the latter.[131]

Hopkins was not himself an advocate for slavery, and he noted his long-standing support for "a plan for its gradual abolition" throughout the whole nation.[132] He simply would not allow the Bible to be manipulated to serve any group's political agenda, no matter how noble. We should nevertheless be thankful that few Christians demonstrate his level of intellectual honesty today. Suppose instead that they acknowledged that the Bible forbids only the specific form of slavery that originates through kidnapping. If Christians wanted to follow the Bible's lead, they could sustain a thriving institution of slavery without needing to kidnap anyone. Over the last hundred years, the US has fought World War II and smaller wars in Korea, Vietnam, Cambodia, Grenada, Panama, Bosnia, Kosovo, Somalia, Iraq (twice), and Afghanistan. Those conflicts yielded prisoners of war from four different continents, and yet Christians never even considered lobbying the American government to turn the war captives into slaves. Christians also never considered resuming the ancient and medieval practice of using slavery to punish someone convicted of a crime.

In acting this way, modern Christians have shown themselves to be the intellectual descendants of the abolitionists. Coming of age during an era that increasingly prioritized liberty and individual rights, abolitionists engaged in elaborate contortions to link their positions to the Bible. Once they crossed the point of no return, abolitionists such as Theodore Weld and Charles Finney became effective political advocates.[133] They could appeal to other Christians, especially those in positions of authority, using a common religious language. These abolitionists essentially proclaimed, "I'm a Christian too, and I can show you why God and the Bible oppose slavery." Such messages, combined with their economic, legal, and pragmatic arguments, allowed them to gradually win more adherents through decades of political struggle. Although they relied on intellectually dishonest readings of the Bible, they were on the right side of history in their moral convictions.

It's impossible to know for sure what would have happened if these abolitionists had read the Bible accurately and decided they could no longer belong to a religion whose holy book sanctioned such a heinous institution. We have reason to believe, however, that legalized slavery would have persisted much longer. As it played out, the various Christian groups and denominations in Western countries contained both proslavery and antislavery members. If all the antislavery members had become nonbelievers, there would have been no one left to push for abolition from a Christian standpoint. In a battle between apostates promoting abolition and Christians defending slavery, the latter would have held the upper hand politically. The cause of abolition certainly benefited from the activism of freethinkers and Unitarians, along with Quakers and other nontraditional Christians, but it also needed traditional Christians to join a broad-based coalition.

The experience of these Christian abolitionists calls to mind a quote often attributed to German leader Otto von Bismarck. In a line most scholars think is apocryphal, he supposedly said that legislation is like sausage in that you should never watch it being made.[134] The sentiment is valid regardless of whether it originated with Bismarck, and we could add religion to the comparison. No religion, even a book-based one such as Christianity, is ever fixed in stone. Christians regularly revisit their texts and traditions, and the result is not only differing interpretations within every era but also entirely new interpretations at certain moments. Some beliefs and moral stances that the biblical authors took for granted win little support among Christians today. It's not pretty to watch, but Christians can read modern values into the Bible and thereby eliminate its worst features. As the abolitionists proved, Christians who manipulate the Bible can sometimes become committed and effective social reformers.

Incidentally, those abolitionists could have preserved their intellectual integrity and still mounted a limited attack on slavery. Other than sentencing for a crime, someone got transported to the Americas as a slave through two primary channels. As historians such as John Thornton have shown, the majority of enslaved people originated as war captives from the numerous military conflicts in western and central Africa.[135] Wars between African chiefdoms and kingdoms yielded a steady stream of slaves from the losing groups, an outcome entirely consistent with ancient customs and the Bible. An abolitionist committed to following the Bible would have to accept, as did the New Testament authors living in the Roman Empire, the morality of converting prisoners of war into slaves. A minority of New World slaves, however, had been kidnapped by European and African slave traders and then sold on the international markets. The abolitionists could have fought against those practices while maintaining fidelity to the Bible.

As a practical matter, though, attacking one type of slavery while accepting another would have created a muddled message. It was simpler and probably more persuasive for abolitionists to assert that all forms of chattel slavery were immoral and contrary to God's will. Many challenges of implementation would have emerged if abolitionists had instead sought to free only those individuals who either entered bondage through kidnapping or were born into it as the offspring of a kidnapped person. What would happen to enslaved people for whom the documentary record wasn't strong enough to determine their entry point? To work on a practical level, abolition had to apply to the entire population of slaves.

THE BIBLE AND HOMOSEXUALITY

Some Christians have reinterpreted the Bible not just on religious freedom and slavery but also on homosexuality. The Bible condemns sexual activity between two people of the same sex in six passages, beginning with Genesis 19:1–29. In the story told there, Lot provided shelter for two male travelers who were actually angels posing as human beings. The men of Sodom surrounded Lot's house and demanded that he bring his houseguests outside "so that we may know them" (Genesis 19:5), with "know" being a common biblical allusion to engaging in sexual relations. Lot offered his two virgin daughters instead. The men of Sodom refused the offer, and the angels had to strike them with blindness to prevent them from knocking down the house's door. Shortly thereafter, God destroyed both Sodom and its sister city of Gomorrah with "sulfur and fire" (Genesis 19:24).

The next biblical reference to homosexual behavior occurs in the law code of Leviticus, where Moses conveyed to the Israelites the following command: "You shall not lie with a male as with a woman; it is an abomination" (Leviticus 18:22). Moses also told them God's punishment for that crime: "If a man lies with a male as with a woman, both of them have committed an abomination; they shall be put to death; their blood is upon them" (Leviticus 20:13).

The New Testament also casts homosexual behavior in a negative light. In the first chapter of Romans, Paul described the consequences for gentiles who denied God's truth and worshipped false idols. "For this reason," Paul wrote, "God gave them up to degrading passions. Their women exchanged natural intercourse for unnatural, and in the same way also the men, giving up natural intercourse with women, were consumed with passion for one another. Men committed shameless acts with men and received in their own persons the due penalty for their error" (Romans 1:26–27).

In one of the other passages, 1 Corinthians 6:9–10, Paul writes, "Do you not know that wrongdoers will not inherit the kingdom of God? Do not be deceived! Fornicators, idolaters, adulterers, *malakoi*, *arsenokoitai*, thieves, the greedy, drunkards, revilers, robbers—none of these will inherit the kingdom of God." I have left the words *malakoi* and *arsenokoitai* untranslated from the original Greek, and I'll return shortly to disputes over what they mean. The final reference to homosexual activity occurs in 1 Timothy 1:9–11, which also disparages *arsenokoitai*: "This means understanding that the law is laid down not for the innocent but for the lawless and disobedient, for the godless and sinful, for the unholy and profane, for those who kill their father or mother, for murderers, fornicators, *arsenokoitai*, slave traders, liars, perjurers, and whatever else is contrary to the sound teaching that conforms to the glorious gospel of the blessed God, which he entrusted to me."

For more than nineteen centuries, theologians and biblical interpreters were consistent in thinking these six references demonstrate that God abhors sexual relations between two people of the same sex. In commenting in the fourth century on Romans 1:26–27, John Chrysostom lamented "the men leaving the natural use of the woman." Chrysostom linked back to the creation account in Genesis to argue "that the two should be one, I mean the woman and the man."[136] Augustine, who was Chrysostom's contemporary, held that "offenses against nature are everywhere and at all times to be held in detestation and should be punished," with his prime example being the Sodomites.[137]

Martin Luther agreed, adding that only the devil's influence could lead a man to have sex with another man.[138] John Calvin commented on Romans 1:26–27 and decried the "dreadful crime of unnatural lust." In that passage, Calvin noted, people "became degraded beyond the beasts, since they reversed the whole order of nature."[139] English theologian Matthew Poole subsequently observed that 1 Corinthians 6:9–10 referred to "the sin of Sodom, a sin not to be named amongst Christians."[140] Historian John Boswell has claimed that the Church tolerated and even honored same-sex relationships at certain times, but other scholars find his evidence unpersuasive.[141] In any event, no one has discovered any writers from before the twentieth century who thought the Bible—as opposed to particular Christian officials—allowed homosexual behavior.

NEW INTERPRETATIONS OF HOMOSEXUALITY

Beginning in the 1960s, revisionist scholars studying ancient cultures and languages began claiming the Bible condemns only certain forms of homosexual activity. The fruits of this research can be seen in three recent books: Matthew Vines, *God and the Gay Christian: The Biblical Case in Support of Same-Sex Relationships*; Ken Wilson, *A Letter to My Congregation: An Evangelical Pastor's Path to Embracing People Who Are Gay, Lesbian, Bisexual and Transgender into the Company of Jesus*; and James Brownson, *Bible, Gender, Sexuality: Reframing the Church's Debate on Same-Sex Relationships*.[142] Vines, Wilson, and Brownson are an activist, pastor, and scholar, respectively, but all three are deeply versed in the relevant research, some of which has been conducted by Brownson himself. The books by Vines, Wilson, and Brownson collectively present the most widely accepted arguments on behalf of the revisionist position.

Interestingly, all three authors identify as evangelicals. "Like most theologically conservative Christians," Vines explains, "I hold what is called a 'high' view of the Bible. That means I believe all of Scripture is inspired by God and authoritative for my life."[143] Wilson describes his long-standing "involvement in the evangelical movement" and notes, "As a follower of Jesus, His book is my book."[144] Brownson also calls himself a "theological conservative" and teaches at a seminary that defines its identity as "an evangelical and ecumenical community of faith in the Reformed tradition that serves the church of Jesus Christ."[145]

Vines, Wilson, Brownson, and other revisionists hold that the biblical authors intended to prohibit only certain kinds of same-sex behaviors, which Wilson describes as "orgy-sex, temple prostitution, pederasty, and slave-sex."[146] He and other revisionists think the Bible does not speak to "modern-day monogamous gay relationships."[147] One can apply that approach to each of the six passages that form the core of the debate. For the first of these passages, God's destruction of Sodom and Gomorrah, Brownson reasons that the men sinned only through their "humiliation, violence, and inhospitality toward strangers."[148] Brownson rejects an alternative interpretation holding that the biblical authors disparaged those acts *and* the homosexual behavior through which they were manifested. Contrary to Brownson's claim, Jewish writers around the time of the New Testament often mentioned the same-sex actions as either the entire offense or one component of it.[149] Throughout Christian history, theologians such as John Chrysostom, Augustine, and Martin Luther used the "sin of the Sodomites" as a shorthand for homosexuality, and they were certain the Bible forbade it in both the Old and New Testaments.

Moving next to the two Leviticus verses, Vines contends they are not normative because they appear in the Old Testament in "a law code that has never applied to Christians."[150] Vines's statement is misleading, for Christians historically have viewed the law code's moral teachings to be binding even as Jesus's death and resurrection abrogated its civil and ceremonial requirements. Vines counters that "the Old Testament itself never makes those distinctions,"[151] which is true but irrelevant because the distinctions appear in the New Testament and in Christian theological works from every era.[152] Paul affirmed that circumcision was not required for Christians (Galatians 5:3–6), and Jesus overturned the Jewish dietary code and Sabbath restrictions (Mark 7:1–23; Luke 6:1–11, 13:10–17). Yet Jesus also stressed the need to obey God's commandments (Matthew 19:16–19), and his Sermon on the Mount (Matthew 5–7) drew from the moral instruction of the Old Testament.

Showing that early Christians accepted the Old Testament's moral rules, Tertullian (155–240) explained that God gave Adam in embryonic form "all the precepts which afterwards sprouted forth when given through Moses; that is, You shall love the Lord your God from your whole heart and out of your whole soul; You shall love your neighbour as yourself; You shall not kill; You shall not commit adultery; You shall not steal; False witness you shall not utter; Honour your father and mother; and, That which is another's, shall you not covet."[153] Tertullian insisted that those moral rules applied to all of humanity even though the Israelites' sacrifices, circumcision, food restrictions, and Sabbath observance did not.[154] Subsequent theologians including Augustine, Aquinas, and Calvin all distinguished between the moral teachings of the Old Testament, which Christians must obey, and its civil and ceremonial requirements that were limited to ancient Israel.[155]

For the specific case of homosexual behavior, the New Testament ratified and reinforced the teachings from Leviticus. To defend their position, revisionists therefore attempt to overturn the traditional understanding of the relevant New Testament passages. Brownson does this for Romans 1:26–27 by arguing that Paul disparaged not all same-sex behaviors but only those flowing from "excessive lust."[156] According to Brownson, "When interpreting scriptural commands or prohibitions, we must ask not only *what* is commanded or prohibited but *why*."[157] As other Christians have long recognized, however, there are two problems with this approach. First, it requires one to reconstruct Paul's motivations, a process that can never reach closure among all interpreters. Second, Paul used general and encompassing language to cast aspersions on the same-sex relations of both women and men. Had he intended to say that two women or two men could engage in sex flowing out of love and mutual commitment, he could have done so.

Revisionists use different kinds of arguments to overcome the messages of 1 Corinthians 6:9–10 and 1 Timothy 1:9–11. Wilson holds that the crucial words in those two verses, *malakoi* and *arsenokoitai*, "are notoriously difficult to translate."[158] As documented in works such as *Strong's Concordance*, a standard tool for biblical study, *malakos* means soft or effeminate, or morally weak.[159] The noun form *malakoi* therefore denotes the individuals having those qualities. As for the other word in question, *arsenokoitai*, scholars widely agree that Paul either coined it or borrowed it from one of his contemporaries, as it does not appear in any surviving documents from earlier times.[160]

Vines tries to discern the meaning of *arsenokoitai* by examining its usage in authors writing more than a hundred years after Paul. Based on these later authors, Vines concludes that the term refers only to exploitative male-to-male relationships such as pederasty, male prostitution, and the sexual abuse of slaves by their masters.[161] The problem with this method of understanding a word, as every linguist knows, is that meanings can change over time, a process known as "semantic change" or "semantic drift."[162] Think, for example, of the connotations of *ping*, *swipe*, *troll*, and *tweet* in the Internet age compared to earlier decades. Vines's method for uncovering the meaning of *arsenokoitai* would require studying its usage among Paul's contemporaries, not his successors.

We therefore need a better way to understand Paul's intended meaning, and many scholars begin by observing that he was a Greek-speaking Jew.[163] His scriptures were thus contained in the Septuagint, the ancient translation of sacred Jewish writings into Greek. In the Septuagint (presented for present purposes in the Roman alphabet), Leviticus 20:13 reads: "kai os an koimeetee meta *arsenos koiten* gynaikos bdelugma epoieesan amphoteroi thanatousthoosan enokhoi eisin."[164] I have italicized the two words, *arsenos* ("male") and *koiten* ("bed," often in a sexual sense) that Paul has joined together to yield *arsenokoiten*. The specific word he uses in 1 Corinthians 6:9 is *arsenokoitai*, the plural noun form of *arsenoskoiten*. A literal translation of *arsenoskoitai* based on its component parts would be "male bedders" or, in more familiar language, "those who sleep with males."[165]

Nobody thinks that Paul wanted to condemn married women who slept with their husbands. Given that he was deriving *arsenoskoitai* from verses in the Septuagint that called male-to-male intercourse an abomination, he clearly had in mind males (not females) who had sex with males. Females who slept with males to whom they were not married were already covered within the *pornoi* ("the sexually immoral" or "fornicators") that Paul also condemned in 1 Corinthians 6:9–10. Ancient Christians, for their part, had no trouble figuring out what Paul meant by *arsenokoitai*. Jerome, whose translation became the standard Bible for Christians in the West for over a millennium, rendered *arsenokoitai* into Latin as *masculorum concubitores*, a phrase meaning "males who sleep with males."[166]

Different questions arise for the term *malakoi*, which Paul paired with *arsenokoitai* in 1 Corinthians 6:9–10. Paul could have intended *malakoi* to refer to the passive partners in male same-sex relations, with *arsenokoitai* indicating the active partners. Alternatively, he might have meant for *arsenokoitai* to include both partners, with *malakoi* denoting a different category of men who are soft, effeminate, or morally weak.[167] Either way, Paul covers the full set of those who engage in male-to-male sex. There is no hint in the text itself that he is distinguishing between exploitative and consensual behaviors, both of which existed in the ancient world. Although most scholars agree that the ancient world lacked the concept of sexual orientation as a fixed and stable trait, the ancients did know about people who maintained adult, long-term, and consensual sexual relationships with someone of the same sex.[168] The standard reading of 1 Corinthians 6:9–10 in which Paul declares immoral all male-to-male sex is consistent with what he says in Romans 1:26–27, where he condemns the homosexual behavior of men (and women).

BIBLICAL REVISIONISM AND GOD

As we have seen, revisionists distort what the Bible teaches about homosexuality. Even more problematic, however, is how the standard conception of God must change if their interpretations are correct. During most of Christian history, theologians and biblical scholars believed the Bible prohibited all types of homosexual behavior. People who acted on any desires for a person of the same sex were consistently labeled as moral degenerates, and they commonly feared persecution from political and religious authorities.[169] Even if they escaped formal punishment through legal or social means, such people carried shame for their entire lives. To the revisionists, who think God approves of homosexuality within the context of a loving and monogamous relationship, all of that suffering didn't have to happen. It could have been avoided if only Christians had interpreted the Bible correctly.

When every interpreter for nearly two thousand years makes the same mistake, however, one begins to think the problem lies with the text and the God who supposedly inspired it. Recall that Vines, Wilson, Brownson, and other revisionists accept the Bible as the Word of God and deem it authoritative in telling us how to act. Their stance therefore requires believing that the Bible only *appears* to forbid homosexual activity in all its forms. Any God who did such a poor job conveying his message that nobody before the revisionists could figure it out must be devious or incompetent, either of which would render him unworthy of worship. Why should Christians put their faith in a God who has caused needless suffering by failing to communicate effectively?

This same problem arises with the issues of slavery and religious freedom. Today's apologists are convinced the Bible prohibits chattel slavery and requires a comprehensive right to religious freedom. The leading theologians disagreed for over sixteen centuries, which leads one to wonder why God inspired a Bible so cryptic that nobody discovered his true beliefs on those issues until the Age of Reason. Think of all the people who suffered up to and beyond the seventeenth century as an enslaved person or a member of a religious minority. If there is a God who wanted rulers to outlaw slavery and establish religious freedom, he could have made himself clear to the biblical authors and, through their writings, to later generations of Christians. Christians could then have pushed for those policies once they gained strong influence over emperors, kings, and princes beginning in the fourth century.

The fact that none of the great minds of the Church could discern such a message suggests a simpler explanation: The Bible contains the words of human beings, not God. Through commission (on homosexuality and slavery) and omission and contradictory messages (on religious freedom), the biblical authors took indefensible moral stances on many subjects. Modern Christians who cannot accept certain aspects of the Bible's morality have to perform mental gymnastics to convince themselves that it teaches what they want to believe. Rather than acknowledging that the biblical authors got some aspects of morality wrong, twenty-first-century believers use eisegesis to preserve the illusion of a morally perfect Bible and God.

Nearly all Christians now oppose slavery and support religious freedom, but many traditionalists still think homosexual behavior is inherently sinful. They point out, correctly, the errors in the revisionist interpretations. Yet those same traditionalists thoroughly misread the Bible on other issues. After you've already discarded sixteen centuries of biblical interpretations on slavery and religious freedom, you're going to hold the line at nineteen centuries of interpretations on homosexuality?

The traditionalists will surely search for a way to reconcile their inconsistencies, and they could try to invoke the Christian concept of sin. The ravages of sin, a traditionalist could argue, prevented all the interpreters from the first sixteen centuries from grasping the Bible's teachings about slavery and religious freedom, which explains why those interpreters got it wrong. Such an argument is easily refuted, however, with the traditionalists' own doctrines. Within the Catholic, Protestant, and Orthodox branches of Christianity, all people are affected by sin. How can traditionalists, wracked by sin just like everyone else, see the truth that Augustine, Aquinas, Luther, Calvin, and other leading lights of the Church overlooked? Moreover, why did sin corrupt the ways theologians historically read the Bible on slavery and religious freedom but failed to taint their interpretations on homosexuality? Traditionalists cannot answer these questions and will thus remain trapped in a web of contradictions.

Meanwhile, Vines, Wilson, Brownson, and other revisionists disagree with traditionalists about the morality of homosexuality. These revisionists are fighting for the full inclusion of gays and lesbians in Christian churches. They rely on intellectually dishonest interpretations of the Bible, and yet I hope they succeed in their larger mission. They can probably do more good inside rather than outside of Christianity. For the most part, people unaffiliated with any religion already accept gays and lesbians as ordinary members of society.[170] The last bastion of opposition in the West comes from organized religion, especially the conservative branches of Christianity. In order for those branches to change, they need advocates from within their own faith communities to press for reforms. The revisionists provide intellectual cover for other Christians who haven't studied the relevant biblical passages but assume that God can't possibly consider homosexual behavior to be inherently immoral.

Of course, Christians could simply admit that they must look outside their religion for guidance on these kinds of questions. The malleability of Christian positions on homosexuality, slavery, religious freedom, and other topics points to the need for an alternative source of morality. I elaborated such a source in chapter 3, and I will develop it further in the next chapter. We'll see that my approach, which is derived from humanism and based on inclusive deliberation, allows us to attain objectivity and understand moral progress.

CHAPTER 6

Achieving Moral Progress

ANNE FRANK SECURED A PERMANENT PLACE IN HISTORY THROUGH HER famous diary documenting her life while hiding from the Nazis. Compelling stories can also be found in the people who assisted her family, most notably Miep and Jan Gies. They brought food and supplies to the Frank family and four other Jews for over two years, no small feat in occupied Holland where essential goods were tightly rationed. Jan was a member of the Dutch resistance movement, through which he acquired the counterfeit ration cards needed to buy extra groceries. To avoid attracting suspicion, Miep used the cards and her family's resources to make small purchases from different stores and delivered the goods only at night. Both Miep and Jan knew they could be tortured and executed if they were caught assisting Jews.[1]

As Miep explains in her book describing these events, both she and Jan were atheists. Jan had been an atheist for many years, and Miep lost her faith in God during the war. They risked their lives for others not because they thought some divine being commanded it, or because they expected a reward in heaven, but simply because it was the right thing to do. After the war, they lived a quiet life and sought to avoid calling attention to themselves. Miep later insisted in interviews that she was "not a hero" and merely "did what any decent person would have done."[2]

Some Christians also sheltered Jews during the Nazi occupation and participated in the resistance movement. Although leaders of the official churches generally acquiesced to the reality of Nazi rule, individual

Christians made their own decisions.[3] A few of them, most famously Dietrich Bonhoeffer, gave their lives to the resistance.[4] Their actions demonstrate that you don't have to be an atheist to be moral. Within any large population, whether it be atheists, Christians, or some other religious grouping, one can find many generous, compassionate, and courageous people along with others who are stingy, callous, and cowardly.

This chapter is not about moral virtues or behaviors, however, but rather the origins of morality. I will argue that Christians cannot persuasively account for the source of their moral beliefs or make sense of moral progress. Again, Christians are just as capable as anyone else of acting morally, but their religion does not give them the resources to articulate a system of objective morality or understand how moral progress happens. Only atheism, which quickly leads to humanism, allows us to discover an objective moral code that transcends particular individuals, groups, and societies. The concept of moral progress, I will argue, fits easily within humanism but cannot be accommodated within a Christian worldview.

DELIBERATION AND THE BIBLE

An investigation of moral progress can usefully begin with the Bible, whose moral teachings manifestly did not result from deliberation or any other process based on reason. Many biblical characters, including Moses, Ezekiel, and the other prophets, instead claimed to be conveying commands they received directly from God.[5] Paul sometimes referred to teachings originating with Jesus, and Christians later came to believe that Paul and the other New Testament authors had been inspired by God to write what they did.[6] The upshot is that nobody thinks the Bible reflected a deliberative process whereby authors had to defend on rational grounds the morality they proclaimed. That's the point of a divine morality: It rests on God's nature and commands rather than substantive reasons that humans can discuss, evaluate, and critique.

Leaving aside its nondeliberative character, does the Bible offer an objective morality untainted by the unique perspectives of particular individuals and cultures? To the contrary, the Bible's morality is highly subjective. It presents as universal what are really just the parochial beliefs of ancient Christians and Jews. Of course, some of the Bible's morality is widely shared across societies and has stood the test of time. For example, both the Old and New Testaments offer a version of the Golden Rule, which has been independently discovered within many different philosophical and religious traditions. The Bible also prohibits murder and incest, demands fidelity to one's promises, and requires care for infants and children. All of these aspects of morality are readily accepted not only by Christians and Jews but also by atheists, agnostics, Buddhists, Muslims, Hindus, and members of other religious groups.

Some aspects of the Bible's morality, however, are particularistic rather than universal. Reflecting the distinctive features of their history, economic system, and social organization, ancient Christians and Jews developed their beliefs about subjects such as slavery, genocide, homosexuality, blasphemy, divorce, capital punishment, moneylending at interest, and corporal punishment of children. Honest observers now recognize that on these and other topics, the Bible presents the subjective perspectives of the groups that produced it. If there really was a God who created the world, sent his son into it, and inspired a group of writers, he surely would have ensured that his scriptures escaped the limitations of the time and place of their composition.

The Bible also fails a test of inclusivity from within its own cultural milieu. In other words, it captures not the sentiments of all ancient Christians and Jews but only those who gained a following within their religious communities. This flaw is readily apparent in how the Bible addresses questions related to gender. All of the prophets who pronounce on morality are men, as are Jesus and his twelve disciples. The women who appear in the Bible are mostly minor characters who provide the supporting cast to the men who carry the story forward. Even God is portrayed as male, which makes no sense if he is a one-of-a-kind being not limited to the human gender binary.

We can understand why the Bible envisions a God who is male once we think about the characteristics of the people who wrote it. The Bible includes sixty-six different books accepted by both Protestants and Catholics, and scholars do not attribute the authorship of any of them to a woman.[7] It should surprise no one that the male writers conceived a God who is also male. The authors include men such as Amos, Jeremiah,

Hosea, Matthew, Luke, and Paul. The books of Ruth and Esther, which might seem to be exceptions, are about women but give no statements of authorship within the texts themselves. Jewish tradition identifies the two authors as Samuel and Mordecai.[8]

What kind of moral system would we expect a group of exclusively male authors to construct? One giving women a subordinate status. We don't have to read much of the Bible to discover its biases in that area. For example, Moses revealed God's decree that a woman is ceremonially unclean after giving birth, and she is unclean for twice as long if she birthed a girl as opposed to a boy (Leviticus 12:1–8). Those girls, in turn, could be sold into slavery by their fathers (Exodus 21:7). Upon becoming women, they had the further ignominy of being subordinate within the Ten Commandments, which were presented with the male reader and listener in mind. In the tenth of the commandments, wives are listed along with a man's slaves, farm animals, and other property that another man should not covet (Exodus 20:17). If a woman is discovered on her wedding night not to be a virgin, she must be stoned to death (Deuteronomy 22:13–21).

But it gets worse. The Bible treats the rape of an Israelite girl or woman as an offense against her *father*. If she is unmarried, she must marry her rapist, whose punishment involves paying her father a fine and losing the right to ever divorce her (Deuteronomy 22:28–29). Just imagine being forced to spend the rest of your life with the man who raped you. Moses also conveyed God's wartime requirement for Israelite soldiers to kill all the boys, men, and nonvirgin women but to "keep alive for yourselves" the virgins (Numbers 31:17–18). The Bible thus gives a wink and a nod to a practice that has existed throughout human history: rape during and after warfare.[9] Notice that the virgins had no choice in what happened to them, which makes the command look like an open invitation for Israelite soldiers to rape them either once, in the aftermath of the battles, or repeatedly through a forced marriage.

Lest one think the New Testament elevated women to an equal status with men, the texts indicate otherwise. Peter tells wives to "accept the authority of your husbands" (1 Peter 3:1), and Paul instructs those wives to "be subject to your husbands" (Colossians 3:18; Ephesians 5:22).

Such a command makes sense in light of Paul's declaration that "man was not made from woman, but woman from man. Neither was man created for the sake of woman, but woman for the sake of man" (1 Corinthians 11:8–9). Paul also requires women to "be silent in the churches. For they are not permitted to speak, but should be subordinate, as the law also says. If there is anything they desire to know, let them ask their husbands at home. For it is shameful for a woman to speak in church" (1 Corinthians 14:34–35). The New Testament thus mandates the subjugation of women not only at home but also within their religious communities.

The lowly status of women in church continues in 1 Timothy 2:11–15: "Let a woman learn in silence with full submission. I permit no woman to teach or to have authority over a man; she is to keep silent. For Adam was formed first, then Eve; and Adam was not deceived, but the woman was deceived and became a transgressor. Yet she will be saved through childbearing, provided they continue in faith and love and holiness, with modesty." The Bible here manages to combine a retrograde view of women with the group-based guilt and punishment that recurs throughout the Old and New Testaments. Linking back to Genesis 3:16, the author of 1 Timothy charges all women with the sin of the first woman, Eve. The text of 1 Timothy doesn't explicitly say that the role of women in society is to be barefoot and pregnant, but that's clearly the implication of requiring them to stay silent in church and find their calling "through childbearing." Other biblical books portray a world in which men do and should hold the vast majority of the leadership positions in politics, the economy, and religious affairs.

Apologists who want to praise the Bible's teachings on gender (and other subjects) often cite Paul's words in Galatians 3:28, "There is no longer Jew or Greek, there is no longer slave or free, there is no longer male and female; for all of you are one in Christ Jesus." This verse proclaims the spiritual unity of all people in Jesus but manifestly does not call for social equality. When placed against other biblical teachings that establish and affirm hierarchies, Galatians 3:28 amounts to a call for quiescence. Don't worry about the inequality around you, the verse suggests, for everyone is equal spiritually. Such a message offers cold comfort to the people who suffer daily indignities in the material world.

MORALITY DURING THE MIDDLE AGES

The Bible's subjectivity on women, slavery, and other topics had little consequence in the days when Christians were a tiny minority within the Roman Empire. Their morality competed with that of other religious and philosophical systems. After Roman emperors made Christianity the official religion of the empire in the fourth century, and especially after Christianity came to dominate Europe in the following centuries, the stakes increased. The Bible became, in effect, the moral guidebook of the West. Not everyone during the Middle Ages accepted its moral code, but the Bible nevertheless wielded enormous influence over all of society's institutions.[10]

The conditions of medieval Europe were not conducive to reconsidering any aspect of the Bible's morality. Consistent with the Bible's teachings, Europeans believed that God himself had placed kings onto the throne.[11] The Old Testament consistently described God choosing the rulers of Israel and other nations. In the books of 1 and 2 Samuel, for example, God worked through his prophet to anoint the first king of Israel, Saul. When Saul proved to be a disappointment, God replaced him with David and pronounced that all subsequent kings would come from the Davidic line. God also identified the larger principle those episodes illustrated: "By me kings reign, and rulers decree what is just; by me rulers rule, and nobles, all who govern rightly" (Proverbs 8:15–16).

The New Testament reaffirmed the teachings of these Old Testament passages. As Paul explained, "Let every person be subject to the governing authorities; for there is no authority except from God, and those authorities that exist have been instituted by God. Therefore whoever resists authority resists what God has appointed, and those who resist will incur judgment" (Romans 13:1–2). Paul thereby endorsed the Old Testament conception of providence in which God guides human affairs by directly choosing rulers, which makes disobedience against them a sin. Paul's fellow apostle, Peter, made a similar point: "For the Lord's sake accept the authority of every human institution, whether of the emperor as supreme, or of governors, as sent by him to punish those who do wrong and to praise those who do right" (1 Peter 2:13–14).

The Bible thus provided the theological justification for what came to be called the divine right of kings. Ordinary people were expected to obey their rulers, not to question them, and certainly not to usurp their authority. Adomnan of Iona (624–704) spoke for many of his contemporaries in condemning regicide as a violation of the political order God had established.[12] Monarchs were not shy about pointing to God as the source of their authority. King Richard I of England (1157–1199) proclaimed, "I am born in a rank which recognizes no superior but God, to whom alone I am responsible for my actions."[13] Martin Luther would later cite Paul's letter to the Romans in calling upon God's appointed rulers to quash the Peasant Rebellion of 1525.[14]

The masses had little opportunity to develop a religious perspective that could challenge these dominant understandings. As I explained in chapter 5, theologians before Roger Williams did not think the Bible required rulers to establish and protect religious freedom. Theologians instead denied that individuals had the right to publicly proclaim whatever religious and moral beliefs they wished. Pagans faced social ostracism and the destruction of their temples, while Jews often endured pogroms, expulsions, and forced conversions. Christian heretics, meanwhile, could be sent to one of the various institutions of the Inquisition. Within this climate of religious repression, few dared to openly dispute the Bible's moral teachings.

Intellectual life was no more hospitable to a moral rethinking, partly because writers assumed rather than investigated the truth of the biblical texts. They thought faith was the fundamental starting point for any intellectual activity. As Augustine (354–430) said, "Understanding is the reward of faith. Therefore do not seek to understand in order to believe, but believe that you may understand."[15] Anselm (1033–1109) captured the essence of this idea through his famous phrase, "faith seeking understanding."[16] Such an approach turned intellectual works into mere extensions of the Christian worldview. Bonaventure (1221–1274) went even further in asserting that "all divisions of knowledge are handmaidens to theology," with reading and studying serving as a means through which "faith may be strengthened, God may be honored."[17] With faith as their foundational assumption, intellectuals of the Middle Ages could not conceive of grounding morality on anything other than God's revelation.

Any writers who might have been inclined to reject some aspects of biblical morality knew they would face the full might of the Church. As early as the ninth century, Christian leaders worked to suppress the printing, distribution, and reading of books advancing heretical ideas. In 1559 Pope Paul IV formalized this practice through his List of Prohibited Books ("Index Librorum Prohibitorum") that contained the names of several hundred authors.[18] Galileo had already learned what happened when a person questioned a belief the Church held dear. For suggesting that the earth revolved around the sun, Galileo was tried by the Inquisition, threatened with torture, and placed under house arrest for the remainder of his life.[19] A person who found flaws in the Bible's moral teachings could expect far worse, which greatly narrowed the scope of intellectual inquiry. As of 1600, then, the moral system of the West was drawn from the Bible, elaborated by the Church, and enforced through rigid hierarchies.

SHIFTING TOWARD A MORALITY BASED ON DELIBERATION

Several forces combined to make it possible in the modern era to discover moral truths through a deliberative process. The Protestant Reformation divided Christendom and gave rise to competing authorities on religious and moral questions. Protestants attacked Catholic beliefs about salvation, the sacraments, and other aspects of Christian theology and practice, and Catholics responded by saying Protestants were risking eternal damnation by abandoning the institutional life that had sustained Christians for centuries. Protestants themselves soon splintered into groups of Calvinists, Lutherans, Anabaptists, and others making different and often contradictory assertions. Ordinary people could easily become confused by the various charges and countercharges.

Intellectuals witnessed this fracturing of society and searched for a method to establish truths that would not depend on a person's prior religious commitments. Could knowledge be founded on grounds simultaneously accepted by Catholics, Protestants, Jews, and other religious groups?[20] Through his *Discourse on the Method*, René Descartes

(1596–1650) offered reason as the solution. Prior to Descartes, intellectuals typically defended a claim by saying it was supported by authorities, including the great minds before them. The medieval practice of scholasticism, for example, rested on reconciling apparent contradictions among the accepted authorities on a topic. Descartes instead proposed using deductive reasoning to discover what could not be doubted, which led to his famous starting point of "I think, therefore I am." He proceeded to explain in a step-by-step fashion the conclusions that he thought logically followed.

Other writers included empiricism and induction, especially through the scientific method, as a means to discover truth. Francis Bacon (1561–1626) propounded scientific inquiry through observation, with contentious religious beliefs set aside so that investigations could proceed through empirical means alone. Hugo Grotius (1583–1645) drew from history to establish the principles of international law that would hold even if "there is no God" or "the affairs of men are of no concern to him."[21] Like other intellectuals of his era, Grotius sought a kind of knowledge that did not require any religious assumptions. John Locke (1632–1704) later stated that "reason must be our last judge and guide in everything."[22] Descartes, Bacon, Grotius, and Locke were all Christians, but their method of establishing truth empowered their intellectual descendants to question key aspects of Christianity, including the Bible's moral system.

Those challenges could not emerge until there were at least some protections in place for the freedom of speech and religion. It's never easy for someone to argue against an accepted consensus. Such people are often seen by their contemporaries as a threat to the social order, and they risk estrangement from family and friends. If the state persecutes them, it will usually be difficult for their ideas to spread. The gradual development of political freedoms was thus a prerequisite to a more open discussion about moral questions. In order to deliberate over morality, people must be free to state their views without fear of persecution. As various countries began expanding the boundaries of permissible speech and religion during the Enlightenment, intellectuals pushed new ideas about morality and other subjects.

For example, Italian jurist and philosopher Cesare Beccaria (1738–1794) applied Enlightenment principles to the realm of criminal justice. Beccaria held that the justice system must be reformed so that penalties would be levied in a manner proportional to each crime. He rejected the concept of retribution and thought punishment could be justified only for purposes of reforming the offender, deterring future crime, or protecting society while the offender was incapacitated. Hundreds of crimes at that time were subject to the death penalty, but he called for eliminating its use entirely, and he also wanted to ban the use of torture to extract confessions.[23]

English philosopher Jeremy Bentham (1748–1832) advocated reforms across an even broader range of domains. Denying that religion should control discussions over moral questions, Bentham proposed an alternative system based on what he called the "greatest happiness of the greatest number." He made a strong case for the freedom of speech and religion as tools that promote human flourishing. Bentham wanted to abolish not only the death penalty but also slavery and the use of corporal punishment, even for children. Bentham was also an early advocate for respecting animals as sentient beings.[24]

MAKING DELIBERATION MORE INCLUSIVE

Beccaria, Bentham, and other intellectuals of the Enlightenment read each other's works and communicated through a system historians have called the "Republic of Letters."[25] The correspondence between them, much of it preserved in archives and libraries in Europe and North America, served as a kind of intellectual activity in itself. Intellectuals would stake claims, make arguments, and comment on the works of both their direct correspondent and other writers. The Republic of Letters was thus a forum for deliberation, complementing the communication that occurred through books, journals, periodicals, and the meetings of literary and scientific academies. Within these assorted outlets for communication, knowledge had to be justified through reason rather than faith, tradition, and authority.[26] In intellectual life one could no longer defend a claim by saying, "This is what the Bible teaches," or "I'm just affirming what Christians have always believed."

Boosted by the spread of literacy and the growth of the publishing industry, the works of Enlightenment authors circulated well beyond their fellow intellectuals. Starting from a base of approximately 20 percent when averaged across European countries in 1600, literacy doubled to about 40 percent by 1700.[27] The number of books published in English rose fourfold between the beginning of the seventeenth and eighteenth centuries, and similar patterns can be seen in German and other European languages.[28] People could not only read the books in private but also discuss them in salons, cafés, coffeehouses, and Masonic lodges. These new venues combined to form what philosopher and social theorist Jürgen Habermas has described as a "public sphere."[29]

Although it provided a forum for deliberation and thereby improved on what had previously existed, the public sphere nevertheless included only a limited range of voices. As Habermas himself acknowledges, the public sphere reflected the values and mindsets of the rising middle class of male property owners as opposed to wage laborers or the enslaved. Women were also largely excluded from its venues. English writer Mary Wollstonecraft (1759–1797) highlighted that problem in her *Vindication of the Rights of Woman*. She held that women were just as capable as men of engaging in the rational thought that characterized the Enlightenment. She acknowledged that women had not made as many intellectual contributions, which she explained through a lack of opportunities rather than a lack of abilities.[30]

Over the next two centuries, participation in deliberative venues expanded greatly. The literacy and education gap between men and women shrank, and authors such as Jane Austen, Marie-Anne de Bovet, and Concepción Arenal found a receptive audience in Western countries.[31] The shift from monarchies to democratic republics proceeded in the manner of two steps forward, one step backward. First white men with property, then white men without property, then men of all races, and finally—in the twentieth century—women gained the right to vote in Western countries. Periods when democratic rights were taken from racial and ethnic minorities were typically followed by periods in which their rights expanded.[32] Mass education and nearly universal literacy gave more people than ever the opportunity to express their views about moral questions.[33]

As deliberation over morality became more inclusive starting in the eighteenth century, pressure mounted against one of the oldest of all human institutions: slavery. Men and women of all races pressed for abolition through pamphlets, essays, letters, novels, plays, and argumentative books. Former slaves publicized their experiences and unique insights through memoirs, speeches, and other means.[34] After nearly three hundred years of struggle, humanity eventually made moral progress in reaching a consensus that slavery is wrong. This consensus cuts across lines of nationality, race, gender, religion, language, income, region, and political affiliation. Every country on earth banned human bondage during either the nineteenth or twentieth centuries.[35]

We can now say that the biblical authors were not just wrong in judging slavery to be morally permissible, they were *objectively* wrong. The problem with the Bible is that it teaches the subjective morality of its authors rather than an objective morality for all of humanity. An objective morality must rise above the limited perspectives of any individual or group. Inclusive deliberation, a natural outgrowth of humanism, is a powerful method for fostering this objectivity. When diverse people with different identities interact as fellow human beings and subject their ideas to public scrutiny, they learn from each other, gain the opportunity to reconsider their views, and grow in their understanding of difficult topics. Although deliberation as it actually happens invariably fails to incorporate all relevant information and include all voices on equal terms, the kind of deliberation that has existed for the last few centuries has been sufficiently robust for us to conclude that it's immoral for one person to own another as property.

HUMANISM AND MORAL PROGRESS

The example of slavery points to a more general problem with the Christian worldview. If the Bible is the Word of God, as Christians believe, they cannot account for moral progress. God doesn't make mistakes, and you can't improve on a revelation that is already perfect. As stated by Kenneth Samples, a Senior Research Scholar at the apologetics ministry

Reasons to Believe, "The Bible reveals moral principles as being objective, universal, and unchanging."[36] It follows that mere mortals cannot discover a better moral code than the one the Bible presents. Christians have to accept whatever rules and commands God has communicated through his revelation even if they find them to be objectionable.

Such a stance eliminates the very possibility of moral progress, as the practice of slavery illustrates. The Bible was not unique in endorsing it, for virtually every ancient society and most medieval ones allowed holding someone as property so long as they were not a member of your own ethnic group and religion. During the last three centuries, humanity has accomplished something nearly everyone now views as moral progress: outlawing slavery worldwide and greatly shrinking its incidence. Christians have no means to make sense of this moral progress. They are compelled by the logic of their worldview to claim the Bible opposed slavery all along; otherwise, it could not have taught the "objective, universal, and unchanging" morality that Kenneth Samples and other apologists insist it contains.

A humanist, by contrast, can understand moral progress without engaging in verbal contortions to make the Bible say something it doesn't. To talk about moral progress, however, a humanist needs a standard by which to determine whether it has occurred. My definition of contractarian morality gives us that standard. Moral progress happens when beliefs about right and wrong emerge through inclusive deliberation instead of instinct, tradition, assertion, dogma, authority, power, conventional wisdom, or some other nondeliberative means. If we more closely approximate the ideals of inclusive deliberation, moral progress will follow.

This deliberation can only be as good as the information on which it relies, so advances in general knowledge often lead to a better morality. Some of the information a deliberation requires is empirical but not necessarily scientific. For example, a moral rethinking can be prompted by widespread learning about the lives of people in one's own and other societies. Such information can be acquired through face-to-face contact or from books, documentaries, news reports, or other sources. Other kinds of information that feed into deliberation are both empirical and scientific. As scientific knowledge accumulates, we can often improve on what was formerly considered moral. Whereas we might think an institution or practice is helping people, better science or a more rigorous investigation might demonstrate the opposite. We would then need to modify our actions to keep pace with the expanding knowledge.

Scientific and moral knowledge, then, are intimately connected. Conversely, an inaccurate understanding of the natural world can lead someone to harm other people, as we can see with respect to the Bible. It includes the instruction, "Thou shalt not suffer a witch to live" (Exodus 22:18). Through that command, the biblical authors implied that witches are, in fact, real and deserve to die. The Bible thereby helped create the conditions for the immoral behaviors of subsequent generations. You can't act morally if you base your actions on false beliefs about what is and is not present in your community.

Those false beliefs led to atrocities during the long era predating a scientific understanding of the world. In times of social and economic anxieties, Christians could point to witchcraft as the cause of whatever went wrong in their lives. If your cow died, or your crops failed, or your daughter caught a mysterious disease, you might conclude that witches in your village had cavorted with the devil and put a hex on you. That way of thinking brought hundreds of years of literal witch hunts in Europe and later the American colonies. Historians estimate that approximately forty thousand people, mostly women, were tortured and executed as alleged witches from the fifteenth through the eighteenth centuries. Many more lived in constant fear of facing false accusations.[37]

Most Christians today don't invoke witchcraft as their explanation for adverse events. They can appeal to biology, chemistry, geology, and other sciences to explain sickness, death, and natural disasters. As science writer Michael Shermer observes, scientific understanding about the causes of various phenomena enabled the subsequent moral progress in eliminating witch hunts.[38] The mistake the biblical authors made was in giving the command to kill witches in the first place, which encouraged people to indulge their fantasies. If there really was an omniscient God who inspired the Bible, he would have known that witches with the power to put a hex on people are a figment of the human imagination.

The Bible makes another scientific (and hence moral) mistake in how it handles epilepsy, which it portrays as a form of demon possession. Other ancient cultures held similar misunderstandings. The Babylonians linked seizures to the body's invasion by specific named spirits, while the Romans explained epilepsy as a generic curse of the gods.[39] The gospel stories show Jesus casting out the demons who caused epilepsy, including one from a boy who had regularly experienced convulsions since early childhood (Mark 9:14–29; see also Matthew 17:14–20 and Luke 9:37–43). The Bible's accounts led to systematic mistreatment of epileptics within Christian cultures. People with epilepsy have often been abused, shunned, and forced to undergo painful exorcisms by communities who attributed their seizures to demon possession.[40]

Through advances in science, we now know that epilepsy is a neurological condition with both genetic and environmental causes. It can't be cured, but medications can lessen the frequency and intensity of the seizures.[41] A person believed to be suffering from excess electrical activity in the brain is likely to be treated far better than someone understood to be harboring a demon. Although some Christians with epilepsy continue to be condemned by their family and community for demon possession, most now receive love, sympathy, and medical treatment.[42] That change is a prime example of moral progress.

Scientific advances, however, are not the only path to moral progress. Moral progress also happens when more people gain access to the centers of power in different societies around the world. If a narrow elite controls a particular society in an authoritarian or totalitarian manner, the accepted morality within it will be skewed toward their interests and beliefs. Any apparent consensus within such a system does not qualify as contractarian. When we see greater participation in political, economic, and social institutions from the full range of each society's inhabitants, the moral code that emerges will move closer to the ideals of contractarian morality.[43]

THE ERA OF HOMOSEXUALITY AS A SIN

The issue of homosexuality shows how moral progress happens. It is worth spending some time examining this progress, because it illustrates all of the key points of this chapter. Societies historically have differed greatly in how they viewed same-sex attractions and behaviors. In some Melanesian cultures, sexual experimentation with young men was a coming-of-age expectation for adolescent boys.[44] Love poetry between women testifies to lesbian relationships in ancient Greece and Rome.[45] Certain Native American cultures historically conceived of a "third gender," people who might serve in spiritual and ceremonial roles and engage in sexual acts with those whom outsiders might consider members of the same sex.[46]

Other cultures, most notably those of ancient Jews and Christians, have deemed homosexuality immoral, and the Bible records their beliefs on this subject. Most of the Bible's references do not provide the reasons why homosexuality must be condemned. In Leviticus 18:22, for example, the act of a man lying with another man is simply denounced as an "abomination." Leviticus 20:13 requires the death penalty for violators without explaining why the offense is so grievous that such a punishment is appropriate. Within the New Testament, male homosexuals appear on Paul's lists of sinners in 1 Corinthians 6:9–10 and 1 Timothy 1:9–11, but he doesn't tell the reader why he placed them with adulterers, drunkards, thieves, and liars. The only exception to the Bible's sparse treatment of homosexuality occurs in Romans 1:26–27 and the surrounding text, where Paul offers a sketch of an argument involving creation, nature, and degrading passions.

Modern Christians such as theologian Robert Gagnon have attempted to reconstruct in great detail the reasons lying behind the biblical system, but the reasons are ultimately irrelevant.[47] Christians hold that the Bible is the Word of God, meaning that the biblical authors worked under divine inspiration to write what they did. Once those authors declared sexual activity between two people of the same sex to be sinful, their writings settled the matter for subsequent generations of Christians. If you think disputes over whether homosexuality is moral or immoral can only be resolved through publicly articulated reasons that can be discussed and debated, you're working within a humanist rather than a Christian framework.

After Christianity became the dominant religion of the West, its teachings about homosexuality (and other topics) went largely unquestioned. Rulers and local communities used many different means to enforce the biblical morality. Depending on where they lived, men during the Middle Ages caught engaging in homosexual acts could be tortured, castrated, and executed.[48] Some people managed to carry out the forbidden behaviors in secret. Scholars have documented indications of covert same-sex love among people who knew better than to openly and flagrantly violate the Christian ethics of their society.[49] Demonstrating broad assent to those ethics, writers of the Middle Ages did not challenge them.[50] The moral code on homosexuality rested not on public deliberation or any other form of reason but rather on the tradition, power, and authority of the Church and its scriptures. Accordingly, the societal consensus of that era does not meet the definition of contractarian morality I elaborated in chapter 3.

The dawn of the Enlightenment opened up possibilities for rethinking some moral questions, but not homosexuality. For fear of a backlash, Jeremy Bentham decided not to release his essay using utilitarian principles to call for repealing antisodomy laws, and his thoughts on the matter lay dormant until scholars published his essay in 1978.[51] Those who violated the accepted sexual ethics of Bentham's time continued to face criminal prosecution and social ostracism. After a long period when it received little public attention, homosexuality finally became a subject of interest to a handful of medical professionals at the end of the nineteenth century.[52] Most of them agreed with Austro-German psychiatrist Richard von Krafft-Ebing in calling it a form of perversion.[53]

The leading edge of a moral revolution occurred in 1897 when German doctor and scientist Magnus Hirschfeld founded the Scientific-Humanitarian Committee, the first LGBT advocacy organization in history. Hirschfeld thus kickstarted a long process whereby moral beliefs about homosexuality would eventually come to be formed through the means I have advocated, inclusive deliberation. The Scientific-Humanitarian Committee worked to decriminalize sodomy, promote scientific research, and influence public opinion. In 1919 Hirschfeld proceeded to found the Institute for Sexual Science. Until the Nazis closed it down in 1933 and staged a public burning of its library and archival collections, the Institute collected research materials, published journals, served as a clearinghouse of information, and offered counseling services.[54] The Nazis later conducted a systematic campaign to arrest gays and send them to concentration camps, where they were frequently beaten, castrated, and killed.[55]

The rest of the Western world was no more ready to engage the subject of homosexuality through open-ended discussion and dialogue. During World War II, the United States government sought to purge gays from the military, and several thousand service members were discharged. A few years later the government attempted to locate and fire all gays working in federal departments and agencies.[56] In reviewing and summarizing these efforts, the US Senate in 1950 reported that "considerable progress has been made in removing homosexuals and similar undesirable employees from positions in the Government."[57] Meanwhile, the police in major cities regularly made arrests in the bars, beaches, and parks where gays congregated.[58] News articles at midcentury covering homosexuality typically included words like "perversion," "the underworld," and "sexual deviancy."[59]

MORAL PROGRESS ON HOMOSEXUALITY

These cultural perceptions could not change until a conversation *about* gays and lesbians began to include them as participants in a deliberative process. Fearing prosecution by the state and hostility from employers, landlords, businesses, and even their own family and friends, gays and lesbians often stayed closeted during the first half of the century.[60] After World War II, a small vanguard formed organizations to share experiences, create solidarity, promote research and education, and advocate for their rights. These groups included Arcadie (France), the League of 1948 (Denmark), and the Center for Culture and Recreation (Netherlands).[61] All of them operated on shoestring budgets and struggled to gain attention and support from other members of their own community, let alone the larger public. Within the United States, the Mattachine Society (formed in 1950) and Daughters of Bilitis (formed in 1955) attracted a total of only six mentions, most of them fleeting, in the *New York Times* from their founding up to 1965.[62]

The LGBT groups were also fighting an uphill battle for respect from scientists and doctors. In 1952 the American Psychiatric Association (APA) published its *Diagnostic and Statistical Manual* (*DSM*), which soon became the standard reference manual among mental health counselors, therapists, and researchers. The expert committee that constructed and compiled the *DSM* labeled homosexuality a type of "sexual deviation" within the larger category of "sociopathic personality disturbances." To document the disturbances each patient presented, the *DSM* instructed clinicians to "specify the type of the pathologic behavior, such as homosexuality, transvestitism, pedophilia, fetishism and sexual sadism (including rape, sexual assault, mutilation)."[63] Homosexuality's place on that list is a striking indicator of scientific understandings at midcentury.

Beginning in the late 1950s, these scientific understandings started to look shaky. Psychiatrists now agree that the research about homosexuality feeding into the original *DSM* lacked scientific rigor.[64] The *DSM* authors had failed to consider the possibility that gays sometimes exhibited mental disorders not because of anything intrinsic to their sexual orientation but because the larger society had marginalized them. In addition, the research available to the *DSM* authors consisted largely of case reports of gays who had sought psychiatric help for anxiety, depression, schizophrenia, or some other problem. Such individuals were not representative of gays within the larger population. In an effort to study the subject through more reliable methods, UCLA psychologist Evelyn Hooker recruited samples of ordinary gay and straight men and administered tests of their psychological functioning. The pioneering study she published in 1957 showed no differences between the two groups, and her research proved to be the first crack in the scientific consensus.[65]

Meanwhile, gays and lesbians continued organizing. The relatively accommodationist groups of the 1950s gave way to a more confrontational LGBT movement in the late 1960s. Whereas previously the police, national security officials, psychiatrists, and other medical professionals were the dominant actors shaping how society addressed the issue of homosexuality, now gays and lesbians themselves were getting involved.[66] One of their most important efforts came in challenging the *DSM*'s classification of homosexuality as a mental illness. In 1973 the APA's executive board removed the controversial designation from the *DSM*, and its membership ratified the decision in a lopsided vote. Within the revised *DSM*, homosexuality per se was not a mental illness and only became problematic if a person did not accept their sexual orientation.[67]

The APA's machinations were both cause and consequence of what was happening within the larger society. For most of Western history, homosexuality was not a subject to be discussed in polite company. It was instead regarded as a sin that both the Bible and Christian leaders condemned. Beginning in the 1970s, sexual orientation emerged as a subject of public debate. People began making arguments about all aspects of homosexuality, including the fundamental question of whether it should be considered moral or immoral. In short, people began deliberating over the issue. A person in earlier eras could hold their position without ever being asked to defend it, but the need to articulate reasons for one's position increased by the end of the twentieth century. The greater attention to homosexuality made it a subject to be engaged through public deliberation.

This deliberation drew from new research in psychology, neuroscience, genetics, and cognate fields. Simon LeVay's influential 1991 article found differences between gay and straight men in the size and functioning of the hypothalamus region of the brain. His research suggested that sexual orientation originated in, or could be understood through, structural features of the brain.[68] Subsequent research used standard techniques of behavioral genetics involving identical and fraternal twins to document genetic influences on sexual orientation.[69] Research in the twenty-first century by Terrance Williams and his colleagues found biological markers of homosexuality in the ratio of the length of a person's index and ring fingers.[70] In its 2008 statement, the American Psychological Association summarized the accumulated research suggesting that "most people experience little or no sense of choice about their sexual orientation," a disposition that most likely results from a complex interplay of "nature and nurture."[71]

The conclusions of this scientific research gradually filtered into the public consciousness. Although ordinary people do not read scientific journals in their spare time, they can learn about the findings indirectly from the news media, medical professionals, or conversations with friends and family. Over time, more people came to accept the scientific evidence indicating that sexual orientation is not a choice and that it has strong biological influences. In 1977 the Gallup Organization for the first time asked a random sample of Americans the following question: "In your view, is being gay or lesbian something a person is born with, or due to factors such as upbringing and environment?" In 1977, only 13 percent of Americans thought sexual orientation was something a person was born with, a figure that rose all the way to 50 percent by 2018.[72] These changes matter because they affect how people think about other aspects of sexual orientation. As political scientists Mark Joslyn and Donald Haider-Markel have shown, people who believe in genetic causes are more likely to think same-sex attractions and behaviors are moral and to support civil rights for gays and lesbians.[73] In a manner similar to what happened with respect to epilepsy, witches, and other subjects, scientific advances allowed more heterosexuals to form their opinions through empirically supported knowledge as opposed to tradition, prejudice, or appeals to authority.

A second key factor that expanded the pool of information available to heterosexuals was the presence of gays and lesbians in their social networks. For most of the twentieth century, it was uncommon for heterosexuals to believe they personally knew someone who was gay or lesbian.[74] Under those conditions, it was easy for them to presume that the anonymous homosexuals were all perverts and deviants. Beginning in the 1970s, gays and lesbians increasingly came out of the closet to their friends, family, coworkers, and neighbors. A moral and political conversation that formerly excluded them now treated their experiences and perspectives as pertinent information.

The greater inclusiveness of the conversation had important impacts on the conclusions heterosexuals reached. Once they realized they knew individuals who were gay or lesbian, many of them dropped the crude stereotypes they formerly held. They increasingly came to see that gays and lesbians show the same range of variation as straight people on just about any trait one could imagine, differing only in the objects of their romantic attractions. Many studies have shown that heterosexuals with a friend or family member who is gay or lesbian are more liberal on the corresponding moral and political issues.[75] Data collected by the Pew Research Center in 2013 suggests that this correlation is, in fact, causal. In Pew's survey, one of every seven Americans said they had changed their minds in favor of same-sex marriage within the last several years. The most common reason they cited for their change was knowing a person who is gay or lesbian, which prompted them to consider the matter more thoroughly.[76] Inclusive deliberation thus enabled moral progress, just as a humanist would predict.

CHRISTIANITY AND THE WEST

Of course, many Christians still adhere to the Bible's teachings on homosexuality and reject the notion that we have made moral progress on that subject. Virtually all Christians, however, embrace certain ideas that have emerged during the last few centuries in the West and around the world. In fact, Christian apologists such as sociologist Alvin Schmidt assert that Christianity deserves the credit for core elements of the Western mentality. Schmidt writes: "Many today who disparage Christianity may not know or believe that, were it not for Christianity, they would not have the freedom that they presently enjoy. The very freedom of speech and expression that ironically permits them to castigate Christian values is largely a by-product of Christianity's influences that have been incorporated into the social fabric of the Western world."[77]

Theologian and pastor Douglas Wilson similarly asserts that "our institutions of liberty" and "the idea of checks and balances" reflect the influence of Christian doctrines.[78] Philosopher and priest Joseph de Torre holds that "democracy, in its fully developed modern form, is a result of the final political flowering of Gospel values."[79] Beyond their contributions to democracy, those values also supposedly made slavery unthinkable. Melinda Penner of the apologetics ministry Stand to Reason says Christianity is responsible for the belief, now almost universally shared, that it's immoral for one person to own another as a slave.[80] Columnist Ross Douthat echoes Penner in giving Christianity credit for such advances as "abolitionism," "universal human rights," and the "separation of church and state."[81]

Are these assertions correct? Do virtually all positive developments in the West stem from Christianity? To answer these questions, we need to reach back to ancient times. Christianity began to exist immediately after Jesus's death, steadily won converts among former pagans, and in 380 became the official religion of the Roman Empire. Christianity then profoundly shaped the European societies that formed after the empire's breakup. Except within scattered communities that adhered to paganism or Judaism, Christianity was dominant from late antiquity through the Middle Ages. Historian Brad Gregory gives a useful summary of Christianity's power in Europe on the eve of the Reformation, and that power still held as of 1600. Gregory observes that Christianity

> *played a central role in everyday life—from the primary relationships between family and kin to the practice of politics and commerce. Social relationships and gender expectations were inseparable from Christian norms. And both public and private morality were conceived in Christian terms. Rather than standing apart from government or courts of justice, religion informed both politics and law. At the same time, Christianity was not aloof from the buying and selling of goods and pursuit of profit; Christian ethical teachings sought to shape economic transactions and restrain greed. Education, from the teaching of ABCs in humble small-town primary schools through instruction in one of Europe's sixty or so universities, was imbued with Christian ideas.*[82]

In writing this summary, Gregory drew from the work of other historians who have shown how Christian beliefs and principles diffused throughout Europe and affected all aspects of life. To wrap my head around the lengthy period of Christian dominance from roughly 380 through 1600, I find it helpful to reflect on my own genealogy. My mom has acquired records pointing to our earliest known ancestors as Harrison Deal (born 1843) and Sarah Britton (born 1846), who are my great-grandparents. The century and a half separating their births and mine seems like an eternity. In fact, they lived so far in the past that I know nothing about them except their names, and yet the distance between 380 and 1600 was many times greater. Surely that was enough time for the true essence of Christianity to manifest itself. Thus, we can evaluate Christianity's contributions by examining its record as of 1600.

How many of the various achievements that apologists attribute to Christianity existed by then? Let's start with opposition to slavery. As of 1600, not a single theologian had interpreted the Bible as prohibiting the ownership of human beings. Slavery had been replaced with serfdom in Europe despite rather than because of what theologians thought the Bible taught. How about the freedom of speech and religion? Alvin Schmidt and other apologists think these liberties stand among Christianity's greatest gifts to the world. So where were the theologians before 1600 who wanted vigorous protections for blasphemy, heresy, or other kinds of speech that political and religious authorities found offensive? Today's apologists believe that Christian values include not only the freedom of speech and religion but also democracy, which would have been news to earlier generations of theologians. How come nobody before 1600 held that God preferred democracy as the best political system? Why did God instead inspire his biblical writers to demand obedience to the monarchs and emperors that he personally installed into power?

Apologists also routinely assert that Christian doctrines lead to support for universal human rights. They rarely pause to consider why their predecessors before 1600 disagreed. Through late antiquity and the Middle Ages, the concept of rights for anyone barely existed, let alone universal human rights that applied to women, gays and lesbians, and racial and religious minorities. By 1600 Christianity had dominated the West for over a thousand years and had reshaped beliefs and practices relating to family, gender, culture, politics, law, commerce, education, and the arts. If there was something within Christian texts and traditions that called for universal human rights, why didn't any of the great minds of the Church discover it? Why did Augustine, Anselm, Bonaventure, Aquinas, Luther, Zwingli, Calvin, and others all fail to see the doctrine that twenty-first-century apologists so confidently attribute to their religion?

The answer to all of these questions is that Christianity today is not the same religion it was back then, and Christians don't worship the same God. Whether they were Protestant, Catholic, or Orthodox, the Christians of 1600 largely accepted the God of the Bible. That God orders genocide, endorses slavery, intervenes in free will, gives power to tyrants and despots, requires the death penalty for minor offenses, and punishes entire groups for the behavior of one of their members. The God of the Bible does not proclaim the need for democracy, freedom of speech and religion, and universal human rights. He is instead a tribalistic God who commands people to obey the rulers he personally installs on the throne.

The ways in which Christian apologists handle the problematic biblical passages remind me of a book series I enjoyed as a child. In the Choose Your Own Adventure books, the reader gets transported into the world of a traveler, zookeeper, musician, or some other character. The reader takes the perspective of the character (the books are written in the second person) and regularly comes to decision points. If you pick one option, you turn to a certain page to continue the story; if you pick another option, you turn to a different page. In the twenty-first century, these books spawned a broader genre known as "gamebooks" that follow the same approach in allowing readers to decide how they want the story to develop.[83]

It's all in good fun when you Choose Your Own Adventure. It's another matter entirely when apologists think they have the license to Choose Your Own God. Once someone commits to believing in the Christian God as depicted in the Bible, they can't (legitimately, at least) manipulate the biblical passages and stories to obtain a different and more palatable God. Yet as I've shown in previous chapters, that's precisely what apologists do through the Ignore, Rationalize, Reinterpret, and Mystify strategies. Rank-and-file Christians commonly embrace the claims supported by these strategies without realizing the extent to which apologists have refashioned the God of the Bible in their own image.

After observing the state of Christian apologetics, one has to wonder: What happened since 1600 to encourage Christians to create this new God? How have they managed to conceive a better God than the one the Bible portrays? The answer is a combination of factors both external and internal to the practice of Christianity. Among the external causes, the most important is secularization, the process through which religion lost much of its social influence and power.[84] Recall how historian Brad Gregory described the ways in which Christianity used to serve as the overarching framework for all aspects of Western societies. Beginning in the 1600s, Christianity gradually became only one viewpoint among many in the public arena. Descartes and his successors grounded truth in reason rather than tradition, faith, authority, and dogma. Non-Christians and Christian heretics gained the freedom to express their views openly, without fear of persecution. Women and racial minorities fought for their rights and began contributing to the public dialogue on a range of matters. The ideals of inclusive deliberation were more closely approximated through this greater participation across lines of race, ethnicity, gender, religion, and other identities.

Responding to these external forces, Christians reformed their religion from within and began envisioning a new and improved God. In 1644 Roger Williams offered a powerful case for religious freedom, and Christians throughout the West eventually stopped believing that God wanted them to punish people for blasphemy and heresy.[85] Starting with Samuel Sewall in 1701, Christian thinkers began interpreting the Bible to indicate that God opposed slavery and required abolition.[86] By the twentieth century, virtually all Christians came to believe their religion was incompatible with human bondage. Meanwhile, the Puritans' congregational styles of church governance led them to think about democratic practices for the larger society, and other Christian groups followed in their footsteps.[87] Christians also offered innovative interpretations of God's revelation in the Bible to defend free speech, women's rights, and gay and lesbian rights.[88]

To be sure, there were holdouts at every step of the way. During the eighteenth and nineteenth centuries, advocates of slavery could cite chapter and verse to demonstrate God's backing for their position.[89] In 1864 Pope Pius IX released his "Syllabus of Errors" and condemned, among other modern ideas, the freedom of religion and the separation of church and state.[90] Opponents of women's rights argued that God communicated through the Bible the need for women to be politically and socially subservient to men.[91] Even today, many conservative Christians follow the Bible in denouncing homosexuality as a sin. Still, the larger pattern of recent centuries has seen Christians accommodating themselves to the modern age. Inclusive deliberation thus facilitated moral progress not only for society at large but also within Christianity. Christians reformulated their God into a divine being who stands on the right side of all moral questions and actually deserves worship.

THE DYNAMICS OF MORAL REGRESS

Having discussed how, when, and why moral progress happens, I need to also address the opposite process of moral regress. My definition of contractarian morality yields a conception of moral regress as a corollary. Namely, moral regress occurs when societies abandon aspirations for inclusive deliberation and instead establish a code of morality through some other means. Because broad participation in moral dialogue cannot happen without protections for civil liberties, moral regress typically goes hand in hand with eliminating basic freedoms. The modern world has witnessed this process most often when a small and unrepresentative group gained control over a particular society and imposed its ideology on everyone else. That ideology then justified policies, behaviors, and practices that both internal critics and outside observers recognized as atrocities. People holding beliefs disfavored by those in power were harassed, imprisoned, and even killed.

The Soviet Union under the influence of Marxism-Leninism wrote the playbook for this kind of moral regress. After overthrowing the government during the Russian Revolution of 1917, Vladimir Lenin's Bolsheviks banned other parties and turned Soviet Russia (and later the Soviet Union) into a one-party state. The Cheka, Lenin's secret police, arrested and deported intellectuals, scientists, and journalists, paving the way for state control over the media, education, and the worlds of art and culture. The rights to assembly, free speech, freedom of religion, and freedom of the press had already been tightly restricted under the czars, and they disappeared entirely with the rise of Marxism-Leninism. Lenin oversaw what came to be called the Red Terror, a program to exterminate counterrevolutionaries, property owners, and deserters from the Red Army.[92]

Upon Lenin's death in 1924, Joseph Stalin took the reins of power. Among his other abuses, Stalin conducted the Great Purge, a systematic effort to eliminate all threats to himself and the Soviet system more generally. Many writers and artists—the very people most capable of articulating and disseminating a competing moral vision—were rounded up and sent to the Gulag. Leaders of the Communist Party and officers of the Red Army were summarily executed. Others were paraded before the public in show trials through which they were forced to confess to offenses both real and imagined. Massive surveillance by the secret police ferreted out information that could be used against anyone the regime targeted.[93]

Although the level of repression decreased under Stalin's successors, the Soviet Union stands as a prime example of moral regress. Rather than incorporating the perspectives of diverse people through extensive discussion and debate, Soviet leaders rigidly enforced the dogmas of Marxist-Leninist ideology and silenced actual and potential critics. They also exported to countries in the Soviet bloc a justification for squelching dissent through violence, intimidation, and the control of information. When workers and students organized protests in Hungary in 1956 and Czechoslovakia in 1968, the Soviets sent their tanks to crush the uprising. Leaders of the protests were jailed and executed.[94] The seventy-year history of the Soviet Union shows what can happen when revolutionaries backed by a violent ideology gain political power.

The experience of Germany under Adolf Hitler's Nazis would also make anyone's short list of the most notable examples of moral regress. Shortly after gaining power, Hitler dissolved all existing parties and outlawed the founding of new ones. The Nazis also sought to eliminate threats to their rule from civil society. They assumed leadership positions in agricultural, volunteer, professional, and recreational groups, and they pushed to reverse the momentum toward gender equality that had occurred in the previous decades. Asserting that the phrase "Emancipation of women" had been "invented by Jewish intellectuals," Hitler declared that the woman's world "is her husband, her family, her children, and her home."[95] Women's enrollment in institutions of higher education plummeted during the early years of Nazi rule.[96]

Limiting the participation of women in economic and political affairs was just one part of a larger Nazi strategy to control the national dialogue. Capitalizing on the chance to blame a fire in the Reichstag on enemies of the state, Hitler ended the right to assembly and the freedom of the press. The Nazis subsequently conducted a nationwide burning of books deemed un-German. Joseph Goebbels's propaganda ministry banned Jews and those labeled unsympathetic to the regime from working in the areas of art, culture, and media. During the Night of the Long Knives from June 30 to July 2, 1934, the Gestapo and the Schutzstaffel (SS) implemented extrajudicial killings of people designated as threats to the regime. Other political opponents were sent to concentration camps.[97]

Several years before the Holocaust, then, the Nazis had already eliminated civil liberties and ensured that only a narrow range of ideas could be publicly discussed. Like the Marxist-Leninists of the Soviet Union, they treated the party's principles as the undisputed truth rather than contentions that must be examined and evaluated by diverse participants. On questions including homosexuality, the role of women in society, and how Jews should be treated, the acceptable moral positions were established through fiat, not deliberation. The relatively little deliberation that did occur was certainly not inclusive. Within such a repressive climate, most Germans who might have been inclined to object to the Holocaust had learned to keep their views to themselves.

MORAL REGRESS AND MORAL PROGRESS

These examples of the Soviet Union and Nazi Germany illustrate a larger phenomenon, for no country can claim a clean record on the subject of moral regress. The French Revolution empowered a band of radicals whose project of terror included mass executions outside the rule of law. The rise of Marxism-Leninism in China, Cambodia, and North Korea brought a death count rivaling or exceeding that of the Soviet Union.[98] Japan has to answer for the Nanking Massacre, Turkey for its genocide of the Armenians, Rwanda for the Hutu genocide of the Tutsis, and Belgium for exploiting labor and spreading pandemics in the Congo Free State. Canada and Australia have brutalized indigenous peoples through colonization, forced assimilation, and the stealing of land and other resources.[99]

Moral regress has also occurred in my own country, the United States. It has a history of atrocities with respect to Native Americans, including bloody wars, land theft, the Trail of Tears, and the massacre at Wounded Knee. The United States has also practiced slavery, instituted Jim Crow laws, and sent Japanese Americans to internment camps. In recent decades many states have enacted laws and bureaucratic procedures that make it more difficult to vote and, not coincidentally, disproportionately affect members of minority groups.[100] Those actions undermine the ability of many Americans to participate in debates over the moral questions that invariably spill over into politics.

The United States also continues to reckon with its history of state-sanctioned violence against its Black population. For several decades following the end of Reconstruction, sheriffs and local officials in the South enabled and even participated in lynchings and other forms of mob actions.[101] The criminal justice system throughout America developed ingrained biases against Blacks in arrests, prosecutions, and sentencing.[102] Police killings of unarmed Black civilians, a long-standing problem across the country, prompted in recent years a national discussion about structural racism in law enforcement and the broader society. Any moral accounting of the United States has to address atrocities such as these in the country's past and present.

Thus, although the centuries since 1600 have witnessed moral progress in areas such as banning slavery, eliminating witch burnings, accepting same-sex love, promoting women's rights, establishing religious freedom, and humanely treating people with epilepsy and various kinds of mental illness, one cannot overlook the instances of stagnation and even regress. Moreover, the deliberation that exists today is not even close to being fully inclusive, and the empirical and scientific knowledge that feeds into it is partial and incomplete. As humans grow in our knowledge, and as more voices contribute to wide-ranging deliberation over moral disputes, we can expect some areas of current consensus to come under scrutiny.

These possibilities become even more interesting in light of the growth of Islam, which is adding more adherents worldwide than Christianity because of differences in birth rates.[103] These two religions have important similarities beyond their size, monotheistic orientations, and Abrahamic roots. Just as traditional Christian doctrines eventually came into conflict with modern ideas, so too with Islamic doctrines. Although it is not as far along as Christianity in accommodating itself to the modern age, Islam is nevertheless practiced differently now than it was when the Quran was first compiled and disseminated. In the next chapter, we'll see how some Muslims have tried to project their contemporary values back into their holy book.

CHAPTER 7

Intellectual Dishonesty in Islam

HUMANS ARE POLES APART FROM THE HYPER-RATIONALIST VULCANS OF *Star Trek*. We make many mistakes in perception and judgment that prevent us from forming and changing our beliefs based solely on logic, reason, and evidence. One of our most important limitations is confirmation bias, the tendency to seek out and remember the information that confirms what we already believe. Confirmation bias helps explain why people cling so tightly to false beliefs about topics such as science, history, and politics. Through the related phenomenon of motivated reasoning, people begin with their conclusion and then build the justification for it. Rather than following the evidence wherever it leads, people tend to construct a case for the belief they held at the outset while ignoring or distorting any contrary information, arguments, and perspectives.

Intellectual dishonesty happens when someone exhibits an extreme form of these tendencies. Unlike ordinary dishonesty, where someone knowingly misleads others, intellectual dishonesty requires a person to believe their own spin. People who engage in intellectual dishonesty start by deceiving themselves, with any deception of others happening subsequently and unintentionally. The root cause of intellectual dishonesty is someone rejecting any possible challenge to their position. Backed by a self-righteous certitude, the person violates the rules of critical thinking by cherry-picking evidence, introducing red herrings, or resorting to fallacious appeals to tradition, authority, or popularity. When presented with a different view, this misguided thinker will move the goalposts, make an ad hominem attack, or reformulate the opposing position into a straw man.

. Although intellectual dishonesty is a common phenomenon, as any reader of Internet forums can attest, faith commitments make a person especially vulnerable to it. Take the case of parents who have faith that God has a plan for every human being. Now imagine that they learn about a crash involving their daughter's school bus. If she died, they'll say that God has brought her home to a better place. If she was injured and taken to the hospital, they'll say that God is testing them. If she walked away unscathed, they'll praise God for saving her. God gets all the credit for good outcomes but never takes any blame for bad ones. When someone constructs their beliefs to be immune from any possible refutation, they're not engaging in an intellectually honest search for truth.

The problem here isn't religion—it's faith. As I'll explain in my concluding chapter, people can hold a religious identity while maintaining their integrity. Any stance based on faith, however, opens the door to intellectual dishonesty. This danger is evident in Christian and Muslim assumptions about God's revelation through written scriptures. In the words of Pope Paul VI, who served from 1963 to 1978, "The books of both the Old and New Testaments in their entirety, with all their parts, are sacred and canonical because written under the inspiration of the Holy Spirit, they have God as their author."[1] The apologetic website Whyislam.org nicely summarizes the standard Islamic doctrine holding that the Quran "consists of the unaltered and direct words of God, which were revealed through the Angel Gabriel to Muhammad, the final prophet of Islam, more than 1,400 years ago."[2] Under either the Christian or Muslim view of revelation, we have a holy book that communicates God's teachings to us.

If you're not a member of the relevant religions, you don't regard either the Bible or the Quran as God's revelation. You can instead treat them as profoundly human works worthy of the same respect as the writings of Plato, Confucius, and Shakespeare. You can learn from the holy books about the nature of human beings, how we can degenerate into depravity, and how we can aspire to something better. You can recognize their value as historical documents that give us insights into the societies that produced them. You can appreciate their lasting influence in the realms of art, architecture, literature, and popular culture in different parts of the world.

Pious Christians and Muslims, however, must treat their holy books differently. Once you accept through faith that either the Bible or the Quran is the Word of God, you're on the road to intellectual dishonesty. One way to avoid going any further is to remain blissfully ignorant of what your scriptures actually say. Both the Bible and the Quran are complex books that can be difficult to read and understand. Many believers therefore live their lives without seriously engaging their scriptures. Surveys conducted by Christian research organizations indicate that most Christians cannot accurately describe the contents of the text through which, they believe, God speaks to humanity.[3] Muslims, for their part, often memorize parts of the Quran in Arabic without even knowing the meaning of the words. Competitions throughout the Muslim world, including in countries where few people speak Arabic, reward children for their skills in reciting—not explaining or understanding—the Quran in its original language.[4]

Believers who are unaware of their holy book's problems need not engage in intellectual dishonesty to dismiss them. These people could be considered lazy for failing to reckon with their scriptures, but they can at least avoid committing acts of intellectual dishonesty. Apologists don't have that option. They often hold advanced degrees in relevant subjects and study their scriptures carefully. Lacking the ability to credibly claim ignorance, they must find other ways to handle the verses and passages in which God acts immorally himself or commands immoral behaviors among humans. In previous chapters, I have shown the lengths to which Christian apologists will go in attempting to sanitize the Bible. Because they take it on faith that God has revealed himself through a written text, they have to defend the moral system it presents even when doing so forces them into intellectual dishonesty.

In this chapter I extend my analysis to cover Islam, the second largest religion in the world. Many of its teachings are controversial, including those involving jihad, apostasy, blasphemy, homosexuality, religious freedom, personal liberties, and crime and punishment. All of those subjects deserve examination in their own right. To avoid tackling more material than I can reasonably handle in one chapter, I limit my focus to Islamic doctrines and practices relating to women. Doing so allows me to highlight in a concrete way the processes operating across the full set of important topics in Islam.

I further simplify my inquiry by restricting it to the Quran and its interpretations. The broader category of sharia (Islamic law) includes qiyas (analogical reasoning) and ijma (the judicial consensus of scholars). Those scholars, in turn, rely on the hadith (sayings, approvals, and actions attributed to Muhammad by oral tradition) and the sunnah (the example provided to Muslims by Muhammad's teachings and practices). Complications arise in that Islamic scholars disagree on which elements of hadith and sunnah they consider authentic and binding. Discussing, understanding, and evaluating sharia can therefore be difficult because of the complexity of the hadith, sunnah, qiyas, and ijma.

Many of the most controversial Islamic practices affecting women flow from these non-Quranic sources of authority. For example, the Quran requires women to dress modestly and cover their bodies (24:31) but does not prescribe the hijab (headscarf), let alone the niqab (face veil) or burqa (full body covering). The particulars regarding appropriate clothing for women are part of sharia through the hadith, sunnah, and ijma, which means there is no definitive Islamic position.[5] Similarly, there are references to female genital mutilation (FGM) in the hadith but not the Quran. Working from the available materials, the four major schools of jurisprudence in Sunni Islam have reached different conclusions as to whether FGM is mandated or, alternatively, optional but recommended.[6] Shiite leaders have generally derived their positions from forebears such as Ja'Far al-Sadiq, an influential scholar of the eighth century who recommended FGM.[7]

There is also no explicit grounding in the Quran for the Islamic doctrine that a woman needs four male witnesses to accuse a man of rape. This demand seems misogynistic because it makes rape allegations difficult to prove and can lead to an adultery punishment for the rape survivor, who must acknowledge that sex occurred in order to bring charges. The requirement for four male witnesses initially developed from Quranic verses and hadith relating to sexual transgressions other than rape.[8] Other hadith say that women are less intelligent than men, that women comprise most of hell's inhabitants, and that Muhammad married a six-year-old girl and consummated the marriage when she was nine.[9] Muslims who disapprove of those hadith can simply call them inauthentic even though they are just as thoroughly documented as others appearing in the same collections.

By contrast, any mainstream Muslim accepts the Quran as the Word of God. Whether they identify as Sunni or Shiite, whether they live in Pakistan, Somalia, the United States, or somewhere else, all Muslims (in principle, at least) ground their religion in God's revelation as conveyed through Muhammad. The authority of the Quran is typically accepted even by those Muslims who get labeled as "liberal" or "moderate." I therefore focus my investigation on the Quran and its interpretations, thereby avoiding the need to wade into disputes over other sources of authority in Islam.[10]

Just like Christians with respect to the Bible, contemporary Muslims who read the Quran, whether in the original or in translation, will encounter some puzzling moral precepts. Muslim apologists respond in the same four ways as their Christian counterparts. The familiar distinction between literal and metaphorical interpretations does not capture these responses, for the verses in question generally involve direct commands rather than stories or miracles that can be interpreted metaphorically. Instead, the apologetic moves are better understood as applications of the Ignore, Rationalize, Reinterpret, and Mystify strategies. Of course, the Quran also contains content that any modern person can heartily endorse. Muslims don't need to resort to an apologetic strategy when they accept a plain-sense reading of their scriptures. Accordingly, I will start with verses that virtually all Muslims can embrace before turning to the problematic material.[11]

QURANIC VERSES FAVORABLE TO WOMEN
You can learn about the society in which the Quran emerged by examining the text's prohibitions, for they tell us about the temptations of the earliest Muslims. As anthropologist Donald Symons explains, you'll

never read a legal or moral requirement in any society proclaiming, "Thou shalt not eat rocks," even though doing so would surely jeopardize a person's health. As a practical matter, nobody wants to eat rocks, and so there is no need to forbid it. By contrast, the motivations of anger, jealousy, revenge, and self-interest can incline people toward actions such as lying, theft, fraud, assault, and murder. Accordingly, systems of morality have to address those kinds of behaviors.[12]

Knowing this background, we can understand why the Quran tells Muslims to "compel not your female slaves into prostitution if they desire to be chaste" (24:33). A text wouldn't need to ban such a practice unless some slaveholders in the surrounding societies profited from trafficking their female slaves. I'll leave aside the larger question of how to view sacred scriptures that authorize owning human beings as property in the first place. If a slave system is going to exist, presumably everyone can agree that it's morally superior to forbid than allow the sex trafficking of enslaved people.

As another example of a Quranic teaching worthy of respect, consider its appeal to a future in which "the female infant buried alive is asked for what sin she was slain" (81:8–9). The obvious implication is that the female infant has not sinned at all, with the sinners instead being those who buried her. The Quran also mentions someone who must decide, after the birth of a female child, whether to "keep it in humiliation, or bury it in the dust? Behold! Evil indeed is the judgment they make!" (16:58–59). People in the twenty-first century don't need to be told not to commit infanticide by burying their daughters alive, but that was apparently not the case among some of those who first heard Muhammad's message.

The Quran also establishes a basis for women's independent ownership of property, which did not exist in Europe at that time. One verse instructs husbands and their families to "give the women their bridewealth as a free gift" (4:4). It was a common practice then, and still today in many parts of the world, for the bride to receive property from the groom's family, and the Quran allows the wife to retain possession even after a divorce or her husband's death: "It is not lawful for you to inherit women through coercion, nor to prevent them from marrying [again], that you may take away some of what you have given them, unless they commit a flagrant indecency" (4:19). The Quran's establishment of rules for women's ownership of property is often regarded even by Islam's critics as one of the book's pro-woman stances.[13]

Further support for gender equality can be found in the Quran's calls for marital harmony. One verse declares that God "created mates for you from among yourselves, that you might find rest in them, and He established affection and mercy between you" (30:21). Many other verses assume certain kinds of equality between men and women. For example, "believing men and believing women are protectors of one another" (9:71), and God promises that he "shall not let the work of any worker among you, male or female, be in vain; each of you is like the other" (3:195). Men and women have similar spiritual destinations in that "whosoever performs righteous deeds, whether male or female, and is a believer, such shall enter the Garden" (4:124; see also 16:97 and 40:40).

DOMESTIC VIOLENCE

If the Quran included only the verses above that seem to promote gender equality, it would be easy for a person with modern values to embrace the book's teachings. However, the Quran is patriarchal and misogynistic in many other places, and any honest appraisal of its morality must grapple with that content. I addressed problematic aspects of the Bible's teachings regarding women in chapter 6, and here I do the same for the Quran.

It will be instructive to begin with the domestic violence of husbands against wives, which is a problem not just for Islam but for all of humanity. Countries around the world have historically overlooked, tolerated, or even legitimized this practice. Yuhong Zhao, a law professor at the Chinese University of Hong Kong, observes that "throughout China's long history of civilization, domestic violence was seen neither as a crime nor as a societal problem to be addressed by courts or legislative bodies."[14] The World Health Organization estimates that the current incidence of intimate partner abuse is higher in the area containing India, Bangladesh, Sri Lanka, and Maldives than in any other world region.[15]

Nevertheless, every region has domestic violence in its past and present. Works of art and literature testify to how the subject was understood in medieval Europe. A French painting from the fourteenth century, for example, depicts a husband beating his wife with a stick as if the practice was ordinary and accepted.[16] In explaining the common law in England, William Blackstone in the eighteenth century noted, "The husband also (by the old law) might give his wife moderate correction," so long as he did not apply force "otherwise than lawfully and reasonably belongs to the husband for the due government and correction of his wife." The civil law, Blackstone observed, gave a husband the "same, or a larger authority over his wife." Depending on the severity of her infraction, the husband could either "beat his wife severely with scourges and sticks" or "use moderate chastisement."[17]

In 1641 the Massachusetts Bay Colony enacted the first known law outlawing domestic violence. The colony's law code stipulated, "Every married woman shall be free from bodily correction or stripes by her husband, unless it be in his own defence upon her assault. If there be any just cause of correction complaint shall be made to Authority assembled in some Court, from which only she shall receive it."[18] Among the other colonies and later the American states, however, there were no legal restrictions on wife beating until Tennessee outlawed the practice in 1850.[19] Other states soon followed, though domestic violence was rarely reported, let alone prosecuted, until the end of the twentieth century. Despite greater attention to the problem in the United States and other countries, the World Health Organization estimated in 2013 that 35 percent of all women worldwide had experienced intimate partner violence.[20]

Amid the global phenomenon of domestic violence, Islam has posed a particular challenge. The leading scholar of this subject is Ayesha Chaudhry, a professor of Islamic Studies and Gender Studies at the University of British Columbia. Chaudhry was raised Muslim in Canada by Pakistani immigrants, and she retained her adherence to Islam as an adult. She wrote an entire book on the Quranic verse (4:34) that discusses domestic violence. In Chaudhry's preferred translation, where she highlights the key Arabic words and how she renders them into English, the verse reads

Men are qawwāmūn (in authority) over women, because God has preferred some over others and because they spend of their wealth. Righteous women are obedient and guard in [their husbands] absence what God would have them guard. Concerning those women from whom you fear nushūz (disobedience/rebellion), admonish them, and/or abandon them in bed, and/or wa-ḍribūhunna (hit them). If they obey you, do not seek a means against them. God is most High, Great.[21]

Any observer can see why this verse puts Muslims in a bind, for it states that God grants men authority over women and requires wives to obey their husbands. Both of those provisions are nonstarters among people who believe in gender equality. To make matters worse, the Quran gives a husband the right to hit his disobedient wife as one of three possible ways to bring her to heel. Every Quranic translation before the last few decades rendered the operative word as "hit," "beat," "strike," "scourge," or something equivalent, though a handful of translators now try to eliminate the problem by picking a verb with an entirely different meaning.

The Quran's stance on wife beating should not be surprising, for the book originated in the cultural milieu of seventh-century Arabia. You wouldn't bat an eye if you discovered a similarly worded document from the seventh century in England, Poland, China, India, or anywhere else in the world. The difficulty here is that Muslims treat the Quran as sacred scripture. The ordinary laws, norms, and practices of a society can all be changed by later generations. To Muslims, however, the Quran reflects God's final revelation in his own language, and it has normative force for all time. A Muslim can't discard God's words merely because they conflict with the values of people living today.

Recognizing this dilemma, Chaudhry spent several years wrestling with the Quran's teaching. Long before she began her formal investigation, she prescribed the permissible answers it could yield, for she reports feeling "unsettled and defensive" upon first learning about the problematic verse while in middle school.[22] The verse implied that Islam rejected gender equality, elevated men over women, and allowed husbands to hit their wives—and yet, Chaudhry reports, "I did not believe any of these things to be true about Islam."[23] During her high school and college years, she talked to Muslim leaders who tried to justify the verse. They told her that God created men and women to be different from but complementary to each other, that husbands could not use excessive force while striking their wives, and that Islamic scholars through the ages had explained the justice of God's commands.[24]

Chaudhry tells her readers that she thought those responses failed to capture the full richness of the Islamic tradition.[25] For her doctoral research, she therefore studied the history of Islamic commentary and interpretation regarding the verse in Arabic, Urdu, and English. She expected to find alternative positions through which she could bring "to light egalitarian interpretations that treat men and women with equal human worth."[26] Yet her painstaking research left her disappointed. Although some Islamic jurists and scholars before the twentieth century thought the verse authorized only modest correction that did not cause injury, none of them "interpreted Q. 4:34 in a way that forbids husbands from hitting their wives."[27] However, she discovered in modern times a minority of voices who developed "fresh, creative, and resourceful" interpretations that reject the received wisdom from Islamic history.[28] According to these new readings, the Quran does not authorize any physical force, whether light or severe, and instead the command in question tells husbands to "have sexual intercourse" with their wives, "leave the marriage," or "travel."[29]

To any ordinary person, these reinterpretations are a transparent attempt to turn the Quran into a ventriloquist's dummy. Such a strategy is appealing to someone who wants the Quran to align with their personal values. By giving credence to the reinterpretations, Chaudhry is acting as an apologist. She decided way back in middle school what Islam teaches, and as an adult she learned the academic jargon and theories through which she could dress up her views. She takes a postmodern approach to interpretation and begins her book with an epigraph from Jacques Derrida. Chaudhry asserts that "religious texts mean what their communities say they mean. Texts do not have a voice of their own."[30] Accordingly, Muslims can reinterpret the Quran as a text condemning domestic violence simply by wanting it to be true.

Chaudhry's approach has allowed her to imprint her own outlook—which she calls "gender egalitarianism"—onto her holy book. Her solution, however, requires her to believe in a God unlike the one Muslims have historically worshipped. If domestic violence is a moral evil, as Chaudhry believes, why didn't God just say so clearly and explicitly in his scriptures? A competent human, let alone an omnipotent God, could convey that principle in one or two sentences. Why did God instead give us a Quran that expresses the opposite view, and which nobody interpreted any differently until some adventurous postmodernists came onto the scene in recent times? Just think about all the abuse of women that God, through his inarticulate utterances, authorized and enabled in the intervening centuries. Would anyone really want to worship such a God?

In contrast to modern Muslims such as Chaudhry, atheists have a coherent response: There is no God and therefore the Quran is of human rather than divine origins. When Muhammad made his regular trips to the cave to receive God's revelation, the voice he heard was his own. He might well have thought he was conveying God's message, but we don't have to believe him. The scriptures Muhammad bequeathed were instead shaped by the social environment in which he formed his values. Whereas domestic violence was acceptable to him and other male leaders of his time and place, people of the twenty-first century needn't agree.

RAPE WITHIN SLAVERY

We can observe similar dynamics in the controversy over a 2017 lecture by Jonathan A. C. Brown, who was raised Christian and converted to Islam in 1997. Brown now serves as a professor of Islamic Studies at Georgetown University and director of its Prince Alaweed bin Talal Center for Muslim-Christian Understanding. After listening to his lecture, one of Brown's critics alleged that he "condones rape and slavery under sharia."[31] The fallout from Brown's lecture received media coverage in a range of outlets including the *Washington Post*, *National Review*, and *Crisis Magazine*, a Catholic periodical.

This was not the first time Brown had commented on these subjects. In a Facebook post from two years earlier, he wrote:

I think people have a lot of things mixed up in their minds, forming a sort of outrage soup that they can't deal with. I think one has to proceed in an orderly way 1) slavery is, in general, allowed in Islamic law. 2) It's very possible (and it's actually happened) to declare that slavery is no longer permissible, whether due to consistent failings in treatment of slaves or the decision of governments for the common good of the Muslim community. 3) But it's not possible to say that slavery is inherently, absolutely, categorically immoral in all times and places, since it was allowed by the Quran and Prophet. 4) Slave women do not have agency over their sexual access, so their owner can have sex with them.[32]

It's not difficult to see the explosive potential of Brown's post, and he developed his views further in his controversial lecture. Interestingly, he barely mentioned Islam at all during his formal presentation, focusing instead on the different labor arrangements that historically have been grouped together under the umbrella term "slavery." To Brown, slavery "can mean so many things that it's not very useful for accurate communication."[33] He concluded: "Instead of fixating on a word or an ill-defined category, it is much more useful to focus on regulating conditions and protecting people's rights in order to prevent such extreme debasement. As hopefully my next essay will show, this is precisely what the sharia aimed to do."[34]

If the lecture had ended there, Brown might have avoided public scrutiny of his remarks. Unfortunately for him, the audience forced him to clarify his position during the question-and-answer period. After summarizing one questioner's belief in the universal wrongness of slavery, defined as the ownership of human beings as property, Brown invoked the example of Muhammed: "The prophet of God who lays out Islam had slaves. He had slaves, there's no denying that. Are you more morally mature than the prophet of God? No, you're not."[35] A few minutes later, Brown remarked, "I don't think it's morally evil to own somebody."[36]

Refusing to quit while he was behind, Brown answered a final question involving a male slaveholder's right under Islamic law to have sex with a female slave. The Quranic verse governing this matter (4:24) extends that right to the master even if his female slave is married. The verse tells men that "married women [are forbidden unto you] save those whom your right hands possess," with the phrase "those whom your right hands possess" serving throughout the Islamic scriptures as a euphemism for slaves. As I explained earlier, the Quran bans a slaveholder from forcing a female slave into prostitution, but the same text grants him sexual access to her. The Quran giveth and the Quran taketh away.

The resulting practices are indistinguishable from rape because an enslaved woman has no legal or social standing to reject her owner's demands. The questioner thus put Brown on the hot seat. Can he defend the Quran on this point? Brown replied: "The way I would respond to that is to say that, as, I mean this is just a fact. This isn't a judgment, this is a fact, okay? For most of human history, human beings have not thought of consent as the essential feature of moral, of morally correct sexual activity. And second, we fetishize the idea of autonomy, to the extent that we forget, again, who's really free? Are we really autonomous people? And what does autonomy mean?"[37]

Upon hearing his answers, most people would think Brown is playing word games to defend an abomination. Within the scope of this book, his answer is a clear example of the "Rationalize" strategy. Almost everyone today, regardless of their religious affiliation, will find his rationalizations hard to swallow. Our contemporary expectations of consent in sexual relations have resulted from a centuries-long struggle through which women have fought for equality in the bedroom, courtroom, workplace, and community. If a woman has no power to give or deny consent, as with female slaves in the Quran, outside observers can rightfully call that situation rape.

Of course, rape within slavery is not unique to Islam. Whenever slavery exists, a male slaveholder can easily feel entitled to sex with a female slave, and she cannot realistically say no. Although there is no way to know how often slaveholders historically have wielded this power, we know they did so at least sometimes. Documentary evidence and DNA tests, for example, indicate that Thomas Jefferson had several children with one of his female slaves, Sally Hemmings. As an enslaved person, she lacked the authority to either accept or reject his advances.

It's possible that she sought to make the best of a bad situation, in effect trading sex and intimacy for favorable treatment and better living conditions. Within any slave system, however, the power imbalance between master and slave eliminates the possibility of genuine consent.

The challenging part of this subject lies in the Quran's status as holy scripture, which separates it from other works. Ex-Muslim writer and activist Ali Rizvi notes that nobody thinks Jefferson's words and deeds are binding for us today.[38] We can remember Jefferson's achievements, such as advocating for religious freedom and universal rights to life, liberty, and the pursuit of happiness, while also condemning the ways he violated those principles. Indeed, it is precisely Jefferson's contradictions that make him such an intriguing historical figure. Muslims, by comparison, must treat Muhammad differently. If Muhammad was God's final prophet, then his actions—such as owning slaves—become examples of moral instruction. Furthermore, if Muhammad accurately transmitted the Quran, as Muslims believe, they can't accept the parts they like while discarding the rest. To rationalize a practice that people today recognize as rape, apologists such as Brown therefore have to rely on rhetorical shenanigans.

CHILD MARRIAGE

Similar problems arise for the issue of child marriage, which is still common today—especially for girls—in many countries.[39] Journalists, scholars, and activists have documented its adverse effects. The advocacy group Girls Not Brides explains that a girl who marries young will typically hold little power in her marriage and can suffer domestic violence from an older husband who claims authority over her. The girl might endure social isolation in moving to live with her husband and his family, and girls who marry early often report being coerced into sex by their husbands. Those sexual relationships, in turn, can lead to early pregnancy, which poses serious health risks to girls barely beyond puberty. Once these girls start having children, their educational prospects diminish and they become even more dependent on their husbands.[40]

The United Nations estimates that the highest rates of child marriage by age fifteen occur in Chad (30 percent), Central African Republic (29 percent), Niger (28 percent), and Bangladesh (22 percent).[41] India also historically had high rates of child marriage, though the rates declined greatly in recent decades. According to one ancient authority in India, "A damsel should be given in marriage, before her breasts swell," while another indicated that "the time for giving a girl in marriage is from the sixth year of her age to the period previous to the appearance of her menses."[42] The *Manusmriti*, an ancient legal text, differed in specifying that a girl should be married within three years after onset of puberty, which would still qualify as child marriage by modern standards.[43]

The Quran, for its part, takes child marriage for granted in three verses that cover the waiting period for remarriage after a divorce. As with many matters in the Quran, gender inequality is built into the text: Husbands can remarry immediately but wives cannot. Divorced wives must wait three months before remarrying (2:228) unless the marriage was never consummated, a situation the Quran references euphemistically in saying that a husband has not yet "touched" his wife (33:49). In those instances, she can remarry as soon as the divorce occurs. Other cases are covered in the first part of 65:4: "As for those of your women who no longer await menstruation, if you are unsure, then their waiting period is three months, as it is for those who are yet to menstruate. But as for those who are pregnant, their term is until they deliver."

The standard understanding of these instructions developed shortly after Muhammad's death. Throughout Islamic history, commentaries have stated that the two opening clauses of 65:4 refer, respectively, to post-menopausal women ("those of your women who no longer await menstruation") and prepubescent girls ("those who are yet to menstruate"). Anyone fitting those profiles can get remarried after three months, whereas a pregnant woman must wait until after she gives birth.[44] Note that the prepubescent girls covered in 65:4 ("those who are yet to menstruate") have had sex with their husbands. Otherwise, they would fall under the exception in 33:49 that allows remarriage immediately after divorce for a girl or woman who has never engaged in sexual intercourse with her husband.

The only reason a holy book would create divorce rules for girls who have yet to menstruate is if they can, in fact, get married. Western

Muslims who have formed their values in relatively secular societies are often shocked to learn that the Quran allows child marriage. How can apologists respond if they want to claim that child marriage is actually anti-Islamic? One approach is represented by Arzu Kaya-Uranli, who describes herself as "a broadcaster, adjunct professor and spiritual mentor."[45] She has written several dozen articles for *HuffPost*, where she tries to explain and defend Islam to its largely progressive and non-Muslim readership. In an article titled "Nowhere Does Islam Excuse Child Brides," Urlani bypasses the verses related to child marriage. Through the "Ignore" strategy, she directs people instead to a few Quranic verses that mention marriage but do not give the permissible ages for brides. Taking interpretive license to its limit, Uranli asserts that those ancillary verses forbid child marriage.[46]

Within the larger realm of apologetics, however, Muslims have to confront the problematic verses directly. In Muslim-majority countries, many leaders try to follow the provisions for child marriage in the Quran and other sources of Islamic authority. In 2017, for example, a government agency in Turkey said that sharia allows marriage at age nine for girls and twelve for boys.[47] Muslims in the West, though, typically condemn child marriage and try to invoke the Quran for support. At the apologetics website Discover the Truth, Kaleef Karim asserts that verse 65:4 refers not to prepubescent girls but to adult women who "experience situations where their menstrual cycles have stopped for a long period of time" or "who have reached the age of maturity yet are unable to menstruate due to medical condition(s)."[48] Ro Waseem, another Muslim writer whose work has been published in several American outlets, reinterprets the verse the same way. Waseem freely acknowledges that his reading differs from what he calls the "traditional interpretations" over many centuries.[49]

Have Karim, Waseem, and other Muslim apologists succeeded in overturning the conventional understandings? To answer that question, imagine yourself as a God who communicated with human beings through your final prophet. You knew that a tiny proportion of adult women of reproductive age do not menstruate because of a medical condition. You also knew about the girls who do not menstruate because they have not yet reached puberty. Taking that knowledge into account, you delivered a Quranic verse (65:4) prescribing the waiting period for remarriage after divorce for a wife who has yet to menstruate. How did you think people would understand your instructions? You would surely have expected exactly what happened—namely, that every interpreter for more than a millennium understood your verse to describe child brides. Had you wanted people to think of adults, you could easily have worded your verse differently. Of course, with your divine foreknowledge, you would have known that some Muslim apologists in the twenty-first century would eventually reject the only plausible reading of the text. Such is the reality of being a God whose followers sometimes replace your words with theirs.

OTHER INSTANCES OF FORMALIZED INEQUALITY

In addition to the verses about wife beating, the rape of female slaves, and child marriage, many others in the Quran establish a gender hierarchy. One such verse authorizes polygamy. Whereas a woman can have only one husband, a man can have up to four wives: "marry such women as seem good to you, two, three, or four; but if you fear that you will not deal justly, then only one, or those whom your right hands possess" (4:3). Researchers have shown that polygamy is invariably associated in practice with gender inequality.[50] The women in a polygamous relationship typically assume traditional gender roles and hold little power in their marriage or the larger society.

Within the Quran, women are unequal to men not just in the number of permissible spouses but also in the religious requirements for a marriage. Muslim men are allowed to marry not only fellow Muslims but also "those who were given the Book before you" (5:5), which is the Quran's designation for Christians and Jews. No such provision allows a Muslim woman to marry someone from another religion. Double standards also apply in the realm of inheritance, where the Quran stipulates a son's share to be double that of a daughter (4:11). Elsewhere the Quran delegitimizes the testimony of women in cases involving debts, where authorities must call "two witnesses from among your men, and if there are not two men, then a man and two women from among those whom you approve as witnesses, so that if one of the two errs, the other can remind her" (2:282). Here the Quran takes an essentialist view of women as being inherently prone to either forgetting or lying, which is why the proceedings require a second woman to "remind" the first. The upshot is that it takes the testimony of two women to equal that of one man.

These specific instances of gender inequality flow from the larger hierarchy the Quran prescribes. Men "have a degree over" women (2:228) and serve as their "upholders and maintainers" (4:34). Much of the Quran is directed to men and establishes the rules they must enforce against women. For example, men must "tell the believing women to lower their eyes and to guard their private parts, and to not display their adornment except that which is visible thereof" (24:31). The text also states, "Your women are a tilth to you, and go unto your tilth as you will" (2:223). It's a jarring image. The Quran hereby reduces women to tilth, an old-fashioned word for soil that is ready for raising crops. Just as farmers have control over their soil, so too the husband chooses the time and place of sexual intercourse with his wife. The wife's consent does not enter into the picture, for husbands are told to "go unto your tilth as you will."

How can a Muslim apologist handle all the Quranic verses that promote a gender hierarchy? They can try to rationalize or reinterpret them one by one, and I have shown a sampling of those strategies earlier in this chapter. Alternatively, an apologist can simply ignore the Quran's challenging parts and redirect people's attention to elsewhere in the text. This is the approach taken by Amina Wadud in her article, "Islam Beyond Patriarchy through Gender Inclusive Qur'anic Analysis."[51] Wadud spent most of her career as a professor of religion and philosophy at Virginia Commonwealth University. She is one of the most influential proponents of the view that the Quran, along with Islam more generally, supports gender equality.[52]

Rather than directly confront all the places where the Quran requires unequal treatment, Wadud highlights instead a handful of verses she interprets as teaching the opposite. For example, she stresses the creation story in 4:1: "O mankind! Reverence your Lord, Who created you from a single soul and from it created its mate, and from the two has spread abroad a multitude of men and women." The verse indicates that God first created the male, then created the female from him to be his mate, and then from the two of them God created all of humanity. Wadud infers from that account God's desire for gender equality. She supplements her analysis with other verses, such as the Quran's promise that "whosoever, whether male or female, performs a righteous deed and is a believer shall enter the Garden" (40:40). Similarly, she comments on God's call for "affection and mercy" within a marriage (30:21).

In her eighteen-page article, however, Wadud does not discuss any of the Quranic verses that undermine her case. To be fair, she addresses some of the challenging material in her other published works.[53] Overall, though, her body of scholarship accentuates the positive while quickly dismissing the negative. This is an example of cherry-picking, an intellectually dishonest practice. To evaluate the Quran honestly, you must engage all of it, not just the parts you can read as confirming what you already want to believe. Accordingly, an accurate assessment requires acknowledging the verses that seem both favorable and unfavorable to women. How can those apparent contradictions be reconciled?

Actually, it's not that difficult. Wadud and other apologists emphasize the Quranic teaching that human beings originated from a single soul. My response: So what? Why should that generic verse override others that specifically establish gender inequality? Similarly, it's wonderful that the Quran praises "affection and mercy" between husbands and wives. One can easily have those qualities within the hierarchical marriages the Quran requires in other verses. A husband can hold authority over his wife while still treating her well, and many Muslims have historically treasured the relationships they built within a framework of male headship. Similarly, the fact that the Quran allows both men and women to enter paradise, and thus establishes a kind of spiritual equality, does not change its prescription for unequal relations within the family and society.

Careful readers will note that I am following the same theory of interpretation I have advanced in my earlier chapters. Muslim apologists frequently state that texts can have multiple interpretations, a point on which I fully agree. At the same time, a text imposes limits on which interpretations are plausible. You can claim the Quran teaches that the moon is made of green cheese, but the rest of us don't have to give your interpretation any credence. Furthermore, the fact that people often struggle to decipher a text does not change the fact that the author was trying to communicate something. That's why I have distinguished between exegesis, where a person draws meaning from a text, and eisegesis, where the person reads into it their beliefs, values, and interests. Any Muslim would presumably want to uphold this distinction. With heaven and hell resting in the balance, would a Muslim really want to confront God in the afterlife after essentially rewriting his Word?

Someone aspiring to recover the author's intent, whether we're dealing with a religious text or any other, can follow several guidelines. For starters, you must engage with the whole text and refrain from cherry-picking. You need to understand as much as possible about the cultural environment in which the text was produced. Ideally you read the text in its original language, and you pay attention to matters of genre and literary style. As a check against the temptation for eisegesis, you look toward the history of interpretation. If every interpreter before recent times read the text a certain way, only someone with a cavalier attitude would dismiss them. How you can be confident that all the great minds of the past got it wrong, while you have somehow figured it all out? Isn't it more likely that you're forcing the text to conform to your modern values?

Some Muslim apologists reject my theory of interpretation and start from different assumptions, ones informed by postmodernism. Instead of searching for the meaning intended by a text's author, these apologists locate meaning in the reader's response. Someone proceeding in this manner will state that the Quran can be read as upholding either gender equality or inequality. Since both readings are possible, why not accept the interpretations favoring equality? As an example of this move, consider the way in which Ayesha Chaudhry invokes the concept of "choice." Chaudhry, who explores the competing interpretations on whether or not the Quran allows domestic violence, states that "Muslims may follow whichever interpretation they choose."[54]

My position differs. I have too much respect for texts, starting with my own, to accept whatever interpretation someone chooses. Throughout this book, I have tried to express my points clearly and concisely. No doubt I have failed in some places, but I hope that any reader—even a pious believer—will attempt to accurately summarize my claims before proceeding to either endorse or reject them. I suspect Muslim apologists such as Chaudhry would demand the same treatment for their own works. Rightfully recoiling if someone "chose" to interpret their articles and books in a way that flattered the person's predispositions, they would surely insist that the reader try instead to discern the author's intent. It's easy to take a postmodern approach to somebody else's writings; the true test is whether you take umbrage when a critic does the same to yours.

BLAME THE INTERPRETATIONS
Other Muslim apologists, it should be noted, do not follow Chaudhry in working within a postmodern framework. In fact, most apologists assume there is a correct interpretation to the Quran, and they have it. Proceeding in this way allows them to resolve the cognitive dissonance they would otherwise experience. If someone is a Muslim who believes in gender equality, reading the Quran in its entirety can be dispiriting. What can the person do when encountering verses that contradict their beliefs? The easiest solution is to argue that the verses do not mean what an ordinary reader would think they mean.

This response has become common in recent decades. Reflecting on the work of scholars and activists around the turn of the twenty-first century, Margot Badran wrote a book titled *Feminism in Islam: Secular and Religious Convergences*. Badran, who has held appointments at several universities and research centers, defines Islamic feminism as "a feminist discourse and practice articulated within an Islamic paradigm. Islamic feminism, which derives its understanding and mandate from the Qur'an, seeks rights and justice for women, and for men, in the totality of their existence," with the caveat that "the producers and users of Islamic feminist discourse include those who may or may not accept the Islamic feminist label or identity."[55]

Islamic feminists argue that Islam is not just compatible with, but actually demands, the equality of men and women. According to Amani Al-Khatahtbeh, editor of MuslimGirl.com, "Islam literally founded the principles of gender equality that we call feminism today."[56] We have heard that Islam is "the most feminist religion" from Yassmin

Abdel-Magied, a prominent Muslim activist and writer.[57] Taking one of the satellite TED stages while still a teenager, Eve Ahmad asserted that "Islam, the Quran, [and] Prophet Muhammad were feminists in the sense that they valued women and believed in their equality."[58] Linda Sarsour, an influential activist and co-chair of the Women's March of 2017, has stated, "I don't need people in the West, or people in Europe, or people in the United States of America to teach me what feminism is," because she learned it all from "my beloved Prophet Muhammad."[59]

Interestingly, the leading figures in Islamic feminism embed these bold claims within a theology that is traditional in other respects. As explained by anthropologist Saba Mahmood, Islamic feminists "believe in Islam and the truth of Islam" but also hold that "the subordinate status of women in Islam is a function of the way that these scriptures have been interpreted."[60] Susan Carland, a Muslim intellectual in Australia, argues that people read the Quran as a patriarchal text "because religion is a social institution and sadly, when people come to events, we often see a sexist lens put over it. And particularly if people come with sexism in their hearts or souls or minds, they will want to find a religious justification for that."[61]

Carland gave an illuminating interview to the podcast for *Dumbo Feather*, a magazine based in Melbourne that focuses on popular culture. Amid a discussion about her life and views before a live audience, she stated: "As Muslims, we say you don't read the Quran, the Quran reads you. . . . What you read of those texts and come away with tells us so much more about you and who you are than what the book says." Bringing her remarks to a crescendo, she asserted, "The religion is just like a magnifying glass on the person that just shows us who we really are."[62] The crowd immediately broke into applause, showing that many in the West, Muslim and non-Muslim alike, are desperate to attribute patriarchy to people's interpretations of the Quran rather than the text itself.

It's reasonable to assume that most of Carland's audience had never read the Quran. After all, Muslims typically do not study their own scriptures in a language they can understand, and Quranic literacy is even lower among non-Muslims.[63] The people cheering for Carland were surely aware, however, of the tendency for observers to bring collective guilt on all Muslims for the actions of a few. After every terrorist incident perpetrated by a Muslim individual or group, peaceful Muslims have to defend themselves against the charge that their religion condones violence against innocent civilians. Moderate and progressive thinkers in the West therefore have an instinctive desire to absolve the religion's teachings from any blame. Anything immoral that a particular Muslim believes or does, such as promoting patriarchy, cannot possibly have any justification in the religion or its scriptures. Instead, certain individuals impose their twisted interpretations onto the Quran to justify their pre-existing beliefs and behaviors.

You can see why Westerners lacking knowledge of the Quran would embrace this explanation. It allows them to hold the comforting belief that the Quran aligns with modern perspectives on freedom, justice, women's rights, and other subjects. It's harder to explain why the scholars promoting Islamic feminism, who actually have read the Quran, always blame the interpretations while exonerating the text. How can they make that argument with a straight face?

The answer is faith and the intellectual dishonesty it encourages. Despite being a minority within their own religion, Islamic feminists express a form of faith that is traditional in many ways. Like other Muslims, Islamic feminists see Muhammad as a moral exemplar. Many Muslims grant him such total deference that they ritually invoke the words "Peace Be Upon Him," or "'alayhi-salam" in Arabic, when saying his name.[64] Islamic feminists typically don't go that far, but they nevertheless treat his words and deeds as beyond reproach. Their Muslim faith also leads them to accept the Quran as God's revelation.

Because of these faith commitments, Islamic feminists find themselves forced to say things that would make anyone else blush. They believe that Muhammad could not have endorsed or established patriarchy, for he was the perfect guide to how people should live their lives. By assumption, then, patriarchal doctrines and practices in Islam must have emerged in the centuries after his death as people read their prejudices into the Quran. The text itself is taken to be flawless, something nobody can criticize. Since they are unable or unwilling to challenge anything written in the Quran, Islamic feminists have to twist themselves into logical pretzels to pretend that their values are the ones it has taught all along.

REFORMING ISLAM FROM THE INSIDE

Islamic feminists nevertheless play an important role in elevating the voices of Muslim women. Ayesha Chaudhry explains that she is "interested in the debates that are happening around Muslim women in public contexts. Usually Muslim women are at the center of the debate. They're a subject of the conversation that's happening, but for the most part they are absent contributors to the conversation." Chaudhry tries to counter that problem "by offering alternative narratives and alternative scripts of Muslim women both in the past and in the present."[65] Similarly, Libyan-Canadian physician, social entrepreneur, and human rights leader Alaa Murabit laments, "The decision-maker, the person who gets to control the message, is sitting at the table and unfortunately, in every single world faith, they are not women."[66] Murabit has therefore sought to incorporate Muslim women around the world into the dialogue about Islam.

I can at least partially endorse the mission that Chaudhry, Murabit, and others have defined for themselves. Indeed, their goals overlap heavily with the concept of inclusive deliberation that I have advanced in my earlier chapters. A system of morality will be deeply flawed, I have argued, unless it is built on deliberations that incorporate a diverse array of participants. If women are systematically excluded from decision-making in families, businesses, religious organizations, and the larger political system, the society will develop a moral code biased against them. Chaudhry and Murabit rightly worry that discussions about Islam can quickly degenerate into men telling women what the religion teaches.

Islamic feminists nevertheless find themselves caught in a contradiction. They don't want the Muslim men in their communities to lecture them, but they're perfectly willing to defer to a seventh-century man and the largely male followers who recorded and compiled his words. Islamic feminists can't change the fact that patriarchy has been baked into their religion from its inception. Any realistic assessment of the Quran will conclude that it is manmade—and I do mean *man*made. Muhammad grew up in a patriarchal society, and his own values tainted the revelations he thought he received from God. Islamic feminists who want to elevate women's voices are unfortunately fourteen centuries too late. If your house's foundation is poorly constructed, you can't salvage it by applying a fresh coat of paint to the exterior walls.

Of course, I say all of that while recognizing that I hold zero influence over the worldwide Muslim population of nearly two billion adherents. Islamic feminists differ in that there is a plausible pathway by which they could convince some of their fellow Muslims that God demands gender equality. So long as a person remains a Muslim, isn't it better that they believe their religion forbids domestic violence, child marriage, polygamy, raping female slaves, unequal inheritance and testimony in court, male authority in the home and society, and other forms of gender inequality? True, Islamic feminists have to manipulate the Quran to make it consistent with their beliefs, but would it be better for them to concede the debate to fundamentalists? Although the project of Islamic feminism is intellectually dishonest, it can help to reform the religion from within and promote the well-being of Muslim women.

Still, Islamic feminism is a bridge too far for some believers in gender equality. People who have left the religion in recent decades have often cited women's issues as one of their main concerns. This group includes Sarah Haider, cofounder of Ex-Muslims of North America; Yasmine Mohammed, a Canadian human rights activist; and Maryam Namazie, a British-Iranian activist and intellectual. All of them have spoken about the adversity people face in trying to leave Islam. Haider's organization puts it this way: "Former Muslims find little acceptance from their own family and friends. In fact, many never disclose their lack of faith to anyone, living a lie for fear of the price of telling the truth."[67]

Fortunately for Muslims living in the West, the obstacles to becoming an ex-Muslim do not include persecution by the government. With religious liberty enshrined in the laws and constitutions of every Western country, it is families and communities—not the government—who make it difficult for these Muslims to change religions or identify as atheist or agnostic. It's a different matter elsewhere, where governments, families, and communities work together to oppress actual and potential apostates. Becoming an apostate is a crime in many Muslim-majority countries, and the potential punishments include the death penalty in thirteen of them.[68] Although such punishments are difficult to enforce, they nevertheless establish a context within which people who lose their faith often fear for their lives.

Muslim-majority countries also typically fare poorly on measures of gender equality. The World Economic Forum, an international organization that connects leaders from politics, business, and academia, regularly publishes an index of the male-female gap in life outcomes around the globe. This index includes separate measures on four components covering economic participation and opportunity, educational attainment, health and survival, and political empowerment. The summary measure for 2021 shows Iceland scoring the highest and Afghanistan the lowest.[69] There is a strong relationship between a country's religious composition and its score in the rankings, which do not fluctuate much on a year-to-year basis. Of the top thirty countries on gender equality, none are majority-Muslim. Meanwhile, twenty-four of the bottom thirty slots are taken by countries where a majority of people, more than 95 percent in most cases, are Muslim.[70]

There are thus substantial barriers to increasing gender equality in the Muslim world. Because it's so difficult in those countries to become an ex-Muslim, secular advocates of women's rights will generally be scarce. When more than 95 percent of the population identifies as Muslim, progress on gender equality necessarily must come from within rather than outside of Islam. If ordinary Muslims think Islam teaches a hierarchal approach to gender, political reforms to improve women's health, safety, education, and social status are unlikely to win widespread support. If enough of the rank and file can be convinced that Islam demands gender equality, however, such reforms become possible.

In practice, Islamic feminists are invariably countered by the more numerous and powerful conservative Muslims who do not accept egalitarian interpretations of the Quran. Still, it's hard to see any other path forward in the Muslim world than to make the case for gender equality through Islamic principles and scriptures. On the one hand, it's painful to watch as Islamic feminists distort the Quran and other sources of Islamic authority. On the other hand, Islamic feminists can bring pressure for improving the lives of Muslim women in the here and now. As we saw in chapter 5 with respect to Christianity, moral progress within Islam often requires a sizable amount of intellectual dishonesty.

CHAPTER 8

The Alternative to Traditional Monotheist Religions

René Descartes revolutionized the world of ideas by publishing *Discourse on the Method* in 1637. For many centuries in the West, intellectuals wanting to learn what was true deferred to authorities, especially the Church and its popes, councils, scriptures, and traditions. Such an approach could persist when all of Western Christendom was united under the umbrella of the Catholic Church. The Protestant Reformation and its aftermath, however, raised the question of whether Protestants or Catholics held the correct beliefs about salvation, the clergy, the Bible, and other topics. Protestants themselves soon divided into several branches making contradictory truth claims.

Descartes could have aligned himself with one of the theological orientations of his day, but he took a different approach altogether. Seeking to establish a foundation for knowledge acceptable to anyone, regardless of their religious commitments, Descartes relied on deductive methods akin to those of geometry. His famous phrase *Cogito ergo sum* ("I think, therefore I am") indicated his starting point. He could initially be certain on just one matter: his status as a thinking agent. From there, he articulated a system of axioms, deductions, and conclusions. Should his project succeed, it had the potential to unify the quarrelsome writers and thinkers he considered his peers.

Few philosophers today accept all of the specific conclusions Descartes thought he established beyond all doubt. His treatise nevertheless laid the groundwork for intellectual discourse in the following centuries. Authority gradually became devalued among intellectuals, with reason—both inductive and deductive—taking pride of place. Claims were increasingly accepted because of evidence and argument, not the authority of whoever was advancing them. Norms of open inquiry were especially important in the realm of science, where knowledge expanded beyond what anyone could have expected. Religion, in turn, remained a powerful force in society but became far less central to intellectual life.

My own book would not be possible without the pioneering efforts of Descartes. I'm an advocate of humanism, a worldview that developed in recent centuries alongside intellectual activity more generally. By the turn of the twentieth century, people often self-identified with humanism and organized around it. There have been many statements since then of humanism's core principles, perhaps most famously the Amsterdam Declaration of 2002. Representing humanist organizations from around the world, the drafters affirmed that "humanism is undogmatic, imposing no creed upon its adherents." Humanists instead are united by a commitment to reason, applying "the methods of science and free inquiry to the problems of human welfare."[1]

Through reason, the statement noted, humanists have come to recognize the value of "democracy," "human rights," "personal liberty," "social responsibility," and "artistic creativity and imagination."[2] In proposing "a way of life for everyone everywhere," the drafters embraced humanism as "an alternative to organized religion."[3] Many people think religion—especially religion based on revelation from a God—is necessary for morality. In this book I have joined hands with my fellow humanists in disputing that proposition.

RELIGION AS A CULTURAL ATTACHMENT

Humanists need not reject all aspects of religion, however. In fact, many people who identify with a religion actually do so in a humanist manner. I speak here of those who have lost their faith in divine revelation through a written text but who nevertheless find something of value in their religion. Such people view their scriptures as the words of fallible human beings, not God. After taking that step, they can acknowledge their holy book's mistakes not only in history and science but also in morality.

To be sure, most Christians and Muslims would consider it a radical move to deny the divine origin of their scriptures. It is less radical for Jews, many of whom adhere to Judaism as an identity rather than a religion. You can be Jewish and accept many different views about the supernatural, including the belief that God is a figment of the human imagination. Jews who are atheists (or agnostics, deists, pantheists, etc.) are common in the modern world, and there is no reason we could not see the same phenomenon among Christians and Muslims. True, Judaism is an ethnicity while Christianity and Islam are not, but Judaism parallels the other Abrahamic religions in being an identity. Religious identity serves many of the same functions as ethnicity through its ability to bind people together, give them a shared history, and provide meaning through symbols and rituals.

There are, in fact, a growing number of people who identify as cultural Christians or Muslims. Consider the testimony of Max Sky, a businessman in Australia and New Zealand who says he denies Christianity's supernatural assertions but nevertheless "attempts to live by the teachings of Jesus and the New Testament."[4] A contributor to the Philosophy Forum also calls himself a cultural Christian, saying, "I don't believe in 'literal miracles.' . . . That said, I don't feel the hostility that many atheists have toward Christianity and the various works of the church over the last 2000 years."[5] Journalist Pamela Stone embraces the label of a cultural Christian through her appreciation of "old hymns, religious poetry, [and] church spires."[6] An author at a theology blog enthusiastically calls himself a cultural Christian even though he regards the Bible as a literary work "full of errors, contradictions, and outrageous mythological constructions."[7]

In countries that protect religious freedom, some Muslims also retain cultural aspects of their tradition while discarding or downplaying its supernatural components. In Jean Beaman's book *Citizen Outsider: Children of North African Immigrants in France*, one respondent calls himself "a cultural Muslim, which means in terms of culture I am Muslim, because I was raised that way."[8] Ali Hassan, a comedian in Canada, explains that he has held his identity as a cultural Muslim through his "numerous ups and downs and ins and outs with my faith."[9] One of the contributors to FaithFreedom.org says he is "secular minded" but nevertheless Muslim because "that is the group I feel I belong with."[10] Journalist Fareed Zakaria has similarly felt compelled "to acknowledge the religion into which I was born" even though he characterizes his own views as "somewhere between deism and agnosticism."[11]

These cultural Christians and Muslims, much like their Jewish counterparts, are uniquely positioned to take a clear-eyed view of their scriptures. Because they typically have family and friends with strong faith commitments, they have no desire to make gratuitous attacks on their religion or its scriptures. At the same time, seeing their scriptures as human rather than divine frees them from the need to sugarcoat the objectionable parts. Whereas apologists engage in intellectual dishonesty to uphold all the stories and teachings in the Bible and Quran, cultural Christians and Muslims can see each text as a product of when and where it was composed. They can treat their holy books as a source of ideas for discussion and debate rather than the last word on any topic.

Cultural Christians and Muslims thereby gain the ability to critically engage with their scriptures. This engagement can sometimes amount to picking and choosing, which is not intellectually dishonest so long as people do not claim they are bound by the text. Having abandoned the possibility of divine revelation, a person can self-consciously use principles from outside the text to inform their judgment about which parts to keep and which to discard. To someone who thinks their scriptures spring from the hand of God, however, that option is unavailable. Apologists who believe in divine revelation therefore find themselves forced to pick and choose from their holy books while pretending otherwise.

THE BENEFITS OF COMMUNITY

In a move that might seem surprising, some cultural Christians and Muslims join a church or mosque. Why would they do so, given that they have renounced some or all of their religion's core doctrines? Because religion, for them, is a matter of community rather than belief. Social science demonstrates the wisdom of their attempt to partake in the communal aspects of their religion. A rigorous body of research shows that gaining social support through a religious group contributes positively to a person's happiness and their physical and mental health.[12]

This research has been widely mischaracterized in the news media. According to various articles, "Religion Is a Sure Route to True Happiness" (*Washington Post*); "The Tantalizing Proof That Belief in God Makes You Happier and Healthier" (*Daily Mail*); and "Religious Beliefs Make People Happier" (*HuffPost*).[13] The research actually shows nothing of the kind. The best studies include measures of both religious belief (such as whether a person thinks God exists and accepts certain religious propositions) and religious engagement (such as the frequency of attendance at worship services). When they include both kinds of measures in the same analysis, researchers find positive benefits for religious participation but not belief.[14] Stated differently, a cultural Christian or Muslim who attends services will create social ties and gain the attendant benefits, whereas someone who believes in God will not see any improvements in their well-being unless they become embedded in a religious community.[15]

Many cultural Christians and Muslims go outside their traditions in a search for community, and they sometimes become Unitarian Universalists. I know of such people personally through my own membership in a Unitarian Universalist church. Unitarians emerged in the sixteenth century as a broadly Christian group that denied Jesus's divinity and stressed instead the unity of God. Universalists, meanwhile, have taught since ancient times that all people will eventually be saved. Both Unitarians and Universalists gradually became less Christian, and the two groups merged (organizationally, at least) in the United States and some other countries during the twentieth century.

Congregations that join the Unitarian Universalist Association affirm six sources of insight for how people should relate to each other and the wider world: "direct experience of that transcending mystery and wonder"; "words and deeds of prophetic people"; "wisdom from the world's religions"; "Jewish and Christian teachings"; "humanist teachings"; and "spiritual teachings of earth-centered religions."[16] Unitarian Universalism thereby attracts people with many different religious identities, including atheists, agnostics, pagans, pantheists, Christians, Muslims, Jews, Buddhists, and others.[17] Unitarian Universalism is accordingly a noncreedal religion that focuses on how people act, not what they believe. It offers them the chance to make social connections, support each other, collaborate in volunteer and charitable activities, and find personal and spiritual fulfillment. They accomplish all of that without feeling any pressure to accept a certain book as God's revelation.

Unitarian Universalists thus hold worldviews similar to those of humanists and cultural Christians, Muslims, and Jews. These overlapping groups all reject the category of revelation and rely instead on reason to answer life's fundamental questions. Of course, reason is itself a broad term that must be elaborated before it can be useful. In this book I have defended a specific form of reason—inclusive deliberation—as the means to discover objective morality. My approach, I think, could be embraced by many different humanists, Unitarian Universalists, cultural Christians, Muslims, and Jews, and adherents of non-Abrahamic religions.

That's not to say that members of these groups would necessarily agree once we turned to specific moral controversies. If we were to discuss exactly how to build a just society, strike the right balance between freedom and equality, or handle the challenge of climate change, we would surely see a range of views. Many people would participate in the dialogue, engage with the perspectives of others, and offer their own perspectives on the subject at hand. That's exactly the kind of inclusive deliberation I hope to encourage. No person has all the answers, but if we put our minds together, we can make progress on even the most difficult moral questions.

ACKNOWLEDGMENTS

If anyone had predicted twenty-five years ago that I would someday write this book, I would have insisted that their crystal ball was broken. As a young political scientist, I read, studied, and researched on many topics, but religion was not among them. This being my second book on religion, clearly my interests have shifted. My faculty position at a research university has given me the autonomy and intellectual freedom to change my scholarship's focus, and I never forget how fortunate I am to work in such an environment.

I thank my colleagues at the University of Washington, and especially my recent department chairs Peter May, George Lovell, and John Wilkerson, for encouraging me to explore areas that initially seemed odd for a political scientist. This book accordingly reflects my engagement with ideas and authors in history, philosophy, psychology, anthropology, communication, sociology, and religious studies as well as political science. My department was also supportive as I developed and regularly taught two courses, "Free Will, Nature, and Nurture in Politics and Society" and "Seeking Truth in an Age of Cynicism, Misinformation, and Political Polarization," that pushed me to think in the interdisciplinary ways necessary for this book.

During the writing and revising, I received crucial help from many quarters. John Gastil and Bill Talbott read particular chapters, forcing me to clarify my arguments and saving me from errors both large and small. A discussion in the Political Economy Forum at UW, organized by Victor Menaldo and James Long, generated high-level questions I needed to address. Skye Scofield and Jamie Mayerfeld gave me feedback on drafts of the entire manuscript, and I'm grateful for their suggestions and critiques.

I have also benefited over several years from conversations with members of the Atheists, Humanists, and Agnostics ("AHA") group at Shoreline Unitarian Universalist Church. Two of our monthly meetings focused specifically on my book, giving me a good sense of how people were reacting to my main claims. Other conversations with AHA members also contributed to my thinking.

My greatest gratitude goes to my family. My wife, Kristen Hammerback, was the first reader of every chapter. Thankfully, she helped eliminate the worst problems in those drafts before anybody else spotted them. Beyond the book, she has supported me at every step of our two and a half decades together. Being able to talk with her about anything, anytime, has been one of the comforts of my life.

My daughters, Julie and Ali, had started developing their own intellectual identities by the time I initiated this project. They have consistently demonstrated what I hope to encourage in the book: a thoughtful, reasoned orientation that engages with diverse perspectives on questions of morality, politics, and society. They applied that approach in their careful readings of my manuscript as it neared completion, for which I feel both grateful and proud.

NOTES

PREFACE

1. Stephen Jay Gould, *Rocks of Ages: Science and Religion in the Fullness of Life* (New York: Ballantine Books, 1999), 6.
2. Brian Huffling and Michael Shermer, "If God, Why Evil? A Debate on the Problem of Evil," YouTube video, 2:02:28, March 1, 2019, https://www.youtube.com/watch?v=qH4jIHlMunw, beginning at 1:25:45.

CHAPTER 1

1. *Frontline*, "Two American Families," written by Kathleen Hughes and Bill Moyers, July 9, 2013, http://www.pbs.org/wgbh/frontline/film/two-american-families/transcript/.
2. Ross M. Stolzenberg, Mary Blair-Loy, and Linda J. Waite, "Religious Participation over the Life Course: Age and Family Life Cycle Effects on Church Membership," *American Sociological Review* 60 (1995): 84–103.
3. Penny Edgell, Joseph Gerteis, and Douglas Hartmann, "Atheists as 'Other': Moral Boundaries and Cultural Membership in American Society," *American Sociological Review* 71 (2006): 211–34; Will M. Gervais, Azim F. Shariff, and Ara Norenzayan, "Do You Believe in Atheists? Distrust Is Central to Anti-atheist Prejudice," *Journal of Personality and Social Psychology* 101 (2011): 1189–206.
4. Christians widely misunderstand the moral systems of atheists and other nonreligious people, as shown by Phil Zuckerman, *Living the Secular Life: New Answers to Old Questions* (New York: Penguin Press, 2014).
5. Unless otherwise noted, all biblical quotations in this book are from the New Revised Standard Version.
6. Plato, *Euthyphro*, trans. Benjamin Jowett, Internet Classics Archive, accessed August 2, 2018, http://classics.mit.edu/Plato/euthyfro.html.
7. William Lane Craig, *On Guard: Defending Your Faith with Reason and Precision* (Colorado Springs, CO: David C. Cook, 2010), 135–36.
8. Frank Turek, *Stealing from God: Why Atheists Need God to Make Their Case* (Colorado Springs, CO: NavPress, 2014), 104.
9. Trent Horn, *Answering Atheism: How to Make the Case for God with Logic and Charity* (San Diego: Catholic Answers Press, 2013), 211–12; Paul Copan, "The Moral

Argument," in *The Rationality of Theism*, ed. Paul Copan and Paul K. Moser (New York: Routledge, 2003), 165–66; Alex McFarland, *10 Answers for Skeptics* (Ventura, CA: Regal, 2011), 53.

10. William Lane Craig, "#349 The Moral Argument for God," Reasonable Faith, December 23, 2013, https://www.reasonablefaith.org/question-answer/P40/the-moral -argument-for-god/.

11. William Lane Craig, "#483 Could God Be Amoral?" Reasonable Faith, July 17, 2016, https://www.reasonablefaith.org/writings/question-answer/could-god-be-amoral/.

12. William Lane Craig, "#123 Is the Islamic Conception of God Morally Inadequate?" Reasonable Faith, August 24, 2009, https://www.reasonablefaith.org/writings/question -answer/is-the-islamic-conception-of-god-morally-inadequate/.

13. Ibid.; William Lane Craig, "The Most Gruesome of Guests," in *Is Goodness without God Good Enough?* ed. Robert K. Garcia and Nathan L. King (Lanham, MD: Rowman & Littlefield, 2009), 172.

14. C. S. Lewis, *Mere Christianity*, rev. ed. (New York: HarperOne, 2001), 3–8.

15. Augustine, *The City of God*, in *Nicene and Post-Nicene Fathers*, First Series, vol. 2, ed. Philip Schaff, trans. Marcus Dods (Buffalo, NY: Christian Literature , 1887), 426, Book XIX, chapter 6, revised and edited for New Advent by Kevin Knight, accessed April 2, 2018, http://www.newadvent.org/fathers/1201.htm.

16. Rice Broocks, *God's Not Dead: Evidence for God in an Age of Uncertainty* (Nashville, TN: Thomas Nelson, 2013), 45; Thomas R. Schreiner, *40 Questions about Christians and Biblical Law* (Grand Rapids, MI: Kregel , 2010), 77–78; F. Leroy Forlines, *The Quest for Truth: Answering Life's Inescapable Questions* (Nashville, TN: Randall House , 2001), 34.

17. Gleason L. Archer, *Encyclopedia of Bible Difficulties* (Grand Rapids, MI: Zondervan, 1982), 15.

18. See, for example, Alan Wolfe, *The Transformation of American Religion: How We Actually Live Our Faith* (Chicago: University of Chicago Press, 2003).

19. Lewis, *Mere Christianity*; Josh McDowell, *Evidence That Demands a Verdict*, rev. ed. (San Bernadino, CA: Here's Life, 1979).

20. The figures are calculated from the variable "relig" in the General Social Survey, GSS Data Explorer, accessed March 7, 2022, https://gssdataexplorer.norc.org/variables/287/ vshow. See also Tom W. Smith, Peter Marsden, Michael Hout, and Jibum Kim, *General Social Surveys, 1972–2016: Cumulative Codebook* (Chicago: NORC at the University of Chicago, 2017).

21. Margaret Rouse, "spin (PR, marketing)," WhatIs.com, accessed February 18, 2018, http://whatis.techtarget.com/definition/spin-in-public-relations.

22. Anthony Pagden, *The Enlightenment: And Why It Still Matters* (Oxford: Oxford University Press, 2013).

23. G. R. Evans, *Philosophy and Theology in the Middle Ages* (New York: Routledge, 1993).

24. See, for example, David Instone-Brewer, *Divorce and Remarriage in the Bible: The Social and Literary Context* (Grand Rapids, MI: Wm. B. Eerdmans, 2002).

25. Willem-Jan de Wit, "'Your Little Ones against the Rock!' Modern and Ancient Interpretations of Psalm 137:9," in *Christian Faith and Violence*, vol. 2, ed. Dirk van

Keulen and Martien E. Brinkman (Zoetermeer, The Netherlands: Meinema, 2005), 301–02.

26. James R. White, "Harold Camping," Christian Research Institute, April 14, 2009, http://www.equip.org/articles/harold-camping/.

27. Ian Paul, "Is Allegorical Interpretation a Good Thing?" Psephizo, September 26, 2016, https://www.psephizo.com/biblical-studies/is-allegorical-interpretation-a-good-thing/.

28. William Cowper, "God Moves in a Mysterious Way," hymnary.org, accessed April 17, 2017, http://www.hymnary.org/text/god_moves_in_a_mysterious_way.

29. Catechism of the Catholic Church, second edition (Washington, DC: United States Catholic Conference, 2011), sec. 237, https://www.usccb.org/sites/default/files/flipbooks/catechism/.

30. "What Does It Mean That God Works in Mysterious Ways?" GotQuestions.org, accessed April 17, 2017, https://www.gotquestions.org/God-works-in-mysterious-ways.html.

31. See, for example, the debate between William Lane Craig and Alex Rosenburg at Purdue University, February 1, 2013; and the debate between William Lane Craig and Stephen Law at Westminster Hall, London, on October 17, 2011.

32. Nicholas Kristof, "Am I a Christian, Pastor Timothy Keller?" New York Times, December 23, 2016, https://www.nytimes.com/2016/12/23/opinion/sunday/pastor-am-i-a-christian.html?_r=0.

33. David T. Lamb, God Behaving Badly: Is the God of the Old Testament Angry, Sexist and Racist? (Downers Grove, IL: InterVarsity Press, 2011).

34. Tom Gilson, "'God Behaving Badly' by David T. Lamb," Thinking Christian, July 24, 2011, https://www.thinkingchristian.net/posts/2011/07/god-behaving-badly-by-david-t-lamb/; Jack Dodgen, "Book Review: God Behaving Badly," Start2Finish, accessed April 22, 2017, https://start2finish.org/book-review-god-behaving-badly/ (site discontinued).

35. Lamb, God Behaving Badly, 96.

36. Lamb, God Behaving Badly, 99. This interpretation is not original to Lamb, but he explains it well.

37. Lamb, God Behaving Badly, 97.

38. Lamb, God Behaving Badly, 99.

39. Norman Geisler and Thomas Howe, When Critics Ask: A Popular Handbook on Bible Difficulties (Wheaton, IL: Victor Books, 1992), 191–92.

40. Annotations upon All the Books of the Old and New Testament (London: John Legatt, 1651), Early English Books Online, image 268. I have modernized the spelling and capitalization.

41. Poole completed his commentary on all books up through Isaiah before he died in 1679. The rest of his commentary was completed by friends and colleagues and published posthumously. See Matthew Poole, Annotations upon the Holy Bible Wherein the Sacred Text Is Inserted and Various Readings Annexed, vol. 1, fourth edition (London: Thomas Parkhurst, 1700), Early English Books Online, image 227 of 526. I have modernized the spelling and capitalization.

42. Perez Zagorin, *How the Idea of Religious Tolerance Came to the West* (Princeton, NJ: Princeton University Press, 2003); Graham M. Stanton and Guy G. Stroumsa, eds., *Tolerance and Intolerance in Early Judaism and Christianity* (Cambridge: Cambridge University Press, 2008); Gerd Lüdemann, *Intolerance and the Gospel: Selected Texts from the New Testament* (Amherst, NY: Prometheus Books, 2007); H. A. Drake, *Constantine and the Bishops: The Politics of Intolerance* (Baltimore: Johns Hopkins University Press, 2000).

CHAPTER 2

1. Catholic Church, Catechism of the Catholic Church, second edition (Washington, DC: United States Catholic Conference, 2011), sec. 311, emphasis in original.
2. Among the Catholics, see Peter Kreeft, *Letters to an Atheist: Wrestling with Faith* (Lanham, MD: Rowman & Littlefield, 2014), 146; and Trent Horn, *Answering Atheism: How to Make the Case for God with Logic and Clarity* (San Diego: Catholic Answers Press, 2013), 84–85. Among the Protestants, see Rice Broocks, *God's Not Dead: Evidence for God in an Age of Uncertainty* (Nashville, TN: Thomas Nelson, 2013), 56; Frank Turek, *Stealing from God: Why Atheists Need God to Make Their Case* (Colorado Springs, CO: NavPress, 2014), 129.
3. Examples of this pattern of noncitation include Kreeft, *Letters to an Atheist*, 146; Horn, *Answering Atheism*, 84–85; Broocks, *God's Not Dead*, 56; Turek, *Stealing from God*, 129; William Lane Craig, *On Guard: Defending Your Faith with Reason and Precision* (Colorado Springs, CO: David C. Cook, 2010), 151–58; Stephen Arterburn and John Shore, *Being Christian: Exploring Where You, God, and Life Connect* (Bloomington, MN: Bethany House, 2008), 56–57.
4. Norman Geisler, *Baker Encyclopedia of Christian Apologetics* (Grand Rapids, MI: Baker Books, 1999), 219–24; Randy Alcorn, *If God Is Good: Faith in the Midst of Suffering and Evil* (Colorado Springs, CO: Multnomah Books, 2009), 243–55.
5. Tim LaHaye, *How to Study the Bible for Yourself* (Eugene, OR: Harvest House, 2006), 114.
6. Ronald F. Youngblood, ed., *Nelson's Illustrated Bible Dictionary*, rev. ed. (Nashville, TN: Thomas Nelson, 2014), 450.
7. "What Are the Attributes of God," GotQuestions.org, accessed May 10, 2017, https://www.gotquestions.org/attributes-God.html.
8. Ravi Zacharias and Norman Geisler, eds., *Who Made God? And Answers to Over 100 Other Tough Questions of Faith* (Grand Rapids, MI: Zondervan, 2003); John Ankerberg and Dillon Burroughs, *Why Does God Allow Suffering and Evil?* (Chattanooga, TN: AMG, 2008). Sometimes apologists use the verb "permit" instead of "allow."
9. For example, the verse does not merit a mention in three prominent books that address a wide range of Bible difficulties. See Josh McDowell and Sean McDowell, *The Bible Handbook of Difficult Verses: A Complete Guide to Answering the Tough Questions* (Eugene, OR: Harvest House, 2013); Gleason L. Archer, *Encyclopedia of Bible Difficulties* (Grand Rapids, MI: Zondervan, 1982); Norman L. Geisler and Thomas Howe, *The Big Book of Bible Difficulties: Clear and Concise Answers from Genesis to Revelation* (Grand Rapids, MI: Baker Books, 1992). Another book in this genre mentions the verse but only in the larger context of Romans 13:1–7, and it doesn't address the crucial matter of

God installing all governing authorities. See Walter C. Kaiser Jr., Peter H. Davids, F. F. Bruce, and Manfred T. Brauch, *Hard Sayings of the Bible* (Downers Grove, IL: InterVarsity Press, 1996).

10. R. C. Sproul, "Civil Government," Ligonier Ministries, accessed May 15, 2017, http://www.ligonier.org/learn/devotionals/civil-government/.

11. C. S. Cowles, Eugene H. Merrill, Daniel L. Gard, and Tremper Longman III, *Show Them No Mercy: Four Views on God and Canaanite Genocide* (Grand Rapids, MI: Zondervan, 2003); Eric A. Seibert, *The Violence of Scripture: Overcoming the Old Testament's Troubling Legacy* (Minneapolis: Fortress Press, 2012).

12. Turek, *Stealing from God*, 125; David T. Lamb, *God Behaving Badly: Is the God of the Old Testament Angry, Sexist and Racist?* (Downers Grove, IL: InterVarsity Press, 2011), 39–41, 76–81, and 100–01; Greg Koukl, "The Canaanites: Genocide or Judgment?" Stand to Reason, January 1, 2013, https://www.str.org/publications/the-canaanites-genocide-or-judgment#.WRpyCeXysdU.

13. Clay Jones, "We Don't Hate Sin So We Don't Understand What Happened to the Canaanites: An Addendum to the 'Divine Genocide' Arguments," *Philosophia Christi* 11, no. 1 (2009): 55.

14. Christopher Wright, *The God I Don't Understand: Reflections on Tough Questions of Faith* (Grand Rapids, MI: Zondervan, 2008), 88.

15. Sean McDowell and Jonathan Morrow, *Is God Just a Human Invention? And Seventeen Other Questions Raised by the New Atheists* (Grand Rapids, MI: Kregel , 2010), 179–81.

16. "Genocide," United Nations Office on Genocide Prevention and the Responsibility to Protect, accessed January 3, 2018, http://www.un.org/en/genocideprevention/genocide.html.

17. Matt Flannagan, "*Is God a Moral Monster?* A Review of Paul Copan's Book," MandM, March 17, 2011, http://www.mandm.org.nz/2011/03/is-god-a-moral-monster-a-review-of-paul-copans-book.html.

18. Ikenna Nwachukwu, "Book Review: *Is God a Moral Monster?* by Paul Copan," Christ a Poet, March 25, 2017, https://christapoet.com/2017/03/25/book-review-is-god-a-moral-monster-by-paul-copan/.

19. See, for example, William Lane Craig's debate with Sam Harris in April 2011. The transcript is available at Reasonable Faith, accessed June 12, 2017, http://www.reasonablefaith.org/is-the-foundation-of-morality-natural-or-supernatural-the-craig-harris.

20. The ministry is the Christian Research Institute. The organization's president, Hank Hanegraaff, made the offer on his broadcast "Bible Answer Man" before his interview with Paul Copan on December 29, 2016. A recording of the interview is available at the website of One Place, accessed June 12, 2017, http://www.oneplace.com/ministries/bible-answer-man/listen/is-god-a-moral-monster-with-paul-copan-572841.html.

21. Paul Copan, *Is God a Moral Monster? Making Sense of the Old Testament God* (Grand Rapids, MI: Baker Books, 2011), 175.

22. Joshua Ryan Butler, *The Skeletons in God's Closet: The Mercy of Hell, the Surprise of Judgment, the Hope of Holy War* (Nashville, TN: Thomas Nelson, 2014), 228.

23. William Lane Craig, "Slaughter of the Canaanites," Reasonable Faith, August 6, 2007, http://www.reasonablefaith.org/slaughter-of-the-canaanites.

24. McDowell and Morrow, *Is God Just a Human Invention?*, 166.

25. Ibid., 175.

26. I first heard about this implication of Craig's position in David Fletcher, Jeremy Beahan, Justin Schieber, and Luke Galen, "Summer Genocide Series Part 1," Reasonable Doubts Podcast, Episode 88, 1:19:35, August 10, 2011, https://podcasts.apple.com/us/podcast/rd88-summer-genocide-series-part-1/id266671828?i=1000096358868.

27. Copan, *Is God a Moral Monster?* He covers the Canaanites in chapters 15–17 and the Amalekites on pp. 173–74.

28. Copan, *Is God a Moral Monster?*, 174

29. John Winthrop, "A Model of Christian Charity," The Winthrop Society, accessed May 24, 2017, http://winthropsociety.com/doc_charity.php.

30. Cotton Mather, *Souldiers Counselled and Comforted. A Discourse Delivered unto Some Part of the Forces Engaged in the Just War of New-England Against the Northern & Eastern Indians* (Boston: Samuel Green, 1689), 38.

31. *The Summa Theologica of St. Thomas Aquinas*, trans. Fathers of the English Dominican Province, part 2, vol. 2, issue 4 (New York: Benziger Brothers, 1922), 32.

32. David Eltis and Stanley L. Engerman, "Dependence, Servility, and Coerced Labor in Space and Time," in *The Cambridge World History of Slavery: Volume 3, AD 1420–AD 1804*, ed. David Eltis and Stanley L. Engerman (Cambridge: Cambridge University Press, 2011), 10.

33. "Biblical Hebrew Vocabulary: How Much Is Enough? The Law of Diminishing Returns," Biblical Hebrew Made Easy, December 13, 2012, http://biblicalhebrew-madeeasy.weebly.com/blog/biblical-hebrew-vocabulary-how-much-is-enough-the-law-of-diminishing-returns; "How Many Words Are There in the English Language?" Oxford Living Dictionaries, accessed June 5, 2017, https://en.oxforddictionaries.com/explore/how-many-words-are-there-in-the-english-language.

34. Hank Hanegraaff, *The Complete Bible Answer Book: Collector's Edition* (Nashville, TN: Thomas Nelson, 2008), 45, emphasis in original.

35. Orlando Patterson, *Slavery and Social Death: A Comparative Study* (Cambridge, MA: Harvard University Press, 1982).

36. Robert J. Hutchinson, *The Politically Incorrect Guide to the Bible* (Washington, DC: Regnery, 2007), 157.

37. Copan, *Is God a Moral Monster?*.

38. Steve C. Halbrook, *God Is Just: A Defense of the Old Testament Civil Laws*, second edition (Theonomy Resources Media, 2014).

39. Craig, *On Guard*; Gregory Koukl, *Tactics: A Game Plan for Discussing Your Christian Convictions* (Grand Rapids, MI: Zondervan, 2009); Norman L. Geisler and Thomas Howe, *When Critics Ask: A Popular Handbook on Bible Difficulties* (Grand Rapids, MI: Baker Books, 1992).

40. Nancy Pearcey, *Total Truth: Liberating Christianity from Its Cultural Captivity*, Study Guide Edition (Wheaton, IL: Crossway Books, 2005).

41. The Leon Show, "Is There Any Evidence in the Universe That Demonstrates the Existence of God?" YouTube Video, 28:34, June 22, 2014, https://www.youtube.com/watch?v=NbbrYwhYpjw&ab_channel=Cold-CaseChristianitywithJ.WarnerWallace.
42. Matt Slick and David Smalley, "Debate: Is God a Moral Monster?" Bible & Beer Consortium, Soundcloud, 2:16:41, October 7, 2016, https://soundcloud.com/biblethumpingwingnut/debate-matt-slick-vs-david-smalley-is-god-a-moral-monster.
43. Ibid., beginning at 47:49.
44. Ibid., beginning at 2:02:36. Dillahunty prefaced his question by joking that he was "cheating" by joining the conversation, because he would have the chance to question Slick in a formal debate the following night.
45. Ibid.
46. Matt Slick, "You May Buy Slaves?" Christian Apologetics & Research Ministry, December 9, 2008, https://carm.org/bible-difficulties/genesis-deuteronomy/you-may-buy-slaves.
47. Melinda Penner, "Does the Bible Condone Slavery?" Stand to Reason, February 16, 2012, https://www.str.org/blog/does-the-bible-condone-slavery#.WTYLH2jysdU.
48. Brooke N. Newman, "Historical Perspective: Slavery over the Centuries," in *Human Trafficking: Interdisciplinary Perspectives*, ed. Mary C. Burke (New York: Routledge, 2013), 30–36; Lukas de Blois and R. J. van der Spek, *An Introduction to the Ancient World*, second edition, trans. Susan Mellor (New York: Routledge, 1997), 55–59.
49. Wayne Jackson, "What about the Bible and Slavery," Christian Courier, accessed June 3, 2017, https://www.christiancourier.com/articles/800-what-about-the-bible-and-slavery.
50. Bob Seidensticker, "Yes, Biblical Slavery Was the Same as American Slavery," August 25, 2014, Patheos, http://www.patheos.com/blogs/crossexamined/2014/08/yes-biblical-slavery-was-the-same-as-american-slavery/.
51. Hutchinson, *The Politically Incorrect Guide to the Bible*, 162.
52. Ibid., 161.
53. Slick, "You May Buy Slaves?"
54. McDowell and Morrow, *Is God Just a Human Invention?*, 152.
55. Jack Wellman, "What Does the Bible Say about Slavery? Does It Condone It?" What Christians Want to Know, accessed June 4, 2017, http://www.whatchristianswanttoknow.com/what-does-the-bible-say-about-slavery-does-it-condone-it/. Emphasis in original.
56. Newman, "Historical Perspective: Slavery over the Centuries," 30–36; de Blois and van der Spek, *An Introduction to the Ancient World*, 55–59.
57. Hanegraaff, *The Complete Bible Answer Book*, 45.
58. "The KJV New Testament Greek Lexicon," entry for *andrapodistes*, Bible Study Tools, accessed June 9, 2017, http://www.biblestudytools.com/lexicons/greek/kjv/andrapodistes.html.
59. *The Liberties of the Massachusets Collonie in New England,* Hanover Historical Texts Project, accessed June 10, 2017, https://history.hanover.edu/texts/masslib.html. The provision is number 91.
60. Ibid. The provision is number 94, part 10.

61. Edmund Morgan, *The Puritan Family: Religion and Domestic Relations in Seventeenth-Century New England*, rev. ed. (New York: Harper & Row, 1966), 110.
62. Ronald Bailey, "'Those Valuable People, the Africans': The Economic Impact of the Slave(ry) Trade on Textile Industrialization in New England," in *The Meaning of Slavery in the North*, ed. David Roediger and Martin H. Blatt (New York: Garland, 1998), 7.
63. We see this pattern in blog posts, which typically do not include citations, but sometimes even in books. For example, Hank Hanegraaff does not engage with other interpretations in *The Complete Bible Answer Book*.
64. Endnotes appear in books such as McDowell and Morrow, *Is God Just a Human Invention?*, and Copan, *Is God a Moral Monster?*.
65. Biblical commentaries are the best place to search for interpretations. A list of commentaries, many of them written before the Enlightenment, can be found at the Wikipedia entry for "List of Biblical Commentaries."
66. Melissa Snell, "Slavery in the Middle Ages," ThoughtCo, accessed June 11, 2017, https://www.thoughtco.com/chains-in-medieval-times-1788699.
67. Tim Rayborn, *The Violent Pilgrimage: Christians, Muslims and Holy Conflicts, 850–1150* (Jefferson, NC: McFarland, 2013).
68. Hector Zagal, "Aquinas on Slavery: An Aristotelian Puzzle," *ROMA* (September 2003), http://www.e-aquinas.net/pdf/zagal.pdf.
69. Pierre Bonnassie, *From Slavery to Feudalism in South-Western Europe* (New York: Cambridge University Press, 1991).
70. Georges Duby, *The Early Growth of the European Economy: Warriors and Peasants from the Seventh to the Twelfth Century* (Ithaca, NY: Cornell University Press, 1974).
71. Pope Eugene IV, "Sicut Dudum," Papal Encyclicals Online, accessed June 11, 2017, http://www.papalencyclicals.net/Eugene04/eugene04sicut.htm.
72. Pope Nicholas V, "Dum Diversas," Unam Sanctum Catholicam, accessed June 11, 2017, http://unamsanctamcatholicam.blogspot.de/2011/02/dum-diversas-english-translation.html.
73. Pope Paul III, "Sublimus Dei," Papal Encyclicals Online, accessed June 11, 2017, http://www.papalencyclicals.net/Paul03/p3subli.htm.
74. Gregory, Bishop of Nyssa, "Homilies on Ecclesiastes," in *Gregory of Nyssa Homilies on Ecclesiastes: An English Version with Supporting Studies*, ed. Stuart George Hall, trans. Stuart George Hall and Rachel Moriarty (Berlin: Walter de Gruyter, 1993), 31–144.
75. I address this point in greater depth in chapter 5.
76. Genesis 9:6, Leviticus 24:17, Leviticus 20:10, Leviticus 24:10–16, Exodus 22:19, Leviticus 20:15–16, Exodus 21:17, Leviticus 20:9, Exodus 31:14, Exodus 35:2, Leviticus 20:13, Deuteronomy 19:16–21, Deuteronomy 22:13–21.
77. I searched through the available records from each of these organizations and could not find any support for adhering to all biblical rules regarding capital punishment.
78. St. Thomas Aquinas, *Summa Theologica*, trans. Fathers of the English Dominican Province, 1947, First Part of the Second Part, Questions 98–108, Internet Sacred Text Archive, accessed June 18, 2017, http://www.sacred-texts.com/chr/aquinas/summa/index.htm.

79. Bill Jones, *Putting Together the Puzzle of the Old Testament* (Atlanta: Authentic, 2007), 63–65; Amy Orr-Ewing, *Is the Bible Intolerant? Sexist? Oppressive? Homophobic? Outdated? Irrelevant?* (Downers Grove, IL: InterVarsity Press, 2005), 117–18; Thomas R. Schreiner, *40 Questions about Christians and Biblical Law* (Grand Rapids, MI: Kregel , 2010), 89–94.

80. James White, *Contemporary Moral Problems*, tenth edition (Belmont, CA: Wadsworth, 2011); Lewis Vaughn, *Contemporary Moral Arguments: Readings in Ethical Issues*, second edition (New York: Oxford University Press, 2012); Judith A. Boss, *Analyzing Moral Issues*, sixth edition (New York: McGraw Hill, 2013); Mark Timmons, *Disputed Moral Issues: A Reader*, fourth edition (New York: Oxford University Press, 2016).

81. Lydia Saad, "Four Moral Issues Sharply Divide Americans," Gallup, May 26, 2010, http://www.gallup.com/poll/137357/four-moral-issues-sharply-divide-americans.aspx.

82. "Moral Relativism," *Stanford Encyclopedia of Philosophy*, April 20, 2015, https://plato .stanford.edu/entries/moral-relativism/.

83. Phil Fernandes, *The Atheist Delusion: A Christian Response to Christopher Hitchens and Richard Dawkins* (Maitland, FL: Xulon Press, 2009), 99.

84. David Silverman, who became president of American Atheists in 2010, is a prominent example. See David Silverman, *Fighting God: An Atheist Manifesto for a Religious World* (New York: St. Martin's Press, 2015).

85. See, for example, Sam Harris, *The Moral Landscape: How Science Can Determine Human Values* (New York: Free Press, 2010); Massimo Pigliucci, *Answers for Aristotle: How Science and Philosophy Can Lead Us to a More Meaningful Life* (New York: Basic Books, 2012); Michael Shermer, *The Moral Arc: How Science and Reason Lead Humanity toward Truth, Justice, and Freedom* (New York: Henry Holt, 2015).

86. The examples I use in chapters 2 and 4 overlap with those from Elizabeth Anderson, "If God Is Dead, Is Everything, Permitted?" in *Philosophers without Gods: Meditations on Atheism and the Secular Life*, ed. Louise Antony (New York: Oxford University Press, 2007), 215–30.

87. See, for example, Quran 2:191–93, 4:74, 4:89, 9:5, 17:16, 61:4, 61:9 (on jihad); Quran 4:34, 38:44, Sahih Bukhari 72:715, Sahih Muslim 4:2127 (on wife beating); Quran 4:24, 8:69, 23:5–6, and 33:50 (on slavery for prisoners of war); Sahih al-Burkari 4:52:260, 9:83:17, 9:83:271, Sahih Muslim 16:4152, 16:4154, 20:4490 (on the death penalty for apostates).

CHAPTER 3

1. Penny Edgell, Douglas Hartmann, Evan Stewart, and Joseph Gerteis, "Atheists and Other Cultural Outsiders: Moral Boundaries and the Non-Religious in the United States," *Social Forces* 95 (2016): 607–38.

2. Justin McCarthy, "In U.S., Socialist Presidential Candidates Least Appealing," Gallup, June 15, 2015, http://www.gallup.com/poll/183713/socialist-presidential-candidates -least-appealing.aspx.

3. Greta Christina, *Coming Out Atheist: How to Do It, How to Help Each Other, and Why* (Durham, NC: Pitchstone, 2014).

4. Michael Wallace, Bradley R. E. Wright, and Allen Hyde, "Religious Affiliation and Hiring Discrimination in the American South: A Field Experiment," *Social Currents* 1 (2014): 189–207; Bradley R. E. Wright, Michael Wallace, John Bailey, and Allen Hyde, "Religious Affiliation and Hiring Discrimination in New England: A Field Experiment," *Research in Social Stratification and Mobility* 34 (2013): 111–26.

5. Will M. Gervais, "Everything Is Permitted? People Intuitively Judge Immorality as Representative of Atheists," *PLoS One* 9, no. 4 (April 2014).

6. Gregory A. Smith, "A Growing Share of Americans Say It's Not Necessary to Believe in God to Be Moral," Pew Research Center, October 16, 2017, http://www.pewresearch.org/fact-tank/2017/10/16/a-growing-share-of-americans-say-its-not-necessary-to-believe-in-god-to-be-moral/.

7. William Lane Craig, "First Rebuttal," in *Is Goodness without God Good Enough? A Debate on Faith, Secularism, and Ethics*, ed. Robert K. Garcia and Nathan L. King (Lanham, MD: Rowman & Littlefield, 2009), 36.

8. William Lane Craig, "Can We Be Good without God?" Reasonable Faith, accessed August 9, 2017, http://www.reasonablefaith.org/can-we-be-good-without-god.

9. Matt Slick, "Can Atheists Be Ethical?" Christian Apologetics and Research Ministry, December 9, 2008, https://carm.org/can-atheists-be-ethical.

10. Larry Alex Taunton, *The Faith of Christopher Hitchens: The Restless Soul of the World's Most Notorious Atheist* (Nashville, TN: Thomas Nelson, 2016). See also Matt Nelson, "How Not to Talk to Atheists: 3 Essential Points from Matt Fradd's Interview with Dr. Randal Rauser," Reasonable Catholic, July 15, 2015, https://www.reasonablecatholic.com/how-not-to-talk-to-atheists-3-essential-points-from-matt-fradds-interview-with-dr-randal-rauser/.

11. Rice Broocks, *God's Not Dead: Evidence for God in an Age of Uncertainty* (Nashville, TN: Thomas Nelson, 2013), 44.

12. Dennis Prager, "If There Is No God," *The Dennis Prager Show*, August 19, 2008, http://www.dennisprager.com/if-there-is-no-god/.

13. Chad Meister, "Atheists and the Quest for Objective Morality," Christian Research Institute, January 31, 2011, http://www.equip.org/article/atheists-and-the-quest-for-objective-morality/.

14. Craig J. Hazen, "Can We Be Good without God?" *Biola Magazine*, Summer 2011, http://magazine.biola.edu/article/11-summer/can-we-be-good-without-god/.

15. J. M. Njoroge, "Must the Moral Law Have a Lawgiver?" *Faithandthelaw's Blog*, August 21, 2016, https://faithandthelaw.wordpress.com/2016/08/21/must-the-moral-law-have-a-lawgiver/.

16. Dinesh D'Souza, *What's So Great about Christianity* (Washington, DC: Regnery, 2007), 214–20; Larry Alex Taunton, *The Grace Effect: How the Power of One Life Can Reverse the Corruption of Unbelief* (Nashville, TN: Thomas Nelson, 2011), chs. 8–9.

17. Christel Manning, *Losing Our Religion: How Unaffiliated Parents Are Raising Their Children* (New York: New York University Press, 2015); Elizabeth Drescher, *Choosing Our Religion: The Spiritual Lives of America's Nones* (New York: Oxford University Press, 2016); Phil Zuckerman, *Faith No More: Why People Reject Religion* (New York: Oxford University Press, 2012); Phil Zuckerman, *Society without God: What the Least Religious*

Nations Can Tell Us about Contentment, second edition (New York: New York University Press, 2020).

18. Peter Kreeft, *Letters to an Atheist: Wrestling with Faith* (Lanham, MD: Rowman & Littlefield, 2014).

19. Jason Lisle, "Atheism: An Irrational Worldview," in *A Pocket Guide to Atheism: Understanding the Inherent Problems of a No-God Worldview* (Petersburg, KY: Answers in Genesis, 2014), 51–59.

20. Alister McGrath, *The Twilight of Atheism: The Rise and Fall of Disbelief in the Modern World* (New York: Doubleday, 2006), 145.

21. Lance Waldie, *A Christian Apologetic for Christian Apologists* (Cypress, TX: Lulu, 2012), 61.

22. Norman L. Geisler and Frank Turek, *I Don't Have Enough Faith to Be an Atheist* (Wheaton, IL: Crossway Books, 2004), 225.

23. Ricky Gervais, @rickygervais, "Saying 'Atheism Is a Belief System,' Is Like Saying 'Not Going Skiing, Is a Hobby,'" Twitter, May 6, 2014, 8:00 a.m., https://twitter.com/gervaisquotes/status/463694901482639361.

24. Callum G. Brown, *Becoming Atheist: Humanism and the Secular West* (London: Bloomsbury Academic, 2017).

25. "Defining 'Humanism,'" Humanists UK, accessed August 19, 2017, https://humanism.org.uk/humanism/.

26. Stephen Law, *Humanism: A Very Short Introduction* (New York: Oxford University Press, 2011).

27. OED Online, "objective, adj. and n.," June 2017, Oxford University Press, http://www.oed.com.offcampus.lib.washington.edu/view/Entry/129634?redirectedFrom=objective.

28. Ibid.

29. Eric Wielenberg, *Robust Ethics: The Metaphysics and Epistemology of Godless Normative Reason* (New York: Oxford University Press, 2014); Michael Martin, *Atheism, Morality, and Meaning* (Amherst, NY: Prometheus Books, 2002); Julian Baggini, *Atheism: A Very Short Introduction* (New York: Oxford University Press, 2003), ch. 3; and Paul Kurtz, *Forbidden Fruit: The Ethics of Secularism* (Amherst, NY: Prometheus Books, 2008).

30. Broocks, *God's Not Dead*, 54.

31. Meister, "Atheists and the Quest for Objective Morality."

32. Hazen, "Can We Be Good without God?"

33. "The 'Golden Rule' (a.k.a. Ethics of Reciprocity) Part 1: Passages in Religious Texts in 14 Faiths from the Bahá'í Faith to Satanism," Religious Tolerance, accessed September 23, 2017, http://www.religioustolerance.org/reciproc2.htm; Zia H. Shah, "The Golden Rule in Islam," *Muslim Times*, October 27, 2013, https://themuslimtimes.info/2013/10/27/the-golden-rule-in-islam/.

34. On the history of social contract thinking, see Patrick Riley, "How Coherent Is the Social Contract Tradition?" *Journal of the History of Ideas* 34 (1973): 543–62.

35. Thomas Hobbes, *Leviathan*, revised edition, ed. A. P. Martinich and Brian Battiste (Toronto: Broadview Press, 2011 [1668]), 126.

36. John Rawls, *A Theory of Justice*, revised edition (Cambridge, MA: Harvard University Press, 1999 [1971], 118.

37. Rawls, *A Theory of Justice*, 119.

38. *The Histories of Herodotus Interlinear English Translation*, ed. Heinrich Stein, trans. George Macaulay (Lighthouse Digital, 2013); Alexis de Tocqueville, *Democracy in America*, trans. Harvey Mansfield and Delba Winthrop (Chicago: University of Chicago Press, 2000 [1835, 1840]); Kwame Anthony Appiah, *Cosmopolitanism: Ethics in a World of Strangers* (New York: W. W. Norton, 2006).

39. Mary M. Dwyer and Courtney K. Peters, "The Benefits of Study Abroad: New Study Confirms Significant Gains," *Transitions Abroad*, March/April 2004, 56–57, IES Abroad, https://www.iesabroad.org/system/files/Benefits%20%28Dwyer%2C%20Peters %29%20%28Transitions%20Abroad%29.pdf.

40. David Hume, "Essay XI: Of the Original Contract," in David Hume, *Essays and Treatises on Several Subjects* (London: A. Millar, 1758), 252–62.

41. Robert Nozick, *Anarchy, State, and Utopia* (New York: Basic Books, 2013 [1974]), 287.

42. Donald E. Brown, *Human Universals* (Boston: McGraw-Hill, 1991).

43. John Hick, "The Universality of the Golden Rule," in *Ethics, Religion, and the Good Society: New Directions in a Pluralistic World*, ed. Joseph Runzo (Louisville, KY: Westminster/John Knox Press, 1992), 155–66.

44. Mitchel P. Roth, *An Eye for an Eye: A Global History of Crime and Punishment* (Chicago: University of Chicago Press, 2014).

45. Arthur P. Wolf and William H. Durham, eds., *Inbreeding, Incest, and the Incest Taboo: The State of Knowledge at the Turn of the Century* (Stanford, CA: Stanford University Press, 2004); "Adultery," *New World Encyclopedia*, accessed September 23, 2017, http://www.newworldencyclopedia.org/entry/Adultery.

46. Clifford Christians and Michael Traber, eds., *Communication Ethics and Universal Values* (Thousand Oaks, CA: Sage, 1997); Marshall Sahlins, *Stone Age Economics* (New York: Routledge, 1972); Morris B. Hoffman, *The Punisher's Brain: The Evolution of Judge and Jury* (New York: Cambridge University Press, 2014).

47. Philip Lieberman, *Uniquely Human: The Evolution of Speech, Thought, and Selfless Behavior* (Cambridge, MA: Harvard University Press, 1991), ch. 6.

48. Christine Gross-Loh, *Parenting without Borders: Surprising Lessons Parents around the World Can Teach Us* (New York: Penguin Group, 2013).

49. Frans de Waal, *The Bonobo and the Atheist: In Search of Humanism among the Primates* (New York: W. W. Norton, 2013).

50. Paul Finkelman and Joseph Calder Miller, *Macmillan Encyclopedia of World Slavery*, vols. 1 and 2 (New York: Macmillan Library Reference, 1999).

51. International Labor Office, Walk Free Foundation, and International Organization for Migration, *Global Estimates of Modern Slavery* (Geneva: International Labor Office, 2017), Alliance 8.7, http://www.alliance87.org/global_estimates_of_modern_slavery -forced_labour_and_forced_marriage.pdf.

52. Aina Gallego, *Unequal Political Participation Worldwide* (New York: Cambridge University Press, 2015).

53. Eli Pariser, *The Filter Bubble: How the New Personalized Web Is Changing What We Read and How We Think* (New York: Penguin Press, 2011).
54. James S. Fishkin, *Democracy and Deliberation: New Directions for Democratic Reform* (New Haven, CT: Yale University Press, 1991).
55. Tina Nabatchi, "An Introduction to Deliberative Civic Engagement," in *Democracy in Motion: Evaluating the Practice and Impact of Deliberative Civic Engagement*, ed. Tina Nabatchi, John Gastil, G. Michael Weiksner, and Matt Leighninger (New York: Oxford University Press, 2012), 3–18.
56. Jürg Steiner, *The Foundations of Deliberative Democracy: Empirical Research and Normative Implications* (Cambridge: Cambridge University Press, 2012).
57. Laura Black, "How People Communicate during Deliberative Events," in *Democracy in Motion*, 59–82.
58. James Fishkin and Cynthia Farrar, "Deliberative Polling*: From Experiment to Community Resource," in *The Deliberative Democracy Handbook: Strategies for Effective Civic Engagement in the Twenty-First Century*, ed. John Gastil and Peter Levine (San Francisco: Jossey-Bass, 2005), 68–79.
59. Helene Landemore, *Democratic Reason: Politics, Collective Intelligence, and the Rule of the Many* (Princeton, NJ: Princeton University Press, 2017).
60. See, for example, A. C. Grayling, *Meditations for the Humanist: Ethics for a Secular Age* (New York: Oxford University Press, 2003); Greg Epstein, *Good without God: What a Billion Nonreligious People Do Believe* (New York: HarperCollins, 2009); and Dan Barker, *The Good Atheist: Living a Purpose-Filled Life without God* (Berkeley, CA: Ulysses Press, 2011).
61. Jürgen Habermas, *Moral Consciousness and Communication Action*, trans. Christian Lenhardt and Shierry Weber Nicholsen (New York: Polity Press, 1990).
62. Brooke N. Newman, "Historical Perspective: Slavery over the Centuries," in *Human Trafficking: Interdisciplinary Perspectives*, ed. Mary C. Burke (New York: Routledge, 2013), 30–36; Lukas de Blois and R. J. van der Spek, *An Introduction to the Ancient World*, second edition, trans. Susan Mellor (New York: Routledge, 1997), 55–59.
63. Manisha Sinha, *The Slave's Cause: A History of Abolition* (New Haven, CT: Yale University Press, 2016).
64. Harriet Beecher Stowe, *Uncle Tom's Cabin; or, Life among the Lowly* (Boston: John Jewett, 1852); Dion Boucicault, *The Octoroon, or, Life in Louisiana: A Play in Five Acts* (Salem, NH: Ayer, 1992 [1859]); Herman Melville, "Benito Cereno," in Herman Melville, *The Piazza Tales* (New York: Dix & Edwards, 1856); Gertrudis Gómez de Avellaneda, *Sab* (Madrid: Imprenta Calle Del Barco, 1841).
65. Seymour Drescher, *Abolition: A History of Slavery and Antislavery* (Cambridge: Cambridge University Press, 2009).
66. William J. Talbott, *Which Rights Should Be Universal?* (New York: Oxford University Press, 2005).
67. Edward O. Wilson, *Consilience: The Unity of Knowledge* (New York: Alfred A. Knopf: 1998); Steven Pinker, *The Blank Slate: The Modern Denial of Human Nature* (New York: Penguin Group, 2002); Edward Slingerland, *What Science Offers the Humanities: Integrating Body and Culture* (New York: Cambridge University Press, 2008).

68. Robert Rosenthal, "The File Drawer Problem and Tolerance for Null Results," *Psychological Bulletin* 86, no. 3 (1979): 638–41.

69. Elisabeth A. Lloyd, *The Case of the Female Orgasm: Bias in the Science of Evolution* (Cambridge, MA: Harvard University Press, 2005).

70. C. Glenn Begley and John P. A. Ioannidis, "Reproducibility in Science: Improving the Standard for Basic and Preclinical Research," *Circulation Research* 116 (2015): 116–26.

71. Janet D. Stemwedel, "The Objectivity Thing (or, Why Science Is a Team Sport," *Scientific American*, July 20, 2011, https://blogs.scientificamerican.com/doing-good-science/httpblogsscientificamericancomdoing-good-science20110720the-objectivity-thing-or-why-science-is-a-team-sport/. See also Miriam Soloman, *Social Empiricism* (Cambridge, MA: MIT Press, 2001).

72. David Harker, *Creating Scientific Controversies: Uncertainty and Bias in Science and Society* (Cambridge: Cambridge University Press, 2015).

73. John R. Huizenga, *Cold Fusion: The Scientific Fiasco of the Century* (New York: Oxford University Press, 1992).

74. Henry R. Frankel, *The Continental Drift Controversy: Volume I: Wegener and the Early Debate* (Cambridge: Cambridge University Press, 2012).

75. For a summary of plate tectonics and the evidence supporting it, see Peter Molnar, *Plate Tectonics: A Very Short Introduction* (Oxford: Oxford University Press, 2015).

76. William Lane Craig often uses this hypothetical—albeit for a different purpose—during his debates. See, for example, Sam Harris and William Lane Craig, "The God Debate II: Harris vs. Craig," YouTube Video, 2:06:54, April 12, 2011, https://www.youtube.com/watch?v=yqaHXKLRKzg.

77. Ravi Zacharias, *The End of Reason: A Response to the New Atheists* (Grand Rapids, MI: Zondervan, 2008), 55.

78. Phil Fernandes, *No Other Gods: A Defense of Biblical Christianity* (Maitland, FL: Xulon Press, 2002), 81; David Limbaugh, *Jesus on Trial: A Lawyer Affirms the Truth of the Gospel* (Washington, DC: Regnery, 2014), 272; Doug Powell, *Holman Quicksource Guide to Christian Apologetics* (Nashville, TN: Holman Reference, 2006), 89.

79. Christopher Akers, "God and Objective Morality," The Catholic Thing, July 8, 2017, https://www.thecatholicthing.org/2017/07/08/god-and-objective-morality/.

80. William H. Frye, "Is There a God (Part 3)—Is Morality Real or Just Opinion and Preference," whfrye.com, accessed September 21, 2017, http://whfrye.com/is-there-a-god-part-3-is-morality-real-or-just-opinion-and-preference/.

81. Jordan Peterson, Rebecca Goldstein, and William Lane Craig, "Is There Meaning to Life?" YouTube Video, 2:07:30, January 26, 2018, https://www.youtube.com/watch?v=pDDQOCXBrAw&t=6960s, beginning at 13:11.

82. United Nations, "Universal Declaration of Human Rights," accessed September 23, 2017, http://www.ohchr.org/EN/UDHR/Documents/UDHR_Translations/eng.pdf.

83. Johannes Morsink, *The Universal Declaration of Human Rights: Origins, Drafting, and Intent* (Philadelphia: University of Pennsylvania Press, 2000).

84. Turek, *Stealing from God*, 98.

85. Michael Novak, *No One Sees God: The Dark Night of Atheists and Believers* (New York: Doubleday, 2008), 53.
86. John Mizzoni, *Ethics: The Basics*, second edition (Hoboken, NJ: John Wiley & Sons, 2017).
87. P. Alex Linley, Susan Harrington, and Nicola Garcea, eds., *The Oxford Handbook of Positive Psychology and Work* (New York: Oxford University Press, 2013); George E. Vaillant, *Triumphs of Experience: The Men of the Harvard Grant Study* (Cambridge, MA: Harvard University Press, 2012); Michael Eid and Randy J. Larsen, eds., *The Science of Subjective Well-Being* (New York: Guilford Press, 2008).
88. Mona Chalabi, "Are Prisoners Less Likely to Be Atheists?" FiveThirtyEight, March 12, 2015, https://fivethirtyeight.com/features/are-prisoners-less-likely-to-be-atheists/; Alex Daniels, "Religious Americans Give More, New Study Finds," *Chronicle of Philanthropy*, November 25, 2013, https://www.philanthropy.com/article/Religious-Americans-Give-More/153973.
89. Sean McDowell and Jonathan Morrow, *Is God Just a Human Invention? And Seventeen Other Questions Raised by the New Atheists* (Grand Rapids, MI: Kregel , 2010), 212.
90. Turek, *Stealing from God*, 90. Emphasis in original.
91. William Lane Craig and Louise Antony, "Is God Necessary for Morality," The Veritas Forum, YouTube Video, June 22, 2012, https://www.youtube.com/watch?v=6wKk-bquUDSM, beginning at 13:13.
92. Ibid., beginning at 12:46.
93. Gregg Allison and Chris Castaldo, *The Unfinished Reformation: What Unites and Divides Catholics and Protestants after 500 Years* (Grand Rapids, MI: Zondervan, 2016), ch. 6.
94. Quran 2:82, 2:177.
95. Quran 2:82, 2:177, 89:17–30.
96. Quran 7:7–9, 101:5–6.

CHAPTER 4
1. These branches of Christianity differ over whether the Old Testament Apocrypha should be included as scripture, but none of them accept anything written after the final New Testament books.
2. For more on this point, see my earlier book *Secular Faith: How Culture Has Trumped Religion in American Politics* (Chicago: University of Chicago Press, 2015).
3. David Berreby, *Us and Them: The Science of Identity* (Chicago: University of Chicago Press, 2008).
4. Bruce Bridgeman, *Psychology and Evolution: The Origins of Mind* (Thousand Oaks, CA: Sage , 2013).
5. Robert M. Sapolsky, *Behave: The Biology of Humans at Our Best and Worst* (New York: Penguin Press, 2017), ch. 11.
6. Brian M. Howell and Jenell Williams Paris, *Introducing Cultural Anthropology: A Christian Perspective* (Grand Rapids, MI: Baker Academic, 2011), 78.
7. Ann McElroy, *Nunavut Generations: Change and Continuity in Canadian Inuit Communities* (Long Grove, IL: Waveland Press, 2008), 8.

8. Karen Wynn, Paul Bloom, Ashley Jordan, Julia Marshall, and Mark Sheskin, "Not Noble Savages After All: Limits to Early Altruism," *Current Directions in Psychological Science* 27 (2018): 3–8.

9. J. Kiley Hamlin, Neha Mahajan, Zoe Liberman, and Karen Wynn, "Not Like Me = Bad: Infants Prefer Those Who Harm Dissimilar Others," *Psychological Science* 24 (2013): 589–94.

10. Henri Tajfel, "Experiments in Intergroup Discrimination," *Scientific American* 223 (1970): 96–102.

11. Brian Mullen, Rupert Brown, and Colleen Smith, "Ingroup Bias as a Function of Salience, Relevance, and Status: An Integration," *European Journal of Social Psychology* 22 (1992): 103–22.

12. Celia de Anca, *Beyond Tribalism: Managing Identity in a Diverse World* (New York: Palgrave Macmillan, 2012); Lyndon Storey, *Humanity or Sovereignty: A Political Roadmap for the 21st Century* (New York: Peter Lang, 2012).

13. Sebastian Junger, *Tribe: On Homecoming and Belonging* (New York: Hachette Book Group, 2016); Robert D. Putnam, *Bowling Alone: The Collapse and Revival of American Community* (New York: Simon & Schuster, 2000).

14. Duke Sherman, *A Soldier's Thoughts: A Collection of Poems* (Bloomington, IN: Xlibris Corporation, 2012), 164.

15. Christie Davies, *Ethnic Humor around the World: A Comparative Analysis* (Bloomington: Indiana University Press, 1990).

16. Gordon Hodson, Jonathan Rush, and Cara C. MacInnis, "A Joke Is Just a Joke (Except When It Isn't): Cavalier Humor Beliefs Facilitate the Expression of Group Dominance Motives," *Journal of Personality and Social Psychology* 99 (2010): 660–82.

17. Brooke N. Newman, "Historical Perspective: Slavery over the Centuries," in *Human Trafficking: Interdisciplinary Perspectives*, ed. Mary C. Burke (New York: Routledge, 2013), 30–36; Lukas de Blois and R. J. van der Spek, *An Introduction to the Ancient World*, second edition, trans. Susan Mellor (New York: Routledge, 1997), 55–59.

18. Mary E. Kite and Bernard E. Whitley Jr., *Psychology of Prejudice and Discrimination*, third edition (New York: Routledge, 2016), ch. 3.

19. Jackson J. Spielvogel, *Western Civilization: A Brief History, Volume I: To 1715*, ninth edition (Boston: Centage Learning, 2017), 154.

20. Mark Edward Lewis, *Sanctioned Violence in Early China* (Albany: State University of New York Press, 1990), 91–94; Klaus Muhlhahn, *Criminal Justice in China: A History* (Cambridge, MA: Harvard University Press, 2009), 61.

21. Anne Applebaum, *Gulag: A History* (New York: Doubleday, 2003).

22. Committee for Human Rights in North Korea, *The Hidden Gulag: The Lives and Voices of "Those Sent to the Mountains,"* second edition (Washington, DC: David Hawk, 2012), 4–9.

23. Conor Friedersdorf, "The Obama Administration's Drone-Strike Dissembling," *Atlantic*, March 14, 2016, https://www.theatlantic.com/politics/archive/2016/03/the-obama-administrations-drone-strike-dissembling/473541/.

24. Agence France-Presse, "Malala Condemns Donald Trump's 'Ideology of Hatred,'" Public Radio International, December 16, 2015, https://www.pri.org/stories/2015-12 -16/malala-condemns-donald-trumps-ideology-hatred.

25. Maggie Haberman, "Donald Trump Reverses Position on Torture and Killing Terrorists' Families," New York Times, March 4, 2016, https://www.nytimes.com/politics/ first-draft/2016/03/04/donald-trump-reverses-position-on-torture-and-killing-terrorists -families/.

26. John Piper, "How God Visits Sins on the Third and Fourth Generations," Desiring God, March 6, 2009, https://www.desiringgod.org/articles/how-god-visits-sins-on-the -third-and-fourth-generation. Emphasis in original.

27. "Are Children Punished for the Sins of Their Parents," GotQuestions.org, accessed November 18, 2017, https://www.gotquestions.org/parents-sin.html.

28. Susan S. Kuo, "'Not Only Injurious to Individuals, but Dangerous to the State': A Theory of Disaster Crime," in Disasters, Hazards, and Law, ed. Mathieu Deflam (Bingley, UK: Emerald Group, 2012), 31–32.

29. Jyoti Grewal, Betrayed by the State: The Anti-Sikh Pogrom of 1984 (New York: Penguin Books India, 2007).

30. Mukul Kesavan, "Murderous Majorities," New York Review of Books, January 18, 2018, 37–40; Max Bearak, "Rohingya Militants in Burma: Terrorists or Freedom Fighters?" Washington Post, September 11, 2017, https://www.washingtonpost.com/news/ worldviews/wp/2017/09/11/rohingya-militants-in-burma-terrorists-or-freedom-fighters /?utm_term=.55f464793414.

31. David Smith, Sherman's March to the Sea 1864: Atlanta to Savannah (Oxford, UK: Osprey, 2007).

32. David M. Kennedy, ed., The Library of Congress World War II Companion (New York: Simon & Schuster, 2007), ch. 8.

33. Leslie Alan Horvitz and Christopher Catherwood, Encyclopedia of War Crimes and Genocide (New York: Facts on File, 2006), 89–90.

34. Wilson D. Miscamble, The Most Controversial Decision: Truman, the Atomic Bombs, and the Defeat of Japan (New York: Cambridge University Press, 2011).

35. Thomas Hippler, Bombing the People: Giulio Douhet and the Foundations of Air-Power Strategy, 1884–1939 (Cambridge, UK: Cambridge University Press, 2013).

36. Rushanara Ali, "157 Parliamentarians Call on Government to Suspend and Review British Military Training Programs with Burmese Military," Burma Campaign UK, September 10, 2017, http://burmacampaign.org.uk/157-parliamentarians-call-on -government-to-suspend-and-review-british-military-training-programs-with-burmese -military/.

37. Su-am Kim, The North Korean Penal Code, Criminal Procedures, and Their Actual Application (Seoul: Korea Institute for National Unification, 2006).

38. Andrew Rudalevige, "What Can Watergate Teach Us about the Trump White House?" Washington Post, May 18, 2017, https://www.washingtonpost.com/news/mon-key-cage/wp/2017/05/18/what-can-watergate-teach-us-about-the-trump-white-house/ ?utm_term=.1346b5ff1494.

39. "Roald Dahl: The Day I Lost Faith in 'the Boss,'" *The Telegraph*, August 6, 2010, http://www.telegraph.co.uk/culture/books/biographyandmemoirreviews/7930223/Roald -Dahl-on-God-the-day-I-lost-faith-in-the-Boss.html.

40. Rachel Kneen, "Subacute Sclerosing Pan-encephalitis," Encephalitis Society, accessed November 19, 2017, https://www.encephalitis.info/subacute-sclerosing-pan -encephalitis-sspe.

41. Khurram Zarin, "10 Deadliest Natural Disasters of 21st Century," Scienceve, accessed November 5, 2017, http://www.scienceve.com/10-deadliest-natural-disasters -of-21st-century/; Mamta Bhatt, "The Most Devastating Natural Disasters of the 21st Century," All That Is Interesting, August 28, 2011. http://all-that-is-interesting.com/the -most-devastating-natural-disasters-of-the-21st.

42. Rich Deem, "Where Is God When Bad Things Happen? Why Natural Evil Must Exist," Evidence for God, February 13, 2013, http://www.godandscience.org/apologetics /natural_evil_theodicity.html.

43. J. Warner Wallace, *God's Crime Scene: A Cold-Case Detective Examines the Evidence for a Divinely Created Universe* (Colorado Springs, CO: David C. Cook, 2015), ch. 8.

44. "The Problem of Evil," Ongoing Ambassadors for Christ, September 21, 2017, http: //www.oafc.org/apologetics-witnessing-resources/the-problem-of-evil.

45. Frank Turek, *Stealing from God: Why Atheists Need God to Make Their Case* (Colorado Springs, CO: NavPress, 2014), 129.

46. Kenneth Boa, *God, I Don't Understand: Answers to Difficult Questions of the Christian Faith* (Eugene, OR: Wipf & Stock, 2012), 100–01.

47. Robert Velarde, "How Can God Allow So Much Evil and Suffering?" Focus on the Family, January 1, 2009, https://www.focusonthefamily.com/faith/becoming-a-christian/ is-christ-the-only-way/how-can-god-allow-so-much-evil-and-suffering.

48. Catholic Church, Catechism of the Catholic Church, second edition, sec. 417 (Washington, DC: United States Catholic Conference, 2011), https://www.usccb.org/ sites/default/files/flipbooks/catechism/.

49. The Augsburg Confession, Article 2, Zion Evangelical Lutheran Church, accessed November 19, 2017, http://atlanta.clclutheran.org/bibleclass/bookofconcord/article2 .html.

50. Greg Koukl, "Why Are Natural Disasters an Evil with No Connection to Free Will," Stand to Reason, YouTube Video, 8:03, February 23, 2015, https://www.youtube .com/watch?v=0_YHNQCdqo8&ab_channel=StandtoReason.

51. Matthew Tingblad, "The Problem of Natural Disasters," Josh McDowell Ministry, April 6, 2017, https://www.josh.org/problem-natural-disasters/.

52. Seth Stephens-Davidowitz, *Everybody Lies: Big Data, New Data, and What the Internet Can Tell Us about Who We Really Are* (New York: HarperCollins, 2017), introduction.

53. Michael Mann, *The Sources of Social Power: A History of Power from the Beginning to A.D. 1760*, vol. 1 (New York: Cambridge University Press, 1986), 260–61; Sandra R. Joshel, *Slavery in the Roman World* (New York: Cambridge University Press, 2010), 8.

54. "Over 40 Million People Caught in Modern Slavery, 152 Million in Child Labor— UN," UN News Centre, September 19, 2017, http://www.un.org/apps/news/story.asp ?NewsID=57550#.WibhWEqnEdV.

55. Hans van Wees, "Genocide in the Ancient World," in *The Oxford Handbook of Genocide Studies*, ed. Donald Bloxham and A. Dirk Moses (Oxford: Oxford University Press, 2010), 239–58.

56. Peter Singer, *The Expanding Circle: Ethics, Evolution, and Moral Progress* (Princeton, NJ: Princeton University Press, 1981).

57. K. J. Dover, *Greek Popular Morality in the Time of Plato and Aristotle* (New York: Hackett, 1994), 280.

58. *The Dialogues of Plato*, trans. B. Jowett, vol. 1 (New York: Random House, 1892), 734.

59. Ibid., 732.

60. Lionel Casson, *Travel in the Ancient World* (Baltimore: Johns Hopkins University Press, 1994).

61. Ian Morris and Walter Scheidel, eds., *The Dynamics of Ancient Empires: State Power from Assyria to Byzantium* (Oxford: Oxford University Press, 2009).

62. Gordon Allport, *The Nature of Prejudice* (New York: Perseus Books, 1954).

63. Morton Deutsch and Mary Evans Collins, *Interracial Housing: A Psychological Evaluation of a Social Experiment* (Minneapolis: University of Minnesota Press, 1951).

64. Kendrick T. Brown, Tony N. Brown, James S. Jackson, Robert M. Sellers, and Warde J. Manuel, "Teammates On and Off the Field? Contact with Black Teammates and the Racial Attitudes of White Student Athletes," *Journal of Applied Social Psychology* 33 (July 2003): 1379–403.

65. Daniel Cox, Juhem Navarro-Rivera, and Robert P. Jones, *A Shifting Landscape: A Decade of Change in American Attitudes about Same-Sex Marriage and LGBT Issues* (Washington, DC: Public Religion Research Institute, 2014).

66. Robert D. Putnam and David E. Campbell, *American Grace: How Religion Divides and Unites Us* (New York: Simon & Schuster, 2010).

67. Thomas F. Pettigrew and Linda R. Tropp, "A Meta-Analytic Test of Intergroup Contact Theory," *Journal of Personality and Social Psychology* 90 (2006): 751–83.

68. Inga J. Hoever, Daan van Knippenberg, Wendy P. van Ginkel, and Harry G. Barkema, "Fostering Team Creativity: Perspective Taking as Key to Unlocking Diversity's Potential," *Journal of Applied Psychology* 97 (2012): 982–96; Katherine W. Phillips, "How Diversity Makes Us Smarter," *Scientific American*, October 1, 2014, https://www.scientificamerican.com/article/how-diversity-makes-us-smarter/.

69. William V. Harris, *Ancient Literacy* (Cambridge, MA: Harvard University Press, 1991).

70. Mary Beard, "Writing and Religion," in *Religions of the Ancient World: A Guide*, ed. Sarah Iles Johnston (Cambridge, MA: Harvard University Press, 2014), 128–29. Since few women were literate, the literacy rate for the population as a whole was roughly half the rate for men.

71. United Nations Educational, Scientific and Cultural Organization, *Reading the Past, Writing the Future: Fifty Years of Promoting Literacy* (Paris: United Nations Educational, Scientific and Cultural Organization, 2017).

72. Lynn Hunt, *Inventing Human Rights: A History* (New York: W. W. Norton, 2007), ch. 1.

73. Ibid., ch. 5.

74. Michael Shermer, "Why Smart People Believe Weird Things," September 2002, https://michaelshermer.com/2002/09/smart-people-believe-weird-things/.

75. Leonard W. Levy, *Blasphemy: Verbal Offense against the Sacred, from Moses to Salman Rushdie* (Chapel Hill: University of North Carolina Press, 1995).

76. Paul Cliteur, *The Rise and Fall of Blasphemy Law* (Leiden, The Netherlands: Leiden University Press, 2017).

CHAPTER 5

1. Andy Rau, "Understand Your Bible Better: How to Use Commentaries, Study Bibles, and More at Bible Gateway," Bible Gateway, July 26, 2017, https://www.biblegateway.com/blog/2017/07/understand-your-bible-better-how-to-use-commentaries-study-bibles/.

2. Terry Johnson, "Just Me and My Bible?" Ligonier Ministries, accessed March 28, 2018, https://www.ligonier.org/learn/articles/just-me-and-my-bible/.

3. Terance Espinoza, "Exegesis versus Eisegesis," February 16, 2017, Thought Hub, Southwestern Assemblies of God University, https://www.sagu.edu/thoughthub/exegesis-versus-eisegesis.

4. "5 Steps to Understanding Any Biblical Text: The Interpretive Journey from 'Grasping God's Word,'" Zondervan Academic, June 10, 2015, https://zondervanacademic.com/blog/5-steps-to-understanding-any-biblical-text/.

5. Wyman Lewis Richardson, *Walking Together: A Congregational Reflection on Biblical Church Discipline* (Eugene, OR: Wipf & Stock, 2007), 30.

6. S. Michael Houdmann, *Questions about the Bible: The 100 Most Frequently Asked Questions about the Bible* (Bloomington, IN: WestBow Press, 2015).

7. Richardson, *Walking Together,* 49.

8. Jonathan G. Koomey, "What Is Intellectual Honesty and Why Is It Important?" June 18, 2012, http://www.koomey.com/post/25385125958.

9. Gleason L. Archer, *Encyclopedia of Bible Difficulties* (Grand Rapids, MI: Zondervan, 1982), 15.

10. Steven Pinker, *The Better Angels of Our Nature: Why Violence Has Declined* (New York: Penguin Books, 2011), 367.

11. Christopher H. Evans, *The Social Gospel in American Religion* (New York: New York University Press, 2017).

12. John Rustin, "Religious Liberty Has Its Roots in the Bible," NC Family Policy Council, July 5, 2018, http://www.ncfamily.org/religious-liberty-has-its-roots-in-the-bible/.

13. Bart Barber, "The Biblical Case for Religious Liberty," Praisegod Barebones, July 30, 2015, http://praisegodbarebones.blogspot.com/2015/07/the-biblical-case-for-religious-liberty.html.

14. Hugh Whelchel, "Is Religious Liberty Biblical?" Institute for Faith, Work & Economics, April 25, 2016, https://tifwe.org/is-religious-liberty-biblical/.

15. Tertullian, *The Apology,* in *Ante-Nicene Fathers,* vol. 3, ed. Alexander Roberts, James Donaldson, and A. Cleveland Coxe, trans. S. Thelwall (Buffalo, NY: Christian Literature

, 1885), rev. and ed. for New Advent by Kevin Knight, http://www.newadvent.org/fathers/0301.htm, ch. 39.

16. Ibid., ch. 24.

17. Andrew Pettegree, "The Politics of Toleration in the Free Netherlands, 1572–620," in *Tolerance and Intolerance in the European Reformation*, ed. Ole Peter Grell and Bob Scribner (Cambridge: Cambridge University Press, 1996), 198.

18. Bernard Green, *Christianity in Ancient Rome: The First Three Centuries* (London: T&T Clark International, 2010), ch. 3.

19. Donald MacGillivray Nicol and J. F. Matthews, "Constantine I," in *Encyclopedia Brittannica*, accessed April 26, 2018, https://www.britannica.com/biography/Constantine-I-Roman-emperor.

20. Erwin Fahlbusch, Jan Milic Lochman, John Mbiti, and Jaroslav Pelikan, eds., *The Encyclopedia of Christianity*, vol. 5 (Grand Rapids, MI: Wm. B. Eerdsman, 2008), 189.

21. Augustine, "Letter 34 (AD 396) to Eusebius," par. 1, New Advent, accessed April 26, 2018, http://www.newadvent.org/fathers/1102034.htm.

22. Augustine, "Letter 173 (AD 416) to Donatus," par. 10, New Advent, accessed April 26, 2018, http://www.newadvent.org/fathers/1102173.htm.

23. Ibid.

24. Ibid., par. 3.

25. Ibid.

26. Augustine, "Letter 93 (AD 408) to Vicentius," ch. 6, par. 20, New Advent, accessed April 26, 2018, https://www.newadvent.org/fathers/1102093.htm.

27. Ibid., ch. 2, par. 6.

28. Ibid., ch. 2, par. 8.

29. John Chrysostom, "Homily 46 (on Matthew)," in *Nicene and Post-Nicene Fathers*, First Series, vol. 10, ed. Philip Schaff, trans. George Prevost, rev. M. B. Riddle (Buffalo, NY: Christian Literature, 1888), rev. and ed. for New Advent by Kevin Knight, http://www.newadvent.org/fathers/200146.htm.

30. Perez Zagorin, *How the Idea of Religious Toleration Came to the West* (Princeton, NJ: Princeton University Press, 2005), 28–29. The primary source is apparently unavailable in English translation, so I rely on Zagorin's characterization of it.

31. Ibid., 31–32.

32. Mark Vessey, ed., *A Companion to Augustine* (Malden, MA: Blackwell, 2012).

33. Zagorin, *How the Idea of Religious Toleration Came to the West*, 32.

34. Codex Theodosianus, Early Church Texts, accessed April 29, 2018, http://www.earlychurchtexts.com/public/codex_theodosianus.htm.

35. Joan Mervyn Hussey, "Justinian I," in *Encyclopedia Britannica*, accessed April 29, 2018, https://www.britannica.com/biography/Justinian-I.

36. Alcuin, Epistles 110 and 113, in *Christianity and Religious Freedom: A Sourcebook of Scriptural, Theological, and Legal Texts*, ed. Karen Taliaferro (Washington, DC: Berkeley Center for Religion, Peace & World Affairs of Georgetown University, 2014), 41.

37. Thomas Aquinas, *Summa Theologica*, trans. Fathers of the English Dominican Province (New York: Benzinger Brothers: 1947), Second Part of the Second Part, Question 11, Article 3, Dominican House of Studies, Priory of the Immaculate

Conception, accessed May 4, 2018, https://dhspriory.org/thomas/summa/SS/SS011
.html#SSQ11OUTP1.

38. Catholic Church, *Twelfth Ecumenical Council: Lateran IV 1215*, canon 68, in
Fordham University, *Medieval Sourcebook*, accessed May 4, 2018, https://sourcebooks
.fordham.edu/basis/lateran4.asp.

39. Ibid., canon 3.

40. As quoted in Alan Cross, *When Heaven and Earth Collide: Racism, Southern Evangelicals, and the Better Way of Jesus* (Montgomery, AL: NewSouth Books, 2014), 76.

41. Martin Luther, "On Governmental Authority," in *The Protestant Reformation*, ed.
Hans J. Hillerbrand (London: Palgrave Macmillan, 1968), 58.

42. Ibid., 48.

43. Martin Luther, "On War against Islamic Reign of Terror (On War against the
Turk)," Martin Luther og hans skrifter, accessed May 4, 2018, http://www.lutherdansk
.dk/On%20war%20against%20Islamic%20reign%20of%20terror/On%20war%20against
%20Islamic%20reign%20of%20terror1.htm.

44. Martin Luther, "Letter to George Spalatin, January or February 1514," in *Luther's
Correspondence and Other Contemporary Letters*, vol. 1, 1507–1521, ed. and trans.
Preserved Smith and Charles M. Jacobs (Philadelphia: Lutheran Publication Society,
1913), 29.

45. Martin Luther, Wayback Machine, accessed July 8, 2021, https://web.archive.org/
web/20050103042654/http://jdstone.org/cr/pages/sss_mluther.html.

46. Jaroslav Pelikan, ed., *Luther's Works, vol. 13: Selected Psalms II* (St. Louis: Concordia,
1956), 61.

47. Ibid., 61–62.

48. Ibid., 62.

49. Robert von Friedeburg, *Luther's Legacy: The Thirty Years War and the Modern Notion
of "State" in the Empire, 1530s to 1790s* (Cambridge: Cambridge University Press, 2016),
109.

50. Taliaferro, *Christianity and Religious Freedom*, 56.

51. John Calvin, *The Institutes of the Christian Religion*, trans. Henry Beveridge, Christian Classics Ethereal Library, accessed May 5, 2018, http://www.ccel.org/ccel/calvin/
institutes.pdf?url=.

52. Ibid., 1174.

53. See, for example, Calvin's remarks about Leviticus 24:15–26 in *Calvin's Commentary
on the Bible*, studylight.org, accessed June 3, 2018, https://www.studylight.org/commentaries/cal/leviticus-24.html.

54. John Calvin, "Letter to Farel, 1553," in *Letters of John Calvin*, vol. 2, ed. and trans.
Jules Bonnet (Philadelphia: Presbyterian Board of Publication, 1868), 417.

55. Thomas Helwys, *A Short Declaration of the Mystery of Iniquity* (Macon, GA: Mercer
University Press, 1998 [1611/1612]; John Murton, *A Most Humble Supplication of Many
the Kings Maiesties Loyall Subiects, Ready to Testifie All Civill Obedience, by the Oath, as the
Law of This Realme Requireth, and That of Conscience* (EEOB Editions, 2011 [1621]).

56. Roger Williams, *The Bloudy Tenent of Persecution*, reprint ed. (London: Forgotten Books, 2018 [1644]), 243. I have updated the spelling and capitalization to make it consistent with modern usage.

57. Ibid., 3.

58. Ibid., 334.

59. Ibid., 106.

60. Ibid., 252.

61. Ibid., 3.

62. David Platt, "Christians Need to Fight for the Religious Freedom of Everyone," *Relevant*, March 15, 2017, https://relevantmagazine.com/god/christians-need-to-fight-for-the-religious-freedom-of-everyone/.

63. Sean McDowell, "A Simple Case for Religious Liberty," July 25, 2017, http://sean-mcdowell.org/blog/a-secular-case-for-religious-liberty.

64. Wayne Grudem, *Politics According to the Bible: A Comprehensive Resource for Understanding Modern Political Issues in Light of Scripture* (Grand Rapids, MI: Zondervan, 2010), 99.

65. "Is Freedom of Religion a Biblical Concept?" GotQuestions.org, accessed May 21, 2018, https://www.gotquestions.org/freedom-of-religion.html.

66. "Biblical Christianity: The Origin of the Rights to Conscience," WallBuilders, accessed May 21, 2018, https://wallbuilders.com/biblical-christianity-origin-rights-conscience/.

67. Augustine, "Letter 173 (AD 416) to Donatus," par. 10, New Advent, accessed April 26, 2018, http://www.newadvent.org/fathers/1102173.htm.

68. Bart D. Ehrman, *Jesus: Apocalyptic Prophet of the New Millennium* (Oxford: Oxford University Press, 1999).

69. Henry Kamen, *The Rise of Toleration* (New York: McGraw-Hill, 1972).

70. Zagorin, *How the Idea of Religious Toleration Came to the West*.

71. Miklós Molnár, *A Concise History of Hungary*, trans. Anna Magyar (Cambridge: Cambridge University Press, 2001), 110.

72. Joke Spaans, "Religious Policies in the Seventeenth-Century Dutch Republic," in *Calvinism and Religious Toleration in the Dutch Golden Age*, ed. R. Po-Chia Hsia and H. F. K. Van Nierop (Cambridge: Cambridge University Press, 2002), 72–86.

73. Thomas D. Hamm, *The Quakers in America* (New York: Columbia University Press, 2003), 23.

74. William G. McLoughlin, *Rhode Island: A History* (New York: W. W. Norton, 1986), ch. 1.

75. Andrew Bradstock, *Radical Religion in Cromwell's England: A Concise History from the English Civil War to the End of the Commonwealth* (London: I. B. Tauris, 2011).

76. Bruce T. Murray, *Religious Liberty in America: The First Amendment in Historical and Contemporary Perspective* (Amherst: University of Massachusetts Press, 2008).

77. Lloyd P. Gartner, *History of the Jews in Modern Times* (Oxford: Oxford University Press, 2001), ch. 5.

78. Edward J. Eberle, *Church and State in Western Society: Established Church, Cooperation and Separation* (Farnham, UK: Ashgate, 2016).

79. Scott A. Merriman, *When Religious and Secular Interests Collide: Faith, Law, and the Religious Exemption Debate* (Santa Barbara, CA: Praeger, 2017).

80. Timothy Samuel Shah, Thomas F. Farr, and Jack Friedman, eds., *Religious Freedom and Gay Rights: Emerging Conflicts in North America and Europe* (Oxford: Oxford University Press, 2016).

81. Luke Timothy Johnson, "Religious Rights and Christian Texts," in *Religious Human Rights in Global Perspective: Religious Perspectives*, ed. John Witte Jr. and Johan D. van der Vyver (The Hague, The Netherlands: Matinus Nijhoff, 1996), 66.

82. On the surprisingly large number of Christians in America who believe in reincarnation, see "Many Americans Mix Multiple Faiths," Pew Research Center, December 9, 2009, http://www.pewforum.org/2009/12/09/many-americans-mix-multiple-faiths/.

83. For the purposes of this chapter, I follow tradition and call Paul the author of Colossians, Ephesians, and 1 Timothy. Regardless of who wrote them, those books are in the Bible, and Christians have to reckon with them.

84. Philip de Souza, *Piracy in the Greco-Roman World* (Cambridge: Cambridge University Press, 1999), 62.

85. Walter Scheidel, "The Roman Slave Supply," in *The Cambridge History of World Slavery, Volume 1: The Ancient Mediterranean World*, ed. Keith Bradley and Paul Cartledge (Cambridge: Cambridge University Press, 2011), 287–310.

86. Hector Avalos, *Slavery, Abolitionism, and the Ethics of Biblical Scholarship* (Sheffield, England: Sheffield Phoenix Press, 2013), chs. 7–16.

87. Rodney Stark, *For the Glory of God: How Monotheism Led to Reformations, Science, Witch-Hunts, and the End of Slavery* (Princeton, NJ: Princeton University Press, 2003); Rodney Stark, *The Victory of Reason: How Christianity Led to Freedom, Capitalism, and Western Success* (New York: Random House, 2005). On Stark as an apologist, see Alan Wolfe, "The Reason for Everything," *New Republic*, January 15, 2006, https://newrepublic.com/article/65229/the-reason-everything.

88. Avalos, *Slavery, Abolitionism, and the Ethics of Biblical Scholarship*, chs. 7–9.

89. See, for example, Sean McDowell's comments during his discussion with Matthew Vines, "What Does the Bible Say about Homosexuality? Sean McDowell and Matthew Vines in Conversation," YouTube Video, 2:10:34, February 3, 2018, https://www.youtube.com/watch?v=yFY4VtCWgyI&t=3206s.

90. See, for example, Clement of Alexandria, *The Stromata*, book 2, New Advent, accessed April 2, 2018, http://www.newadvent.org/fathers/02102.htm. Clement of Alexandria, *The Stromata*, in *Ante-Nicene Fathers*, vol. 2., ed. Alexander Roberts, James Donaldson, and A. Cleveland Coxe, trans. William Wilson (Buffalo, NY: Christian Literature., 1885), rev. and ed. for New Advent by Kevin Knight, accessed April 2, 2018, http://www.newadvent.org/fathers/02102.htm.

91. *The Epistle of Barnabas* 19:7, trans. J. B. Lightfoot, Early Christian Writings, accessed April 2, 2018, http://www.earlychristianwritings.com/text/barnabas-lightfoot.html.

92. *The Didache* 4:11, accessed April 2, 2018, thedidache.com.

93. Cyprian, *Treatise V: An Address to Demetrianus*, Christian Classics Ethereal Library, accessed April 2, 2018, https://www.ccel.org/ccel/schaff/anf05.iv.v.v.html.

94. Chris L. de Wet, "The Cappadocian Fathers on Slave Management," The Scientific Electronic Library Online, accessed April 2, 2018, http://www.scielo.org.za/pdf/she/v39n1/17.pdf.

95. The document is apparently available only in Latin, and I have taken the quote from Marc Bloch's translation. See Marc Bloch, "How and Why Ancient Slavery Came to an End," in *Critical Readings in Global Slavery*, vol. 4, ed. Damian Alan Pargas and Felicia Roşu (Leiden, The Netherlands: Brill, 2018), 487.

96. Synod of Gangra, in *Nicene and Post-Nicene Fathers*, Second Series, vol. 14, ed. Philip Schaff and Henry Wace, trans. Henry Percival (Buffalo, NY: Christian Literature, 1900), rev. and ed. for New Advent by Kevin Knight. http://www.newadvent.org/fathers/3804.htm.

97. The Council of Chalcedon, Papal Encyclicals Online, accessed April 3, 2018, http://www.papalencyclicals.net/councils/ecum04.htm.

98. Gregory, Bishop of Nyssa, "Homilies on Ecclesiastes," in *Gregory of Nyssa Homilies on Ecclesiastes: An English Version with Supporting Studies*, ed. Stuart George Hall, trans. Stuart George Hall and Rachel Moriarty (Berlin: Walter de Gruyter, 1993), 31–144.

99. Augustine, *The City of God*, in *Nicene and Post-Nicene Fathers*, First Series, vol. 2., ed. Philip Schaff, trans. Marcus Dods (Buffalo, NY: Christian Literature, 1887 [426]), rev. and ed. for New Advent by Kevin Knight, accessed April 2, 2018, http://www.newadvent.org/fathers/1201.htm, ch. 15.

100. Ibid.

101. Ibid.

102. I rely on the translation in Hector Avalos, *Slavery, Abolitionism, and the Ethics of Biblical Scholarship* (Sheffield, England: Sheffield Phoenix Press, 2013), 168.

103. "Decrees on Sale of Unfree Christians, c. 922–1171," in Fordham University, *Medieval Sourcebook*, accessed April 3, 2018, https://sourcebooks.fordham.edu/source/1171latrsale.asp.

104. Rachel Stone, *Morality and Masculinity in the Carolingian Empire* (Cambridge: Cambridge University Press, 2012), 179.

105. Thomas Aquinas, *Summa Theologica*, trans. Fathers of the English Dominican Province (New York: Benzinger Brothers, 1947), First Part, Question 96, Article 4, Dominican House of Studies, Priory of the Immaculate Conception, https://dhspriory.org/thomas/summa/FP/FP096.html#FPQ96OUTP1, accessed April 4, 2018.

106. Ibid., First Part of the Second Part, Question 94, Article 5, accessed April 4, 2018, https://dhspriory.org/thomas/summa/FS/FS094.html#FSQ94OUTP1.

107. Ibid., Second Part of the Second Part, Question 57, Article 3, accessed April 4, 2018, https://dhspriory.org/thomas/summa/SS/SS057.html#SSQ57OUTP1.

108. Ibid., Second Part of the Second Part, Question 104, Article 6, accessed April 4, 2018, https://dhspriory.org/thomas/summa/SS/SS104.html#SSQ104OUTP1.

109. Pope Eugene IV, "Sicut Dudum," Papal Encyclicals Online, accessed April 11, 2018, http://www.papalencyclicals.net/Eugene04/eugene04sicut.htm.

110. Joseph F. O'Callaghan, *The Last Crusade in the West: Castile and the Conquest of Granada* (Philadelphia: University of Pennsylvania Press, 2014), 84–85.

111. Pope Nicholas V, "Dum Diversas," Unam Sanctum Catholicam, accessed April 16, 2018, http://unamsanctamcatholicam.blogspot.de/2011/02/dum-diversas-english-translation.html; Pope Nicholas V, "Romanus Pontifex," Native Web, accessed April 16, 2018, https://www.nativeweb.org/pages/legal/indig-romanus-pontifex.html.

112. David Brion Davis, *The Problem of Slavery in Western Culture* (Oxford: Oxford University Press, 1966), 100–01.

113. Pope Paul III, "Sublimus Dei," Papal Encyclicals Online, accessed April 13, 2018, http://www.papalencyclicals.net/Paul03/p3subli.htm.

114. John T. Noonan Jr., *A Church That Can and Cannot Change: The Development of Catholic Moral Teaching* (Notre Dame, IN: University of Notre Dame Press, 2005), 79.

115. Hilton C. Oswald, ed., *Luther's Works, vol. 28: Commentaries on 1 Corinthians 7, 1 Corinthians 15, Lectures on 1 Timothy* (St. Louis: Concordia, 1973), 237–38.

116. John Calvin, *Commentaries on the Epistles to Timothy, Titus, and Philemon*, trans. William Pringle (Edinburgh, UK: Calvin Translation Society, 1856), 31.

117. John Calvin, *Commentaries on St. Paul's Epistles to the Galatians and Ephesians*, trans. John King (Charleston, SC: Createspace, 2015), 226.

118. Ibid.

119. *Annotations upon All the Books of the Old and New Testament* (London: John Legatt, 1651), 364. I have modernized the spelling and capitalization.

120. *The Liberties of the Massachusets Collonie in New England*, provisions 91 and 94, part 10, Hanover Historical Texts Project, accessed April 15, 2018, https://history.hanover.edu/texts/masslib.html.

121. Edmund Morgan, *The Puritan Family: Religion and Domestic Relations in Seventeenth-Century New England*, rev. ed. (New York: Harper & Row, 1966), 110.

122. The document is available only in Latin. I rely here on the summary in John Francis Maxwell, *Slavery and the Catholic Church: The History of Catholic Teaching Concerning the Moral Legitimacy of the Institution of Slavery* (Chichester, England: Barry Rose, 1975), 78.

123. Victoria Johnson, *Bible Study for Busy Women* (Detroit, MI: Dabar, 1998), 38.

124. Samuel Sewall, *The Selling of Joseph: A Memorial* (Boston: Bartholomew Green and John Allen, 1700), Massachusetts Historical Society, accessed April 2, 2018, http://www.masshist.org/database/53.

125. Paul Copan, *Is God a Moral Monster? Making Sense of the Old Testament God* (Grand Rapids, MI: Baker Books, 2011); Robert J. Hutchinson, *The Politically Incorrect Guide to the Bible* (Washington, DC: Regnery, 2007).

126. George Bourne, *A Condensed Antislavery Bible Argument* (New York: S. W. Benedict, 1845); Albert Barnes, *An Inquiry into the Scriptural Views of Slavery* (Philadelphia: Perkins & Purves, 1846).

127. John Henry Hopkins, *A Scriptural, Ecclesiastical, and Historical View of Slavery, from the Days of Patriarch Abraham, to the Nineteenth Century* (New York: W. I. Pooley, 1864), 6.

128. Ibid., 7.

129. Ibid., 11.

130. Ibid., 10, 80–81, 217–18.

131. Ibid., 4.

132. Ibid., 40–41.

133. J. Brent Morris, *Oberlin, Hotbed of Abolitionism: College, Community, and the Fight for Freedom and Equality in Antebellum America* (Chapel Hill, NC: University of North Carolina Press, 2014); Owen W. Muelder, *Theodore Dwight Weld and the American Anti-Slavery Society* (Jefferson, NC: McFarland, 2011).

134. Fred R. Shapiro, ed., *The Yale Book of Quotations* (New Haven, CT: Yale University Press, 2006), 86.

135. John Thornton, *Africa and Africans in the Making of the Atlantic World, 1400–1800*, second edition (Cambridge: Cambridge University Press, 1998), 98–102.

136. John Chrysostom, "Homily 4 on Romans," in *Nicene and Post-Nicene Fathers*, First Series, vol. 11, ed. Philip Schaff, trans. J. Walker, J. Sheppard, and H. Browne, rev. George B. Stevens (Buffalo, NY: Christian Literature, 1889), rev. and ed. for New Advent by Kevin Knight, http://www.newadvent.org/fathers/210204.htm.

137. Augustine. *Confessions*, in *Nicene and Post-Nicene Fathers*, First Series, vol. 1, book 3, Chapter 8, Point 15, ed. Philip Schaff, trans. J. G. Pilkington (Buffalo, NY: Christian Literature Publishing, 1887 [397–400]), rev. and ed. for New Advent by Kevin Knight, accessed April 7, 2018, http://www.newadvent.org/fathers/1101.htm.

138. Ewald Martin Plass, *What Luther Says: An Anthology* (St. Louis: Concordia, 1959), 1:134.

139. John Calvin, *Commentary on Romans*, "Romans 1:24–32," Christian Classics Ethereal Library, accessed April 7, 2018, https://www.ccel.org/ccel/calvin/calcom38.v.vii.html.

140. Matthew Poole, *Annotations upon the Holy Bible Wherein the Sacred Text Is Inserted and Various Readings Annexed*, vol. 2, fourth edition (London: Thomas Parkhurst, 1700), Early English Books Online, image 444 of 629.

141. Paul Halsall, "Reviewing Boswell," in Fordham University, *People with a History: An Online Guide to Lesbian, Gay, Bisexual, and Trans* History*, December 17, 1995, https://sourcebooks.fordham.edu/halsall/pwh/bosrevdisc-kennedy1.asp.

142. Matthew Vines, *God and the Gay Christian: The Biblical Case in Support of Same-Sex Relationships* (New York: Convergent Books, 2014); Ken Wilson, *A Letter to My Congregation: An Evangelical Pastor's Path to Embracing People Who Are Gay, Lesbian, Bisexual and Transgender into the Company of Jesus* (Canton, MI: Spirit Books, 2014); and James Brownson, *Bible, Gender, Sexuality: Reframing the Church's Debate on Same-Sex Relationships* (Grand Rapids, MI: William B. Eerdmans, 2013).

143. Vines, *God and the Gay Christian*, 2.

144. Wilson, *A Letter to My Congregation*, 9, 51.

145. Brownson, *Bible, Gender, Sexuality*, 4; Western Theological Seminary, "Mission and Vision," accessed April 7, 2018, https://www.westernsem.edu/about/mission-vision/.

146. Wilson, *A Letter to My Congregation*, 73.

147. Wilson, *A Letter to My Congregation*, 77.

148. Brownson, *Bible, Gender, Sexuality*, 268.

149. William Loader, *Making Sense of Sex: Attitudes towards Sexuality in Early Jewish and Christian Literature* (Grand Rapids, MI: William B. Eerdmans, 2013), 132–37.

150. Vines, *God and the Gay Christian*, 130.

151. Vines, *God and the Gay Christian*, 82.

152. Jonathan McLatchie, "Cherry Picking the Bible? Are Christians Expected to Follow the Levitical Laws," December 10, 2011, CrossExamined.org, https://crossexamined.org/cherry-picking-the-bible-are-christians-expected-to-follow-the-levitical-laws/.

153. Tertullian, *An Answer to the Jews*, in *Ante-Nicene Fathers*, vol. 3, ed. Alexander Roberts, James Donaldson, and A. Cleveland Coxe, trans. S. Thelwall (Buffalo, NY: Christian Literature , 1885), rev. and ed. for New Advent by Kevin Knight. http://www.newadvent.org/fathers/0308.htm, ch. 2.

154. Ibid., chapters 3–6.

155. Jonathan F. Bayes, *The Threefold Division of the Law* (Newcastle upon Tyne, UK: Christian Institute, 2017), The Christian Institute, http://www.christian.org.uk/wp-content/uploads/the-threefold-division-of-the-law.pdf.

156. Brownson, *Bible, Gender, Sexuality*, 266.

157. Brownson, *Bible, Gender, Sexuality*, 259. Italics in original.

158. Wilson, *A Letter to My Congregation*, 60.

159. *Strong's Concordance*, Bible Hub, accessed April 8, 2018, http://biblehub.net/search-strongs.php?q=malakos.

160. James B. DeYoung, *Homosexuality: Contemporary Claims Examined in Light of the Bible and Other Ancient Literature and Law* (Grand Rapids, MI: Kregel , 2000), 198–99.

161. Vines, *God and the Gay Christian*, 124–25.

162. Elizabeth Closstraugott and Richard B. Dasher, *Regularity in Semantic Change* (Cambridge: Cambridge University Press, 2004).

163. National Council of Churches of Singapore, *A Christian Response to Homosexuality* (Kent Ridge, Singapore: Genesis Books, 2004), 14–17.

164. Petri Paavola, "What Does the Bible Say about Homosexuality?" accessed April 8, 2018, http://www.kotipetripaavola.com/homosexual.html.

165. *Strong's Concordance*, Bible Hub, accessed April 8, 2018, http://biblehub.com/greek/733.htm.

166. Michael L. Brown, *Can You Be Gay and Christian? Responding with Love and Truth to Questions about Homosexuality* (Lake Mary, FL: Front Line, 2014), 167.

167. Robert A. J. Gagnon, *The Bible and Homosexual Practice: Texts and Hermeneutics* (Nashville, TN: Abingdon Press, 2001), ch. 4.

168. William Loader, *Sexuality in the New Testament: Understanding the Key Texts* (Louisville, KY: Westminster John Knox Press, 2010), ch. 2.

169. Louis Crompton, *Homosexuality and Civilization* (Cambridge, MA: Harvard University Press, 2003).

170. See the public opinion data on how different religious groups (including the unaffiliated) think about homosexuality in Pew Research Center, 2014 Religions Landscape Survey, http://www.pewforum.org/religious-landscape-study/views-about-homosexuality/.

CHAPTER 6

1. Miep Gies and Alison Leslie Gold, *Anne Frank Remembered: The Story of the Woman Who Helped to Hide the Frank Family* (New York: Simon & Schuster Paperbacks, 2009), 105, 110–11, and 120–21.

2. Ibid., 241; Michael T. Kaufman, "The Woman Who Saved the Diary of a Young Girl," *New York Times*, March 11, 1995, https://www.nytimes.com/1995/03/11/nyregion /about-new-york-the-woman-who-saved-the-diary-of-a-young-girl.html. On the principles of humanism, see Greg M. Epstein, *Good without God: What a Billion Nonreligious People Do Believe* (New York: William Morrow Paperbacks, 2010).

3. Robert P. Ericksen, *Complicity in the Holocaust: Churches and Universities in Nazi Germany* (Cambridge: Cambridge University Press, 2012).

4. Eric Metaxas, *Bonhoeffer: Pastor, Martyr, Prophet, Spy* (Nashville, TN: Thomas Nelson, 2010).

5. See, for example, Exodus 20:1, Ezekiel 36:13, and Isaiah 48:17.

6. John F. Walvoord, "Is the Bible the Inspired Word of God," Bible.org, January 1, 2008, https://bible.org/seriespage/1-bible-inspired-word-god.

7. Jeffrey Kranz, "The 35 Authors Who Wrote the Bible," OverviewBible, August 9, 2018, https://overviewbible.com/authors-who-wrote-bible/.

8. "Encyclopedia of the Bible—Book of Ruth," Bible Gateway, accessed August 17, 2018, https://www.biblegateway.com/resources/encyclopedia-of-the-bible/Book-Ruth; "Encyclopedia of the Bible—Book of Esther," Bible Gateway, accessed August 17, 2018, https://www.biblegateway.com/resources/encyclopedia-of-the-bible/Book-Esther.

9. Kathy L. Gaca, "The Martial Rape of Girls and Women in Antiquity and Modernity," in *The Oxford Handbook of Gender and Conflict*, ed. Fionnuala Ní Aoláin, Naomi Cahn, Dina Francesca Haynes, and Nahla Valji (New York: Oxford University Press, 2018), 305–15.

10. Robert E. McNally, *The Bible in the Early Middle Ages* (Eugene, OR: Wipf & Stock, 1959).

11. "Divine Right of Kings," Credo, accessed August 18, 2018, https://search.credoreference.com/content/topic/divine_right_of_kings.

12. "Adamnan: Life of St. Columba," in Fordham University, *Medieval Sourcebook*, accessed August 18, 2018, https://sourcebooks.fordham.edu/basis/columba-e.asp.

13. As quoted in Jonathan Duncan, *The Dukes of Normandy from the Time of Rollo to the Expulsion of King John by Philip Augustus of France* (London: Joseph Rickerby, Sherbourn Lane, and Harvey and Darton, 1839), 290.

14. Martin Luther, "Against the Robbing and Murdering Hordes of Peasants," trans. Charles M. Jacobs, Scroll Publishing, accessed July 9, 2021, https://www.scrollpublishing.com/store/Luther-Peasants.html.

15. Augustine of Hippo, "Tractate 29 (John 7:14–18)," par. 6, New Advent, accessed August 18, 2018, http://www.newadvent.org/fathers/1701029.htm.

16. Brian Davies and G. R. Evans, eds., *Anselm of Canterbury: The Major Works* (Oxford: Oxford University Press, 1998), 82–104.

17. As quoted in Edward J. Ondrako, *Progressive Illumination: A Journey with John Henry Cardinal Newman, 1980–2005* (Binghamton, NY: Global Academic, 2006), 189.

18. Joseph Hilgers, "Index of Prohibited Books," in *The Catholic Encyclopedia*, vol. 7. (New York: Robert Appleton Company, 1910), accessed July 8, 2021, http://www.newadvent.org/cathen/07721a.htm.

19. Maurice A. Finocchiaro, *Retrying Galileo, 1633–1992* (Berkeley, CA: University of California Press, 2005).

20. Jeffrey Stout, *The Flight from Authority: Religion, Morality, and the Quest for Autonomy* (Notre Dame, IN: University of Notre Dame Press, 1981).

21. Hugo Grotius, *The Rights of War and Peace*, vol. 1, ed. Richard Tuck (Indianapolis: Liberty Fund, 2005 [1625]), Online Library of Liberty, http://oll.libertyfund.org/titles/grotius-the-rights-of-war-and-peace-2005-ed-vol-1-book-i.

22. John Locke, *An Essay Concerning Human Understanding*, ed. Jonathan Bennett, 2017 [1690], book 4, chapter 19,, 280, Early Modern Texts, accessed July 9, 2021, http://www.earlymoderntexts.com/assets/pdfs/locke1690book4_3.pdf.

23. Cesare Bonesana di Beccaria, *An Essay on Crimes and Punishments*, Online Library of Liberty, accessed August 19, 2018, http://oll.libertyfund.org/titles/beccaria-an-essay-on-crimes-and-punishments.

24. J. H. Burns and H. L. A. Hart, eds., *The Collected Works of Jeremy Bentham* (Oxford: Oxford University Press, 2005).

25. Dena Goodman, *The Republic of Letters: A Cultural History of the French Enlightenment* (Ithaca, NY: Cornell University Press, 1994).

26. Anthony Pagden, *The Enlightenment: And Why It Still Matters* (Oxford: Oxford University Press, 2013).

27. Max Roser and Esteban Ortiz-Ospina, "Literacy," Our World in Data, accessed August 18, 2018, https://ourworldindata.org/literacy.

28. Olaf Simons, "The English Market of Books: Title Statistics and a Comparison with German Data," June 7, 2013, Critical Threads, https://criticalthreads.wordpress.com/2013/07/06/4-the-english-market-of-books-title-statistics-and-a-comparison-with-german-data/.

29. Jürgen Habermas, *The Structural Transformation of the Public Square: An Inquiry into the Category of Bourgeois Society*, trans. Thomas Burger (Cambridge, MA: MIT Press, 1991).

30. Mary Wollstonecraft, *A Vindication of the Rights of Woman* (Mineola, NY: Dover , 1996 [1792]).

31. Ann Harmon, "Women Writers of the Nineteenth Century," August 5, 2012, The New Agenda, http://thenewagenda.net/2012/08/05/women-writers-of-the-nineteenth-century/; Kristian Wilson, "25 Books by Modernist Women Writers," August 19, 2016, Bustle, https://www.bustle.com/articles/169948-25-books-by-modernist-women-writers.

32. Rogers M. Smith and Philip A. Klinkner, *The Unsteady March: The Rise and Decline of Racial Equality in America* (Chicago: University of Chicago Press, 1999).

33. David Vincent, *The Rise of Mass Literacy: Reading and Writing in Modern Europe* (Cambridge: Polity Press, 2000).

34. Manisha Sinha, *The Slave's Curse: A History of Abolition* (New Haven, CT: Yale University Press, 2016).

266

35. Seymour Drescher, *Abolition: A History of Slavery and Antislavery* (Cambridge: Cambridge University Press, 2009).

36. Kenneth Richard Samples, *Without a Doubt: Answering the 20 Toughest Faith Questions* (Grand Rapids, MI: Baker Books, 2004), 237.

37. Malcolm Gaskill, *Witchcraft: A Very Short Introduction* (Oxford: Oxford University Press, 2010), 76.

38. Michael Shermer, *The Moral Arc: How Science and Reason Lead Humanity toward Truth, Justice, and Freedom* (New York: Henry Holt, 2015), ch. 3.

39. *Atlas: Epilepsy Care in the World, 2005* (Geneva: World Health Organization, 2005), 16.

40. Krzysztof Owczarek and Joanna Jędrzejczak, "Christianity and Epilepsy," *Neurologia i Neurochirurgia Polska* 47 (2013): 271–77.

41. Patricia O. Shafer, "About Epilepsy: The Basics," 2014, Epilepsy Foundation, accessed August 17, 2018, https://www.epilepsy.com/learn/about-epilepsy-basics.

42. See, for example, Emily Armstrong, "What God's Teaching Me through Epilepsy," *Blogging Theologically*, February 12, 2013, https://www.bloggingtheologically.com/2013/02/12/what-gods-teaching-me-through-epilepsy/.

43. On human flourishing in the absence of religion, see Phil Zuckerman, *Society without God: What the Least Religious Nations Can Tell Us about Contentment*, second edition (New York: New York University Press, 2020).

44. Gilbert H. Herdt, ed., *Ritualized Homosexuality in Melanesia* (Berkeley, CA: University of California Press, 1984).

45. *People with a History: An Online Guide to Lesbian, Gay, Bisexual, and Trans History*, in Fordham University, Internet History Sourcebooks Project, accessed August 18, 2018, https://sourcebooks.fordham.edu/pwh/index-anc.asp.

46. Sue-Ellen Jacobs, Wesley Thomas, and Sabine Lang, eds., *Two-Spirit People: Native American Identity, Sexuality, and Spirituality* (Urbana: University of Illinois Press, 1997).

47. Robert A. J. Gagnon, *The Bible and Homosexual Practice: Texts and Hermeneutics* (Nashville, TN: Abingdon Press, 2001).

48. Rita J. Simon and Alison Brooks, *Gay and Lesbian Communities the World Over* (Lanham, MD: Lexington Books, 2009), 30–31.

49. Jeffrey Richards, *Sex, Dissidence, and Damnation: Minority Groups in the Middle Ages* (New York: Routledge, 1991), ch. 7.

50. Louis Crompton, *Homosexuality and Civilization* (Cambridge, MA: Harvard University Press, 2003), ch. 7.

51. Jeremy Bentham, "Offences against One's Self," Stonewall and Beyond, accessed August 19, 2018, http://www.columbia.edu/cu/lweb/eresources/exhibitions/sw25/bentham/index.html.

52. George E. Haggerty, ed., *Gay Histories and Cultures: An Encyclopedia* (New York: Routledge, 2012), 713.

53. Richard von Krafft-Ebing, *Psychopathia Sexualis: The Classic Study of Deviant Sex*, trans. Franklin S. Klaf (New York: Skyhorse, 2011).

54. Ralf Dose, *Magnus Hirschfeld and the Origins of the Gay Liberation Movement*, trans. Edward H. Willis (New York: Monthly Review Press, 2014), 51–67.

55. Richard Plant, *The Pink Triangle: The Nazi War against Homosexuals* (New York: Henry Holt, 1986).

56. David K. Johnson, *The Lavender Scare: The Cold War Persecution of Gays and Lesbians in the Federal Government* (Chicago: University of Chicago Press, 2004).

57. US Senate, "Employment of Homosexuals and Other Sex Perverts in the US Government," reprinted (selections) in Mark Blasius and Shane Phelan, eds., *We Are Everywhere: A Historical Sourcebook of Gay and Lesbian Politics* (New York: Routledge, 1997), 251.

58. Joey L. Mogul, Andrea J. Ritchie, and Kay Whitlock, *Queer (In)Justice: The Criminalization of LGBT People in the United States* (Boston: Beacon Press, 2012), ch. 2.

59. *Readers' Guide to Periodical Literature* 20 (March 1955 to February 1957): 1144–45.

60. Steven Seidman, *Beyond the Closet: The Transformation of Gay and Lesbian Life* (New York: Routledge, 2004), ch. 1.

61. Leila J. Rupp, "The European Origins of Transnational Organizing: The International Committee for Sexual Equality," in *LGBT Activism and the Making of Europe: A Rainbow Europe?* ed. Phillip M. Ayoub and David Paternotte (New York: Palgrave Macmillan, 2014), 29–49.

62. Based on word searches of the *New York Times* Archive, accessed November 4, 2011, http://www.nytimes.com/ref/membercenter/nytarchive.html.

63. American Psychiatric Association, *Diagnostic and Statistical Manual: Mental Disorders* (Washington, DC: American Psychiatric Association, 1952), 38–39.

64. Stuart A. Kirk and Herb Kutchins, *The Selling of DSM: The Rhetoric of Science in Psychiatry* (New York: Routledge, 2017), ch. 4.

65. Evelyn Hooker, "The Adjustment of the Male Overt Homosexual," *Journal of Projective Techniques* 21 (1957): 18–31.

66. Lisa M. Stulberg, *LGBTQ Social Movements* (Cambridge: Polity Press, 2018), ch. 2.

67. Herb Kutchins and Stuart A. Kirk, *Making Us Crazy: DSM: The Psychiatric Bible and the Creation of Mental Disorders* (New York: Free Press, 1997), ch. 3.

68. Simon LeVay, "A Difference in Hypothalmic Structure between Heterosexual and Homosexual Men," *Science* 253 (August 1991): 1034–37.

69. J. M. Bailey, M. P. Dunne, and N. G. Martin, "Genetic and Environmental Influences on Sexual Orientation and Its Correlates in an Australian Twin Sample," *Journal of Personality and Social Psychology* 78 (March 2000): 524–36.

70. Terrance J. Williams, Michelle E. Pepitone, Scott E. Christensen, Bradley Cooke, Andrew D. Huberman, Nicholas J. Breedlove, Tessa J. Breedlove, Cynthia Jordan, and Stephen Breedlove, "Finger-Length Ratios and Sexual Orientation," *Nature* 404 (2000): 455–56.

71. American Psychological Association, "Answers to Your Questions for a Better Understanding of Sexual Orientation and Homosexuality," 2008, accessed August 19, 2018, http://www.apa.org/topics/lgbt/orientation.pdf.

72. "Gay and Lesbian Rights," Gallup, accessed August 19, 2018, https://news.gallup.com/poll/1651/gay-lesbian-rights.aspx.

73. Mark R. Joslyn and Donald P. Haider-Markel, "Genetic Attributions, Immutability, and Stereotypical Judgments: An Analysis of Homosexuality," *Social Science Quarterly* 97

(2016): 377–90; Mark R. Joslyn and Donald P. Haider-Markel, "Beliefs about Homosexuality and Support for Gay Rights: An Empirical Test of Attribution Theory," *Public Opinion Quarterly* 72 (2018): 291–310.

74. Seidman, *Beyond the Closet*, ch. 1.

75. Melanie C. Steffens and Christof Wagner, "Attitudes toward Lesbians, Gay Men, Bisexual Women, and Bisexual Men in Germany," *Journal of Sex Research* 41 (2004): 137–49; *Gallup Poll: Public Opinion 2009* (Lanham, MD: Rowman & Littlefield, 2010), 190–91.

76. "Growing Support for Gay Marriage: Changed Minds and Changing Demographics," Pew Research Center, March 20, 2013, http://www.people-press.org/2013/03/20/growing-support-for-gay-marriage-changed-minds-and-changing-demographics/.

77. Alvin J. Schmidt, *How Christianity Changed the World* (Grand Rapids, MI: Zondervan, 2001).

78. Christopher Hitchens and Douglas Wilson, *Is Christianity Good for the World? A Debate* (Moscow, ID: Canon Press, 2008), 29.

79. Joseph M. de Torre, "The Influence of Christianity on Modern Democracy, Equality, and Freedom," 1997, Catholic Education Resource Center, accessed August 17, 2018, https://www.catholiceducation.org/en/culture/catholic-contributions/the-influence-of-christianity-on-modern-democracy-equality-and-freedom.html.

80. Melinda Penner, "The Church and Slavery," Stand to Reason, July 17, 2015, https://www.str.org/blog/the-church-and-slavery#.W3cI2uhKgdU.

81. Ross Douthat, "Liberalism Is Stuck Halfway between Heaven and Earth," *Slate*, April 19, 2012, http://www.slate.com/articles/arts/the_book_club/features/2012/ross_douthat_s_bad_religion/bad_religion_by_ross_douthat_reviewed_liberalism_and_christianity_.html.

82. Brad S. Gregory, *Rebel in the Ranks: Martin Luther, the Reformation, and the Conflicts That Continue to Shape Our World* (New York: Harper One, 2017), 5.

83. "A Brief History of Gamebooks," Games vs Play, accessed August 17, 2018, http://gamesvsplay.com/a-brief-history-of-gamebooks/.

84. Bryan R. Wilson, *Religion in Sociological Perspective* (Oxford: Oxford University Press, 1982).

85. See my chapter 5.

86. Ibid.

87. Joshua Miller, *The Rise and Fall of Democracy in Early America, 1630–1789: The Legacy for Contemporary Politics* (University Park, PA: Pennsylvania State University Press, 1991), ch 2.

88. See my chapter 5; see also Mark A. Smith, *Secular Faith: How Culture Has Trumped Religion in American Politics* (Chicago: University of Chicago Press, 2015).

89. Smith, *Secular Faith*, ch. 2.

90. Pope Pius IX, "The Syllabus of Errors," Papal Encyclicals Online, accessed June 27, 2018, https://www.papalencyclicals.net/pius09/p9syll.htm. See especially propositions 15 and 55.

91. Smith, *Secular Faith*, ch. 6.

92. Daniel Pipes, *Russia under the Bolshevik Regime* (New York: Vintage, 1994), ch. 5; Lesley Chamberlain, *Lenin's Private War: The Voyage of the Philosophy Steamer and the Exile of the Intelligentsia* (New York: St. Martin's Press, 2007); James Ryan, *Lenin's Terror: The Ideological Origins of Early Soviet State Violence* (New York: Routledge, 2012), ch. 5.

93. Robert W. Thurston, *Life and Terror in Stalin's Russia, 1934–1941* (New Haven, CT: Yale University Press, 1996), chs. 3–5; Isaiah Berlin, "The Arts in Russia under Stalin," *New York Review of Books*, October 19, 2000, https://www.nybooks.com/articles/2000/10/19/the-arts-in-russia-under-stalin/.

94. Tom Buchanan, *Europe's Troubled Peace: 1945 to the Present*, second edition (New York: Wiley-Blackwell, 2012), ch. 6.

95. Adolf Hitler, "Hitler's Speech to the National Socialist Women's League," September 8, 1934, German History in Documents and Images, http://ghdi.ghi-dc.org/sub_document.cfm?document_id=1557.

96. Lisa Pine, *Education in Nazi Germany* (Oxford, UK: Oberg, 2010), 28.

97. Guenter Lewy, *Harmful and Undesirable: Book Censorship in Nazi Germany* (New York: Oxford University Press, 2016), ch. 2; David Welch, *The Third Reich: Politics and Propaganda*, second edition (London: Routledge, 2002), chs. 3–4; Paul R. Maracin, *The Night of the Long Knives: Forty-Eight Hours That Changed the History of the World* (Guilford, CT: Lyons Press, 2004); Nikolaus Wachsmann, *KL: A History of the Nazi Concentration Camps* (New York: Farrar, Straus and Giroux, 2015), chs. 1–2.

98. Stéphane Courtois, et al., *The Black Book of Communism: Crimes, Terror, Repression* (Cambridge, MA: Harvard University Press, 1999).

99. Paul Havemann, *Indigenous Peoples' Rights in Australia, Canada, and New Zealand* (Oxford: Oxford University Press, 1999).

100. Carol Anderson, *One Person, No Vote: How Voter Suppression Is Destroying Our Democracy* (New York: Bloomsbury, 2018).

101. William Fitzhugh Brundage, *Lynching in the New South: Georgia and Virginia, 1880–1930* (Champaign: University of Illinois Press, 2012).

102. Michelle Alexander, *The New Jim Crow: Mass Incarceration in the Age of Colorblindness* (New York: New Press, 2012).

103. Pew Research Center, "The Future of World Religions: Population Growth Projections, 2010–2015," accessed August 14, 2018, http://www.pewforum.org/2015/04/02/religious-projections-2010-2050/.

CHAPTER 7

1. Pope Paul VI, "Dei Verbum," November 18, 1965, The Vatican, accessed June 26, 2019, http://www.vatican.va/archive/hist_councils/ii_vatican_council/documents/vat-ii_const_19651118_dei-verbum_en.html.

2. "Quran: The Word of God," Whyislam.org, accessed June 26, 2019, https://www.whyislam.org/quran/quran-the-word-of-god/.

3. Wendy Wilson, "Barna Research Finds Many Americans Still Read Bible, but What Are They Learning," August 23, 2018, Illinois Family Institute, https://illinoisfamily

.org/faith/barna-research-finds-many-americans-still-read-bible-but-what-are-they
-learning/.

4. The practice is detailed in the documentary *Koran by Heart: One Chance to Remember*, directed by Greg Barker (New York: HBO Home Entertainment, 2011).

5. Sahar Amer, *What Is Veiling?* (Chapel Hill: University of North Carolina Press, 2014).

6. Quentin Wodon, "Islamic Law, Women's Rights, and State Law: The Cases of Female Genital Cutting and Child Marriage," *Review of Faith and International Affairs* 13, no. 3 (2015): 85–86.

7. S. A. Aldeeb Abu-Sahlieh, "Muslims' Genitalia in the Hands of the Clergy: Religious Arguments about Male and Female Circumcision," in *Male and Female Circumcision: Medical, Legal, and Ethical Considerations in Pediatric Practice*, ed. George C. Denniston, Frederick Mansfield Hodges, and Marilyn Fayre Milos (New York: Kluwer Academic, 1999), 131–72.

8. Quran 24:4, 24:13; Sahih al-Bukhari 5:59:462.

9. On women's intelligence: see Sahih al-Bukhari 1:6:301, 2:24:541, and 3:48:826; on women in hell, see Sahih Muslim 241 and 2048; on Aisha's ages at marriage and consummation, see Sahih al-Bukhari 5:58:236, 7:62:64, and 8:73:151, Sahih Muslim 8:3310 and 3311, Ibn Majah 3:1877, and Sunan Abu Dawud 2116.

10. Unless otherwise indicated, I will be using text from *The Study Quran*. Its translation team was led by Seyyed Hossein Nasr, a widely respected scholar of philosophy and Islamic studies. *The Study Quran* has quickly become one of the most popular translations used in academic institutions in the English-speaking world. See Celene Ibrahim, "The Study Quran: A New Translation and Commentary," *Journal of Islamic and Muslim Studies* 1, no. 2 (2000): 89–92.

11. Unless I'm quoting another author, I use a minimalist approach in transliterating Arabic words into the Roman alphabet. Thus, I refer in this chapter to the "Quran" rather than the "Qur'ān"; "qiyas" rather than "qiyās"; etc.

12. See Don Symons's correspondence with Julie Metz in her book *Perfection: A Memoir of Betrayal and Renewal* (New York: Voice, 2009), 294.

13. Azhar Aslam and Shaista Kazmi, "Muslim Women and Property Rights," Institute of Economic Affairs, July 16, 2009, https://iea.org.uk/blog/muslim-women-and-property-rights.

14. Yuhong Zhao, "Domestic Violence in China: In Search of Legal and Social Responses," *UCLA Pacific Basin Law Journal* 18, no. 2 (2000): 212–13.

15. World Health Organization, *Global and Regional Estimates of Violence against Women: Prevalence and Health Effects of Intimate Partner Violence and Non-Partner Sexual Violence* (Geneva: World Health Organization: 2013), 17, World Health Organization, https://apps.who.int/iris/bitstream/handle/10665/85239/9789241564625_eng.pdf;jsessionid=F3F35B7F7CABB56C5CF8D50743224189?sequence=1.

16. The image is available at Wikimedia Commons, accessed July 4, 2019, https://commons.wikimedia.org/wiki/File:A_Husband_Beating_his_Wife_with_a_Stick_-_Google_Art_Project.png.

17. William Blackstone, *Commentaries on the Laws of England*, vol. 1, ed. William Carey Jones (San Francisco: Bancroft-Whitney, 1915), 633–34.

18. *The Liberties of the Massachusets Collonie in New England*, 1641, no. 80, Hanover Historical Texts Project, accessed August 31, 2019, https://history.hanover.edu/texts/masslib.html.

19. S. J. Kleinberg, *Women in the United States, 1830–1945* (Houndmills, UK: Macmillan, 1999), 143.

20. World Health Organization, *Global and Regional Estimates of Violence against Women*, 2.

21. Ayesha S. Chaudhry, *Domestic Violence and the Islamic Tradition* (Oxford: Oxford University Press, 2013), 2.

22. Ibid.

23. Ibid.

24. Ibid., 3–5.

25. Ibid, 4–5.

26. Ibid., 8.

27. Ibid.

28. Ibid., 223.

29. Ibid., 136.

30. Ayesha Chaudhry, "Does the Koran Allow Wife-Beating? Not If Muslims Don't Want It To," *Toronto Globe and Mail*, March 27, 2014, https://www.theglobeandmail.com/opinion/its-muslims-who-give-voice-to-verse/article17684163/.

31. Meira Svirsky, "Georgetown Professor Condones Rape and Slavery under Sharia," Clarion Project, February 12, 2017, https://clarionproject.org/georgetown-professor-condones-rape-and-slavery-under-sharia/.

32. See Haras Rafiq's screenshot of Brown's post at Haras Rafiq, (@HarasRafiq), "@MaajidNawaz @mwphnh Further Points from the @Georgetown Professor—I Wonder What the Uni Has to Say about This, Especially Point 4," Twitter, February 11, 2017, 1:50 a.m. https://twitter.com/HarasRafiq/status/830353315665952770.

33. Jonathan A. C. Brown, "Islam and the Problem of Slavery," YouTube Video, 1:21:57. February 9, 2017, https://www.youtube.com/watch?v=MpFatRwdPm0, beginning at 47:36.

34. Ibid., beginning at 48:12.

35. Ibid., beginning at 1:00:01.

36. Ibid., beginning at 1:10:38.

37. Ibid., beginning at 1:18:03.

38. Ali A. Rizvi, *The Atheist Muslim: A Journey from Religion to Reason* (New York: St. Martin's Press, 2016), 190–92.

39. United Nations Children's Fund, *Ending Child Marriage: Progress and Prospects* (New York: UNICEF, 2014).

40. Girls Not Brides, under "What Is the Impact of Child Marriage," sections on Conflict and Humanitarian Crises, Education, Health, Human Rights and Justice, Poverty, Sustainable Development Goals (SDGs), and Violence Against Girls, accessed August 31, 2019, https://www.girlsnotbrides.org/what-is-the-impact/.

41. Data downloaded from the website of UNICEF, Child Marriage, accessed July 16, 2019. https://data.unicef.org/topic/child-protection/child-marriage/.
42. Shyámacharan Sarkár Vidyá-Bhúshan, *Vyavasthá-Darpana: A Digest of Hindú Law, as Current in Bengal*, third edition (Calcutta: Shanhope Press, 1883), 168.
43. *The Laws of Manu*, trans. Georg Bühler, chapter 9, no. 90, Internet Sacred Text Archive, accessed July 16, 2019, http://www.sacred-texts.com/hin/manu/manu09.htm.
44. "The Quran; Commentaries for 65:4; Al Talaq (Divorce)," QuranX.com, accessed July 7, 2021, https://quranx.com/tafsirs/65.4.
45. Arzu Kaya-Uranli, profile at LinkedIn, accessed August 30, 2019, https://www.linkedin.com/in/arzu-kaya-uranli-b4612a28.
46. Arzu Kaya-Uranli, "Nowhere Does Islam Excuse Child Brides," *Huffpost*, June 18, 2014, https://www.huffpost.com/entry/nowhere-does-islam-excuse_b_5176425.
47. "Turkish Child Marriage Religious Document Sparks Anger," BBC News, January 3, 2018, https://www.bbc.com/news/world-europe-42558328.
48. Kaleef K. Karim, "Quran 65:4—The Child Marriage Claim," Discover the Truth, March 12, 2016, https://discover-the-truth.com/2016/03/12/quran-654-the-child-marriage-claim/.
49. Ro Waseem, "Ideology vs. Islam," WVoice, July 8, 2014, http://www.womensvoices-now.org/wvoice/ideology-vs-islam/.
50. Rose McDermott, *The Evils of Polygyny: Evidence of Its Harm to Women, Men, and Society* (Ithaca, NY: Cornell University Press, 2018).
51. Amina Wadud, "Islam Beyond Patriarchy through Gender Inclusive Qur'anic Analysis," Musawah, accessed August 31, 2019, http://arabic.musawah.org/sites/default/files/Wanted-AW-EN.pdf.
52. Amina Wadud, *Qur'an and Woman: Rereading the Sacred Text from a Woman's Perspective* (New York: Oxford University Press, 1999).
53. Ibid.; Amina Wadud, *Inside the Gender Jihad: Women's Reform in Islam* (London: Oneworld , 2006).
54. Chaudhry, "Does the Koran Allow Wife-Beating?"
55. Margot Badran, *Feminism in Islam: Secular and Religious Convergences* (Oxford: Oneworld, 2009), 242, 244.
56. Astronauts Wanted, "Episode 6: Can You Be a Muslim Feminist?" Girl on Girl, YouTube Video, April 25, 2016, https://www.youtube.com/watch?v=tmLXk4fkjbs, beginning at 3:12.
57. ABC News, "Sharia Law Debated by Yassmin Abdel-Magied and Jacqui Lambie on Q&A," YouTube Video, 4:46, February 13, 2017, https://www.youtube.com/watch?v=Xn6WKOJDzuI, beginning at 0:45.
58. Eve Ahmad, "I Am a Muslim Feminist," TEDxPasadenaWomen, YouTube Video, 10:32, November 23, 2016, https://www.youtube.com/watch?v=LCuAu67OCDk, beginning at 4:46.
59. Linda Sarsour, "2018 SALAM Annual Banquet_Linda Sarsour," YouTube Video, 35:52, December 13, 2018, https://www.youtube.com/watch?v=WnfyBgGcZuU, beginning at 14:40.

60. NowThisWorld, "What Does It Mean to Be a Feminist in Islam," YouTube Video, 4:02, January 30, 2016, https://www.youtube.com/watch?v=MpdXrKqWx14, beginning at 1:49.

61. No Filter podcast, "Susan Carland on Being a Muslim Feminist," episode 147, 59:33, May 22, 2017, omny.fm, https://omny.fm/shows/no-filter/susan-carland-on-being-a-muslim-feminist, beginning at 17:41.

62. Dumbo feather podcast, "Susan Carland: Activist, Muslim, Mother," episode 1, 53:27, April 27, 2016, Stitcher, https://www.stitcher.com/podcast/dumbo-feather-podcast/e/1-susan-carland-activist-muslim-mother-44322273, beginning at 51:06.

63. Pew Forum on Religion and Public Life, *U.S. Religious Knowledge Survey* (Washington, DC: Pew Research Forum, 2010).

64. Khwaja Mohammed Zubair, "Why Muslims Say 'Peace Be Upon Him' When Muhammad's Name Is Mentioned," *Khaleej Times*, June 18, 2016, https://www.khaleejtimes.com/ramadan-2016/why-muslims-say-peace-be-upon-him-when-muhammads-name-is-mentioned.

65. UBC Faculty of Arts, "Ayesha S. Chaudhry, Associate Professor of Gender and Islam," YouTube Video, 0:59, October 30, 2018, https://www.youtube.com/watch?v=WPcoEZw2hz0.

66. Alaa Murabit, "What Islam Really Says about Women," YouTube Video, 12:23, July 21, 2015, https://www.youtube.com/watch?v=FETryXMpDl8, beginning at 6:30.

67. Ex-Muslims of North America, "Support Communities," accessed August 31, 2019, https://exmuslims.org/community/.

68. Victor Kiprop, "Countries Where Apostasy Is Illegal," WorldAtlas, December 13, 2018, https://www.worldatlas.com/articles/countries-where-apostasy-is-illegal.html.

69. World Economic Forum, *Global Gender Gap Report 2021* (Geneva: World Economic Forum, 2021), 10, https://www.weforum.org/reports/global-gender-gap-report-2021/in-full.

70. Figures on the percentage of Muslims by country can be found in Pew Research Center, *The Future of World Religions: Population Growth Projections, 2010–2050*, April 2, 2015, 234–44, https://assets.pewresearch.org/wp-content/uploads/sites/11/2015/03/PF_15.04.02_ProjectionsFullReport.pdf.

CHAPTER 8

1. "The Amsterdam Declaration," Humanists International, accessed April 2, 2020, https://humanists.international/what-is-humanism/the-amsterdam-declaration/.

2. Ibid.

3. Ibid.

4. Max Sky, "Cultural Christians Should Defend Judeo-Christian Values," *Whaleoil*, April 28, 2019, https://www.whaleoil.net.nz/2019/04/cultural-christians-should-defend-judeo-christian-values/.

5. Bitter Crank, "Why Doesn't the Mosaic God Lead by Example?" The Philosophy Forum, accessed April 2, 2020, https://thephilosophyforum.com/discussion/6254/why-doesnt-the-mosaic-god-lead-by-example/p2.

6. Harold Zwier, "We Need Religion, but God Is Optional," ABC News, September 28, 2010, https://www.abc.net.au/news/2009-12-22/27778.

7. Bruce Gerencser, "Why I Am Still in the Ministry: A Guest Post by John Calvin," The Life and Times of Bruce Gerencser, July 31, 2019, https://brucegerencser.net/2019/07/why-i-am-still-in-the-ministry-a-guest-post-by-john-calvin/.

8. Jean Beaman, *Citizen Outsider: Children of North African Immigrants in France* (Oakland: University of California Press, 2017), 51.

9. Guy MacPherson, "Ali Hassan Mines Muslim Culture for Comedy," *Georgia Straight*, February 15, 2017, https://www.straight.com/arts/868891/ali-hassan-mines-muslim-culture-comedy.

10. Ali Sina, "Debate with Mr. Muhammad K," FaithFreedom.org, accessed April 2, 2020, http://www.faithfreedom.org/debates/arif.htm.

11. Fareed Zakaria, "I Am a Muslim. But Trump's Views Appall Me Because I Am an American," *Washington Post*, December 10, 2015, https://www.washingtonpost.com/opinions/i-am-a-muslim-but-trumps-views-appall-me-because-i-am-an-american/2015/12/10/fcba9ea6-9f6d-11e5-8728-1af6af208198_story.html.

12. Tyler J. VanderWeele, "On the Promotion of Human Flourishing," *Proceedings of the National Academy of Sciences of the United States of America* 114 (August 2017): 8148–56; Tyler J. VanderWeele, "Religion and Health: A Synthesis," in *Spirituality and Religion within the Culture of Medicine: From Evidence to Practice*, ed. Michael J. Balboni and John R. Peteet (New York: Oxford University Press, 2017), 347–401; Scott Schieman, Alex Bierman, and Christopher G. Ellison, "Religion and Mental Health," in *Handbook of the Sociology of Mental Health*, second edition, ed. Carol S. Aneshensel, Jo C. Phelan, and Alex Bierman (New York: Springer, 2013), 457–78.

13. Sally Quinn, "Religion Is a Sure Route to True Happiness," *Washington Post*, January 24, 2014, https://www.washingtonpost.com/national/religion/religion-is-a-sure-route-to-true-happiness/2014/01/23/f6522120-8452-11e3-bbe5-6a2a3141e3a9_story.html; Tom Knox, "The Tantalising Proof That Belief in God Makes You Happier and Healthier," *Daily Mail*, February 18, 2011, https://www.dailymail.co.uk/femail/article-1358421/The-tantalising-proof-belief-God-makes-happier-healthier.html; "Religious Beliefs Make People Happier," *HuffPost*, December 6, 2017, https://www.huffpost.com/entry/religious-beliefs-happier-_n_4725269.

14. Jibum Kim, Tom Smith, and Jeong-han Kang, "Religious Affiliation, Religious Service Attendance, and Mortality," *Journal of Religion and Health* 54 (June 2015): 2052–72; Chaeyoon Lim and Robert D. Putnam, "Religion, Social Networks, and Life Satisfaction," *American Sociological Review* 75 (December 2010): 914–33.

15. Luke W. Galen, "Focusing on the Nonreligious Reveals Secular Mechanisms Underlying Well-Being and Prosociality," *Psychology of Religion and Spirituality* 10 (2018): 296–306.

16. Unitarian Universalist Association, "Sources of Our Living Tradition," Unitarian Universalist Association, accessed April 2, 2020, https://www.uua.org/beliefs/what-we-believe/sources.

17. Unitarian Universalists Association, "We Are Unitarian Universalists," YouTube Video, 3:17, October 6, 2016, https://www.youtube.com/watch?v=-3UYWnngiEo, beginning at 1:20.

Bibliography

ABC News. "Sharia Law Debated by Yassmin Abdel-Magied and Jacqui Lambie on Q&A." YouTube Video, 4:46. February 13, 2017. https://www.youtube.com/watch?v=Xn6WKOJDzuI.

Abu-Sahlieh, S. A. Aldeeb. "Muslims' Genitalia in the Hands of the Clergy: Religious Arguments about Male and Female Circumcision." In *Male and Female Circumcision: Medical, Legal, and Ethical Considerations in Pediatric Practice*, edited by George C. Denniston, Frederick Mansfield Hodges, and Marilyn Fayre Milos, 131–72. New York: Kluwer Academic, 1999.

"Adamnan: Life of St. Columba." In Fordham University, Medieval *Sourcebook*. Accessed August 18, 2018. https://sourcebooks.fordham.edu/basis/columba-e.asp.

Agence France-Presse. "Malala Condemns Donald Trump's 'Ideology of Hatred.'" Public Radio International, December 16, 2015. https://www.pri.org/stories/2015-12-16/malala-condemns-donald-trumps-ideology-hatred.

Ahmad, Eve. "I Am a Muslim Feminist." TEDxPasadenaWomen. YouTube Video, 10:32. November 23, 2016. https://www.youtube.com/watch?v=LCuAu67OCDk.

Akers, Christopher. "God and Objective Morality." The Catholic Thing. July 8, 2017. https://www.thecatholicthing.org/2017/07/08/god-and-objective-morality/.

Alcorn, Randy. *If God Is Good: Faith in the Midst of Suffering and Evil*. Colorado Springs, CO: Multnomah Books, 2009.

Alcuin. Epistles 110 and 113. In *Christianity and Religious Freedom: A Sourcebook of Scriptural, Theological, and Legal Texts*, edited by Karen Taliaferro. Washington, DC: Berkeley Center for Religion, Peace & World Affairs of Georgetown University, 2014.

Alexander, Michelle. *The New Jim Crow: Mass Incarceration in the Age of Colorblindness*. New York: New Press, 2012.

Ali, Rushanara, "157 Parliamentarians Call on Government to Suspend and Review British Military Training Programs with Burmese Military." Burma Campaign UK, September 10, 2017. http://burmacampaign.org.uk/157-parliamentarians-call-on-government-to-suspend-and-review-british-military-training-programs-with-burmese-military/.

Allison, Gregg, and Chris Castaldo. *The Unfinished Reformation: What Unites and Divides Catholics and Protestants after 500 Years*. Grand Rapids, MI: Zondervan, 2016.

Allport, Gordon. *The Nature of Prejudice*. New York: Perseus Books, 1954.

Amer, Sahar. *What Is Veiling?* Chapel Hill: University of North Carolina Press, 2014.

American Psychiatric Association. *Diagnostic and Statistical Manual: Mental Disorders.* Washington, DC: American Psychiatric Association, 1952.

American Psychological Association. "Answers to Your Questions for a Better Understanding of Sexual Orientation and Homosexuality." 2008. http://www.apa.org/topics/lgbt/orientation.pdf.

Anca, Celia de. *Beyond Tribalism: Managing Identity in a Diverse World.* New York: Palgrave Macmillan, 2012.

Anderson, Carol. *One Person, No Vote: How Voter Suppression Is Destroying Our Democracy.* New York: Bloomsbury, 2018.

Anderson, Elizabeth. "If God Is Dead, Is Everything Permitted?" In *Philosophers without Gods: Meditations on Atheism and the Secular Life,* edited by Louise Antony, 215–30. New York: Oxford University Press, 2007.

Ankerberg, John, and Dillon Burroughs. *Why Does God Allow Suffering and Evil?* Chattanooga, TN: AMG, 2008.

Annotations upon All the Books of the Old and New Testament. London: John Legatt, 1651.

Appiah, Kwame Anthony. *Cosmopolitanism: Ethics in a World of Strangers.* New York: W.W. Norton, 2006.

Applebaum, Anne. *Gulag: A History.* New York: Doubleday, 2003.

Aquinas, Thomas. *Summa Theologica.* Translated by the Fathers of the English Dominican Province. New York: Benzinger Bros., 1947. Internet Sacred Text Archive. Accessed June 18, 2017. http://www.sacred-texts.com/chr/aquinas/summa/index.htm.

Archer, Gleason L. *Encyclopedia of Bible Difficulties.* Grand Rapids, MI: Zondervan, 1982.

"Are Children Punished for the Sins of Their Parents." GotQuestions.org. Accessed November 18, 2017. https://www.gotquestions.org/parents-sin.html.

Armstrong, Emily. "What God's Teaching Me Through Epilepsy." *Blogging Theologically.* February 12, 2013. https://www.bloggingtheologically.com/2013/02/12/what-gods-teaching-me-through-epilepsy/

Arterburn, Stephen, and John Shore. *Being Christian: Exploring Where You, God, and Life Connect.* Bloomington, MN: Bethany House, 2008.

Aslam, Azhar, and Shaista Kazmi. "Muslim Women and Property Rights." Institute of Economic Affairs. July 16, 2009. https://iea.org.uk/blog/muslim-women-and-property-rights.

Astronauts Wanted. "Episode 6: Can You Be a Muslim Feminist?" Girl on Girl. YouTube Video, 9:38. April 25, 2016. https://www.youtube.com/watch?v=tmLXk4fk-jbs.

Atlas: Epilepsy Care in the World, 2005. Geneva: World Health Organization, 2005.

The Augsburg Confession. Zion Evangelical Lutheran Church. Accessed November 19, 2017. http://atlanta.clclutheran.org/bibleclass/bookofconcord/article2.html.

Augustine. "Letter 173 (AD 416) to Donatus." New Advent. Accessed April 26, 2018. http://www.newadvent.org/fathers/1102173.htm.

———. "Letter 34 (AD 396) to Eusebius." New Advent. Accessed April 26, 2018. http://www.newadvent.org/fathers/1102034.htm.

———. "Letter 93 (AD 408) to Vicentius." New Advent. Accessed April 26, 2018. https://www.newadvent.org/fathers/1102093.htm.

———. "Tractate 29 (John 7:14–18)." New Advent. Accessed August 18, 2018. http://www.newadvent.org/fathers/1701029.htm.

———. *The City of God*. In *Nicene and Post-Nicene Fathers*, First Series. Vol. 2. Edited by Philip Schaff. Translated by Marcus Dods. Buffalo, NY: Christian Literature, 1887 [426]. Revised and edited for New Advent by Kevin Knight. Accessed April 2, 2018. http://www.newadvent.org/fathers/1201.htm.

———. *Confessions*. In *Nicene and Post-Nicene Fathers*, First Series. Vol. 1. Edited by Philip Schaff. Translated by J.G. Pilkington. Buffalo, NY: Christian Literature., 1887 [397–400]. Revised and edited for New Advent by Kevin Knight. Accessed April 7, 2018. http://www.newadvent.org/fathers/1101.htm.

Avalos, Hector. *Slavery, Abolitionism, and the Ethics of Biblical Scholarship*. Sheffield, England: Sheffield Phoenix Press, 2013.

Avellaneda, Gertrudis Gómez de. *Sab*. Madrid: Imprenta Calle Del Barco, 1841.

Badran, Margot. *Feminism in Islam: Secular and Religious Convergences*. Oxford: Oneworld, 2009.

Baggini, Julian. *Atheism: A Very Short Introduction*. New York: Oxford University Press, 2003.

Bailey, J. M., M. P. Dunne, and N. G. Martin. "Genetic and Environmental Influences on Sexual Orientation and Its Correlates in an Australian Twin Sample." *Journal of Personality and Social Psychology* 78 (March 2000): 524–36.

Bailey, Ronald. "'Those Valuable People, the Africans': The Economic Impact of the Slave(ry) Trade on Textile Industrialization in New England." In *The Meaning of Slavery in the North*, edited by David Roediger and Martin H. Blatt. New York: Garland, 1998.

Barber, Bart. "The Biblical Case for Religious Liberty." Praisegod Barebones. July 30, 2015. http://praisegodbarebones.blogspot.com/2015/07/the-biblical-case-for-religious-liberty.html.

Barker, Dan. *The Good Atheist: Living a Purpose-Filled Life without God*. Berkeley, CA: Ulysses Press, 2011.

Barnes, Albert. *An Inquiry into the Scriptural Views of Slavery*. Philadelphia: Perkins & Purves, 1846.

Bayes, Jonathan F. *The Threefold Division of the Law*. Newcastle upon Tyne, UK: The Christian Institute, 2017. Accessed April 8, 2018. http://www.christian.org.uk/wp-content/uploads/the-threefold-division-of-the-law.pdf.

Beaman, Jean. *Citizen Outsider: Children of North African Immigrants in France*. Oakland: University of California Press, 2017.

Beard, Mary. "Writing and Religion." In *Religions of the Ancient World: A Guide*, edited by Sarah Iles Johnston, 128–29. Cambridge, MA: Harvard University Press, 2014.

Beccaria, Cesare Bonesana di. *An Essay on Crimes and Punishments*. Online Library of Liberty. Accessed August 19, 2018. http://oll.libertyfund.org/titles/beccaria-an -essay-on-crimes-and-punishments.

Begley, C. Glenn, and John P. A. Ioannidis. "Reproducibility in Science: Improving the Standard for Basic and Preclinical Research." *Circulation Research* 116 (2015): 116–26.

Bentham, Jeremy. "Offences against One's Self." Stonewall and Beyond. Accessed August 19, 2018. http://www.columbia.edu/cu/lweb/eresources/exhibitions/sw25/ bentham/index.html.

Berlin, Isaiah. "The Arts in Russia under Stalin." *New York Review of Books*, October 19, 2000, https://www.nybooks.com/articles/2000/10/19/the-arts-in-russia-under -stalin/.

Berreby, David. *Us and Them: The Science of Identity*. Chicago: University of Chicago Press, 2008.

Bhatt, Mamta. "The Most Devastating Natural Disasters of the 21st Century." All That Is Interesting. August 28, 2011. http://all-that-is-interesting.com/the-most -devastating-natural-disasters-of-the-21st.

"Biblical Christianity: The Origin of the Rights to Conscience." WallBuilders. Accessed May 21, 2018. https://wallbuilders.com/biblical-christianity-origin-rights -conscience/.

"Biblical Hebrew Vocabulary: How Much Is Enough? The Law of Diminishing Returns." Biblical Hebrew Made Easy. December 13, 2012. http://biblicalhebrew-madeeasy.weebly.com/blog/biblical-hebrew-vocabulary-how-much-is-enough-the -law-of-diminishing-returns.

Bitter Crank. "Why Doesn't the Mosaic God Lead by Example?" The Philosophy Forum. Accessed April 2, 2020. https://thephilosophyforum.com/discussion/6254 /why-doesnt-the-mosaic-god-lead-by-example/p2.

Black, Laura. "How People Communicate during Deliberative Events." In *Democracy in Motion: Evaluating the Practice and Impact of Deliberative Civic Engagement*, edited by Tina Nabatchi, John Gastil, G. Michael Weiksner, and Matt Leighninger, 59–82. New York: Oxford University Press, 2012.

Blackstone, William. *Commentaries on the Laws of England*. Vol. 1. Edited by William Carey Jones. San Francisco, Bancroft-Whitney Company, 1915 [1765].

Bloch, Marc. "How and Why Ancient Slavery Came to an End." In *Critical Readings in Global Slavery*. Vol. 4. Edited by Damian Alan Pargas and Felicia Roşu. Leiden, The Netherlands: Brill, 2018.

Blois, Lukas de, and R. J. van der Spek. *An Introduction to the Ancient World*. second edtion. Translated by Susan Mellor. New York: Routledge, 1997.

Boa, Kenneth. *God, I Don't Understand: Answers to Difficult Questions of the Christian Faith*. Eugene, OR: Wipf & Stock, 2012.

Bonnassie, Pierre. *From Slavery to Feudalism in South-Western Europe*. New York: Cambridge University Press, 1991.

Boss, Judith A. *Analyzing Moral Issues*. Sixth edition. New York: McGraw Hill, 2013.

Boucicault, Dion. *The Octoroon; or, Life in Louisiana: A Play in Five Acts.* Salem, NH: Ayer, 1992 [1859].

Bourne, George. *A Condensed Antislavery Bible Argument.* New York: S. W. Benedict, 1845.

Bradstock, Andrew. *Radical Religion in Cromwell's England: A Concise History from the English Civil War to the End of the Commonwealth.* London: I. B. Tauris, 2011.

Bridgeman, Bruce. *Psychology and Evolution: The Origins of Mind.* Thousand Oaks, CA: Sage , 2013.

"A Brief History of Gamebooks." Games vs Play. Accessed August 17, 2018. http:// gamesvsplay.com/a-brief-history-of-gamebooks/.

Broocks, Rice. *God's Not Dead: Evidence for God in an Age of Uncertainty.* Nashville, TN: Thomas Nelson, 2013.

Brown, Callum G. *Becoming Atheist: Humanism and the Secular West.* London: Bloomsbury Academic, 2017.

Brown, Donald E. *Human Universals.* Boston: McGraw-Hill, 1991.

Brown, Jonathan A. C. "Islam and the Problem of Slavery." YouTube Video, 1:21:57. February 9, 2017. https://www.youtube.com/watch?v=MpFatRwdPm0.

Brown, Kendrick T., Tony N. Brown, James S. Jackson, Robert M. Sellers, and Warde J. Manuel. "Teammates On and Off the Field? Contact with Black Teammates and the Racial Attitudes of White Student Athletes." *Journal of Applied Social Psychology* 33 (July 2003): 1379–403.

Brown, Michael L. *Can You Be Gay and Christian? Responding with Love and Truth to Questions about Homosexuality.* Lake Mary, FL: Front Line, 2014.

Brownson, James. *Bible, Gender, Sexuality: Reframing the Church's Debate on Same-Sex Relationships.* Grand Rapids, MI: William B. Eerdmans, 2013.

Brundage, William Fitzhugh. *Lynching in the New South: Georgia and Virginia, 1880–1930.* Champaign: University of Illinois Press, 2012.

Buchanan, Tom. *Europe's Troubled Peace: 1945 to the Present.* Second edition. New York: Wiley-Blackwell, 2012.

Burns, J. H., and H. L. A. Hart, eds. *The Collected Works of Jeremy Bentham.* Oxford: Oxford University Press, 2005.

Butler, Joshua Ryan. *The Skeletons in God's Closet: The Mercy of Hell, the Surprise of Judgment, the Hope of Holy War.* Nashville, TN: Thomas Nelson, 2014.

Calvin, John. "Letter to Farel, 1553." In *Letters of John Calvin.* Vol. 2. Edited by Jules Bonnet. Translated by Jules Bonnet. Philadelphia: Presbyterian Board of Publication, 1868.

———. *Calvin's Commentary on the Bible.* studylight.org. Accessed June 3, 2018. https:// www.studylight.org/commentaries/eng/cal.html.

———. *Commentaries on St. Paul's Epistles to the Galatians and Ephesians.* Translated by John King. Charleston, SC: Createspace, 2015.

———. *Commentaries on the Epistles to Timothy, Titus, and Philemon.* Translated by William Pringle. Edinburgh, Scotland: The Calvin Translation Society, 1856.

———. *Commentary on Romans.* Christian Classics Ethereal Library. Accessed April 7, 2018. https://www.ccel.org/ccel/calvin/calcom38.v.vii.html.

———. *The Institutes of the Christian Religion.* Translated by Henry Beveridge. Christian Classics Ethereal Library. Accessed May 5, 2018. http://www.ccel.org/ccel/calvin/institutes.pdf?url=.

Casson, Lionel. *Travel in the Ancient World.* Baltimore: Johns Hopkins University Press, 1994.

Catholic Church. Catechism of the Catholic Church. Second edition. Washington, DC: United States Catholic Conference, 2011. https://www.usccb.org/sites/default/files/flipbooks/catechism/

———. *Twelfth Ecumenical Council: Lateran IV 1215.* In Fordham University, *Medieval Sourcebook.* Accessed May 4, 2018. https://sourcebooks.fordham.edu/basis/lateran4.asp.

Chalabi, Mona. "Are Prisoners Less Likely to Be Atheists?" FiveThirtyEight. March 12, 2015. https://fivethirtyeight.com/features/are-prisoners-less-likely-to-be-atheists/.

Chamberlain, Lesley. *Lenin's Private War: The Voyage of the Philosophy Steamer and the Exile of the Intelligentsia.* New York: St. Martin's Press, 2007.

Chaudhry, Ayesha. "Does the Koran Allow Wife-Beating? Not If Muslims Don't Want It To." *Toronto Globe and Mail,* March 27, 2014. https://www.theglobeandmail.com/opinion/its-muslims-who-give-voice-to-verse/article17684163/.

———. *Domestic Violence and the Islamic Tradition.* Oxford: Oxford University Press, 2013.

Christians, Clifford, and Michael Traber, eds. *Communication Ethics and Universal Values.* Thousand Oaks, CA: Sage, 1997.

Christina, Greta. *Coming Out Atheist: How to Do It, How to Help Each Other, and Why.* Durham, NC: Pitchstone, 2014.

Chrysostom, John. "Homily 4 on Romans." In *Nicene and Post-Nicene Fathers,* First Series. Vol. 11. Edited by Philip Schaff. Translated by J. Walker, J. Sheppard and H. Browne, and revised by George B. Stevens. Buffalo, NY: Christian Literature , 1889. Revised and edited for New Advent by Kevin Knight. http://www.newadvent.org/fathers/210204.htm.

———. "Homily 46 (on Matthew)." In *Nicene and Post-Nicene Fathers,* First Series. Vol. 10. Edited by Philip Schaff. Translated by George Prevost and revised by M. B. Riddle. Buffalo, NY: Christian Literature, 1888. Revised and edited for New Advent by Kevin Knight. http://www.newadvent.org/fathers/200146.htm.

Clement of Alexandria. *The Stromata.* In *Ante-Nicene Fathers.* Vol. 2. Edited by Alexander Roberts, James Donaldson, and A. Cleveland Coxe. Translated by William Wilson. Buffalo, NY: Christian Literature , 1885. Revised and edited for New Advent by Kevin Knight. Accessed April 2, 2018. http://www.newadvent.org/fathers/02102.htm.

Cliteur, Paul. *The Rise and Fall of Blasphemy Law.* Leiden, The Netherlands: Leiden University Press, 2017.

Closstraugott, Elizabeth, and Richard B. Dasher. *Regularity in Semantic Change.* Cambridge: Cambridge University Press, 2004.

Codex Theodosianus. Early Church Texts. Accessed April 29, 2018. http://www.earlychurchtexts.com/public/codex_theodosianus.htm.

Committee for Human Rights in North Korea. *The Hidden Gulag: The Lives and Voices of "Those Sent to the Mountains."* Second edition. Washington, DC: David Hawk, 2012.

Copan, Paul. *Is God a Moral Monster? Making Sense of the Old Testament God.* Grand Rapids, MI: Baker Books, 2011.

———. "The Moral Argument." In *The Rationality of Theism*, edited by Paul Copan and Paul K. Moser, 165–66. New York: Routledge, 2003.

The Council of Chalcedon. Papal Encyclicals Online. Accessed April 3, 2018. http://www.papalencyclicals.net/councils/ecum04.htm.

Courtois, Stéphane, Nicolas Werth, Jean-Louis Panné, Andrzej Paczkowski, Karel Bartošek, and Jean-Louis Margolin. *The Black Book of Communism: Crimes, Terror, Repression*, edited by Mark Kramer. Translated by Jonathan Murphy. Cambridge, MA: Harvard University Press, 1999.

Cowles, C. S., Eugene H. Merrill, Daniel L. Gard, and Tremper Longman III. *Show Them No Mercy: Four Views on God and Canaanite Genocide.* Grand Rapids, MI: Zondervan, 2003.

Cowper, William. "God Moves in a Mysterious Way." hymnary.org. Accessed April 17, 2017. http://www.hymnary.org/text/god_moves_in_a_mysterious_way.

Cox, Daniel, Juhem Navarro-Rivera, and Robert P. Jones. *A Shifting Landscape: A Decade of Change in American Attitudes about Same-Sex Marriage and LGBT Issues.* Washington, DC: Public Religion Research Institute, 2014.

Craig, William Lane. "#123 Is the Islamic Conception of God Morally Inadequate?" Reasonable Faith. August 24, 2009. https://www.reasonablefaith.org/writings/question-answer/is-the-islamic-conception-of-god-morally-inadequate/.

———. "#349 The Moral Argument for God." Reasonable Faith. December 23, 2013. https://www.reasonablefaith.org/question-answer/P40/the-moral-argument-for-god/.

———. "#483 Could God Be Amoral?" Reasonable Faith. July 17, 2016. https://www.reasonablefaith.org/writings/question-answer/could-god-be-amoral/.

———. "Can We Be Good without God?" Reasonable Faith. Accessed August 9, 2017. http://www.reasonablefaith.org/can-we-be-good-without-god.

———. "First Rebuttal." In *Is Goodness without God Good Enough? A Debate on Faith, Secularism, and Ethics*, edited by Robert K. Garcia and Nathan L. King, 36–38. Lanham, MD: Rowman & Littlefield, 2009.

———. "The Most Gruesome of Guests." In *Is Goodness without God Good Enough?* edited by Robert K. Garcia and Nathan L. King. Lanham, MD: Rowman & Littlefield, 2009.

———. *On Guard: Defending Your Faith with Reason and Precision.* Colorado Springs, Colorado: David C. Cook, 2010.

———. "Slaughter of the Canaanites." Reasonable Faith. August 6, 2007. http://www.reasonablefaith.org/slaughter-of-the-canaanites.

Craig, William Lane, and Louise Antony. "Is God Necessary for Morality." The Veritas Forum. YouTube Video, 1:24:36. June 22, 2012. https://www.youtube.com/watch?v=6wKkbquUDSM.

Crompton, Louis. *Homosexuality and Civilization*. Cambridge, MA: Harvard University Press, 2003.

Cross, Alan. *When Heaven and Earth Collide: Racism, Southern Evangelicals, and the Better Way of Jesus*. Montgomery, AL: NewSouth Books, 2014.

Cyprian. *Treatise V: An Address to Demetrianus*. Christian Classics Ethereal Library. Accessed April 2, 2018. https://www.ccel.org/ccel/schaff/anf05.iv.v.v.html.

Daniels, Alex. "Religious Americans Give More, New Study Finds." *Chronicle of Philanthropy*, November 25, 2013. https://www.philanthropy.com/article/Religious -Americans-Give-More/153973.

Davies, Brian, and G. R. Evans, eds. *Anselm of Canterbury: The Major Works*. Oxford: Oxford University Press, 1998.

Davies, Christie. *Ethnic Humor around the World: A Comparative Analysis*. Bloomington: Indiana University Press, 1990.

Davis, David Brion. *The Problem of Slavery in Western Culture*. Oxford: Oxford University Press, 1966.

"Decrees on Sale of Unfree Christians, c. 922–1171." In Fordham University, *Medieval Sourcebook*. Accessed April 3, 2018. https://sourcebooks.fordham.edu/source /1171latrsale.asp.

Deem, Rich. "Where Is God When Bad Things Happen? Why Natural Evil Must Exist." Evidence for God. February 13, 2013. http://www.godandscience.org/ apologetics/natural_evil_theodicity.html.

"Defining 'Humanism.'" Humanists UK. Accessed August 19, 2017. https://humanism .org.uk/humanism/.

Deutsch, Morton, and Mary Evans Collins. *Interracial Housing: A Psychological Evaluation of a Social Experiment*. Minneapolis: University of Minnesota Press, 1951.

DeYoung, James B. *Homosexuality: Contemporary Claims Examined in Light of the Bible and Other Ancient Literature and Law*. Grand Rapids, MI: Kregel, 2000.

The Didache. thedidache.com. Accessed April 2, 2018. http://thedidache.com/.

Dodgen, Jack. "Book Review: *God Behaving Badly*." Start2Finish. Accessed April 22, 2017. https://start2finish.org/book-review-god-behaving-badly/ (site discontinued).

Dose, Ralf. *Magnus Hirschfeld and the Origins of the Gay Liberation Movement*. Translated by Edward H. Willis. New York: Monthly Review Press, 2014.

Douthat, Ross. "Liberalism Is Stuck Halfway between Heaven and Earth." *Slate*. April 19, 2012. http://www.slate.com/articles/arts/the_book_club/features/2012/ross _douthat_s_bad_religion/bad_religion_by_ross_douthat_reviewed_liberalism_and _christianity_.html.

Dover, K. J. *Greek Popular Morality in the Time of Plato and Aristotle*. New York: Hackett, 1994.

Drake, H. A. *Constantine and the Bishops: The Politics of Intolerance*. Baltimore: Johns Hopkins University Press, 2000.

Drescher, Elizabeth. *Choosing Our Religion: The Spiritual Lives of America's Nones*. New York: Oxford University Press, 2016.

Drescher, Seymour. *Abolition: A History of Slavery and Antislavery*. Cambridge: Cambridge University Press, 2009.

D'Souza, Dinesh. *What's So Great about Christianity*. Washington, DC: Regnery, 2007.

Duby, Georges. *The Early Growth of the European Economy: Warriors and Peasants from the Seventh to the Twelfth Century*. Ithaca, NY: Cornell University Press, 1974.

Dumbo feather podcast. "Susan Carland: Activist, Muslim, Mother." Episode 1. April 27, 2016. Stitcher, 53:27, April 27, 2016. https://www.stitcher.com/podcast/ dumbo-feather-podcast/e/1-susan-carland-activist-muslim-mother-44322273.

Duncan, Jonathan. *The Dukes of Normandy from the Time of Rollo to the Expulsion of King John by Philip Augustus of France*. London: Joseph Rickerby, Sherbourn Lane, and Harvey and Darton, 1839.

Dwyer, Mary M., and Courtney K. Peters. "The Benefits of Study Abroad: New Study Confirms Significant Gains." *Transitions Abroad* (March/April 2004), 56–57. https://www.iesabroad.org/system/files/Benefits%20%28Dwyer%2C%20Peters %29%20%28Transitions%20Abroad%29.pdf.

Eberle, Edward J. *Church and State in Western Society: Established Church, Cooperation and Separation*. Farnham, UK: Ashgate, 2016.

Edgell, Penny, Joseph Gerteis, and Douglas Hartmann. "Atheists as 'Other': Moral Boundaries and Cultural Membership in American Society." *American Sociological Review* 71 (2006): 211–34.

Edgell, Penny, Douglas Hartmann, Evan Stewart, and Joseph Gerteis. "Atheists and Other Cultural Outsiders: Moral Boundaries and the Non-Religious in the United States." *Social Forces* 95 (2016): 607–38.

Ehrman, Bart D. *Jesus: Apocalyptic Prophet of the New Millennium*. Oxford: Oxford University Press, 1999.

Eid, Michael, and Randy J. Larsen, eds. *The Science of Subjective Well-Being*. New York: Guilford Press, 2008.

Eltis, David, and Stanley L. Engerman. "Dependence, Servility, and Coerced Labor in Space and Time." In *The Cambridge World History of Slavery: Volume 3, AD 1420–AD 1804*. Edited by David Eltis and Stanley L. Engerman. Cambridge: Cambridge University Press, 2011.

The Epistle of Barnabas. Translated by J. B. Lightfoot. Early Christian Writings. Accessed April 2, 2018. http://www.earlychristianwritings.com/text/barnabas -lightfoot.html.

Epstein, Greg. *Good without God: What a Billion Nonreligious People Do Believe*. New York: HarperCollins, 2009.

Ericksen, Robert P. *Complicity in the Holocaust: Churches and Universities in Nazi Germany*. Cambridge: Cambridge University Press, 2012.

Espinoza, Terance. "Exegesis versus Eisegesis." Thought Hub, Southwestern Assemblies of God University. February 16, 2017. https://www.sagu.edu/thoughthub/exegesis -versus-eisegesis.

Evans, Christopher H. *The Social Gospel in American Religion*. New York: New York University Press, 2017.

Evans, G. R. *Philosophy and Theology in the Middle Ages*. New York: Routledge, 1993.

Ex-Muslims of North America. "Support Communities." Accessed August 31, 2019. https://exmuslims.org/community/.

Fahlbusch, Erwin, Jan Milic Lochman, John Mbiti, and Jaroslav Pelikan, eds. *The Encyclopedia of Christianity*. Vol. 5. Grand Rapids, MI: Wm. B. Eerdsman, 2008.

Fernandes, Phil. *No Other Gods: A Defense of Biblical Christianity*. Maitland, FL: Xulon Press, 2002.

———. *The Atheist Delusion: A Christian Response to Christopher Hitchens and Richard Dawkins*. Maitland, FL: Xulon Press, 2009.

Finkelman, Paul, and Joseph Calder Miller. *Macmillan Encyclopedia of World Slavery*, vols. 1 and 2. New York: Macmillan Library Reference, 1999.

Finocchiaro, Maurice A. *Retrying Galileo, 1633–1992*. Berkeley: University of California Press, 2005.

Fishkin, James S. *Democracy and Deliberation New Directions for Democratic Reform*. New Haven, CT: Yale University Press, 1991.

Fishkin, James, and Cynthia Farrar. "Deliberative Polling: From Experiment to Community Resource." In *The Deliberative Democracy Handbook: Strategies for Effective Civic Engagement in the Twenty-First Century*, edited by John Gastil and Peter Levine, 68–79. San Francisco, CA: Jossey-Bass, 2005.

"5 Steps to Understanding Any Biblical Text: The Interpretive Journey from 'Grasping God's Word.'" *Zondervan Academic* (blog). June 10, 2015. https://zondervanacademic.com/blog/5-steps-to-understanding-any-biblical-text/.

Flannagan, Matt. "Is God a Moral Monster? A Review of Paul Copan's Book." M and M, March 17, 2011. http://www.mandm.org.nz/2011/03/is-god-a-moral-monster-a-review-of-paul-copans-book.html.

Fletcher, David, Jeremy Beahan, Justin Schieber, and Luke Galen. "Summer Genocide Series Part 1." Reasonable Doubts Podcast. Episode 88, 1:19:35, August 10, 2011. https://podcasts.apple.com/us/podcast/rd88-summer-genocide-series-part-1/id266671828?i=1000096358868.

Forlines, F. Leroy. *The Quest for Truth: Answering Life's Inescapable Questions*. Nashville, TN: Randall House, 2001.

Frankel, Henry R. *The Continental Drift Controversy: Volume I: Wegener and the Early Debate*. Cambridge: Cambridge University Press, 2012.

Friedeburg, Robert von. *Luther's Legacy: The Thirty Years War and the Modern Notion of 'State' in the Empire, 1530s to 1790s*. Cambridge: Cambridge University Press, 2016.

Friedersdorf, Conor. "The Obama Administration's Drone-Strike Dissembling." *Atlantic*, March 14, 2016. https://www.theatlantic.com/politics/archive/2016/03/the-obama-administrations-drone-strike-dissembling/473541/.

Frontline. "Two American Families." Written by Kathleen Hughes and Bill Moyers. July 9, 2013. http://www.pbs.org/wgbh/frontline/film/two-american-families/transcript/.

Frye, William H. "Is There a God (Part 3)—Is Morality Real or Just Opinion and Preference." whfrye.com. Accessed September 21, 2017. http://whfrye.com/is-there-a-god-part-3-is-morality-real-or-just-opinion-and-preference/.

"The Future of World Religions: Population Growth Projections, 2010–2015." Pew Research Center. August 14, 2018. http://www.pewforum.org/2015/04/02/religious-projections-2010-2050/.

Gaca, Kathy L. "The Martial Rape of Girls and Women in Antiquity and Modernity." In *The Oxford Handbook of Gender and Conflict*, edited by Fionnuala Ní Aoláin, Naomi Cahn, Dina Francesca Haynes, and Nahla Valji, 305–15. New York: Oxford University Press, 2018.

Gagnon, Robert A. J. *The Bible and Homosexual Practice: Texts and Hermeneutics.* Nashville, TN: Abingdon Press, 2001.

Galen, Luke W. "Focusing on the Nonreligious Reveals Secular Mechanisms Underlying Well-Being and Prosociality." *Psychology of Religion and Spirituality* 10 (2018): 296–306.

Gallego, Aina. *Unequal Political Participation Worldwide.* New York: Cambridge University Press, 2015.

Gallup Poll: Public Opinion 2009. Lanham, MD: Rowman & Littlefield, 2010.

Gartner, Lloyd P. *History of the Jews in Modern Times.* Oxford: Oxford University Press, 2001.

Gaskill, Malcolm. *Witchcraft: A Very Short Introduction.* Oxford: Oxford University Press, 2010.

"Gay and Lesbian Rights." Gallup. Accessed August 19, 2018. https://news.gallup.com/poll/1651/gay-lesbian-rights.aspx.

Geisler, Norman L., and Thomas Howe. *When Critics Ask: A Popular Handbook on Bible Difficulties.* Grand Rapids, MI: Baker Books, 1992.

Geisler, Norman L., and Frank Turek. *I Don't Have Enough Faith to Be an Atheist.* Wheaton, IL: Crossway Books, 2004.

Geisler, Norman. *Baker Encyclopedia of Christian Apologetics.* Grand Rapids, MI: Baker Books, 1999.

Gerencser, Bruce. "Why I Am Still in the Ministry: A Guest Post by John Calvin." The Life and Times of Bruce Gerencser. July 31, 2019. https://brucegerencser.net/2019/07/why-i-am-still-in-the-ministry-a-guest-post-by-john-calvin/.

Gervais, Will M. "Everything Is Permitted? People Intuitively Judge Immorality as Representative of Atheists." *PLoS One* 9:4 (April 2014).

Gervais, Will M., Azim F. Shariff, and Ara Norenzayan. "Do You Believe in Atheists? Distrust Is Central to Anti-atheist Prejudice." *Journal of Personality and Social Psychology* 101 (2011): 1189–1206.

Gies, Miep, and Alison Leslie Gold. *Anne Frank Remembered: The Story of the Woman Who Helped to Hide the Frank Family.* New York: Simon & Schuster Paperbacks, 2009.

Gilson, Tom. "'*God Behaving Badly*' by David T. Lamb." Thinking Christian. July 24, 2011. https://www.thinkingchristian.net/posts/2011/07/god-behaving-badly-by-david-t-lamb/.

Girls Not Brides. "What Is the Impact of Child Marriage." Accessed August 31, 2019. https://www.girlsnotbrides.org/what-is-the-impact/.

Gleason, Archer L. *Encyclopedia of Bible Difficulties*. Grand Rapids, MI: Zondervan, 1982.

"The 'Golden Rule' (a.k.a. Ethics of Reciprocity) Part 1: Passages in Religious Texts in 14 Faiths from the Bahá'í Faith to Satanism." Religious Tolerance. Accessed September 23, 2017. http://www.religioustolerance.org/reciproc2.htm.

Goodman, Dena. *The Republic of Letters: A Cultural History of the French Enlightenment*. Ithaca, NY: Cornell University Press, 1994.

Gould, Stephen Jay. *Rocks of Ages: Science and Religion in the Fullness of Life*. New York: Ballantine Books, 1999.

Grayling, A. C. *Meditations for the Humanist: Ethics for a Secular Age*. New York: Oxford University Press, 2003.

Green, Bernard. *Christianity in Ancient Rome: The First Three Centuries*. London: T&T Clark International, 2010.

Gregory, Bishop of Nyssa. "Homilies on Ecclesiastes." In *Gregory of Nyssa Homilies on Ecclesiastes: An English Version with Supporting Studies*. Edited by Stuart George Hall, 31–144. Translated by Stuart George Hall and Rachel Moriarty. Berlin: Walter de Gruyter, 1993.

Gregory, Brad S. *Rebel in the Ranks: Martin Luther, the Reformation, and the Conflicts That Continue to Shape Our World*. New York: Harper One, 2017.

Grewal, Jyoti. *Betrayed by the State: The Anti-Sikh Pogrom of 1984*. New York: Penguin Books India, 2007.

Gross-Loh, Christine. *Parenting without Borders: Surprising Lessons Parents around the World Can Teach Us*. New York: Penguin Group, 2013.

Grotius, Hugo. *The Rights of War and Peace*. Vol. 1. Edited and with an introduction by Richard Tuck. Indianapolis: Liberty Fund, 2005 [1625]. Online Library of Liberty. http://oll.libertyfund.org/titles/grotius-the-rights-of-war-and-peace-2005-ed-vol-1-book-i.

"Growing Support for Gay Marriage: Changed Minds and Changing Demographics." Pew Research Center. March 20, 2013. http://www.people-press.org/2013/03/20/growing-support-for-gay-marriage-changed-minds-and-changing-demographics/.

Grudem, Wayne. *Politics According to the Bible: A Comprehensive Resource for Understanding Modern Political Issues in Light of Scripture*. Grand Rapids, MI: Zondervan, 2010.

Haberman, Maggie. "Donald Trump Reverses Position on Torture and Killing Terrorists' Families." *New York Times*, March 4, 2016. https://www.nytimes.com/politics/first-draft/2016/03/04/donald-trump-reverses-position-on-torture-and-killing-terrorists-families/.

Habermas, Jürgen. *Moral Consciousness and Communication Action*. Translated by Christian Lenhardt and Shierry Weber Nicholsen. New York: Polity Press, 1990.

———. *The Structural Transformation of the Public Square: An Inquiry into the Category of Bourgeois Society*. Translated by Thomas Burger. Cambridge, MA: MIT Press, 1991.

Haggerty, George E., ed. *Gay Histories and Cultures: An Encyclopedia*. New York: Routledge, 2012.

Halbrook, Steve C. *God Is Just: A Defense of the Old Testament Civil Laws*. second edition. Theonomy Resources Media, 2014.

Halsall, Paul. "Reviewing Boswell." In Fordham University, *People with a History: An Online Guide to Lesbian, Gay, Bisexual, and Trans History*. December 17, 1995. https://sourcebooks.fordham.edu/halsall/pwh/bosrevdisc-kennedy1.asp

Hamlin, J. Kiley, Neha Mahajan, Zoe Liberman, and Karen Wynn. "Not Like Me = Bad: Infants Prefer Those Who Harm Dissimilar Others." *Psychological Science* 24 (2013): 589–94.

Hamm, Thomas D. *The Quakers in America*. New York: Columbia University Press, 2003.

Hanegraaff, Hank. *The Complete Bible Answer Book: Collector's Edition*. Nashville, TN: Thomas Nelson, 2008.

Harker, David. *Creating Scientific Controversies: Uncertainty and Bias in Science and Society*. Cambridge: Cambridge University Press, 2015.

Harmon, Ann. "Women Writers of the Nineteenth Century." The New Agenda. August 5, 2012. http://thenewagenda.net/2012/08/05/women-writers-of-the-nineteenth-century/.

Harris, Sam. *The Moral Landscape: How Science Can Determine Human Values*. New York: Free Press, 2010.

Harris, Sam, and William Lane Craig. "The God Debate II: Harris vs. Craig." YouTube Video, 2:06:54, April 12, 2011. https://www.youtube.com/watch?v=yqaHXKL-RKzg.

Harris, William V. *Ancient Literacy*. Cambridge, MA: Harvard University Press, 1991.

Havemann, Paul. *Indigenous Peoples' Rights in Australia, Canada, and New Zealand*. Oxford: Oxford University Press, 1999.

Hazen, Craig J. "Can We Be Good without God?" *Biola Magazine* (Summer 2011). http://magazine.biola.edu/article/11-summer/can-we-be-good-without-god/.

Helwys, Thomas. *A Short Declaration of the Mystery of Iniquity*. Macon, GA: Mercer University Press, 1998 [1611/1612].

Herdt, Gilbert H., ed. *Ritualized Homosexuality in Melanesia*. Berkeley: University of California Press, 1984.

Herodotus. *The Histories of Herodotus Interlinear English Translation*. Edited by Heinrich Stein. Translated by George Macaulay. Austin, TX: Lighthouse Digital, 2013.

Hick, John. "The Universality of the Golden Rule." In *Ethics, Religion, and the Good Society: New Directions in a Pluralistic World*, edited by Joseph Runzo, 155–66. Louisville, KY: Westminster/John Knox Press, 1992.

Hilgers, Joseph. "Index of Prohibited Books." *The Catholic Encyclopedia*. Vol. 7. New York: Robert Appleton, 1910. Accessed July 8, 2021, http://www.newadvent.org/cathen/07721a.htm.

Hippler, Thomas. *Bombing the People: Giulio Douhet and the Foundations of Air-Power Strategy, 1884–1939*. Cambridge: Cambridge University Press, 2013.

Hitchens, Christopher, and Douglas Wilson. *Is Christianity Good for the World? A Debate*. Moscow, ID: Canon Press, 2008.

Hitler, Adolf. "Hitler's Speech to the National Socialist Women's League." German History in Documents and Images. September 8, 1934. http://ghdi.ghi-dc.org/sub_document.cfm?document_id=1557.

Hobbes, Thomas, *Leviathan*. Edited by A. P. Martinich and Brian Battiste. Toronto: Broadview Press, 2011 [1668].

Hodson, Gordon, Jonathan Rush, and Cara C. MacInnis. "A Joke Is Just a Joke (Except When It Isn't): Cavalier Humor Beliefs Facilitate the Expression of Group Dominance Motives." *Journal of Personality and Social Psychology* 99 (2010): 660–82.

Hoever, Inga J., Daan van Knippenberg, Wendy P. van Ginkel, and Harry G. Barkema. "Fostering Team Creativity: Perspective Taking as Key to Unlocking Diversity's Potential." *Journal of Applied Psychology* 97 (2012): 982–96.

Hoffman, Morris B. *The Punisher's Brain: The Evolution of Judge and Jury*. New York: Cambridge University Press, 2014.

Hooker, Evelyn. "The Adjustment of the Male Overt Homosexual." *Journal of Projective Techniques* 21 (1957): 18–31.

Hopkins, John Henry. *A Scriptural, Ecclesiastical, and Historical View of Slavery, from the Days of Patriarch Abraham, to the Nineteenth Century*. New York: W. I. Pooley, 1864.

Horn, Trent. *Answering Atheism: How to Make the Case for God with Logic and Charity*. San Diego: Catholic Answers Press, 2013.

Horvitz, Leslie Alan, and Christopher Catherwood. *Encyclopedia of War Crimes and Genocide*. New York: Facts on File, 2006.

Houdmann, S. Michael. *Questions about the Bible: The 100 Most Frequently Asked Questions about the Bible*. Bloomington, IN: WestBow Press, 2015.

Howell, Brian M., and Jenell Williams Paris. *Introducing Cultural Anthropology: A Christian Perspective*. Grand Rapids, MI: Baker Academic, 2011.

Huffling, Brian, and Michael Shermer. "If God, Why Evil? A Debate on the Problem of Evil." YouTube Video, 2:02:28. March 1, 2019. https://www.youtube.com/watch?v=qH4jIHlMunw.

Huizenga, John R. *Cold Fusion: The Scientific Fiasco of the Century*. New York: Oxford University Press, 1992.

Humanists International. "The Amsterdam Declaration." Accessed April 2, 2020. https://humanists.international/what-is-humanism/the-amsterdam-declaration/.

Hume, David. "Essay XI: Of the Original Contract." In David Hume, *Essays and Treatises on Several Subjects*, 252–62. London: A. Millar, 1758.

Hunt, Lynn, *Inventing Human Rights: A History*. New York: W.W. Norton, 2007.

Hussey, Joan Mervyn. "Justinian I." In *Encyclopedia Britannica. Accessed* April 29, 2018, https://www.britannica.com/biography/Justinian-I.

Hutchinson, Robert J. *The Politically Incorrect Guide to the Bible*. Washington, DC: Regnery, 2007.

Ibrahim, Celene. "The Study Quran: A New Translation and Commentary." *Journal of Islamic and Muslim Studies* 1, no. 2 (2000): 89–92.

Instone-Brewer, David. *Divorce and Remarriage in the Bible: The Social and Literary Context*. Grand Rapids, MI: Wm. B. Eerdmans, 2002.

International Labor Office, Walk Free Foundation, and International Organization for Migration. "Global Estimates of Modern Slavery, 2017." Geneva: International Labour Organization and Walk Free Foundation, 2017. http://www.alliance87 .org/global_estimates_of_modern_slavery-forced_labour_and_forced_marriage .pdf.

"Is Freedom of Religion a Biblical Concept?" GotQuestions.org. Accessed May 21, 2018. https://www.gotquestions.org/freedom-of-religion.html.

Jackson, Wayne. "What about the Bible and Slavery." Christian Courier. Accessed June 3, 2017. https://www.christiancourier.com/articles/800-what-about-the-bible-and -slavery.

Jacobs, Sue-Ellen, Wesley Thomas, and Sabine Lang, eds. *Two-Spirit People: Native American Identity, Sexuality, and Spirituality*. Urbana: University of Illinois Press, 1997.

Johnson, David K. *The Lavender Scare: The Cold War Persecution of Gays and Lesbians in the Federal Government*. Chicago: University of Chicago Press, 2004.

Johnson, Luke Timothy. "Religious Rights and Christian Texts." In *Religious Human Rights in Global Perspective: Religious Perspectives*, edited by John Witte Jr. and Johan D. van der Vyver, The Hague, The Netherlands: Matinus Nijhoff, 1996.

Johnson, Terry. "Just Me and My Bible?" Ligonier Ministries. Accessed March 28, 2018. https://www.ligonier.org/learn/articles/just-me-and-my-bible/.

Johnson, Victoria. *Bible Study for Busy Women*. Detroit, MI: Dabar, 1998.

Jones, Bill. *Putting Together the Puzzle of the Old Testament*. Atlanta, GA: Authentic, 2007.

Jones, Clay. "We Don't Hate Sin So We Don't Understand What Happened to the Canaanites: An Addendum to the 'Divine Genocide' Arguments." *Philosophia Christi* 11, no. 1 (2009): 53–72.

Joshel, Sandra R. *Slavery in the Roman World*. New York: Cambridge University Press, 2010.

Joslyn, Mark R., and Donald P Haider-Markel. "Beliefs about Homosexuality and Support for Gay Rights: An Empirical Test of Attribution Theory." *Public Opinion Quarterly* 72 (2018): 291–310.

———. "Genetic Attributions, Immutability, and Stereotypical Judgments: An Analysis of Homosexuality." *Social Science Quarterly* 97 (2016): 377–90.

Junger, Sebastian. *Tribe: On Homecoming and Belonging*. New York: Hachette Book Group, 2016.

Kaiser, Walter C., Peter H. Davids, F. F. Bruce, and Manfred T. Brauch. *Hard Sayings of the Bible*. Downers Grove, IL: InterVarsity Press, 1996.

Kamen, Henry. *The Rise of Toleration*. New York: McGraw-Hill, 1972.

Karim, Kaleef K. "Quran 65:4—The Child Marriage Claim." Discover the Truth. March 12, 2016. https://discover-the-truth.com/2016/03/12/quran-654-the-child -marriage-claim/, accessed August 30, 2019.

Kaufman, Michael T. "The Woman Who Saved the Diary of a Young Girl." *New York Times*, March 11, 1995. https://www.nytimes.com/1995/03/11/nyregion/about-new-york-the-woman-who-saved-the-diary-of-a-young-girl.html.

Kaya-Uranli, Arzu. "Nowhere Does Islam Excuse Child Brides." *Huffpost*, June 18, 2014. Accessed August 30, 2019. https://www.huffpost.com/entry/nowhere-does-islam-excuse_b_5176425.

Kennedy, David M., ed. *The Library of Congress World War II Companion*. New York: Simon & Schuster, 2007.

Kesavan, Mukul. "Murderous Majorities." *New York Review of Books*, January 18, 2018, 37–40.

Kim, Jibum, Tom Smith, and Jeong-han Kang. "Religious Affiliation, Religious Service Attendance, and Mortality." *Journal of Religion and Health* 54 (June 2015): 2052–72.

Kim, Su-am. *The North Korean Penal Code, Criminal Procedures, and Their Actual Application*. Seoul: Korea Institute for National Unification, 2006.

Kiprop, Victor. "Countries Where Apostasy Is Illegal." WorldAtlas. December 13, 2018. https://www.worldatlas.com/articles/countries-where-apostasy-is-illegal.html.

Kirk, Stuart A., and Herb Kutchins. *The Selling of DSM: The Rhetoric of Science in Psychiatry*. New York: Routledge, 2017.

Kite, Mary E., and Bernard E. Whitley Jr. *Psychology of Prejudice and Discrimination*. Third edition. New York: Routledge, 2016.

Kleinberg, S. J. *Women in the United States, 1830–1945*. Houndmills, UK: Macmillan Press, 1999.

Kneen, Rachel. "Subacute Sclerosing Pan-encephalitis." Encephalitis Society. Accessed November 19, 2017. https://www.encephalitis.info/subacute-sclerosing-pan-encephalitis-sspe.

Knox, Tom. "The Tantalising Proof That Belief in God Makes You Happier and Healthier." *Daily Mail*, February 18, 2011. https://www.dailymail.co.uk/femail/article-1358421/The-tantalising-proof-belief-God-makes-happier-healthier.html.

Koomey, Jonathan G. "What Is Intellectual Honesty and Why Is It Important?" June 18, 2012. http://www.koomey.com/post/25385125958.

Koran by Heart: One Chance to Remember. Directed by Greg Barker. New York: HBO Home Entertainment, 2011.

Koukl, Greg. "The Canaanites: Genocide or Judgment?" Stand to Reason. January 1, 2013. https://www.str.org/publications/the-canaanites-genocide-or-judgment#.WRpyCeXysdU.

———. *Tactics: A Game Plan for Discussing Your Christian Convictions*. Grand Rapids, MI: Zondervan, 2009.

———. "Why Are Natural Disasters an Evil with No Connection to Free Will." Stand to Reason. YouTube Video, 8:03, February 23, 2015. https://www.youtube.com/watch?v=0_YHNQCdqo8&ab_channel=StandtoReason.

Krafft-Ebing, Richard von. *Psychopathia Sexualis: The Classic Study of Deviant Sex*. Translated by Franklin S. Klaf. New York: Skyhorse, 2011 [1886].

Kranz, Jeffrey. "The 35 Authors Who Wrote the Bible." OverviewBible. August 9, 2018. https://overviewbible.com/authors-who-wrote-bible/.

Kreeft, Peter. *Letters to an Atheist: Wrestling with Faith.* Lanham, MD: Rowman & Littlefield, 2014.

Kristof, Nicholas. "Am I a Christian, Pastor Timothy Keller?" *New York Times*, December 23, 2016. https://www.nytimes.com/2016/12/23/opinion/sunday/pastor-am-i-a-christian.html?_r=0.

Kuo, Susan S. "'Not Only Injurious to Individuals, but Dangerous to the State': A Theory of Disaster Crime." In *Disasters, Hazards, and Law*, edited by Mathieu Deflam, Bingley, UK: Emerald Group Limited, 2012.

Kurtz, Paul. *Forbidden Fruit: The Ethics of Secularism.* Amherst, NY: Prometheus Books, 2008.

Kutchins, Herb, and Stuart A. Kirk. *Making Us Crazy: DSM: The Psychiatric Bible and the Creation of Mental Disorders.* New York: Free Press, 1997.

LaHaye, Tim. *How to Study the Bible for Yourself.* Eugene, OR: Harvest House, 2006.

Lamb, David T. *God Behaving Badly: Is the God of the Old Testament Angry, Sexist and Racist?* Downers Grove, IL: InterVarsity Press, 2011.

Landemore, Helene. *Democratic Reason: Politics, Collective Intelligence, and the Rule of the Many.* Princeton, NJ: Princeton University Press, 2017.

Law, Stephen. *Humanism: A Very Short Introduction.* New York: Oxford University Press, 2011.

The Laws of Manu. Translated by Georg Bühler. Internet Sacred Text Archive. Accessed July 16, 2019. http://www.sacred-texts.com/hin/manu/manu09.htm.

The Leon Show. "Is There Any Evidence in the Universe That Demonstrates the Existence of God?" YouTube Video, 28:34. June 22, 2014. https://www.youtube.com/watch?v=NbbrYwhYpjw&ab_channel=Cold-CaseChristianitywithJ.WarnerWallace.

LeVay, Simon. "A Difference in Hypothalmic Structure between Heterosexual and Homosexual Men." *Science* 253 (August 1991): 1034–37.

Levy, Leonard W. *Blasphemy: Verbal Offense against the Sacred, from Moses to Salman Rushdie.* Chapel Hill: University of North Carolina Press, 1995.

Lewis, C. S. *Mere Christianity.* Rev. ed. New York: HarperOne, 2001.

Lewis, Mark Edward. *Sanctioned Violence in Early China.* Albany: State University of New York Press, 1990.

Lewy, Guenter. *Harmful and Undesirable: Book Censorship in Nazi Germany.* New York: Oxford University Press, 2016.

The Liberties of the Massachusets Collonie in New England. Hanover Historical Texts Project. Accessed April 15, 2018. https://history.hanover.edu/texts/masslib.html.

Lieberman, Philip. *Uniquely Human: The Evolution of Speech, Thought, and Selfless Behavior.* Cambridge, MA: Harvard University Press, 1991.

Lim, Chaeyoon, and Robert D. Putnam. "Religion, Social Networks, and Life Satisfaction." *American Sociological Review* 75 (December 2010): 914–33.

Limbaugh, David. *Jesus on Trial: A Lawyer Affirms the Truth of the Gospel.* Washington, DC: Regnery, 2014.

Linley, P. Alex, Susan Harrington, and Nicola Garcea, eds. *The Oxford Handbook of Positive Psychology and Work*. New York: Oxford University Press, 2013.

Lisle, Jason. "Atheism: An Irrational Worldview." In *A Pocket Guide to Atheism: Understanding the Inherent Problems of a No-God Worldview*, 51–59. Petersburg, KY: Answers in Genesis, 2014.

Lloyd, Elisabeth A. *The Case of the Female Orgasm: Bias in the Science of Evolution*. Cambridge, MA: Harvard University Press, 2005.

Loader, William. *Making Sense of Sex: Attitudes towards Sexuality in Early Jewish and Christian Literature*. Grand Rapids, MI: William B. Eerdman, 2013.

———. *Sexuality in the New Testament: Understanding the Key Texts*. Louisville, KY: Westminster John Knox Press, 2010.

Locke, John. *An Essay Concerning Human Understanding*. Edited by Jonathan Bennett, 2017 [1690]. Early Modern Texts. Accessed July 9, 2021. http://www.earlymoderntexts.com/authors/locke.

Lüdemann, Gerd. *Intolerance and the Gospel: Selected Texts from the New Testament*. Amherst. NY: Prometheus Books, 2007.

Luther, Martin. "Against the Robbing and Murdering Hordes of Peasants." Translated by Charles M. Jacobs. Accessed August 18, 2018. https://www.scrollpublishing.com/store/Luther-Peasants.html.

———. "Letter to George Spalatin, January or February 1514." In *Luther's Correspondence and Other Contemporary Letters*. Vol. 1, 1507–1521. Edited by Preserved Smith and Charles M. Jacobs. Translated by Preserved Smith and Charles M. Jacobs. Philadelphia, PA: Lutheran Publication Society, 1913.

——— *Luther's Works, Vol. 28: Commentaries on 1 Corinthians 7, 1 Corinthians 15, Lectures on 1 Timothy*, edited by Hilton C. Oswald. St. Louis: Concordia House, 1973.

———. "On Governmental Authority." In *The Protestant Reformation*, edited by Hans J. Hillerbrand, London: Palgrave Macmillan, 1968.

———*On the Jews and Their Lies*. Wayback Machine. Accessed July 8, 2021. https://web.archive.org/web/20050103042654/http://jdstone.org/cr/pages/sss_mluther.html.

———. "On War against Islamic Reign of Terror (On War against the Turk)." Martin Luther og hans skrifter. Accessed May 4, 2018. http://www.lutherdansk.dk/On%20war%20against%20Islamic%20reign%20of%20terror/On%20war%20against%20Islamic%20reign%20of%20terror1.htm.

MacPherson, Guy. "Ali Hassan Mines Muslim Culture for Comedy." *The Georgia Straight*. February 15, 2017. https://www.straight.com/arts/868891/ali-hassan-mines-muslim-culture-comedy.

Mann, Michael. *The Sources of Social Power: A History of Power from the Beginning to A.D. 1760*. Vol. 1. New York: Cambridge University Press, 1986.

Manning, Christel. *Losing Our Religion: How Unaffiliated Parents Are Raising Their Children*. New York: New York University Press, 2015.

"Many Americans Mix Multiple Faiths." Pew Research Center. December 9, 2009. http://www.pewforum.org/2009/12/09/many-americans-mix-multiple-faiths/.

Maracin, Paul R. *The Night of the Long Knives: Forty-Eight Hours That Changed the History of the World.* Guilford, CT: Lyons Press, 2004.

Martin, Michael. *Atheism, Morality, and Meaning.* Amherst, NY: Prometheus Books, 2002.

Mather, Cotton. *Souldiers Counselled and Comforted. A Discourse Delivered unto Some Part of the Forces Engaged in the Just War of New-England Against the Northern and Eastern Indians.* Boston: Samuel Green, 1689.

Bearak, Max. "Rohingya Militants in Burma: Terrorists or Freedom Fighters?" *Washington Post,* September 11, 2017, https://www.washingtonpost.com/news/worldviews/wp/2017/09/11/rohingya-militants-in-burma-terrorists-or-freedom-fighters/?utm_term=.55f464793414.

Maxwell, John Francis. *Slavery and the Catholic Church: The History of Catholic Teaching Concerning the Moral Legitimacy of the Institution of Slavery.* Chichester, England: Barry Rose, 1975.

McCarthy, Justin. "In U.S., Socialist Presidential Candidates Least Appealing." Gallup. June 22, 2015. http://www.gallup.com/poll/183713/socialist-presidential-candidates-least-appealing.aspx.

McDermott, Rose. *The Evils of Polygyny: Evidence of Its Harm to Women, Men, and Society.* Ithaca, NY: Cornell University Press, 2018.

McDowell, Josh. *Evidence That Demands a Verdict.* Rev. ed. San Bernadino, CA: Here's Life, 1979.

McDowell, Josh, and Sean McDowell. *The Bible Handbook of Difficult Verses: A Complete Guide to Answering the Tough Questions.* Eugene, OR: Harvest House, 2013.

McDowell, Sean. "A Simple Case for Religious Liberty." July 25, 2017. http://seanmcdowell.org/blog/a-secular-case-for-religious-liberty.

McDowell, Sean, and Jonathan Morrow. *Is God Just a Human Invention? And Seventeen Other Questions Raised by the New Atheists.* Grand Rapids, MI: Kregel, 2010.

McDowell, Sean, and Matthew Vines. "What Does the Bible Say about Homosexuality? Sean McDowell and Matthew Vines in Conversation." YouTube Video, 2:10:34, Feb. 3, 2018. https://www.youtube.com/watch?v=yFY4VtCWgyI&t=3206s.

McElroy, Ann. *Nunavut Generations: Change and Continuity in Canadian Inuit Communities.* Long Grove, IL: Waveland Press, 2008.

McFarland, Alex. *10 Answers for Skeptics.* Ventura, CA: Regal, 2011.

McGrath, Alister. *The Twilight of Atheism: The Rise and Fall of Disbelief in the Modern World.* New York: Doubleday, 2006.

McLatchie, Jonathan. "Cherry Picking the Bible? Are Christians Expected to Follow the Levitical Laws." CrossExamined.org. December 10, 2011. https://crossexamined.org/cherry-picking-the-bible-are-christians-expected-to-follow-the-levitical-laws/.

McLoughlin, William G. *Rhode Island: A History.* New York: W.W. Norton, 1986.

McNally, Robert E. *The Bible in the Early Middle Ages.* Eugene, OR: Wipf & Stock, 1959.

Meister, Chad. "Atheists and the Quest for Objective Morality." Christian Research Institute. January 31, 2011. http://www.equip.org/article/atheists-and-the-quest-for-objective-morality/.

Melville, Herman. "Benito Cereno." In *The Piazza Tales*, by Herman Melville. New York: Dix & Edwards, 1856.

Merriman, Scott A. *When Religious and Secular Interests Collide: Faith, Law, and the Religious Exemption Debate.* Santa Barbara, CA: Praeger, 2017.

Metaxas, Eric. *Bonhoeffer: Pastor, Martyr, Prophet, Spy.* Nashville, TN: Thomas Nelson, 2010.

Metz, Julie. *Perfection: A Memoir of Betrayal and Renewal.* New York: Voice, 2009.

Miller, Joshua. *The Rise and Fall of Democracy in Early America, 1630–1789: The Legacy for Contemporary Politics.* University Park, PA: Pennsylvania State University Press, 1991.

Miscamble, Wilson D. *The Most Controversial Decision: Truman, the Atomic Bombs, and the Defeat of Japan.* New York: Cambridge University Press, 2011.

Mizzoni, John. *Ethics: The Basics.* Second edition. Hoboken, NJ: John Wiley & Sons, 2017.

Mogul, Joey L., Andrea J. Ritchie, and Kay Whitlock. *Queer (In)Justice: The Criminalization of LGBT People in the United States.* Boston: Beacon Press, 2012.

Molnár, Miklós. *A Concise History of Hungary.* Translated by Anna Magyar. Cambridge: Cambridge University Press, 2001.

Molnar, Peter. *Plate Tectonics: A Very Short Introduction.* Oxford: Oxford University Press, 2015.

Morgan, Edmund. *The Puritan Family: Religion and Domestic Relations in Seventeenth-Century New England.* Rev. ed. New York: Harper & Row, 1966.

Morris, Ian, and Walter Scheidel, eds. *The Dynamics of Ancient Empires: State Power from Assyria to Byzantium.* Oxford: Oxford University Press, 2009.

Morris, J. Brent. *Oberlin, Hotbed of Abolitionism: College, Community, and the Fight for Freedom and Equality in Antebellum America.* Chapel Hill: University of North Carolina Press, 2014.

Morsink, Johannes. *The Universal Declaration of Human Rights: Origins, Drafting, and Intent.* Philadelphia: University of Pennsylvania Press, 2000.

Muelder, Owen W. *Theodore Dwight Weld and the American Anti-Slavery Society.* Jefferson, NC: McFarland, 2011.

Muhlhahn, Klaus. *Criminal Justice in China: A History.* Cambridge, MA: Harvard University Press, 2009.

Mullen, Brian, Rupert Brown, and Colleen Smith. "Ingroup Bias as a Function of Salience, Relevance, and Status: An Integration." *European Journal of Social Psychology* 22 (1992): 103–22.

Murabit, Alaa. "What Islam Really Says about Women." YouTube Video, 12:23, July 21, 2015. https://www.youtube.com/watch?v=FETryXMpDl8.

Murray, Bruce T. *Religious Liberty in America: The First Amendment in Historical and Contemporary Perspective.* Amherst, MA: University of Massachusetts Press, 2008.

Murton, John. *A Most Humble Supplication of Many the Kings Maiesties Loyall Subiects, Ready to Testifie All Civill Obedience, by the Oath, as the Law of This Realme Requireth, and That of Conscience.* EEOB Editions, 2011 [1621].

Nabatchi, Tina. "An Introduction to Deliberative Civic Engagement." In *Democracy in Motion: Evaluating the Practice and Impact of Deliberative Civic Engagement,* edited by Tina Nabatchi, John Gastil, G. Michael Weiksner, and Matt Leighninger, 3–18. New York: Oxford University Press, 2012.

National Council of Churches of Singapore. *A Christian Response to Homosexuality.* Kent Ridge, Singapore: Genesis Books, 2004.

Nelson, Matt. "How Not to Talk to Atheists: 3 Essential Points from Matt Fradd's Interview with Dr. Randal Rauser." Reasonable Catholic. July 15, 2015. https://www.reasonablecatholic.com/how-not-to-talk-to-atheists-3-essential-points-from-matt-fradds-interview-with-dr-randal-rauser/.

Newman, Brooke N. "Historical Perspective: Slavery over the Centuries." In *Human Trafficking: Interdisciplinary Perspectives,* edited by Mary C. Burke, 30–36. New York: Routledge, 2013.

Nicol, Donald MacGillivray, and J. F. Matthews. "Constantine I." In *Encyclopedia Britannica,* accessed April 26, 2018, https://www.britannica.com/biography/Constantine-I-Roman-emperor.

Njoroge, J. M. "Must the Moral Law Have a Lawgiver?" *Faithandthelaw's Blog.* August 21, 2016. https://faithandthelaw.wordpress.com/2016/08/21/must-the-moral-law-have-a-lawgiver/.

No Filter podcast. "Susan Carland on Being a Muslim Feminist." Episode 147, 59:33, May 22, 2017. omny.fm. https://omny.fm/shows/no-filter/susan-carland-on-being-a-muslim-feminist.

Noonan, John T., Jr. *A Church That Can and Cannot Change: The Development of Catholic Moral Teaching.* Notre Dame, IN: University of Notre Dame Press, 2005.

Novak, Michael. *No One Sees God: The Dark Night of Atheists and Believers.* New York: Doubleday, 2008.

NowThisWorld. "What Does It Mean to Be a Feminist in Islam." YouTube Video, 4:02, January 30, 2016. https://www.youtube.com/watch?v=MpdXrKqWx14.

Nozick, Robert. *Anarchy, State, and Utopia.* New York: Basic Books, 2013 [1974].

Nwachukwu, Ikenna. "Book Review: *Is God a Moral Monster?* by Paul Copan." Christ a Poet. March 25, 2017. https://christapoet.com/2017/03/25/book-review-is-god-a-moral-monster-by-paul-copan/.

O'Callaghan, Joseph F. *The Last Crusade in the West: Castile and the Conquest of Granada.* Philadelphia: University of Pennsylvania Press, 2014.

Ondrako, Edward J. *Progressive Illumination: A Journey with John Henry Cardinal Newman, 1980–2005.* Binghamton, NY: Global Academic, 2006.

Orr-Ewing, Amy. *Is the Bible Intolerant? Sexist? Oppressive? Homophobic? Outdated? Irrelevant?* Downers Grove, IL: InterVarsity Press, 2005.

Owczarek, Krzysztof, and Joanna Jędrzejczak. "Christianity and Epilepsy." *Neurologia i Neurochirurgia Polska* 47 (2013): 271–77.

Paavola, Petri. "What Does the Bible Say about Homosexuality?" Accessed April 8, 2018. http://www.kotipetripaavola.com/homosexual.html.

Pagden, Anthony. *The Enlightenment: And Why It Still Matters*. Oxford: Oxford University Press, 2013.

Pariser, Eli. *The Filter Bubble: How the New Personalized Web Is Changing What We Read and How We Think*. New York: Penguin Press, 2011.

Patterson, Orlando. *Slavery and Social Death: A Comparative Study*. Cambridge, MA: Harvard University Press, 1982.

Paul, Ian. "Is Allegorical Interpretation a Good Thing?" September 26, 2016. Psephizo. https://www.psephizo.com/biblical-studies/is-allegorical-interpretation-a-good-thing/.

Pearcey, Nancy. *Total Truth: Liberating Christianity from Its Cultural Captivity*. Study Guide Edition. Wheaton, IL: Crossway Books, 2005.

Pelikan, Jaroslav, ed. *Luther's Works, vol. 13: Selected Psalms II*. St. Louis: Concordia House, 1956.

Penner, Melinda. "The Church and Slavery." Stand to Reason. July 17, 2015. https://www.str.org/blog/the-church-and-slavery#.W3cI2uhKgdU.

Penner, Melinda. "Does the Bible Condone Slavery?" Stand to Reason. February 16, 2012. https://www.str.org/blog/does-the-bible-condone-slavery#.WTYLH2jysdU.

People with a History: An Online Guide to Lesbian, Gay, Bisexual, and Trans History, Fordham University. Internet History Sourcebooks Project. Accessed August 18, 2018, https://sourcebooks.fordham.edu/pwh/index-anc.asp.

Peterson, Jordan, Rebecca Goldstein, and William Lane Craig. "Is There Meaning to Life?" YouTube Video, 2:07:30, January 26, 2018. https://www.youtube.com/watch?v=pDDQOCXBrAw&t=6960s.

Pettegree, Andrew. "The Politics of Toleration in the Free Netherlands, 1572–1620." In *Tolerance and Intolerance in the European Reformation*, edited by Ole Peter Grell and Bob Scribner. Cambridge: Cambridge University Press, 1996.

Pettigrew, Thomas F., and Linda R. Tropp. "A Meta-Analytic Test of Intergroup Contact Theory." *Journal of Personality and Social Psychology* 90 (2006): 751–83.

Pew Forum on Religion and Public Life. *U.S. Religious Knowledge Survey*. Washington, DC: Pew Research Forum, 2010.

Pew Research Center. *The Future of World Religions: Population Growth Projections, 2010–2050*. April 2, 2015. https://assets.pewresearch.org/wp-content/uploads/sites/11/2015/03/PF_15.04.02_ProjectionsFullReport.pdf.

———. 2014 Religious Landscape Survey. Accessed April 9, 2018. https://www.pewforum.org/religious-landscape-study/.

Phillips, Katherine W. "How Diversity Makes Us Smarter." *Scientific American*, October 1, 2014. https://www.scientificamerican.com/article/how-diversity-makes-us-smarter/.

Pigliucci, Massimo. *Answers for Aristotle: How Science and Philosophy Can Lead Us to a More Meaningful Life*. New York: Basic Books, 2012.

Pine, Lisa. *Education in Nazi Germany*. Oxford: Oberg, 2010.

Pinker, Steven. *The Better Angels of Our Nature: Why Violence Has Declined*. New York: Penguin Books, 2011.

———. *The Blank Slate: The Modern Denial of Human Nature*. New York: Penguin Group, 2002.

Piper, John. "How God Visits Sins on the Third and Fourth Generations." Desiring God. March 6, 2009. https://www.desiringgod.org/articles/how-god-visits-sins -on-the-third-and-fourth-generation.

Pipes, Daniel. *Russia under the Bolshevik Regime*. New York: Vintage, 1994.

Plant, Richard. *The Pink Triangle: The Nazi War against Homosexuals*. New York: Henry Holt , 1986.

Plass, Ewald Martin. *What Luther Says: An Anthology*. St. Louis: Concordia House, 1959.

Plato. *The Dialogues of Plato*. Vol. 1. Translated by B. Jowett. New York: Random House, 1892.

———. *Euthyphro*. Translated by Benjamin Jowett. Internet Classics Archive. Accessed August 2, 2018. http://classics.mit.edu/Plato/euthyfro.html.

Platt, David. "Christians Need to Fight for the Religious Freedom of Everyone." *Relevant*, March 15, 2017. https://relevantmagazine.com/god/christians-need-to-fight -for-the-religious-freedom-of-everyone/.

Poole, Matthew. *Annotations upon the Holy Bible Wherein the Sacred Text Is Inserted and Various Readings Annexed*, vols. 1–2. Fourth edition. London: Thomas Parkhurst, 1700. Early English Books Online.

Pope Eugene IV. "Sicut Dudum." Papal Encyclicals Online. Accessed June 11, 2017. http://www.papalencyclicals.net/Eugene04/eugene04sicut.htm.

Pope Nicholas V. "Dum Diversas." Unam Sanctum Catholicam. Accessed June 11, 2017. http://unamsanctamcatholicam.blogspot.de/2011/02/dum-diversas-english -translation.html.

———. "Romanus Pontifex." Native Web. Accessed April 16, 2018. https://www .nativeweb.org/pages/legal/indig-romanus-pontifex.html.

Pope Paul III. "Sublimus Dei." Papal Encyclicals Online. Accessed June 11, 2017. http: //www.papalencyclicals.net/Paul03/p3subli.htm.

Pope Paul VI. "Dei Verbum." The Vatican. November 18, 1965. http://www.vatican.va/ archive/hist_councils/ii_vatican_council/documents/vat-ii_const_19651118_dei -verbum_en.html.

Pope Pius IX. "The Syllabus of Errors." Papal Encyclicals Online. Accessed June 27, 2018. https://www.papalencyclicals.net/pius09/p9syll.htm.

Powell, Doug. *Holman Quicksource Guide to Christian Apologetics*. Nashville, TN: Holman Reference, 2006.

Prager, Dennis. "If There Is No God." *The Dennis Prager Show*. August 19, 2008. http:// www.dennisprager.com/if-there-is-no-god/.

"The Problem of Evil." Ongoing Ambassadors for Christ. September 21, 2017. http:// www.oafc.org/apologetics-witnessing-resources/the-problem-of-evil.

Putnam, Robert D. *Bowling Alone: The Collapse and Revival of American Community*. New York: Simon & Schuster, 2000.

Putnam, Robert D., and David E. Campbell. *American Grace: How Religion Divides and Unites Us.* New York: Simon & Schuster, 2010.

Quinn, Sally. "Religion Is a Sure Route to True Happiness." *Washington Post,* January 24, 2014. https://www.washingtonpost.com/national/religion/religion-is-a-sure-route-to-true-happiness/2014/01/23/f6522120-8452-11e3-bbe5-6a2a3141e3a9_story.html.

"Quran: The Word of God." Whyislam.org. Accessed June 26, 2019. https://www.whyislam.org/quran/quran-the-word-of-god/.

"The Quran; Commentaries for 65:4; Al Talaq (Divorce)." QuranX.com. Accessed July 7, 2021. https://quranx.com/tafsirs/65.4.

Rau, Andy. "Understand Your Bible Better: How to Use Commentaries, Study Bibles, and More at Bible Gateway." Bible Gateway. July 26, 2017. https://www.biblegateway.com/blog/2017/07/understand-your-bible-better-how-to-use-commentaries-study-bibles/.

Rawls, John. *A Theory of Justice.* Revised edition. Cambridge, MA: Harvard University Press, 1999 [1971].

Rayborn, Tim. *The Violent Pilgrimage: Christians, Muslims and Holy Conflicts, 850–1150.* Jefferson, NC: McFarland, 2013.

Richards, Jeffrey. *Sex, Dissidence, and Damnation: Minority Groups in the Middle Ages.* New York: Routledge, 1991.

Richardson, Wyman Lewis. *Walking Together: A Congregational Reflection on Biblical Church Discipline.* Eugene, OR: Wipf & Stock, 2007.

"Religious Beliefs Make People Happier." *HuffPost,* December 6, 2017. https://www.huffpost.com/entry/religious-beliefs-happier-_n_4725269.

Riley, Patrick. "How Coherent Is the Social Contract Tradition?" *Journal of the History of Ideas* 34 (1973): 543–62.

Rizvi, Ali A. *The Atheist Muslim: A Journey from Religion to Reason.* New York: St. Martin's Press, 2016.

"Roald Dahl: The Day I Lost Faith in 'the Boss.'" *The Telegraph,* August 6, 2010. http://www.telegraph.co.uk/culture/books/biographyandmemoirreviews/7930223/Roald-Dahl-on-God-the-day-I-lost-faith-in-the-Boss.html.

Rosenthal, Robert. "The File Drawer Problem and Tolerance for Null Results." *Psychological Bulletin* 86, no. 3 (1979): 638–41.

Roser, Max, and Esteban Ortiz-Ospina. "Literacy." Our World in Data. Accessed August 18, 2018. https://ourworldindata.org/literacy.

Roth, Michael P. *An Eye for an Eye: A Global History of Crime and Punishment.* Chicago: University of Chicago Press, 2014.

Rouse, Margaret. "spin (PR, marketing)." WhatIs.com. Accessed February 28, 2018. http://whatis.techtarget.com/definition/spin-in-public-relations.

Rudalevige, Andrew. "What Can Watergate Teach Us about the Trump White House?" *Washington Post,* May 18, 2017. https://www.washingtonpost.com/news/monkey-cage/wp/2017/05/18/what-can-watergate-teach-us-about-the-trump-white-house/?utm_term=.1346b5ff1494.

Rupp, Leila J. "The European Origins of Transnational Organizing: The International Committee for Sexual Equality." In *LGBT Activism and the Making of Europe: A Rainbow Europe?* edited by Phillip M. Ayoub and David Paternotte, 29–49. New York: Palgrave Macmillan, 2014.

Rustin, John. "Religious Liberty Has Its Roots in the Bible." NC Family Policy Council. July 5, 2018. http://www.ncfamily.org/religious-liberty-has-its-roots-in-the-bible/.

Ryan, James. *Lenin's Terror: The Ideological Origins of Early Soviet State Violence.* New York: Routledge, 2012.

Saad, Lydia. "Four Moral Issues Sharply Divide Americans." Gallup. May 26, 2010. http://www.gallup.com/poll/137357/four-moral-issues-sharply-divide-americans.aspx.

Sahlins, Marshall. *Stone Age Economics.* New York: Routledge, 1972.

Samples, Kenneth Richard. *Without a Doubt: Answering the 20 Toughest Faith Questions.* Grand Rapids, MI: Baker Books, 2004.

Sapolsky, Robert M. *Behave: The Biology of Humans at Our Best and Worst.* New York: Penguin Press, 2017.

Sarsour, Linda. "2018 SALAM Annual Banquet_Linda Sarsour." YouTube Video, 35:52, December 13, 2018. https://www.youtube.com/watch?v=WnfyBgGcZuU.

Scheidel, Walter. "The Roman Slave Supply." In *The Cambridge History of World Slavery, Volume I: The Ancient Mediterranean World,* edited by Keith Bradley and Paul Cartledge, 287–310. Cambridge: Cambridge University Press, 2011.

Schieman, Scott, Alex Bierman, and Christopher G. Ellison. "Religion and Mental Health." In *Handbook of the Sociology of Mental Health.* Second edition. Edited by Carol S. Aneshensel, Jo C. Phelan, and Alex Bierman, 457–78. New York: Springer, 2013.

Schmidt, Alvin J. *How Christianity Changed the World.* Grand Rapids, MI: Zondervan, 2001.

Schreiner, Thomas R. *40 Questions about Christians and Biblical Law.* Grand Rapids, MI: Kregel, 2010.

Seibert, Eric A. *The Violence of Scripture: Overcoming the Old Testament's Troubling Legacy.* Minneapolis: Fortress Press, 2012.

Seidenstickler, Bob. "Yes, Biblical Slavery Was the Same as American Slavery." Patheos. August 25, 2014. http://www.patheos.com/blogs/crossexamined/2014/08/yes-biblical-slavery-was-the-same-as-american-slavery/.

Seidman, Steven. *Beyond the Closet: The Transformation of Gay and Lesbian Life.* New York: Routledge, 2004.

Sewall, Samuel. *The Selling of Joseph: A Memorial.* Boston: Bartholomew Green and John Allen, 1700. Massachusetts Historical Society. Accessed April 2, 2018. http://www.masshist.org/database/53.

Shafer, Patricia O. "About Epilepsy: The Basics." Epilepsy Foundation. Accessed August 17, 2018. https://www.epilepsy.com/learn/about-epilepsy-basics.

Shah, Timothy Samuel, Thomas F. Farr, and Jack Friedman, eds. *Religious Freedom and Gay Rights: Emerging Conflicts in North America and Europe*. Oxford: Oxford University Press, 2016.

Shah, Zia H. "The Golden Rule in Islam." *Muslim Times*, October 27, 2013. https://themuslimtimes.info/2013/10/27/the-golden-rule-in-islam/.

Shapiro, Fred R., ed. *The Yale Book of Quotations*. New Haven, CT: Yale University Press, 2006.

Sherman, Duke. *A Soldier's Thoughts: A Collection of Poems*. Bloomington, IN: Xlibris Corporation, 2012.

Shermer, Michael. *The Moral Arc: How Science and Reason Lead Humanity Toward Truth, Justice, and Freedom*. New York: Henry Holt, 2015.

———. "Why Smart People Believe Weird Things." September 2002. https://michaelshermer.com/2002/09/smart-people-believe-weird-things/.

Silverman, David. *Fighting God: An Atheist Manifesto for a Religious World*. New York: St. Martin's Press, 2015.

Simon, Rita J., and Alison Brooks. *Gay and Lesbian Communities the World Over*. Lanham, MD: Lexington Books, 2009.

Simons, Olaf. "The English Market of Books: Title Statistics and a Comparison with German Data." Critical Threads. June 7, 2013. https://criticalthreads.wordpress.com/2013/07/06/4-the-english-market-of-books-title-statistics-and-a-comparison-with-german-data/.

Sina, Ali. "Debate with Mr. Muhammad K." FaithFreedom.org. Accessed April 2, 2020. http://www.faithfreedom.org/debates/arif.htm.

Singer, Peter. *The Expanding Circle: Ethics, Evolution, and Moral Progress*. Princeton, NJ: Princeton University Press, 1981.

Sinha, Manisha. *The Slave's Curse: A History of Abolition*. New Haven, CT: Yale University Press, 2016.

Sky, Max. "Cultural Christians Should Defend Judeo-Christian Values." Whaleoil, April 28, 2019. https://www.whaleoil.net.nz/2019/04/cultural-christians-should-defend-judeo-christian-values/.

Slick, Matt. "Can Atheists Be Ethical?" Christian Apologetics and Research Ministry. December 9, 2008. https://carm.org/can-atheists-be-ethical.

———. "You May Buy Slaves?" Christian Apologetics and Research Ministry. December 9, 2008. https://carm.org/bible-difficulties/genesis-deuteronomy/you-may-buy-slaves.

Slick, Matt, and David Smalley. "Debate: Is God a Moral Monster?" Bible and Beer Consortium. Soundcloud, 2:16:41, October 1, 2016. https://soundcloud.com/biblethumpingwingnut/debate-matt-slick-vs-david-smalley-is-god-a-moral-monster.

Slingerland, Edward. *What Science Offers the Humanities: Integrating Body and Culture*. New York: Cambridge University Press, 2008.

Smith, David. *Sherman's March to the Sea 1864: Atlanta to Savannah*. Oxford, UK: Osprey, 2007.

Smith, Gregory A. "A Growing Share of Americans Say It's Not Necessary to Believe in God to Be Moral." Pew Research Center. October 16, 2017. http://www

.pewresearch.org/fact-tank/2017/10/16/a-growing-share-of-americans-say-its-not
-necessary-to-believe-in-god-to-be-moral/.

Smith, Mark A. *Secular Faith: How Culture Has Trumped Religion in American Politics*. Chicago: University of Chicago Press, 2015.

Smith, Rogers M., and Philip A. Klinkner. *The Unsteady March: The Rise and Decline of Racial Equality in America*. Chicago: University of Chicago Press, 1999.

Smith, Tom W., Peter Marsden, Michael Hout, and Jibum Kim. *General Social Surveys, 1972–2016: Cumulative Codebook*. Chicago: NORC at the University of Chicago, 2017.

Snell, Melissa. "Slavery in the Middle Ages." ThoughtCo. Accessed June 11, 2017. https://www.thoughtco.com/chains-in-medieval-times-1788699.

Soloman, Miriam. *Social Empiricism*. Cambridge, MA: MIT Press, 2001.

Souza, Philip de. *Piracy in the Greco-Roman World*. Cambridge: Cambridge University Press, 1999.

Spaans, Joke. "Religious Policies in the Seventeenth-Century Dutch Republic." In *Calvinism and Religious Toleration in the Dutch Golden Age*, edited by R. Po-Chia Hsia and H. F. K. Van Nierop, 72–86. Cambridge: Cambridge University Press, 2002.

Spielvogel, Jackson J. *Western Civilization: A Brief History, Volume I: To 1715*. Ninth edition. Boston: Centage Learning, 2017.

Sproul, R. C. "Civil Government." Ligonier Ministries. Accessed May 15, 2017. http://www.ligonier.org/learn/devotionals/civil-government/.

Stanton, Graham M., and Guy G. Stroumsa, eds. *Tolerance and Intolerance in Early Judaism and Christianity*. Cambridge: Cambridge University Press, 2008.

Stark, Rodney. *For the Glory of God: How Monotheism Led to Reformations, Science, Witch-Hunts, and the End of Slavery*. Princeton, NJ: Princeton University Press, 2003.

———. *The Victory of Reason: How Christianity Led to Freedom, Capitalism, and Western Success*. New York: Random House, 2005.

Steffens, Melanie C., and Christof Wagner. "Attitudes toward Lesbians, Gay Men, Bisexual Women, and Bisexual Men in Germany." *Journal of Sex Research* 41 (2004): 137–49.

Steiner, Jürg. *The Foundations of Deliberative Democracy: Empirical Research and Normative Implications*. Cambridge: Cambridge University Press, 2012.

Stemwedel, Janet D. "The Objectivity Thing (or, Why Science Is a Team Sport)." *Scientific American* (blog). July 20, 2011. https://blogs.scientificamerican.com/doing-good-science/httpblogsscientificamericancomdoing-good-science20110720the-objectivity-thing-or-why-science-is-a-team-sport/.

Stephens-Davidowitz, Seth. *Everybody Lies: Big Data, New Data, and What the Internet Can Tell Us about Who We Really Are*. New York: HarperCollins, 2017.

Stolzenberg, Ross M., Mary Blair-Loy, and Linda J. Waite. "Religious Participation over the Life Course: Age and Family Life Cycle Effects on Church Membership." *American Sociological Review* 60 (1995): 84–103.

Stone, Rachel. *Morality and Masculinity in the Carolingian Empire*. Cambridge, England: Cambridge University Press, 2012.

Storey, Lyndon. *Humanity or Sovereignty: A Political Roadmap for the 21st Century.* New York: Peter Lang, 2012.

Stout, Jeffrey. *The Flight from Authority: Religion, Morality, and the Quest for Autonomy.* Notre Dame, IN: University of Notre Dame Press, 1981.

Stowe, Harriet Beecher. *Uncle Tom's Cabin; or, Life among the Lowly.* Boston: John Jewett, 1852.

The Study Quran: A New Translation and Commentary, edited by Seyyed Hossein Nasr, Caner K. Dagli, Maria Massi Dakake, Joseph E. B. Lumbard, and Mohammed Rustom. New York: HarperCollins, 2015.

Stulberg, Lisa M. *LGBTQ Social Movements.* Cambridge: Polity Press, 2018.

Svirsky, Meira. "Georgetown Professor Condones Rape and Slavery under Sharia." Clarion Project. February 12, 2017. https://clarionproject.org/georgetown -professor-condones-rape-and-slavery-under-sharia/.

Synod of Gangra. In *Nicene and Post-Nicene Fathers,* Second Series. Vol. 14. Edited by Philip Schaff and Henry Wace. Translated by Henry Percival. Buffalo, NY: Christian Literature , 1900. Revised and edited for New Advent by Kevin Knight. http://www.newadvent.org/fathers/3804.htm.

Tajfel, Henri. "Experiments in Intergroup Discrimination." *Scientific American* 223 (1970): 96–102.

Talbott, William J. *Which Rights Should Be Universal?* New York: Oxford University Press, 2005.

Taunton, Larry Alex. *The Faith of Christopher Hitchens: The Restless Soul of the World's Most Notorious Atheist.* Nashville, TN: Thomas Nelson, 2016.

———. *The Grace Effect: How the Power of One Life Can Reverse the Corruption of Unbelief.* Nashville, TN: Thomas Nelson, 2011.

Tertullian. *An Answer to the Jews.* In *Ante-Nicene Fathers.* Vol. 3. Edited by Alexander Roberts, James Donaldson, and A. Cleveland Coxe. Translated by S. Thelwall. Buffalo, NY: Christian Literature, 1885. Revised and edited for New Advent by Kevin Knight. http://www.newadvent.org/fathers/0308.htm.

———. *The Apology.* In *Ante-Nicene Fathers.* Vol. 3. Edited by Alexander Roberts, James Donaldson, and A. Cleveland Coxe. Translated by S. Thelwall. Buffalo, NY: Christian Literature, 1885. Revised and edited for New Advent by Kevin Knight. http://www.newadvent.org/fathers/0301.htm.

Thornton, John. *Africa and Africans in the Making of the Atlantic World, 1400–1800.* Second edition. Cambridge: Cambridge University Press, 1998.

Thurston, Robert W. *Life and Terror in Stalin's Russia, 1934–1941.* New Haven, CT: Yale University Press, 1996.

Timmons, Mark. *Disputed Moral Issues: A Reader.* Fourth edition. New York: Oxford University Press, 2016.

Tingblad, Matthew. "The Problem of Natural Disasters." Josh McDowell Ministry. April 6, 2017. https://www.josh.org/problem-natural-disasters/.

Tocqueville, Alexis de. *Democracy in America.* Translated by Harvey Mansfield and Delba Winthrop. Chicago: University of Chicago Press, 2000 [1835, 1840].

Torre, Joseph M. de. "The Influence of Christianity on Modern Democracy, Equality, and Freedom." Catholic Education Resource Center. 1997. https://www.catholiceducation.org/en/culture/catholic-contributions/the-influence-of-christianity-on-modern-democracy-equality-and-freedom.html.

Turek, Frank. *Stealing from God: Why Atheists Need God to Make Their Case*. Colorado Springs, CO: NavPress, 2014.

"Turkish Child Marriage Religious Document Sparks Anger." BBC News, January 3, 2018. https://www.bbc.com/news/world-europe-42558328.

Senate. "Employment of Homosexuals and Other Sex Perverts in the US Government." Reprinted (selections) in *We Are Everywhere: A Historical Sourcebook of Gay and Lesbian Politics*, edited by Mark Blasius and Shane Phelan. New York: Routledge, 1997.

UBC Faculty of Arts. "Ayesha S. Chaudhry, Associate Professor of Gender and Islam." YouTube Video, October 30, 2018, 0:59. https://www.youtube.com/watch?v=WPcoEZw2hz0.

Unitarian Universalist Association. "Sources of Our Living Tradition." Accessed April 2, 2010. https://www.uua.org/beliefs/what-we-believe/sources.

———. "We Are Unitarian Universalists." YouTube Video, 3:17, October 6, 2016. https://www.youtube.com/watch?v=-3UYWnngiEo.

United Nations. "Over 40 Million People Caught in Modern Slavery, 152 Million in Child Labor—UN." UN News Centre. September 19, 2017. http://www.un.org/apps/news/story.asp?NewsID=57550#.WibhWEqnEdV.

———. "Universal Declaration of Human Rights." Accessed September 23, 2017. http://www.ohchr.org/EN/UDHR/Documents/UDHR_Translations/eng.pdf.

United Nations Children's Fund. "Child Marriage." Accessed July 16, 2019. https://data.unicef.org/topic/child-protection/child-marriage/.

———. *Ending Child Marriage: Progress and Prospects*. New York: UNICEF, 2014.

United Nations Educational, Scientific and Cultural Organization. *Reading the Past, Writing the Future: Fifty Years of Promoting Literacy*. Paris: United Nations Educational, Scientific and Cultural Organization, 2017.

United Nations Office on Genocide Prevention and the Responsibility to Protect. "Genocide." Accessed January 3, 2018. http://www.un.org/en/genocideprevention/genocide.html.

Vaillant, George E. *Triumphs of Experience: The Men of the Harvard Grant Study*. Cambridge, MA: Harvard University Press, 2012.

van Wees, Hans. "Genocide in the Ancient World." In *The Oxford Handbook of Genocide Studies*, edited by Donald Bloxham and A. Dirk Moses, Oxford: Oxford University Press, 2010.

VanderWeele, Tyler J. "On the Promotion of Human Flourishing." *Proceedings of the National Academy of Sciences of the United States of America* 114 (August 2017): 8148–56.

———. "Religion and Health: A Synthesis." In *Spirituality and Religion within the Culture of Medicine: From Evidence to Practice*, edited by Michael J. Balboni and John R. Peteet, 347–401. New York: Oxford University Press, 2017.

Vaughn, Lewis. *Contemporary Moral Arguments: Readings in Ethical Issues.* Second edition. New York: Oxford University Press, 2012.

Velarde, Robert. "How Can God Allow So Much Evil and Suffering?" Focus on the Family. January 1, 2009. https://www.focusonthefamily.com/faith/becoming -a-christian/is-christ-the-only-way/how-can-god-allow-so-much-evil-and -suffering.

Vessey, Mark, ed. *A Companion to Augustine.* Malden, MA: Blackwell, 2012.

Vidyá-Bhúshan, Shyámacharan Sarkár. *Vyavasthá-Darpana, A Digest of Hindú Law, as Current in Bengal.* Third edition. Calcutta: Shanhope Press, 1883.

Vincent, David. *The Rise of Mass Literacy: Reading and Writing in Modern Europe.* Cambridge: Polity Press, 2000.

Vines, Matthew. *God and the Gay Christian: The Biblical Case in Support of Same-Sex Relationships.* New York: Convergent Books, 2014.

Waal, Frans de. *The Bonobo and the Atheist: In Search of Humanism among the Primates.* New York: W.W. Norton, 2013.

Wachsmann, Nikolaus. *KL: A History of the Nazi Concentration Camps.* New York: Farrar, Straus and Giroux, 2015.

Wadud, Amina. "Islam Beyond Patriarchy through Gender Inclusive Qur'anic Analysis." Musawah. Accessed August 31, 2019. http://arabic.musawah.org/sites/default /files/Wanted-AW-EN.pdf.

———. *Inside the Gender Jihad: Women's Reform in Islam.* London: Oneworld Publications, 2006.

———. *Qur'an and Woman: Rereading the Sacred Text from a Woman's Perspective.* New York: Oxford University Press, 1999.

Waldie, Lance. *A Christian Apologetic for Christian Apologists.* Cypress, TX: Lulu, 2012.

Wallace, J. Warner. *God's Crime Scene: A Cold-Case Detective Examines the Evidence for a Divinely Created Universe.* Colorado Springs, CO: David C. Cook, 2015.

Wallace, Michael, Bradley R. E. Wright, and Allen Hyde. "Religious Affiliation and Hiring Discrimination in the American South: A Field Experiment." *Social Currents* 1 (2014): 189–207.

Walvoord, John F. "Is the Bible the Inspired Word of God." Bible.org. January 1, 2008. https://bible.org/seriespage/1-bible-inspired-word-god.

Waseem, Ro. "Ideology vs. Islam." WVoice. July 8, 2014. http://www.womensvoicesnow .org/wvoice/ideology-vs-islam/.

Welch, David. *The Third Reich: Politics and Propaganda.* Second edition. London: Routledge, 2002.

Wellman, Jack. "What Does the Bible Say about Slavery? Does It Condone It?" What Christians Want to Know. Accessed June 4, 2017. http://www.whatchristian-swanttoknow.com/what-does-the-bible-say-about-slavery-does-it-condone-it/.

Western Theological Seminary. "Mission and Values." Accessed April 7, 2018. https:// www.westernsem.edu/about/mission-vision/.

Wet, Chris L. de. "The Cappadocian Fathers on Slave Management." The Scientific Electronic Library Online. Accessed April 2, 2018. http://www.scielo.org.za/pdf/ she/v39n1/17.pdf.

"What Are the Attributes of God" GotQuestions.org. Accessed May 10, 2017. https://www.gotquestions.org/attributes-God.html.

"What Does It Mean That God Works in Mysterious Ways?" GotQuestions.org. Accessed April 17, 2017. https://www.gotquestions.org/God-works-in-mysterious-ways.html.

Whelchel, Hugh. "Is Religious Liberty Biblical?" Institute for Faith, Work and Economics. April 25, 2016. https://tifwe.org/is-religious-liberty-biblical/.

White, James R. "Harold Camping." April 14, 2009. Christian Research Institute. http://www.equip.org/articles/harold-camping/.

———. *Contemporary Moral Problems.* Tenth edition. Belmont, CA: Wadsworth, 2011.

Wielenberg, Eric. *Robust Ethics: The Metaphysics and Epistemology of Godless Normative Reason.* New York: Oxford University Press, 2014.

Williams, Roger. *The Bloudy Tenent of Persecution.* Reprint ed. London: Forgotten Books, 2018 [1644].

Williams, Terrance J., Michelle E. Pepitone, Scott E. Christensen, Bradley Cooke, Andrew D. Huberman, Nicholas J. Breedlove, Tessa J. Breedlove, Cynthia Jordan, and Stephen Breedlove. "Finger-Length Ratios and Sexual Orientation." *Nature* 404 (2000): 455–56.

Wilson, Bryan R. *Religion in Sociological Perspective.* Oxford: Oxford University Press, 1982.

Wilson, Edward O. *Consilience: The Unity of Knowledge.* New York: Alfred A. Knopf: 1998.

Wilson, Ken. *A Letter to My Congregation: An Evangelical Pastor's Path to Embracing People Who Are Gay, Lesbian, Bisexual and Transgender into the Company of Jesus.* Canton, MI: Spirit Books, 2014.

Wilson, Kristian. "25 Books by Modernist Women Writers." Bustle. August 19, 2016. https://www.bustle.com/articles/169948-25-books-by-modernist-women-writers.

Wilson, Wendy. "Barna Research Finds Many Americans Still Read Bible, but What Are They Learning." Illinois Family Institute. August 23, 2018. https://illinoisfamily.org/faith/barna-research-finds-many-americans-still-read-bible-but-what-are-they-learning/.

Winthrop, John. "A Model of Christian Charity." The Winthrop Society. Accessed May 24, 2017. http://winthropsociety.com/doc_charity.php.

Wit, Willem-Jan de. "'Your Little Ones against the Rock!' Modern and Ancient Interpretations of Psalm 137:9." In *Christian Faith and Violence.* Vol. 2. Edited by Dirk van Keulen and Martien E. Brinkman, Zoetermeer, The Netherlands: Meinema, 2005.

Wodon, Quentin. "Islamic Law, Women's Rights, and State Law: The Cases of Female Genital Cutting and Child Marriage." *Review of Faith and International Affairs* 13, no. 3 (2015): 85–86.

Wolf, Arthur P., and William H. Durham, eds. *Inbreeding, Incest, and the Incest Taboo: The State of Knowledge at the Turn of the Century.* Stanford, CA: Stanford University Press, 2004.

Wolfe, Alan. "The Reason for Everything." *New Republic*, January 15, 2006. https://newrepublic.com/article/65229/the-reason-everything.

———. *The Transformation of American Religion: How We Actually Live Our Faith*. Chicago: University of Chicago Press, 2003.

Wollstonecraft, Mary. *A Vindication of the Rights of Woman*. Mineola, NY: Dover, 1996 [1792].

World Economic Forum. *Global Gender Gap Report 2021*. Geneva: World Economic Forum, 2021. https://www.weforum.org/reports/global-gender-gap-report-2021/in-full.

World Health Organization. *Global and Regional Estimates of Violence against Women: Prevalence and Health Effects of Intimate Partner Violence and Non-Partner Sexual Violence*. Geneva: World Health Organization: 2013. Accessed August 30, 2019. https://apps.who.int/iris/bitstream/handle/10665/85239/9789241564625_eng.pdf;jsessionid=F3F35B7F7CABB56C5CF8D50743224189?sequence=1.

Wright, Bradley R. E., Michael Wallace, John Bailey, and Allen Hyde. "Religious Affiliation and Hiring Discrimination in New England: A Field Experiment." *Research in Social Stratification and Mobility* 34 (2013): 111–26.

Wright, Christopher. *The God I Don't Understand: Reflections on Tough Questions of Faith*. Grand Rapids, MI: Zondervan, 2008.

Wynn, Karen, Paul Bloom, Ashley Jordan, Julia Marshall, and Mark Sheskin. "Not Noble Savages After All: Limits to Early Altruism." *Current Directions in Psychological Science* 27, no. 1 (2018): 3–8.

Youngblood, Ronald F, ed. *Nelson's Illustrated Bible Dictionary*. Rev. ed. Nashville, TN: Thomas Nelson, 2014.

Zacharias, Ravi. *The End of Reason: A Response to the New Atheists*. Grand Rapids, MI: Zondervan, 2008.

Zacharias, Ravi, and Norman Geisler, eds. *Who Made God? And Answers to Over 100 Other Tough Questions of Faith*. Grand Rapids, MI: Zondervan, 2003.

Zagal, Hector. "Aquinas on Slavery: An Aristotelian Puzzle." Paper presented at Congresso Tomista Internationale, Rome, Italy, September 21–25, 2003.

Zagorin, Perez. *How the Idea of Religious Tolerance Came to the West*. Princeton, NJ: Princeton University Press, 2003.

Zakaria, Fareed. "I Am a Muslim. But Trump's Views Appall Me Because I Am an American." *Washington Post*, December 10, 2015. https://www.washingtonpost.com/opinions/i-am-a-muslim-but-trumps-views-appall-me-because-i-am-an-american/2015/12/10/fcba9ea6-9f6d-11e5-8728-1af6af208198_story.html.

Zarin, Khurram. "10 Deadliest Natural Disasters of 21st Century." Scienceve. Accessed November 5, 2017. http://www.scienceve.com/10-deadliest-natural-disasters-of-21st-century/

Zhao, Yuhong. "Domestic Violence in China: In Search of Legal and Social Responses." *UCLA Pacific Basin Law Journal* 18, no. 2 (2000): 211–51.

Zubair, Khwaja Mohammed. "Why Muslims Say 'Peace Be Upon Him' When Muhammad's Name Is Mentioned." *Khaleej Times*, June 18, 2016. https://www

.khaleejtimes.com/ramadan-2016/why-muslims-say-peace-be-upon-him-when
-muhammads-name-is-mentioned.

Zuckerman, Phil. *Faith No More: Why People Reject Religion*. New York: Oxford University Press, 2012.

———. *Living the Secular Life: New Answers to Old Questions*. New York: Penguin Press, 2014.

———. *Society without God: What the Least Religious Nations Can Tell Us about Contentment*. Second edition. New York: New York University Press, 2020.

Zwier, Harold. "We Need Religion, but God Is Optional." ABC News. February 5, 2020. https://www.abc.net.au/news/2009-12-22/27778.

ABOUT THE AUTHOR

Mark Alan Smith is professor of political science and adjunct professor of communication and comparative religion at the University of Washington. His research and teaching focuses on American domestic politics, including religion, public opinion, interest groups, political parties, and public policy. He is the author of two award-winning books, *Secular Faith: How Culture Has Trumped Religion in American Politics* and *American Business and Political Power: Public Opinion, Elections, and Democracy*. He is a regular commentator on national and state politics for print, radio, television, and online outlets.